The Editor

JOANNA LIPKING is Lecturer in English at Northwestern University, where she has taught since 1979. A Columbia Ph.D., she writes on women's emergence in print culture. Her articles and reviews on Aphra Behn and other early women writers appear in *Studies in the Eighteenth Century, The Eighteenth Century: A Current Bibliography*, and the recent Cambridge University Press collection, *Aphra Behn Studies*.

A NORTON CRITICAL EDITION

Aphra Behn

OROONOKO

AN AUTHORITATIVE TEXT

HISTORICAL BACKGROUNDS

CRITICISM

Edited by

JOANNA LIPKING

NORTHWESTERN UNIVERSITY

W • W • NORTON & COMPANY • *New York* • *London*

Copyright © 1997 by W. W. Norton & Company, Inc.

The text of this book is composed in Electra
with the display set in Bernhard Modern.
Composition by PennSet, Inc.
Manufacturing by Courier Companies

Library of Congress Cataloging-in-Publication Data

Behn, Aphra, 1640–1689.
Oroonoko : an authoritative text, historical backgrounds, criticism
Aphra Behn ; edited by Joanna Lipking.
p. cm. — (A Norton critical edition)
Includes bibliographical references.

ISBN 0-393-97014-0 (pbk.)

1. Slaves — Surinam — Fiction. 2. Behn, Aphra, 1640–1689.
Oroonoko. 3. Siave trade — History — Sources. 4. Slavery in
literature. 5. Slaves in literature. I. Lipking, Joanna.
II. Title.
PR3317.07 1996
823'.4 — dc21   96-47186
                                                                     CIP

W. W. Norton & Company, Inc., 500 Fifth Avenue, New York, N.Y. 10110
www.wwnorton.com

W. W. Norton & Company Ltd., Castle House, 75/76 Wells Street,
London W1T 3QT

4 5 6 7 8 9 0

Contents

Criticism

Illustrations

Preface

We know little about the professional woman writer who signed herself "A. Behn," but we know that late in life she was openly ambitious, wanting "Fame" for her plays, "Immortality" for her poems. A few of her plays became favorites in repertory, her poems were praised by later poets, and her fiction was steadily republished through the mid-eighteenth century. But it was *Oroonoko*, the longest of her short tales, that established what she called "the Reputation of my Pen." With her "Royal Slave," a black African prince ensnared in the slave traffic to the Americas, Behn found a subject of such scope and intensity that it kept a niche in the literary histories, even when her other writings were judged indecent and out of date. *Oroonoko* seemed to stand for what was new: the origins of the novel, the growth of empire, the emergence of women writers, interest in non-European "others," the cultivation of sensibility, enlightened ideals of personal freedom. Now this small classic seems to fascinate everyone. But what is it?

There is no settled answer. Critics have differed about its form, its truth, and its sympathies. Placed among traditional genres and currents of thought, *Oroonoko* has seemed an original use of heroic romance and play conventions and the first realistic novel, thirty years before Defoe; like a life of a noble Roman or the life reconnected to nature later idealized by Rousseau; in its politics insistently Royalist or revealing radical undercurrents; a work that brings to light or glosses over the wrongs of the slave trade. Behn's own claim that her tale was a "True History" set off a running dispute among twentieth-century readers for whom history was one thing, fiction another. To some, *Oroonoko* was transparently a tall story, a piece of mythmaking, or perhaps a triumph of fictional imagination and technique; meanwhile the lure of the tale sent scholars from many countries sleuthing through long-forgotten colonial records, gathering evidence that Behn probably visited Surinam and that much of her background detail was accurate or at least plausible, resembling other descriptions of the West Indies. But history, in a more current view, must be understood as an official narrative by privileged voices. New waves of interest in feminist revaluation of women's writing, in gender and race as categories of analysis, and in converging populations of the Atlantic basin and colonialist practices and discourses have led critics to explore another question: how Behn's story is complicit with and resists the weight of old oppressions.

Like some exotic specimen that is yet to be cataloged, *Oroonoko* attracts and challenges. Critics in this volume see blended forms and internal tensions. Perhaps the bold recombining and literalizing of inherited forms for immediate human interest was especially congenial to women and other newcomers to literature. But what the continuing disagreements suggest, above all, is the usefulness of placing Behn's tale among related documents of its time, without regard for their status as literature, their authenticity as history, or their measure of moral clarity. Like *Oroonoko* in their setting and subject and often their anecdotal power, such documents provide a context for the tale—if not a standard account of its origins and influence, at least a fuller sense of its own place and moment. Above all, they invite readers to examine its treatment of slavery and of racial or cultural "others" in relation to events and attitudes in the distant colonial world it represents and in the world of metropolitan Europe where it was read.

Whatever its basis in experience, *Oroonoko* takes place in a world "out there" that was mapped, navigated, interpreted, and settled. Unlike Shakespeare's *Tempest*, *Robinson Crusoe*, or *Gulliver's Travels*, it portrays other peoples who had their own histories, though forever distorted, written by the literate Europeans. As peoples from three continents meet in scenes of curiosity and friendship, Behn explains how they could communicate and gives to each complex and changing views of the others. In her most arresting innovation, she introduces West African slaves during the ill-documented first stages of the slave trade. Behind lay the expansiveness of the sixteenth-century discovery voyages; ahead, the familiar images of planter luxury and slave subjugation, the polarizing of whites and blacks, and the heritage of racialist and sentimental cliché that came with the full development of the slave system. The comparatively sparse records are now the subject of exacting study, so present-day readers need not take their understanding of early slavery from the tale itself or from popular belief. Here an introductory survey—provisional, since the work of reconstruction continues—and selected firsthand reports open a window on scenes that, like *Oroonoko* itself, can often be surprising.

To weigh Behn's debts to the broader range of travel literature would merely encumber a short text with annotations. The available reports, those of America especially, were full of received ideas, common images, and reiterated phrases. The constant springtime with ever-blooming trees was a truism, the wonder that struck observers at the new tropical landscapes apparently unending. Even the 1911 *Encyclopaedia Britannica* account of Guiana (encompassing Surinam) emphasizes the superabundance of its "perpetual" vegetation, "inexhaustible" fine timbers, and "indescribable" birds of plumage. By the time Behn wrote, such details as the Indian priests, or *Peeies*, had been mentioned in many accounts, while selected images, including armadillos and women in feather crowns, had become emblematic of the New World and were drawn in vacant spaces on maps. Native Indian customs, if admittedly strange or cruel, might be seen to reflect an uncomplicated manly ethic, in contrast to the degraded morals and artificial tastes— sometimes termed the "effeminacy"—of Christian Europe. When Montaigne identified the cannibals' two guiding precepts as "Valour towards their enemies and love towards their wives," those could easily be seen as a rude version of traditional noble ideals, the "Fierce warres and faithfull loves" that Spenser invoked in *The Faerie Queene*. Without such details and this idealizing vein, Behn's readers might have felt that she was not presenting a bona fide America.

Her Africa, if romanticized, broadly fits its seventeenth-century profile as a place of wealthy trader kings. No doubt the scene making can seem as fanciful as in a creaky Hollywood epic. When Behn's king acts like an autocrat in an "Oriental" tale, he has for backdrop not just the usual African furnishings of canopy and carpets but a marble bath, and when her hero turns from battle like a latter-day Achilles, he has a pavilion and a couch. But it is not a fancy that in only two years' trading around 1660, English ships carried out to the main station at Cormantine more than thirty-five hundred rugs and about five hundred carpets, among other goods. Not surprisingly, ruling-class Africans might be thought of as partners, while the uprooted, mixed lot of colonists, pursuing fortunes in ill-governed new places, were often stereotyped, noted in the first place for their consumption of drink. Remarks on the slaves are casual and inconsistent, but the first travel accounts in English from the 1650s and 1660s—Richard Ligon's of Barbados, George Warren's of Surinam, John Davies's digest on the Antilles—offer a few repeated notions and catchphrases: that slaves were treated "like dogs" or worse; constituted the colonists' wealth; and showed a striking readiness to die, partly in the belief that they would return to their "own country."

The coincidence among reports is the result not only of shared opinions and habitual ways of seeing but of industrious copying. Title pages do not disclose that works are rough translations, or compilations by nontravelers made up of every sort of material, or recyclings of colorful but long-outdated reports (such as Jean de Léry's on Brazil in 1586 and Pieter De Marees's on West Africa in 1602). Works might be all of those. It is best to think of the writers as compiling a joint encyclopedia, with a generous admixture of folklore and little ever discarded. Even the most independent on-the-scene reporters, those culled for this edition, regularly consulted earlier books, filled out their accounts on matters they did not know, and were appropriated in their turn. Behn does not seem to rely on any particular sources, and she includes practical information that does not seem readily available in Europe, but if she made no use of texts, she would have been very nearly alone.

As a prospect of America, *Oroonoko* resembles Frans Post's landscape on the cover of this volume, painted after his return to Europe. He depicts an identifiable site (a village near Recife in northeast Brazil), arranges typical landscape features and human figures in a New World genre painting (his prints were used to represent Surinam as well), and plainly looks back to established European landscape styles. But in contrast to all of the men who saw and represented the colonies, the woman storyteller introduces new foreground figures, a hero and heroine who are slaves of rank. Although some readers note similar sounds in African languages, their names do not seem recognizably African. It has been suggested that Oroonoko was named after the French romance hero Oroondates in La Calprenède's *Cassandre*, a prince from the rough borderland of Scythia who excels among the cultivated Persians, or, with curious naïveté, for the South American river Orinoco, explored by Sir Walter Ralegh, a few hundred miles north of Surinam. Perhaps an echo of the Virginia colony names—Roanoke, Croonoke, Choanoke—helped to make the name sound suitably foreign to a Europe that blurred ethnographic distinctions. Imoinda's name and the family rivalry she inspires recall Dryden's Indamora, the captive Asian princess in his rhymed heroic play *Aureng-Zebe*. But however they and their names were derived, her noble pair escape the ordinary lot of slaves, whose origins and identities were lost during their transport and breaking in, and are seen with sustained and intimate sympathy. It was they—not the colonists or the detailed colonial background—who caught the imagination of Europe.

They and other black Africans described as noble appeared not only in fiction but in the theater, poems, periodical essays, and assorted other forms. Similar figures are found at the center of what might be called epiphenomena, when a current news item busied many pens with interpretations and elaborations. It was through such figures that Europe began to think or at least to feel its way through the issues of slavery. The accounts are a medley. If they no longer convey much of the colonial scene that Behn called her "other World," they open to view a lively cosmopolitan world that was drawn, much like ours, to stirring or sensational action, glamor, strangeness, sentiment, personal stories and public quarrels. In his essay exploring the "problematical territory" of *Oroonoko*, Robert L. Chibka cites a description of fiction as leaving the reader poised on a knife edge between belief and disbelief. Here we might sometimes think of a diaphanous screen (or perhaps a small fog) with African figures passing from one side to the other, imagined characters taken for historical persons, living persons turned into characters, each reinforcing views of the other. As in *Oroonoko* itself, history and fiction may mingle, their characters sometimes hobnobbing, amid many reminders that the human appetite for striking events may shape what is seen and that a single word meant novel, novelty, and news.

A few of Behn's contemporaries, perhaps playing along with a friendship too novel to disbelieve, claimed that she had often spoken warmly about Oroonoko. Even the faults and difficulties of the 1688 text, as well as its conversational style, can recreate the sense of a tale-teller's circle, the heavy punctuation marking her speech pauses, the ambiguous pronouns, shifting tenses, and unshapely sentences conveying her eager forward motion, her concentration on the immediacy of what she has to tell. For unknown reasons, Oroonoko was also printed in haste, set by two compositors working independently, probably in two different print shops. Both left sentences whose syntax is beyond correction, and the second, during a passage on the marvels of America, appears to have been falling asleep. George Guffey in 1975 suggested that Behn's "Royal Slave" was hurried into print to point up the imminent peril facing James II, his wife, and his new heir, while others cite evidence of Behn's flagging health and need for money. The result, in any case, is that during Oroonoko's dinner conversation with Trefry, the text breaks, a signature is dropped, and the second printer takes up the task using different typographic styles and different, sometimes eccentric habits of spelling. There is no sign that once she supplied the manuscript, Behn had any further role. To provide a readable classroom text, spellings and punctuation that are distracting or confusing have been emended, in most cases following the small corrections (but not the guesswork) of the second and third editions. Emendations are listed in the "Textual Notes," with cruxes marked in the footnotes, so that scholars may have a dependable original text, thus far unavailable in a popular or single-volume edition. With the permission of their authors, quotations within the critical essays have been made consistent with the present Norton text. There has been no attempt to preserve the exact form of the accompanying contextual materials, but they are conservatively modernized (notably by the modernizing of unfamiliar obsolete spellings and misleading punctuation, normalizing of place names, expansion of contractions, removal of some italics and capitalizing not meant for emphasis, and, of course, replacement of old lettering). The spelling in Henry Whistler's journal has required full modernization. Translations of Du Tertre's history, Barbot's 1679 journal, *L'Année Littéraire*, and brief quoted travelers' remarks are mine, with the kind assistance of Tilde Sankovitch.

In attempting to reconstruct Behn's range of reference and conditions on three continents, I have asked help wherever I could, but I have learned in especially practical ways from Edna G. Bay, Paul Breslin, Helen Deutsch, Bernadette Fort, Lawrence Lipking (*maestro di color che sanno*), Russell Maylone of Northwestern Special Collections, Martin Mueller, Barbara Newman, James P. Oakes, Conor Cruise O'Brien, Mary Ann O'Donnell, Stephen Orgel, Hans Panofsky, Rebecca Parker, Orlando Patterson, Johnny Payne, Ruth Perry, William Roberts, Natalie Schmitt, Janet Todd, James G. Turner, M. V. Wakefield-Richmond, Ivor Wilks, David W. Wills, and Garry Wills. It was my good fortune to have at hand the distinguished collection and informed staff of the Herskovits Africana Collection of the Northwestern University Library, and during 1993–94, the shared learning of participants in the Seminars on Race and Gender and on the African Diaspora at the National Humanities Center. Alert help at critical moments by staff members of the Northwestern Library Interlibrary Loan Department and the Newberry Library Photoduplication Department, Michael T. Dumas of the Harvard Theatre Collection, Christopher Fletcher of the British Library Department of Manuscripts, and Northwestern Humanities Bibliographer Jeffrey B. Garrett has amounted to scholarly collaboration. My colleague Douglas Cole was the photographer of Northwestern Library materials.

I am deeply indebted to the six critics in this volume for their willingness and aid in the compression of their arguments to the constraints of a short volume. At Norton, Carol Bemis gave unfailingly patient support through difficulties and delays that could plausibly explain a recourse to two print shops. Over the years, English Department students Heidi Sandige, Elissa Preheim, Becky St. John, and especially Celeste DiNucci have handled early texts with notable care. My current students, with the explanation that they are "the multicultural generation," had such pointed and interesting questions about the art and polemic of *Oroonoko* that I gladly leave this edition to their generation.

July 18, 1996

The Text of
OROONOKO
or, The Royal Slave: A True History

OROONOKO:

OR, THE

Royal Slave.

A TRUE

HISTORY.

By Mrs. *A. BEHN.*

LONDON,

Printed for *Will. Canning,* at his Shop in
the *Temple-Cloysters.* 1688.

The Epistle Dedicatory

To The
Right Honourable
The
Lord MAITLAND.[1]

My Lord,

Since the World is grown so Nice and Critical upon Dedications, and will Needs be Judging the Book, by the Wit of the Patron; we ought, with a great deal of Circumspection, to chuse a Person against whom there can be no Exception; and whose Wit, and Worth, truly Merits all that one is capable of saying upon that Occasion.

The most part of Dedications are charg'd with Flattery; and if the World knows a Man has some Vices, they will not allow one to speak of his Virtues. This, my Lord, is for want of thinking Rightly; if Men wou'd consider with Reason, they wou'd have another sort of Opinion, and Esteem of Dedications; and wou'd believe almost every Great Man has enough to make him Worthy of all that can be said of him there. My Lord, a Picture-drawer, when he intends to make a good Picture, essays the Face many Ways, and in many Lights, before he begins; that he may chuse, from the several turns of it, which is most Agreeable, and gives it the best Grace; and if there be a Scar, an ungrateful Mole, or any little Defect, they leave it out; and yet make the Picture extreamly like: But he who has the good Fortune to draw a Face that is exactly Charming in all its Parts and Features, what Colours or Agreements[2] can be added to make it Finer? All that he can give is but its due; and Glories in a Piece whose Original alone gives it its Perfection. An ill Hand may diminish, but a good Hand cannot augment its Beauty. A Poet is a Painter in his way;[3] he draws to the Life, but in another kind; we draw the Nobler part, the Soul and Mind; the Pictures of the Pen shall out-last those of the Pencil, and even Worlds themselves. 'Tis a short Chronicle of those Lives that possibly wou'd be forgotten by other Historians, or lye neglected there, however deserving an immortal Fame; for Men of eminent Parts[4] are as Exemplary as

---

1. Richard Maitland (1653–1695), later fourth earl of Lauderdale, held important public posts in Scotland. A Jacobite and Roman Catholic, he followed the dethroned James II to France but was both outlawed at home and excluded from the court in exile. The learned Catholic writings Behn refers to are not known, but he was noted for his library and for a verse translation of Virgil.
2. Attractive qualities; from the French *agréments*.
3. The comparison of poets to painters, a commonplace from Horace's *Art of Poetry*, was often cast as a contest by seventeenth-century writers. Richard Lovelace in "Peinture" (1659), his tribute to the court portraitist Sir Peter Lely, used similar terms to elevate painting: "O sacred *Peinture*! That dost fairly draw / What but in Mists deep inward *Poets* saw; / . . . Thou that in frames eternity dost bind, / And art a written and a body'd mind."
4. Abilities.

even Monarchs themselves; and Virtue is a noble Lesson to be learn'd, and 'tis by Comparison we can Judge and Chuse. 'Tis by such illustrious Presidents,[5] as your Lordship, the World can be Better'd and Refin'd; when a great part of the lazy Nobility shall, with Shame, behold the admirable Accomplishments of a Man so Great, and so Young.

Your Lordship has read innumerable Volumes of Men, and Books; not Vainly for the gust[6] of Novelty, but Knowledge, excellent Knowledge: Like the industrious Bee, from every Flower you return Laden with the precious Dew, which you are sure to turn to the Publick Good. You hoard no one Perfection, but lay it all out in the Glorious Service of your Religion and Country; to both which you are a useful and necessary Honour: They both want[7] such Supporters; and 'tis only Men of so elevated Parts, and fine Knowledge; such noble Principles of Loyalty and Religion this Nation Sighs for. [Where is it amongst all our Nobility we shall find so great a Champion for the Catholick Church? With what Divine Knowledge have you writ in Defence of the Faith! How unanswerably have you clear'd all these Intricacies in Religion, which even the Gown-men have left Dark and Difficult! With what unbeaten Arguments you convince the Faithless, and instruct the Ignorant!][8] Where shall we find a Man so Young, like St. *Augustine*, in the midst of all his Youth and Gaiety, Teaching the World divine Precepts, true Notions of Faith, and Excellent Morality, and, at the same time, be also a perfect Pattern of all that accomplish[9] a Great Man? You have, my Lord, all that refin'd Wit that Charms, and the Affability that Obliges; a Generosity that gives a Lustre to your Nobility; that Hospitality, and Greatness of Mind, that ingages the World; and that admirable Conduct, that so well Instructs it. Our Nation ought to regret and bemoan their Misfortunes, for not being able to claim the Honour of the Birth of a Man who is so fit to serve his Majesty, and his Kingdoms, in all Great and Publick Affairs: And to the Glory of your Nation be it spoken, it produces more considerable Men, for all fine Sense, Wit, Wisdom, Breeding, and Generosity (for the generality of the Nobility) than all other Nations can Boast; and the Fruitfulness of your Virtues sufficiently make amends for the Barrenness of your Soil:

---

5. Precedents or models.
6. Relish.
7. Lack.
8. The four bracketed sentences lauding Maitland's Catholic faith survive only as a stop-press variant in the Bodleian Library copy, bound in Behn's *Three Histories* (1688), and may have been removed by Behn or by her publisher. Her most outspoken statement of her Catholic sympathies, they have encouraged speculation that she had a Catholic upbringing or had privately become a Catholic. "Gown-men": the clergy.
9. Complete, fully equip. St. Augustine (354–430), early church father and philosopher. His *Confessions* describe his worldly early years as a student and a teacher of rhetoric in North Africa and Italy, followed by his conversion to Christianity in 386. In his later life (Lord Maitland shows a more precocious wisdom), he often wrote against pagan and Christian enemies of the Church and argued for its authority descended from the Apostles.

Which however cannot be incommode[1] to your Lordship; since your Quality, and the Veneration that the Commonalty naturally pay their Lords, creates a flowing Plenty there—that makes you Happy. And to compleat your Happiness, my Lord, Heaven has blest you with a Lady, to whom it has given all the Graces, Beauties, and Virtues of her Sex; all the Youth, Sweetness of Nature; of a most illustrious Family; and who is a most rare Example to all Wives of Quality, for her eminent Piety, Easiness, and Condescention;[2] and as absolutely merits Respect from all the World, as she does that Passion and Resignation she receives from your Lordship; and which is, on her part, with so much Tenderness return'd. Methinks your tranquil Lives[3] are an Image of the new Made and Beautiful Pair in Paradise: And 'tis the Prayers and Wishes of all, who have the Honour to know you, that it may Eternally so continue, with Additions of all the Blessings this World can give you.

My Lord, the Obligations I have to some of the Great Men of your Nation, particularly to your Lordship, gives me an Ambition of making my Acknowledgments, by all the Opportunities I can; and such humble Fruits, as my Industry produces, I lay at your Lordship's Feet. This is a true Story, of a Man Gallant enough to merit your Protection; and, had he always been so Fortunate, he had not made so Inglorious an end: The Royal Slave I had the Honour to know in my Travels to the other World; and though I had none above me in that Country, yet I wanted power to preserve this Great Man. If there be any thing that seems Romantick, I beseech your Lordship to consider, these Countries do, in all things, so far differ from ours, that they produce unconceivable Wonders; at least, they appear so to us, because New and Strange. What I have mention'd I have taken care shou'd be Truth, let the Critical Reader judge as he pleases. 'Twill be no Commendation to the Book, to assure your Lordship I writ it in a few Hours, though it may serve to Excuse some of its Faults of Connexion; for I never rested my Pen a Moment for Thought: 'Tis purely the Merit of my Slave that must render it worthy of the Honour it begs; and the Author of that of Subscribing herself,

My Lord,
Your Lordship's most oblig'd
and obedient Servant,
A. BEHN.

1. Troublesome. In praising Scotland's feudal traditions, Behn seems to allude not only to the traditional loyalties commanded by Highland chieftains but to the political dominance of the Scottish Privy Council at Edinburgh. Both groups strongly supported the Stuart monarchy.
2. Graciousness.
3. Anne Campbell, daughter of the earl of Argyll, belonged to a Protestant family that led the Scottish opposition to James II, while her husband seems to have resisted some of James's more extreme policies. This tranquility did not continue.

The History of the *Royal Slave*.

I do not pretend, in giving you the History of this *Royal Slave*, to entertain my Reader with the Adventures of a feign'd *Hero*, whose Life and Fortunes Fancy may manage at the Poet's Pleasure; nor in relating the Truth, design to adorn it with any Accidents, but such as arriv'd in earnest to him: And it shall come simply into the World, recommended by its own proper Merits, and natural Intrigues; there being enough of Reality to support it, and to render it diverting, without the Addition of Invention.

I was my self an Eye-Witness to a great part, of what you will find here set down; and what I cou'd not be Witness of, I receiv'd from the Mouth of the chief Actor in this History, the *Hero* himself, who gave us the whole Transactions of his Youth; and though I shall omit, for Brevity's sake, a thousand little Accidents of his Life, which, however pleasant to us, where History was scarce, and Adventures very rare; yet might prove tedious and heavy to my Reader, in a World where he finds Diversions for every Minute, new and strange: But we who were perfectly charm'd with the Character of this great Man, were curious to gather every Circumstance of his Life.

The Scene of the last part of his Adventures lies in a Colony in *America*, called *Surinam*,[4] in the *West-Indies*.

But before I give you the Story of this *Gallant Slave*, 'tis fit I tell you the manner of bringing them to these new *Colonies*; for those they make use of there, are not *Natives* of the place; for those we live with in perfect Amity, without daring to command 'em; but on the contrary, caress 'em with all the brotherly and friendly Affection in the World; trading with 'em for their Fish, Venison, Buffilo's,[5] Skins, and little Rarities; as Marmosets, a sort of *Monkey* as big as a Rat or Weasel, but of a marvellous and delicate shape, and has Face and Hands like an Humane Creature: and *Cousheries*,[6] a little Beast in the form and fashion of a Lion, as big as a Kitten; but so exactly made in all parts like that noble Beast, that it is it in *Miniature*. Then for little *Parakeetoes*, great Parrots, *Muckaws*, and a thousand other Birds and Beasts of wonderful and surprizing Forms, Shapes, and Colours. For Skins of prodigious Snakes, of which there are some threescore Yards in length; as is the Skin of one that may be seen at His Majesty's *Antiquaries*: Where

---

4. An English colony within the larger district of Guiana, on the South American coast east of Venezuela; later Dutch Guiana, now Suriname. During the 1650s it was settled by experienced planters from the main colony at Barbados, where the land supply was exhausted.
5. Buffaloes, or wild oxen of various species.
6. A local animal mentioned in various travel accounts but not consistently described. Probably the lion-headed marmoset, or perhaps the *cujara* (Portuguese), a small rodent known as the rice rat. According to George Warren's *Impartial Description of Surinam* (1667) the "Cusharee" lived in trees and was "black, less than a Marmazet, and shap'd every way perfectly like a Lyon," while John Ogilby's *America* (1671) reported the "Cuscary" to be "a brown four-footed Creature, about the bigness of a little Dog, but hath the shape of a Lyon."

are also some rare Flies,[7] of amazing Forms and Colours, presented to 'em by my self; some as big as my Fist, some less; and all of various Excellencies, such as Art cannot imitate. Then we trade for Feathers, which they order into all Shapes, make themselves little short Habits of 'em, and glorious Wreaths for their Heads, Necks, Arms and Legs, whose Tinctures are unconceivable. I had a Set of these presented to me, and I gave 'em to the King's Theatre, and it was the Dress of the *Indian Queen*,[8] infinitely admir'd by Persons of Quality; and were unimitable. Besides these, a thousand little Knacks, and Rarities in Nature, and some of Art; as their Baskets, Weapons, Aprons, &c. We dealt with 'em with Beads of all Colours, Knives, Axes, Pins and Needles; which they us'd only as Tools to drill Holes with in their Ears, Noses and Lips, where they hang a great many little things; as long Beads, bits of Tin, Brass, or Silver, beat thin; and any shining Trincket. The Beads they weave into Aprons about a quarter of an Ell long, and of the same breadth;[9] working them very prettily in Flowers of several Colours of Beads; which Apron they wear just before 'em, as *Adam* and *Eve* did the Fig-leaves; the Men wearing a long Stripe of Linen, which they deal with us for. They thread these Beads also on long Cotton-threads, and make Girdles to tie their Aprons to, which come twenty times, or more, about the Waist; and then cross, like a Shoulder-belt, both ways, and round their Necks, Arms and Legs. This Adornment, with their long black Hair, and the Face painted in little Specks or Flowers here and there, makes 'em a wonderful Figure to behold. Some of the Beauties which indeed are finely shap'd, as almost all are, and who have pretty Features, are very charming and novel; for they have all that is called Beauty, except the Colour, which is a reddish Yellow; or after a new Oiling, which they often use to themselves, they are of the colour of a new Brick, but smooth, soft and sleek. They are extream modest and bashful, very shy, and nice[1] of being touch'd. And though they are all thus naked, if one lives for ever among 'em, there is not to be seen an indecent Action, or Glance; and being continually us'd to see one another so unadorn'd, so like our first Parents before the Fall, it seems as if they had no Wishes; there being nothing to heighten Curiosity, but all you can see, you see at once, and every Moment see; and where there is no Novelty, there can be no Curiosity. Not but I have seen a

---

7. Butterflies. "*Antiquaries*": probably the new museum or repository of the Royal Society, which had published instructions calling on world travelers to contribute their natural history discoveries.
8. The title character of the rhymed heroic play by Sir Robert Howard and John Dryden, set in Mexico, that opened at the Theatre Royal in January 1664. It was noted for its lavish production, and contemporary accounts mention "speckl'ed plumes" and feather headdresses. However, this opening took place when Behn seems to have been in Surinam (see p. 265), so it is speculated that her costume was used in the 1668 revival and then perhaps in later plays with exotic New World settings.
9. About one foot square. "Ell": an old English measure of about forty-five inches.
1. Careful; with a sense of delicacy.

handsom young *Indian*, dying for Love of a very beautiful young *Indian*
Maid; but all his Courtship was, to fold his Arms, pursue her with his
Eyes, and Sighs were all his Language: While she, as if no such Lover
were present; or rather, as if she desired none such, carefully guarded
her Eyes from beholding him; and never approach'd him, but she
look'd down with all the blushing Modesty I have seen in the most
severe and cautious of our World. And these People represented to me
an absolute *Idea* of the first State of Innocence, before Man knew how
to sin: And 'tis most evident and plain, that simple Nature is the most
harmless, inoffensive and vertuous Mistress. 'Tis she alone, if she were
permitted, that better instructs the World, than all the Inventions of
Man: Religion wou'd here but destroy that Tranquillity, they possess by
Ignorance; and Laws wou'd but teach 'em to know Offence, of which
now they have no Notion. They once made Mourning and Fasting for
the Death of the *English* Governor, who had given his Hand to come
on such a Day to 'em, and neither came, nor sent; believing, when
once a Man's Word was past, nothing but Death cou'd or shou'd prevent his keeping it: And when they saw he was not dead, they ask'd
him, what Name they had for a Man who promis'd a thing he did not
do? The Governor told them, Such a man was a *Lyar*, which was a
Word of Infamy to a Gentleman. Then one of 'em reply'd, *Governor,
you are a Lyar, and guilty of that Infamy.* They have a Native Justice,
which knows no Fraud; and they understand no Vice, or Cunning, but
when they are taught by the *White Men*. They have Plurality of Wives,
which, when they grow old, they serve those that succeed 'em, who are
young; but with a Servitude easie and respected; and unless they take
Slaves in War, they have no other Attendants.

Those on that *Continent* where I was, had no King; but the oldest
War-Captain was obey'd with great Resignation.

A War-Captain is a Man who has led them on to Battel with Conduct,[2] and Success; of whom I shall have Occasion to speak more
hereafter, and of some other of their Customs and Manners, as they
fall in my way.

With these People, as I said, we live in perfect Tranquillity, and good
Understanding, as it behooves us to do; they knowing all the places
where to seek the best Food of the Country, and the Means of getting
it; and for very small and unvaluable Trifles, supply us with what 'tis
impossible for us to get; for they do not only in the Wood, and over
the *Sevana's*,[3] in Hunting, supply the parts of Hounds, by swiftly scour-
ing through those almost impassable places; and by the meer Activity
of their Feet, run down the nimblest Deer, and other eatable Beasts:

2. Capacity to lead.
3. I.e., savannas; open grasslands found in the tropics and subtropics. Lord Willoughby's letter
   to his wife (see p. 99) reports Surinam's "brave savanas, where you may, in coach or on
   horseback, ride thirty or forty miles."

But in the water, one wou'd think they were Gods of the Rivers, or Fellow-Citizens of the Deep; so rare an Art they have in Swimming, Diving, and almost Living in Water; by which they command the less swift Inhabitants of the Floods. And then for Shooting; what they cannot take, or reach with their Hands, they do with Arrows; and have so admirable an Aim, that they will split almost an Hair; and at any distance that an Arrow can reach, they will shoot down Oranges, and other Fruit, and only touch the Stalk with the Dart's Point, that they may not hurt the Fruit. So that they being, on all Occasions, very useful to us, we find it absolutely necessary to caress 'em as Friends, and not to treat 'em as Slaves; nor dare we do other, their Numbers so far surpassing ours in that *Continent*.

Those then whom we make use of to work in our Plantations of Sugar, are *Negro's*, *Black*-Slaves altogether; which are transported thither in this manner.

Those who want Slaves, make a Bargain with a Master, or a Captain of a Ship, and contract to pay him so much a-piece, a matter of twenty Pound a Head for as many as he agrees for, and to pay for 'em when they shall be deliver'd on such a Plantation: So that when there arrives a Ship laden with Slaves, they who have so contracted, go a-board, and receive their Number by Lot;[4] and perhaps in one Lot that may be for ten, there may happen to be three or four Men; the rest, Women and Children: Or be there more or less of either Sex, you are oblig'd to be contented with your Lot.

Coramantien,[5] a Country of *Blacks* so called, was one of those places in which they found the most advantageous Trading for these Slaves; and thither most of our great Traders in that Merchandice traffick'd; for that Nation is very war-like and brave; and having a continual Campaign, being always in Hostility with one neighbouring Prince or other, they had the fortune to take a great many Captives; for all they took in Battel, were sold as Slaves; at least, those common Men who cou'd not ransom themselves. Of these Slaves so taken, the General only has all the profit; and of these Generals, our Captains and Masters of Ships buy all their Freights.

The King of *Coramantien* was himself a Man of a Hundred and odd Years old, and had no Son, though he had many beautiful *Black*-Wives; for most certainly, there are Beauties that can charm of that Colour.

---

4. The contract sale of slaves in lots was a common method of sale, and twenty pounds a frequently mentioned price.
5. Not a country but a fortified English trading station on the Gold Coast of West Africa, in modern-day Ghana, established by agreement with the local Fante ruler in 1632. It became the English trading headquarters until taken by the Dutch in 1665. As the slave trade expanded, all persons shipped out from the region were called Cormantines or Cormantees (variously spelled) and gained a reputation for their beauty and bearing, intelligence and fierceness in war, and extreme dignity under captivity or torture. They would have been mainly but not exclusively Fante, Ashante, and other Akan-speaking peoples.

In his younger Years he had had many gallant Men to his Sons, thirteen of which died in Battel, conquering when they fell; and he had only left him for his Successor, one Grand-Child, Son to one of these dead Victors; who, as soon as he cou'd bear a Bow in his Hand, and a Quiver at his Back, was sent into the Field, to be trained up by one of the oldest Generals, to War; where, from his natural Inclination to Arms, and the Occasions given him, with the good Conduct of the old General, he became, at the Age of Seventeen, one of the most expert Captains, and bravest Soldiers, that ever saw the Field of *Mars*:[6] So that he was ador'd as the Wonder of all that World, and the Darling of the Soldiers. Besides, he was adorn'd with a native Beauty so transcending all those of his gloomy Race, that he strook an Awe and Reverence, even in those that knew not his Quality; as he did in me, who beheld him with Surprize and Wonder, when afterwards he arriv'd in our World.

He had scarce arriv'd at his Seventeenth Year, when fighting by his Side, the General was kill'd with an Arrow in his Eye, which the Prince *Oroonoko* (for so was this gallant *Moor*[7] call'd) very narrowly avoided; nor had he, if the General, who saw the Arrow shot, and perceiving it aim'd at the Prince, had not bow'd his Head between, on purpose to receive it in his own Body rather than it shou'd touch that of the Prince, and so saved him.

'Twas then, afflicted as *Oroonoko* was, that he was proclaim'd General in the old Man's place; and then it was, at the finishing of that War, which had continu'd for two Years, that the Prince came to Court; where he had hardly been a Month together, from the time of his fifth Year, to that of Seventeen; and 'twas amazing to imagine where it was he learn'd so much Humanity; or, to give his Accomplishments a juster Name, where 'twas he got that real Greatness of Soul, those refin'd Notions of true Honour, that absolute Generosity, and that Softness that was capable of the highest Passions of Love and Gallantry, whose Objects were almost continually fighting Men, or those mangl'd, or dead; who heard no Sounds, but those of War and Groans: Some part of it we may attribute to the Care of a *French*-Man of Wit and Learning; who finding it turn to very good Account to be a sort of Royal Tutor to this young *Black*, & perceiving him very ready, apt, and quick of Apprehension, took a great pleasure to teach him Morals, Language and Science; and was for it extreamly belov'd and valu'd by him. Another Reason was, He lov'd, when he came from War, to see all the *English* Gentlemen that traded thither; and did not only learn their

---

6. Battlefield, named after the Roman god of war. The Fante people had a "braffo," or military leader, resembling Behn's general, though not a strong monarchy. Moreover, as Europeans were slow to understand, descent systems of the Akan-speaking peoples of this region were matrilineal.

7. Loosely used for any black-skinned people.

Language, but that of the *Spaniards*[8] also, with whom he traded afterwards for Slaves.

I have often seen and convers'd with this great Man, and been a
Witness to many of his mighty Actions; and do assure my Reader, the
most Illustrious Courts cou'd not have produc'd a braver Man, both for
Greatness of Courage and Mind, a Judgment more solid, a Wit more
quick, and a Conversation more sweet and diverting. He knew almost
as much as if he had read much: He had heard of, and admir'd the
Romans; he had heard of the late Civil Wars in *England*, and the
deplorable Death of our great Monarch;[9] and wou'd discourse of it with
all the Sense, and Abhorrence of the Injustice imaginable. He had an
extream good and graceful Mien, and all the Civility of a well-bred
great Man. He had nothing of Barbarity in his Nature, but in all Points
address'd himself, as if his Education had been in some *European*
Court.

This great and just Character of *Oroonoko* gave me an extream Curiosity to see him, especially when I knew he spoke *French* and *English*,
and that I cou'd talk with him. But though I had heard so much of
him, I was as greatly surpriz'd when I saw him, as if I had heard nothing
of him; so beyond all Report I found him. He came into the Room,
and address'd himself to me, and some other Women, with the best
Grace in the World. He was pretty tall, but of a Shape the most exact
that can be fancy'd: The most famous Statuary[1] cou'd not form the
Figure of a Man more admirably turn'd from Head to Foot. His Face
was not of that brown, rusty Black which most of that Nation are, but
a perfect Ebony, or polish'd Jett. His Eyes were the most awful that
cou'd be seen, and very piercing; the White of 'em being like Snow,
as were his Teeth. His Nose was rising and *Roman*, instead of *African*
and flat. His Mouth, the finest shap'd that cou'd be seen; far from those
great turn'd Lips, which are so natural to the rest of the *Negroes*. The
whole Proportion and Air of his Face was so noble, and exactly form'd,
that, bating[2] his Colour, there cou'd be nothing in Nature more beautiful, agreeable and handsome. There was no one Grace wanting, that
bears the Standard of true Beauty: His Hair came down to his Shoul-

---

8. A version of Portuguese (along with some French and English) became the common trading
   language along the West African coast, but Spain by treaty had no trade in this part of the
   world.
9. King Charles I, tried and beheaded in 1649 at the end of the civil wars between the Royalists
   and Parliamentarians. In 1688, this remark and others would have signaled Behn's ardent
   support of James II, the last of the Stuart kings, who would be forced into exile within the
   year.
1. Sculptor.
2. Except for. The singling out of Africans who met European standards of beauty or character
   is by no means unique to Behn. In the English version of Villault's *Relation of the Coasts of
   Africk called Guinee* (1670), for instance, a Sierra Leone prince is "well proportioned, and
   (bating his complexion) a very handsome man, his aire was courteous, and majestick," while
   some Ivory Coast women show features "so just and regular, that (bate them the unhappiness
   of their complexion) they were absolute beauties."

ders, by the Aids of Art; which was, by pulling it out with a Quill, and
keeping it comb'd; of which he took particular Care. Nor did the Per-
fections of his Mind come short of those of his Person; for his Discourse
was admirable upon almost any Subject; and who-ever had heard him
speak, wou'd have been convinc'd of their Errors, that all fine Wit is
confin'd to the *White* Men, especially to those of *Christendom*; and
wou'd have confess'd that *Oroonoko* was as capable even of reigning
well, and of governing as wisely, had as great a Soul, as politick[3] Maxims, and was as sensible of Power as any Prince civiliz'd in the most
refin'd Schools of Humanity and Learning, or the most Illustrious
Courts.

   This Prince, such as I have describ'd him, whose Soul and Body
were so admirably adorn'd, was (while yet he was in the Court of his
Grandfather) as I said, as capable of Love, as 'twas possible for a brave
and gallant Man to be; and in saying that, I have nam'd the highest
Degree of Love; for sure, great Souls are most capable of that Passion.

   I have already said, the old General was kill'd by the shot of an Arrow,
by the Side of this Prince, in Battel; and that *Oroonoko* was made
General. This old dead *Hero* had one only Daughter left of his Race;
a Beauty that, to describe her truly, one need say only, she was Female
to the noble Male; the beautiful *Black Venus*,[4] to our young *Mars*; as
charming in her Person as he, and of delicate Vertues. I have seen an
hundred *White* Men sighing after her, and making a thousand Vows
at her Feet, all vain, and unsuccessful: And she was, indeed, too great
for any, but a Prince of her own Nation to adore.

   Oroonoko coming from the Wars, (which were now ended) after he
had made his Court to his Grand-father, he thought in Honour he
ought to make a Visit to *Imoinda*, the Daughter of his Foster-father,
the dead General; and to make some Excuses to her, because his Preservation was the Occasion of her Father's Death; and to present her
with those Slaves that had been taken in this last Battel, as the Trophies
of her Father's Victories. When he came, attended by all the young
Soldiers of any Merit, he was infinitely surpriz'd at the Beauty of this
fair Queen of Night, whose Face and Person was so exceeding all he
had ever beheld, that lovely Modesty with which she receiv'd him, that
Softness in her Look, and Sighs, upon the melancholy Occasion of this
Honour that was done by so great a Man as *Oroonoko*, and a Prince of
whom she had heard such admirable things; the Awfulness[5] wherewith
she receiv'd him, and the Sweetness of her Words and Behaviour while
he stay'd, gain'd a perfect Conquest over his fierce Heart, and made
him feel, the Victor cou'd be subdu'd. So that having made his first
Compliments, and presented her an hundred and fifty Slaves in Fetters,

3. Shrewd, sagacious.
4. Goddess of love. According to myth, she and the god of war were lovers.
5. Reverence.

he told her with his Eyes, that he was not insensible of her Charms; while *Imoinda*, who wish'd for nothing more than so glorious a Conquest, was pleas'd to believe, she understood that silent Language of new-born Love; and from that Moment, put on all her Additions to Beauty.

The Prince return'd to Court with quite another Humour than before; and though he did not speak much of the fair *Imoinda*, he had the pleasure to hear all his Followers speak of nothing but the Charms of that Maid; insomuch that, even in the Presence of the old King, they were extolling her, and heightning, if possible, the Beauties they had found in her: So that nothing else was talk'd of, no other Sound was heard in every Corner where there were Whisperers, but *Imoinda! Imoinda!*

'Twill be imagin'd *Oroonoko* stay'd not long before he made his second Visit; nor, considering his Quality, not much longer before he told her, he ador'd her. I have often heard him say, that he admir'd[6] by what strange Inspiration he came to talk things so soft, and so passionate, who never knew Love, nor was us'd to the Conversation[7] of Women; but (to use his own Words) he said, Most happily, some new, and till then unknown Power instructed his Heart and Tongue in the Language of Love, and at the same time, in favour of him, inspir'd *Imoinda* with a Sense of his Passion. She was touch'd with what he said, and return'd it all in such Answers as went to his very Heart, with a Pleasure unknown before: Nor did he use those Obligations[8] ill, that Love had done him; but turn'd all his happy Moments to the best advantage; and as he knew no Vice, his Flame aim'd at nothing but Honour, if such a distinction may be made in Love; and especially in that Country, where Men take to themselves as many as they can maintain; and where the only Crime and Sin with Woman is, to turn her off, to abandon her to Want, Shame and Misery: Such ill Morals are only practis'd in *Christian*-Countries, where they prefer the bare Name of Religion; and, without Vertue or Morality, think that's sufficient. But *Oroonoko* was none of those Professors; but as he had right Notions of Honour, so he made her such Propositions as were not only and barely such; but, contrary to the Custom of his Country, he made her Vows, she shou'd be the only woman he wou'd possess while he liv'd; that no Age or Wrinkles shou'd incline him to change, for her Soul wou'd be always fine, and always young; and he shou'd have an eternal *Idea* in his Mind of the Charms she now bore, and shou'd look into his Heart for that *Idea*, when he cou'd find it no longer in her Face.

After a thousand Assurances of his lasting Flame, and her eternal Empire over him, she condescended to receive him for her Husband;

6. Marveled.
7. Company.
8. Benefits.

or rather, receiv'd him, as the greatest Honour the Gods cou'd do her.

There is a certain Ceremony in these Cases to be observ'd, which I forgot to ask him how perform'd; but 'twas concluded on both sides, that, in Obedience to him, the Grand-father was to be first made acquainted with the Design; for they pay a most absolute Resignation to the Monarch, especially when he is a Parent also.

On the other side, the old King, who had many Wives, and many Concubines, wanted not Court-Flatterers to insinuate in his Heart a thousand tender Thoughts for this young Beauty; and who represented her to his Fancy, as the most charming he had ever possess'd in all the long Race of his numerous Years. At this Character his old Heart, like an extinguish'd Brand, most apt to take Fire,[9] felt new Sparks of Love, and began to kindle; and now grown to his second Childhood, long'd with Impatience to behold this gay thing, with whom, alas! he cou'd but innocently play. But how he shou'd be confirm'd she was this *Wonder*, before he us'd his Power to call her to Court (where Maidens never came, unless for the King's private Use) he was next to consider; and while he was so doing, he had Intelligence brought him, that *Imoinda* was most certainly Mistress to the Prince *Oroonoko*. This gave him some *Shagrien*;[1] however, it gave him also an Opportunity, one Day, when the Prince was a-hunting, to wait on a Man of Quality, as his Slave and Attendant, who shou'd go and make a Present to *Imoinda*, as from the Prince; he shou'd then, unknown, see this fair Maid, and have an Opportunity to hear what Message she wou'd return the Prince for his Present; and from thence gather the state of her Heart, and degree of her Inclination. This was put in Execution, and the old Monarch saw, and burnt: He found her all he had heard, and wou'd not delay his Happiness, but found he shou'd have some Obstacle to overcome her Heart; for she express'd her Sense of the Present the Prince had sent her, in terms so sweet, so soft and pretty, with an Air of Love and Joy that cou'd not be dissembl'd; insomuch that 'twas past doubt whether she lov'd *Oroonoko* entirely. This gave the old King some Affliction; but he salv'd it with this, that the Obedience the People pay their King, was not at all inferior to what they pay'd their Gods: And what Love wou'd not oblige *Imoinda* to do, Duty wou'd compel her to.

He was therefore no sooner got to his Apartment, but he sent the Royal Veil to *Imoinda*; that is, the Ceremony of Invitation: he sends the Lady, he has a Mind to honour with his Bed, a Veil, with which she is cover'd, and secur'd for the King's Use; and 'tis Death to disobey; besides, held a most impious Disobedience.

---

9. Proverbial. As noted in *The Oxford Dictionary of English Proverbs*: "The heat of glowing brands covered with ashes are more fervent and violent when they break out than the flames of blazing brush discovered and dispersed in the open air" (Jacques Yver, *A Courtlie Controversie of Cupids Cautels*, 1578).

1. I.e., chagrin.

'Tis not to be imagin'd the Surprize and Grief that seiz'd this lovely Maid at this News and Sight. However, as Delays in these Cases are dangerous, and Pleading worse than Treason; trembling, and almost fainting, she was oblig'd to suffer her self to be cover'd, and led away.

They brought her thus to Court; and the King, who had caus'd a very rich Bath to be prepar'd, was led into it, where he sate under a Canopy, in State, to receive this long'd for Virgin; whom he having commanded shou'd be brought to him, they (after dis-robing her) led her to the Bath, and making fast the Doors, left her to descend. The King, without more Courtship, bad her throw off her Mantle, and come to his Arms. But *Imoinda*, all in Tears, threw her self on the Marble, on the Brink of the Bath, and besought him to hear her. She told him, as she was a Maid, how proud of the Divine Glory she should have been of having it in her power to oblige her King: but as by the Laws, he cou'd not; and from his Royal Goodness, wou'd not take from any Man his wedded Wife: So she believ'd she shou'd be the Occasion of making him commit a great Sin, if she did not reveal her State and Condition; and tell him, she was anothers, and cou'd not be so happy to be his.

The King, enrag'd at this Delay, hastily demanded the Name of the bold Man, that had marry'd a Woman of her Degree, without his Consent. *Imoinda*, seeing his Eyes fierce, and his Hands tremble; whether with Age, or Anger, I know not; but she fancy'd the last, almost repented she had said so much, for now she fear'd the Storm wou'd fall on the Prince; she therefore said a thousand things to appease the raging of his Flame, and to prepare him to hear who it was with Calmness; but before she spoke, he imagin'd who she meant, but wou'd not seem to do so, but commanded her to lay aside her Mantle, and suffer her self to receive his Caresses; or, by his Gods, he swore, that happy Man whom she was going to name shou'd die, though it were even *Oroonoko* himself. *Therefore* (said he) *deny this Marriage, and swear thy self a Maid. That* (reply'd *Imoinda*) *by all our Powers I do; for I am not yet known to my Husband.* 'Tis enough (said the King); *'tis enough to satisfie both my Conscience, and my Heart.* And rising from his Seat, he went, and led her into the Bath; it being in vain for her to resist.

In this time the Prince, who was return'd from Hunting, went to visit his *Imoinda*, but found her gone; and not only so, but heard she had receiv'd the Royal Veil. This rais'd him to a Storm; and in his Madness, they had much ado to save him from laying violent Hands on himself. Force first prevail'd, and then Reason: They urg'd all to him, that might oppose his Rage; but nothing weigh'd so greatly with him as the King's Old Age uncapable of injuring him with *Imoinda*. He wou'd give way to that Hope, because it pleas'd him most, and flatter'd best his Heart. Yet this serv'd not altogether to make him cease his different Passions, which sometimes rag'd within him, and sometimes softned into Showers. 'Twas not enough to appease him, to tell him, his Grand-father was old, and cou'd not that way injure him, while he retain'd that awful Duty which the young Men are us'd there to pay to their grave Relations. He cou'd not be convinc'd he had no Cause to sigh and mourn for the Loss of a Mistress, he cou'd not with all his Strength and Courage retrieve. And he wou'd often cry, *O my Friends! were she in wall'd Cities, or confin'd from me in Fortifications of the greatest Strength; did Inchantments or Monsters detain her from me, I wou'd venture through any Hazard to free her: But here, in the Arms of a feeble old Man, my Youth, my violent Love, my Trade in Arms, and all my vast Desire of Glory, avail me nothing: Imoinda is as irrecoverably lost to me, as if she were snatch'd by the cold Arms of Death: Oh! she is never to be retriev'd. If I wou'd wait tedious Years, till Fate shou'd bow the old King to his Grave; even that wou'd not leave me Imoinda free; but still that Custom that makes it so vile a Crime for a Son to marry his Father's Wives or Mistresses, wou'd hinder my Happiness; unless I wou'd either ignobly set an ill President to my Successors, or abandon my Country, and fly with her to some unknown World, who never heard our Story.*

But it was objected to him, that his Case was not the same; for *Imoinda* being his lawful Wife, by solemn Contract, 'twas he was the injur'd Man, and might, if he so pleas'd, take *Imoinda* back, the Breach of the Law being on his Grand-father's side; and that if he cou'd circumvent him, and redeem her from the *Otan*,[2] which is the Palace of the King's Women, a sort of *Seraglio*, it was both just and lawful for him so to do.

This Reasoning had some force upon him, and he shou'd have been entirely comforted, but for the Thought that she was possess'd by his Grand-father. However, he lov'd so well, that he was resolv'd to believe what most favour'd his Hope; and to endeavour to learn from *Imoinda*'s own Mouth, what only she cou'd satisfie him in; whether she was robb'd of that Blessing, which was only due to his Faith and Love. But as it was very hard to get a Sight of the Women, for no Men ever enter'd into the *Otan*, but when the King went to entertain himself with some one of his Wives, or Mistresses; and 'twas Death at any other time, for any other to go in; so he knew not how to contrive to get a Sight of her.

While *Oroonoko* felt all the Agonies of Love, and suffer'd under a Torment the most painful in the World, the old King was not exempted from his share of Affliction. He was troubl'd for having been forc'd by an irresistable Passion, to rob his Son[3] of a Treasure, he knew, cou'd not but be extreamly dear to him, since she was the most beautiful that

---

2. *Odan* is a Fante word for "house or apartment," listed in dictionaries of J. Berry (1960), J. Delaney Russell (1910), and others. Behn's *otan* has also been traced to the Turkish word *oda*, "a room in a seraglio," and to the Persian *otagh*, "a tent or pavillion."
3. I.e., grandson.

ever had been seen; and had besides, all the Sweetness and Innocence of Youth and Modesty, with a Charm of Wit surpassing all. He found that, however she was forc'd to expose her lovely Person to his wither'd Arms, she cou'd only sigh and weep there, and think of *Oroonoko*; and oftentimes cou'd not forbear speaking of him, though her Life were, by Custom, forfeited by owning her Passion. But she spoke not of a Lover only, but of a Prince dear to him, to whom she spoke; and of the Praises of a Man, who, till now, fill'd the old Man's Soul with Joy at every Recital of his Bravery, or even his Name. And 'twas this Dotage on our young *Hero*, that gave *Imoinda* a thousand Privileges to speak of him, without offending; and this Condescention in the old King, that made her take the Satisfaction of speaking of him so very often.

Besides, he many times enquir'd how the Prince bore himself; and those of whom he ask'd, being entirely Slaves to the Merits and Vertues of the Prince, still answer'd what they thought conduc'd best to his Service; which was, to make the old King fancy that the Prince had no more Interest in *Imoinda*, and had resign'd her willingly to the Pleasure of the King; that he diverted himself with his Mathematicians, his Fortifications, his Officers, and his Hunting.

This pleas'd the old Lover, who fail'd not to report these things again to *Imoinda*, that she might, by the Example of her young Lover, withdraw her Heart, and rest better contented in his Arms. But however she was forc'd to receive this unwelcome News, in all Appearance, with Unconcern, and Content, her Heart was bursting within, and she was only happy when she cou'd get alone, to vent her Griefs and Moans with Sighs and Tears.

What Reports of the Prince's Conduct were made to the King, he thought good to justifie as far as possibly he cou'd by his Actions; and when he appear'd in the Presence of the King, he shew'd a Face not at all betraying his Heart: So that in a little time the old Man, being entirely convinc'd that he was no longer a Lover of *Imoinda*, he carry'd him with him, in his Train, to the *Otan*, often to banquet with his Mistress. But as soon as he enter'd, one Day, into the Apartment of *Imoinda*, with the King, at the first Glance from her Eyes, notwithstanding all his determin'd Resolution, he was ready to sink in the place where he stood; and had certainly done so, but for the Support of *Aboan*, a young Man, who was next to him; which, with his Change of Countenance, had betray'd him, had the King chanc'd to look that way. And I have observ'd, 'tis a very great Error in those, who laugh when one says, A Negro *can change Colour*; for I have seen 'em as frequently blush, and look pale, and that as visibly as ever I saw in the most beautiful *White*. And 'tis certain that both these Changes were evident, this Day, in both these Lovers. And *Imoinda*, who saw with some Joy the Change in the Prince's Face, and found it in her own, strove to divert the King from beholding either, by a forc'd Caress, with

which she met him; which was a new Wound in the Heart of the poor
dying Prince. But as soon as the King was busy'd in looking on some
fine thing of Imoinda's making, she had time to tell the Prince with
her angry, but Love-darting Eyes, that she resented his Coldness, and
bemoan'd her own miserable Captivity. Nor were his Eyes silent, but
answer'd hers again, as much as Eyes cou'd do, instructed by the most
tender, and most passionate Heart that ever lov'd: And they spoke so
well, and so effectually, as Imoinda no longer doubted, but she was the
only Delight, and the Darling of that Soul she found pleading in 'em
its Right of Love, which none was more willing to resign than she. And
'twas this powerful Language alone that in an Instant convey'd all the
Thoughts of their Souls to each other; that[4] they both found, there
wanted but Opportunity to make them both entirely happy. But when
he saw another Door open'd by Onahal, a former old Wife of the
King's, who now had Charge of Imoinda; and saw the Prospect of a
Bed of State made ready, with Sweets and Flowers for the Dalliance of
the King; who immediately led the trembling Victim from his Sight,
into that prepar'd Repose; What Rage! what wild Frenzies seiz'd his
Heart! which forcing to keep within Bounds, and to suffer without
Noise, it became the more insupportable, and rent his Soul with ten
thousand Pains. He was forc'd to retire, to vent his Groans; where he
fell down on a Carpet, and lay struggling a long time, and only
breathing now and then,—O Imoinda! When Onahal had finish'd her
necessary Affair within, shutting the Door, she came forth to wait, till
the King call'd; and hearing some one sighing in the other Room, she
pass'd on, and found the Prince in that deplorable Condition, which
she thought needed her Aid: She gave him Cordials, but all in vain;
till finding the nature of his Disease, by his Sighs, and naming Imoinda.
She told him, he had not so much Cause as he imagin'd, to afflict
himself; for if he knew the King so well as she did, he wou'd not lose
a Moment in Jealousie, and that she was confident that Imoinda bore,
at this Minute, part in his Affliction. Aboan was of the same Opinion;
and both together, perswaded him to re-assume his Courage; and all
sitting down on the Carpet, the Prince said so many obliging things to
Onahal, that he half perswaded her to be of his Party. And she promis'd
him, she wou'd thus far comply with his just Desires, that she wou'd
let Imoinda know how faithful he was, what he suffer'd, and what he
said.

This Discourse lasted till the King call'd, which gave Oroonoko a
certain Satisfaction; and with the Hope Onahal had made him conceive, he assum'd a Look as gay as 'twas possible a Man in his Circumstances cou'd do; and presently after, he was call'd in with the rest who

4. So that.

waited without. The King commanded Musick to be brought, and several of his young Wives and Mistresses came all together by his Command, to dance before him; where *Imoinda* perform'd her Part with an Air and Grace so passing all the rest, as her Beauty was above 'em; and receiv'd the Present, ordain'd as a Prize. The Prince was every Moment more charm'd with the new Beauties and Graces he beheld in this fair One: And while he gaz'd, and she danc'd, *Onahal* was retir'd to a Window with *Aboan*.

This *Onahal*, as I said, was one of the Cast-Mistresses of the old King; and 'twas these (now past their Beauty) that were made Guardians, or Governants[5] to the new, and the young Ones; and whose Business it was, to teach them all those wanton Arts of Love, with which they prevail'd and charm'd heretofore in their Turn; and who now treated the triumphing happy Ones with all the Severity, as to Liberty and Freedom, that was possible, in revenge of those Honours they rob them of; envying them those Satisfactions, those Gallantries and Presents, that were once made to themselves, while Youth and Beauty lasted, and which they now saw pass regardless by,[6] and were pay'd only to the Bloomings. And certainly, nothing is more afflicting to a decay'd Beauty, than to behold in it self declining Charms, that were once ador'd; and to find those Caresses paid to new Beauties, to which once she laid a Claim; to hear 'em whisper as she passes by, *That once was a delicate Woman*. These abandon'd Ladies therefore endeavour to revenge all the Despights,[7] and Decays of Time, on these flourishing happy Ones. And 'twas this Severity, that gave *Oroonoko* a thousand Fears he shou'd never prevail with *Onahal*, to see *Imoinda*. But, as I said, she was now retir'd to a Window with *Aboan*.

This young Man was not only one of the best Quality, but a Man extreamly well made, and beautiful; and coming often to attend the King to the *Otan*, he had subdu'd the heart of the antiquated *Onahal*, which had not forgot how pleasant it was to be in Love: And though she had some decays in her Face, she had none in her Sense and Wit; she was there agreeable still, even to *Aboan*'s Youth, so that he took pleasure in entertaining her with Discourses of Love. He knew also, that to make his Court to these She-Favourites, was the way to be great; these being the Persons that do all Affairs and Business at Court. He had also observ'd that she had given him Glances more tender and inviting, than she had done to others of his Quality: And now, when he saw that her Favour cou'd so absolutely oblige the Prince, he fail'd not to sigh in her Ear, and to look with Eyes all soft upon her, and give her Hope that she had made some Impressions on his Heart. He

5. Female teachers or caretakers. "Cast": i.e., cast-off.
6. The first editions read "pass were regardless by."
7. Insults.

found her pleas'd at this, and making a thousand Advances to him; but
the Ceremony ending, and the King departing, broke up the Company
for that Day, and his Conversation.

Aboan fail'd not that Night to tell the Prince of his Success, and how
advantageous the Service of Onahal might be to his Amour with Imoinda. The Prince was overjoy'd with this good News, and besought
him, if it were possible, to caress her so, as to engage her entirely; which
he cou'd not fail to do, if he comply'd with her Desires: For then (said
the Prince) her Life lying at your Mercy, she must grant you the Request
you make in my Behalf. Aboan understood him; and assur'd him, he
would make Love so effectually, that he wou'd defie the most expert
Mistress of the Art, to find out whether he dissembl'd it, or had it really.
And 'twas with Impatience they waited the next Opportunity of going
to the Otan.

The Wars came on, the Time of taking the Field approach'd, and
'twas impossible for the Prince to delay his going at the Head of his
Army, to encounter the Enemy: So that every Day seem'd a tedious
Year, till he saw his Imoinda; for he believ'd he cou'd not live, if he
were forc'd away without being so happy. 'Twas with Impatience therefore, that he expected the next Visit the King wou'd make; and, according to his Wish, it was not long.

The Parley of the Eyes of these two Lovers had not pass'd so secretly,
but an old jealous Lover cou'd spy it; or rather, he wanted not Flatterers,
who told him, they observ'd it: So that the Prince was hasten'd to the
Camp, and this was the last Visit he found he shou'd make to the
Otan; he therefore urg'd Aboan to make the best of this last Effort, and
to explain himself so to Onahal, that she, deferring her Enjoyment of
her young Lover no longer, might make way for the Prince to speak to
Imoinda.

The whole Affair being agreed on between the Prince and Aboan,
they attended the King, as the Custom was, to the Otan; where, while
the whole Company was taken up in beholding the Dancing, and an-
tick Postures the Women Royal made, to divert the King, Onahal
singl'd out Aboan, whom she found most pliable to her Wish. When
she had him where she believ'd she cou'd not be heard, she sigh'd to
him, and softly cry'd, Ah, Aboan! When will you be sensible of my
Passion? I confess it with my Mouth, because I wou'd not give my Eyes
the Lye; and you have but too much already perceiv'd they have confess'd
my Flame: Nor wou'd I have you believe, that because I am the abandon'd Mistress of a King, I esteem my self altogether divested of Charms.
No, Aboan; I have still a Rest of Beauty enough engaging, and have
learn'd to please too well, not to be desirable. I can have Lovers still, but
will have none but Aboan. Madam (reply'd the half-feigning Youth) you
have already, by my Eyes, found, you can still conquer; and I believe 'tis
in pity of me, you condescend to this kind Confession. But, Madam,

Words are us'd to be so small a part of our Country-Courtship, that 'tis rare one can get so happy an Opportunity as to tell one's Heart; and those few Minutes we have are forc'd to be snatch'd for more certain Proofs of Love, than speaking and sighing; and such I languish for.

He spoke this with such a Tone, that she hop'd it true, and cou'd not forbear believing it; and being wholly transported with Joy, for having subdu'd the finest of all the King's Subjects to her Desires, she took from her Ears two large Pearls, and commanded him to wear 'em in his. He wou'd have refus'd 'em, crying, *Madam, these are not the Proofs of your Love that I expect; 'tis Opportunity, 'tis a Lone-hour only, that can make me happy.* But forcing the Pearls into his Hand, she whisper'd softly to him, *Oh! Do not fear a Woman's Invention, when Love sets her a-thinking.* And pressing his Hand, she cry'd, *This Night you shall be happy. Come to the Gate of the Orange-Groves, behind the* Otan; *and I will be ready, about Mid-night, to receive you.* 'Twas thus agreed, and she left him, that no notice might be taken of their speaking together.

The Ladies were still dancing, and the King, laid on a Carpet, with a great deal of pleasure, was beholding them, especially *Imoinda;* who that Day appear'd more lovely than ever, being enliven'd with the good Tidings *Onahal* had brought her of the constant Passion the Prince had for her. The Prince was laid on another Carpet, at the other end of the Room, with his Eyes fix'd on the Object of his Soul; and as she turn'd, or mov'd, so did they; and she alone gave his Eyes and Soul their Motions: Nor did *Imoinda* employ her Eyes to any other Use, than in beholding with infinite Pleasure the Joy she produc'd in those of the Prince. But while she was more regarding him, than the Steps she took, she chanc'd to fall; and so near him, as that leaping with extream force from the Carpet, he caught her in his Arms as she fell; and 'twas visible to the whole Presence, the Joy wherewith he receiv'd her: He clasp'd her close to his Bosom, and quite forgot that Reverence that was due to the Mistress of a King, and that Punishment that is the Reward of a Boldness of this nature; and had not the Presence of Mind of *Imoinda* (fonder of his Safety, than her own) befriended him, in making her spring from his Arms, and fall into her Dance again, he had, at that Instant, met his Death; for the old King, jealous to the last degree, rose up in Rage, broke all the Diversion, and led *Imoinda* to her Apartment, and sent out Word to the Prince, to go immediately to the Camp; and that if he were found another Night in Court, he shou'd suffer the Death ordain'd for disobedient Offenders.

You may imagine how welcome this News was to *Oroonoko,* whose unseasonable Transport and Caress of *Imoinda* was blam'd by all Men that lov'd him; and now he perceiv'd his Fault, yet cry'd, *That for such another Moment, he wou'd be content to die.*

All the *Otan* was in disorder about this Accident; and *Onahal* was particularly concern'd, because on the Prince's Stay depended her Happiness; for she cou'd no longer expect that of *Aboan*. So that, e'er they departed, they contriv'd it so, that the Prince and he shou'd come both that Night to the Grove of the *Otan*, which was all of Oranges and Citrons; and that there they shou'd wait her Orders.

They parted thus, with Grief enough, till Night; leaving the King in possession of the lovely Maid. But nothing cou'd appease the Jealousie of the old Lover: He wou'd not be impos'd on, but wou'd have it, that *Imoinda* made a false Step on purpose to fall into *Oroonoko's* Bosom, and that all things look'd like a Design on both sides, and 'twas in vain she protested her Innocence: He was old and obstinate, and left her more than half assur'd that his Fear was true.

The King going to his Apartment, sent to know where the Prince was, and if he intended to obey his Command. The Messenger return'd, and told him, he found the Prince pensive, and altogether unpreparing for the Campaign; that he lay negligently on the Ground, and answer'd very little. This confirm'd the Jealousie of the King, and he commanded that they shou'd very narrowly and privately watch his Motions; and that he shou'd not stir from his Apartment, but one Spy or other shou'd be employ'd to watch him: So that the Hour approaching, wherein he was to go to the Citron-Grove; and taking only *Aboan* along with him, he leaves his Apartment, and was watch'd to the very Gate of the *Otan*; where he was seen to enter, and where they left him, to carry back the Tidings to the King.

Oroonoko and *Aboan* were no sooner enter'd, but *Onahal* led the Prince to the Apartment of *Imoinda*; who, not knowing any thing of her Happiness, was laid in Bed. But *Onahal* only left him in her Chamber, to make the best of his Opportunity, and took her dear *Aboan* to her own; where he shew'd the heighth of Complaisance for his Prince, when, to give him an Opportunity, he suffer'd himself to be caress'd in Bed by *Onahal*.

The Prince softly waken'd *Imoinda*, who was not a little surpriz'd with Joy to find him there; and yet she trembl'd with a thousand Fears. I believe, he omitted saying nothing to this young Maid, that might perswade her to suffer him to seize his own, and take the Rights of Love; and I believe she was not long resisting those Arms, where she so long'd to be; and having Opportunity, Night and Silence, Youth, Love and Desire, he soon prevail'd; and ravish'd in a Moment, what his old Grand-father had been endeavouring for so many Months.

'Tis not to be imagin'd the Satisfaction of these two young Lovers; nor the Vows she made him, that she remain'd a spotless Maid, till that Night; and that what she did with his Grand-father, had robb'd him of no part of her Virgin-Honour, the Gods, in Mercy and Justice, having reserv'd that for her plighted Lord, to whom of Right it belong'd. And 'tis impossible to express the Transports he suffer'd, while he listen'd to a Discourse so charming, from her lov'd Lips; and clasp'd that Body in his Arms, for whom he had so long languish'd; and nothing now afflicted him, but his suddain Departure from her; for he told her the Necessity, and his Commands; but shou'd depart satisfy'd in this, That since the old King had hitherto not been able to deprive him of those Enjoyments which only belong'd to him, he believ'd for the future he wou'd be less able to injure him; so that, abating the Scandal of the Veil, which was no otherwise so, than that she was Wife to another: He believ'd her safe, even in the Arms of the King, and innocent; yet wou'd he have ventur'd at the Conquest of the World, and have given it all, to have had her avoided that Honour of receiving the *Royal Veil*. 'Twas thus, between a thousand Caresses, that both bemoan'd the hard Fate of Youth and Beauty, so liable to that cruel Promotion: 'Twas a Glory that cou'd well have been spar'd here, though desir'd, and aim'd at by all the young Females of that Kingdom.

But while they were thus fondly employ'd, forgetting how Time ran on, and that the Dawn must conduct him far away from his only Happiness, they heard a great Noise in the *Otan*, and unusual Voices of Men; at which the Prince, starting from the Arms of the frighted *Imoinda*, ran to a little Battel-Ax he us'd to wear by his Side; and having not so much leisure, as to put on his Habit, he oppos'd himself against some who were already opening the Door; which they did with so much Violence, that *Oroonoko* was not able to defend it; but was forc'd to cry out with a commanding Voice, *Whoever ye are that have the Boldness to attempt to approach this Apartment thus rudely, know, that I, the Prince* Oroonoko, *will revenge it with the certain Death of him that first enters: Therefore stand back, and know, this place is sacred to Love, and me this Night; to Morrow 'tis the King's.*

This he spoke with a Voice so resolv'd and assur'd, that they soon retir'd from the Door, but cry'd, *'Tis by the King's Command we are come; and being satisfy'd by thy Voice, O Prince, as much as if we had enter'd, we can report to the King the Truth of all his Fears, and leave thee to provide for thy own Safety, as thou art advis'd by thy Friends.*

At these Words they departed, and left the Prince to take a short and sad Leave of his *Imoinda*; who trusting in the strength of her Charms, believ'd she shou'd appease the Fury of a jealous King, by saying, She was surpriz'd, and that it was by force of Arms he got into her Apartment. All her Concern now was for his Life, and therefore she hasten'd him to the Camp; and with much a-do, prevail'd on him to go: Nor was it she alone that prevail'd, *Aboan* and *Onahal* both pleaded, and both assur'd him of a Lye that shou'd be well enough contriv'd to secure *Imoinda*. So that, at last, with a Heart sad as Death, dying Eyes, and sighing Soul, *Oroonoko* departed and took his way to the Camp.

It was not long after the King in Person came to the *Otan*; where beholding *Imoinda* with Rage in his Eyes, he upbraided her Wicked-

ness and Perfidy, and threatning her Royal Lover, she fell on her Face
at his Feet, bedewing the Floor with her Tears, and imploring his
Pardon for a Fault which she had not with her Will committed; as
Onahal, who was also prostrate with her, cou'd testifie: That, unknown
to her, he had broke into her Apartment, and ravish'd her. She spoke
this much against her Conscience; but to save her own Life, 'twas
absolutely necessary she shou'd feign this Falsity. She knew it cou'd
not injure the Prince, he being fled to an Army that wou'd stand by
him, against any Injuries that shou'd assault him. However, this last
Thought of *Imoinda's* being ravish'd, chang'd the Measures of his Revenge; and whereas before he design'd to be himself her Executioner,
he now resolv'd she shou'd not die. But as it is the greatest Crime in
nature amongst 'em to touch a Woman, after having been possess'd by
a Son, a Father, or a Brother; so now he look'd on *Imoinda* as a polluted
thing, wholly unfit for his Embrace; nor wou'd he resign her to his
Grand-son, because she had receiv'd the *Royal Veil*. He therefore re-
moves her from the *Otan*, with *Onahal*; whom he put into safe Hands,
with Order they should be both sold off, as Slaves, to another Country,
either *Christian*, or *Heathen*; 'twas no matter where.

This cruel Sentence, worse than Death, they implor'd, might be
revers'd; but their Prayers were vain, and it was put in Execution accordingly, and that with so much Secrecy, that none, either without,
or within the *Otan*, knew any thing of their Absence, or their Destiny.

The old King, nevertheless, executed this with a great deal of Reluctancy; but he believ'd he had made a very great Conquest over himself,
when he had once resolv'd, and had perform'd what he resolv'd. He
believ'd now, that his Love had been unjust; and that he cou'd not
expect the Gods, or Captain of the Clouds (as they call the unknown
Power) shou'd suffer a better Consequence from so ill a Cause. He
now begins to hold *Oroonoko* excus'd; and to say, he had Reason for
what he did: And now every Body cou'd assure the King, how passion-
ately *Imoinda* was belov'd by the Prince; even those confess'd it now,
who said the contrary before his Flame was abated. So that the King
being old, and not able to defend himself in War, and having no Sons
of all his Race remaining alive, but only this, to maintain him on his
Throne; and looking on this as a Man disoblig'd, first by the Rape of
his Mistress, or rather, Wife; and now by depriving of him wholly of
her, he fear'd, might make him desperate, and do some cruel thing,
either to himself, or his old Grand-father, the Offender; he began to
repent him extreamly of the Contempt he had, in his Rage, put on
Imoinda. Besides, he consider'd he ought in Honour to have kill'd her,
for this Offence, if it had been one: He ought to have had so much
Value and Consideration for a Maid of her Quality, as to have nobly
put her to death; and not to have sold her like a common Slave, the
greatest Revenge, and the most disgraceful of any; and to which they a

thousand times prefer Death, and implore it; as *Imoinda* did, but cou'd not obtain that Honour. Seeing therefore it was certain that *Oroonoko* wou'd highly resent this Affront, he thought good to make some Excuse for his Rashness to him; and to that End he sent a Messenger to the Camp, with Orders to treat with him about the Matter, to gain his Pardon, and to endeavour to mitigate his Grief; but that by no means he shou'd tell him, she was sold, but secretly put to death; for he knew he shou'd never obtain his Pardon for the other.

When the Messenger came, he found the Prince upon the point of Engaging with the Enemy; but as soon as he heard of the Arrival of the Messenger, he commanded him to his Tent, where he embrac'd him, and receiv'd him with Joy; which was soon abated, by the downcast Looks of the Messenger, who was instantly demanded the Cause by *Oroonoko*, who, impatient of Delay, ask'd a thousand Questions in a Breath; and all concerning *Imoinda*: But there needed little Return, for he cou'd almost answer himself of all he demanded, from his Sighs and Eyes. At last, the Messenger casting himself at the Prince's feet, and kissing them, with all the Submission of a Man that had something to implore which he dreaded to utter, he besought him to hear with Calmness what he had to deliver to him, and to call up all his noble and Heroick Courage, to encounter with his Words, and defend himself against the ungrateful[8] things he must relate. *Oroonoko* reply'd, with a deep Sigh, and a languishing voice,—*I am arm'd against their worst Efforts*——; *for I know they will tell me*, Imoinda *is no more*——; *and after that, you may spare the rest.* Then, commanding him to rise, he laid himself on a Carpet, under a rich Pavillion, and remain'd a good while silent, and was hardly heard to sigh. When he was come a little to himself, the Messenger ask'd him leave to deliver that part of his Embassy, which the Prince had not yet divin'd: And the Prince cry'd, *I permit thee*—. Then he told him the Affliction the old King was in, for the Rashness he had committed in his Cruelty to *Imoinda*; and how he deign'd to ask Pardon for his Offence, and to implore the Prince wou'd not suffer that Loss to touch his Heart too sensibly, which now all the Gods cou'd not restore him, but might recompence him in Glory, which he begg'd he wou'd pursue; and that Death, that common Revenger of all Injuries, wou'd soon even the Account between him, and a feeble old Man.

Oroonoko bad him return his Duty to his Lord and Master; and to assure him, there was no Account of Revenge to be adjusted between them; if there were, 'twas he was the Aggressor, and that Death wou'd be just, and, maugre[9] his Age, wou'd see him righted; and he was contented to leave his Share of Glory to Youths more fortunate, and

8. Offensive.
9. In spite of. Oroonoko is saying that he will die first.

worthy of that Favour from the Gods. That henceforth he wou'd never lift a Weapon, or draw a Bow; but abandon the small Remains of his Life to Sighs and Tears, and the continual Thoughts of what his Lord and Grand-father had thought good to send out of the World, with all that Youth, that Innocence, and Beauty.

After having spoken this, whatever his greatest Officers, and Men of the best Rank cou'd do, they cou'd not raise him from the Carpet, or perswade him to Action, and Resolutions of Life; but commanding all to retire, he shut himself into his Pavillion all that Day, while the Enemy was ready to engage; and wondring at the Delay, the whole Body of the chief of the Army then address'd themselves to him, and to whom they had much a-do to get Admittance. They fell on their Faces at the Foot of his Carpet; where they lay, and besought him with earnest Prayers and Tears, to lead 'em forth to Battel, and not let the Enemy take Advantages of them; and implor'd him to have regard to his Glory, and to the World, that depended on his Courage and Con-duct. But he made no other Reply to all their Supplications but this, That he had now no more Business for Glory; and for the World, it was a Trifle not worth his Care. Go, (continu'd he, sighing) and divide it amongst you; and reap with Joy what you so vainly prize, and leave me to my more welcome Destiny.

They then demanded what they shou'd do, and whom he wou'd constitute in his Room, that the Confusion of ambitious Youth and Power might not ruin their Order, and make them a Prey to the Enemy. He reply'd, He wou'd not give himself the Trouble—; but wish'd 'em to chuse the bravest Man amongst 'em, let his Quality or Birth be what it wou'd: For, O my Friends! (said he) it is not Titles make Men brave, or good; or Birth that bestows Courage and Generosity, or makes the Owner happy. Believe this, when you behold Oroonoko, the most wretched, and abandon'd by Fortune, of all the Creation of the Gods. So turning himself about, he wou'd make no more Reply to all they cou'd urge or implore.

The Army beholding their Officers return unsuccessful, with sad Faces, and ominous Looks, that presag'd no good Luck, suffer'd a thou-sand Fears to take Possession of their Hearts, and the Enemy to come even upon 'em, before they wou'd provide for their Safety, by any De-fence; and though they were assur'd by some, who had a mind to animate 'em, that they shou'd be immediately headed by the Prince, and that in the mean time Aboan had Orders to command as General; yet they were so dismay'd for want of that great Example of Bravery, that they cou'd make but a very feeble Resistance; and at last, down-right, fled before the Enemy, who pursu'd 'em to the very Tents, killing 'em: Nor cou'd all Aboan's Courage, which that Day gain'd him im-mortal Glory, shame 'em into a Manly Defence of themselves. The Guards that were left behind, about the Prince's Tent, seeing the Soldiers flee before the Enemy, and scatter themselves all over the Plain, in great Disorder, made such Out-cries as rouz'd the Prince from his amorous Slumber, in which he had remain'd bury'd for two Days, without permitting any Sustenance to approach him: But, in spite of all his Resolutions, he had not the Constancy of Grief to that Degree, as to make him insensible of the Danger of his Army; and in that Instant he leap'd from his Couch, and cry'd,—*Come, if we must die, let us meet Death the noblest Way; and 'twill be more like* Oroonoko *to encounter him at an Army's Head, opposing the Torrent of a conquering Foe, than lazily, on a Couch, to wait his lingering Pleasure, and die every Moment by a thousand wrecking[1] Thoughts; or be tamely taken by an Enemy, and led a whining, Love-sick Slave, to adorn the Triumphs of* Jamoan, *that young Victor, who already is enter'd beyond the Limits I had pre-scrib'd him.*

While he was speaking, he suffer'd his People to dress him for the Field; and sallying out of his Pavillion, with more Life and Vigour in his Countenance than ever he shew'd, he appear'd like some Divine Power descended to save his Country from Destruction; and his People had purposely put on him[2] all things that might make him shine with most Splendor, to strike a reverend Awe into the Beholders. He flew into the thickest of those that were pursuing his Men; and being animated with Despair, he fought as if he came on purpose to die, and did such things as will not be believ'd that Humane Strength cou'd perform; and such as soon inspir'd all the rest with new Courage, and new Order: And now it was, that they began to fight indeed; and so, as if they wou'd not be out-done, even by their ador'd *Hero*; who turning the Tide of the Victory, changing absolutely the Fate of the Day, gain'd an entire Conquest; and *Oroonoko* having the good Fortune to single out *Jamoan*, he took him Prisoner with his own Hand, having wounded him almost to death.

This *Jamoan* afterwards became very dear to him, being a Man very gallant, and of excellent Graces, and fine Parts; so that he never put him amongst the Rank of Captives, as they us'd to do, without distinction, for the common Sale, or Market; but kept him in his own Court, where he retain'd nothing of the Prisoner, but the Name, and return'd no more into his own Country, so great an Affection he took for *Oroonoko*; and by a thousand Tales and Adventures of Love and Gallantry, flatter'd[3] his Disease of Melancholy and Languishment; which I have often heard him say, had certainly kill'd him, but for the Conversation of this Prince and *Aboan*, and the *French* Governor he had from his Childhood, of whom I have spoken before, and who was a Man of admirable Wit, great Ingenuity and Learning; all which he had infus'd

1. Racking (substituted in the next editions).
2. All four seventeenth-century editions read "put him on."
3. Soothed.

into his young Pupil. This *French*-Man was banish'd out of his own
Country, for some Heretical Notions he held; and though he was a
Man of very little Religion, he had admirable Morals, and a brave Soul.

After the total Defeat of *Jamoan's* Army, which all fled, or were left
dead upon the Place, they spent some time in the Camp; *Oroonoko*
chusing rather to remain a while there in his Tents, than enter into a
Place, or live in a Court where he had so lately suffer'd so great a Loss.
The Officers therefore, who saw and knew his Cause of Discontent,
invented all sorts of Diversions and Sports, to entertain their Prince: So
that what with those Amuzements abroad, and others at home, that is,
within their Tents, with the Perswasions, Arguments and Care of his
Friends and Servants that he more peculiarly priz'd, he wore off in time
a great part of that *Shagrien*,[4] and Torture of Despair, which the first
Efforts of *Imoinda's* Death had given him: Insomuch as having receiv'd
a thousand kind Embassies from the King, and Invitations to return to
Court, he obey'd, though with no little Reluctancy; and when he did
so, there was a visible Change in him, and for a long time he was
much more melancholy than before. But Time lessens all Extreams,
and reduces 'em to *Mediums* and Unconcern; but no Motives or Beauties, though all endeavour'd it, cou'd engage him in any sort of Amour,
though he had all the Invitations to it, both from his own Youth, and
others Ambitions and Designs.

Oroonoko was no sooner return'd from this last Conquest, and receiv'd at Court with all the Joy and Magnificence that cou'd be express'd to a young Victor, who was not only return'd triumphant, but
belov'd like a Deity, when there arriv'd in the Port an *English* Ship.

This Person[5] had often before been in these Countries, and was very
well known to *Oroonoko*, with whom he had traffick'd for Slaves, and
had us'd to do the same with his Predecessors.

This Commander was a Man of a finer sort of Address, and Conversation, better bred, and more engaging, than most of that sort of
Men are; so that he seem'd rather never to have been bred out of a
Court, than almost all his Life at Sea. This Captain therefore was always
better receiv'd at Court, than most of the Traders to those Countries
were; and especially by *Oroonoko*, who was more civiliz'd, according
to the *European* Mode, than any other had been, and took more
Delight in the *White* Nations; and, above all, Men of Parts and Wit.
To this Captain he sold abundance of his Slaves; and for the Favour
and Esteem he had for him, made him many Presents, and oblig'd him
to stay at Court as long as possibly he cou'd. Which the Captain seem'd
to take as a very great Honour done him, entertaining the Prince every
Day with Globes and Maps, and Mathematical Discourses and Instru-

4. Not just chagrin but melancholy.
5. The ship's captain.

ments; eating, drinking, hunting and living with him with so much Familiarity, that it was not to be doubted, but he had gain'd very greatly upon the Heart of this gallant young Man. And the Captain, in Return of all these mighty Favours, besought the Prince to honour his Vessel with his Presence, some Day or other, to Dinner, before he shou'd set Sail; which he condescended to accept, and appointed his Day. The Captain, on his part, fail'd not to have all things in a Readiness, in the most magnificent Order he cou'd possibly: And the Day being come, the Captain, in his Boat, richly adorn'd with Carpets and Velvet-Cushions, row'd to the shore to receive the Prince; with another Long-Boat, where was plac'd all his Musick and Trumpets, with which *Oroonoko* was extreamly delighted; who met him on the shore, attended by his *French* Governor, *Jamoan*, *Aboan*, and about an hundred of the noblest of the Youths of the Court: And after they had first carry'd the Prince on Board, the Boats fetch'd the rest off; where they found a very splendid Treat, with all sorts of fine Wines; and were as well entertain'd, as 'twas possible in such a place to be.

The Prince having drunk hard of Punch, and several Sorts of Wine, as did all the rest (for great Care was taken, they shou'd want nothing of that part of the Entertainment) was very merry, and in great Admiration of the Ship, for he had never been in one before; so that he was curious of beholding every place, where he decently might descend. The rest, no less curious, who were not quite overcome with Drinking, rambl'd at their pleasure *Fore* and *Aft*, as their Fancies guided 'em: So that the Captain, who had well laid his Design before, gave the Word, and seiz'd on all his Guests; they clapping great Irons suddenly on the Prince, when he was leap'd down in the Hold, to view that part of the Vessel; and locking him fast down, secur'd him. The same Treachery was us'd to all the rest; and all in one Instant, in several places of the Ship, were lash'd fast in Irons, and betray'd to Slavery. That great Design over, they set all Hands to work to hoise[6] Sail; and with as treacherous and fair a Wind, they made from the Shore with this innocent and glorious Prize, who thought of nothing less than such an Entertainment.

Some have commended this Act, as brave, in the Captain; but I will spare my sense of it, and leave it to my Reader, to judge as he pleases.

It may be easily guess'd, in what manner the Prince resented this Indignity, who may be best resembl'd to a Lion taken in a Toil; so he rag'd, so he struggl'd for Liberty, but all in vain; and they had so wisely manag'd his Fetters, that he cou'd not use a Hand in his Defence, to quit himself of a Life that wou'd by no Means endure Slavery; nor

6. Hoist. The abduction and enslavement of Africans who visited on board ships or traveled as pawns or passengers is recorded with disapproval in many early reports, official and unofficial, if never on this scale. Victims of high rank were sometimes ransomed or returned to avoid retaliation and the closing of trade.

cou'd he move from the Place, where he was ty'd, to any solid part of the Ship, against which he might have beat his Head, and have finish'd his Disgrace that way: So that being depriv'd of all other means, he resolved to perish for want of Food: And pleased at last with that Thought, and toil'd and tired by Rage and Indignation, he laid himself down, and sullenly resolved upon dying, and refused all things that were brought him.

This did not a little vex the Captain, and the more so, because, he found almost all of 'em of the same Humour; so that the loss of so many brave Slaves, so tall and goodly to behold, wou'd have been very considerable: He therefore order'd one to go from him (for he wou'd not be seen himself) to *Oroonoko*, and to assure him he was afflicted for having rashly done so unhospitable a Deed, and which cou'd not be now remedied, since they were far from shore; but since he resented it in so high a nature, he assur'd him he wou'd revoke his Resolution, and set both him and his Friends a-shore on the next Land they shou'd touch at; and of this the Messenger gave him his Oath, provid'd he wou'd resolve to live: And *Oroonoko*, whose Honour was such as he never had violated a Word in his Life himself, much less a solemn Asseveration, believ'd in an instant what this Man said, but reply'd, He expected for a Confirmation of this, to have his shameful Fetters dismiss'd. This Demand was carried to the *Captain*, who return'd him answer, That the Offence had been so great which he had put upon the Prince, that he durst not trust him with Liberty while he remained in the Ship, for fear lest by a Valour natural to him, and a Revenge that would animate that Valour, he might commit some Outrage fatal to himself and the *King* his Master, to whom his Vessel did belong. To this *Oroonoko* replied, he would engage his Honour to behave himself in all friendly Order and Manner, and obey the Command of the *Captain*, as he was Lord of the *King*'s Vessel, and General of those Men under his Command.

This was deliver'd to the still doubting *Captain*, who could not resolve to trust a *Heathen*, he said, upon his Parole,[7] a Man that had no Sense or notion of the God that he Worshipp'd. *Oroonoko* then replied, He was very sorry to hear that the *Captain* pretended to the Knowledge and Worship of any *Gods*, who had taught him no better Principles, than not to Credit as he would be Credited: but they told him the Difference of their Faith occasion'd that Distrust: For the *Captain* had protested to him upon the Word of a *Christian*, and sworn in the Name of a Great G O D; which if he shou'd violate, he would expect eternal Torment in the World to come. *Is that all the Obligation he has to be Just to his Oath? replied Oroonoko. Let him know I Swear by my Honour, which to violate, wou'd not only render me contemptible and de-*

---

7. Word of honor.

*spised by all brave and honest Men, and so give my self perpetual pain,
but it wou'd be eternally offending and diseasing all Mankind, harming,
betraying, circumventing and outraging all Men; but Punishments hereafter are suffer'd by ones self; and the World takes no cognizances
whether this God have revenged 'em, or not, 'tis done so secretly, and
deferr'd so long: While the Man of no Honour, suffers every moment the
scorn and contempt of the honester World, and dies every day ignomin-
iously in his Fame, which is more valuable than Life: I speak not this
to move Belief, but to shew you how you mistake, when you imagine,
That he who will violate his Honour, will keep his Word with his Gods.*
So turning from him with a disdainful smile, he refused to answer him,
when he urg'd him to know what Answer he shou'd carry back to his
Captain; so that he departed without saying any more.

The *Captain* pondering and consulting what to do, it was concluded
that nothing but *Oroonoko*'s Liberty wou'd encourage any of the rest to
eat, except the *French*-man, whom the *Captain* cou'd not pretend to
keep Prisoner, but only told him he was secured because he might act
something in favour of the Prince, but that he shou'd be freed as soon
as they came to Land. So that they concluded it wholly necessary to
free the Prince from his Irons, that he might show himself to the rest;
that they might have an Eye upon him, and that they cou'd not fear a
single Man.

This being resolv'd, to make the Obligation the greater, the Captain
himself went to *Oroonoko*; where, after many Compliments, and Assurances of what he had already promis'd, he receiving from the Prince
his *Parole*, and his Hand, for his good Behaviour, dismiss'd his Irons,
and brought him to his own Cabin; where, after having treated and
repos'd him a while, for he had neither eat[8] nor slept in four Days
before, he besought him to visit those obstinate People in Chains, who
refus'd all manner of Sustenance, and intreated him to oblige 'em to
eat, and assure 'em of their Liberty the first Opportunity.

Oroonoko, who was too generous, not to give Credit to his Words,
shew'd himself to his People, who were transported with Excess of Joy
at the sight of their Darling Prince; falling at his Feet, and kissing and
embracing 'em; believing, as some Divine Oracle, all he assured 'em.
But he besought 'em to bear their Chains with that Bravery that became
those whom he had seen act so nobly in Arms; and that they cou'd not
give him greater Proofs of their Love and Friendship, since 'twas all
the Security the Captain (his Friend) cou'd have, against the Revenge,
he said, they might possibly justly take, for the Injuries sustain'd by
him. And they all, with one Accord, assur'd him, they cou'd not suffer
enough, when it was for his Repose and Safety.

After this they no longer refus'd to eat, but took what was brought

8. The past form of *eat*.

'em, and were pleas'd with their Captivity, since by it they hop'd to
redeem the Prince, who, all the rest of the Voyage, was treated with all
the Respect due to his Birth, though nothing cou'd divert his Melancholy; and he wou'd often sigh for *Imoinda*, and think this a Punishment due to his Misfortune, in having left that noble Maid behind
him, that fatal Night, in the *Otan*, when he fled to the Camp.

Possess'd with a thousand Thoughts of past Joys with this fair young
Person, and a thousand Griefs for her eternal Loss, he endur'd a tedious
Voyage, and at last arriv'd at the Mouth of the River of *Surinam*, a
Colony belonging to the King of *England*, and where they were to
deliver some part of their Slaves. There the Merchants and Gentlemen of
the Country going on Board, to demand those Lots of Slaves they had already agreed on; and, amongst those, the Over-seers of those Plantations
where I then chanc'd to be, the Captain, who had given the Word, order'd his Men to bring up those noble Slaves in Fetters, whom I have spoken of; and having put 'em, some in one, and some in other Lots, with
Women and Children (which they call *Pickaninies*[9]), they sold 'em off, as
Slaves, to several Merchants and Gentlemen; not putting any two in one
Lot, because they wou'd separate 'em far from each other; not daring to
trust 'em together, lest Rage and Courage shou'd put 'em upon con-
triving some great Action, to the Ruin of the Colony.

Oroonoko was first seiz'd on, and sold to our Over-seer, who had the
first Lot, with seventeen more of all sorts and sizes, but not one of
Quality with him. When he saw this, he found what they meant; for,
as I said, he understood *English* pretty well; and being wholly unarm'd
and defenceless, so as it was in vain to make any Resistance, he only
beheld the Captain with a Look all fierce and disdainful, upbraiding
him with Eyes, that forc'd Blushes on his guilty Cheeks, he only cry'd,
in passing over the Side of the Ship, *Farewel, Sir: 'Tis worth my Suffering, to gain so true a Knowledge both of you, and of your Gods by
whom you swear.* And desiring those that held him to forbear their pains,
and telling 'em he wou'd make no Resistance, he cry'd, *Come, my
Fellow-Slaves; let us descend, and see if we can meet with more Honour
and Honesty in the next World we shall touch upon.* So he nimbly leap'd
into the Boat, and shewing no more Concern, suffer'd himself to be
row'd up the River, with his seventeen Companions.

The Gentleman that bought him was a young *Cornish* Gentleman,
whose Name was *Trefry*; a Man of great Wit, and fine Learning, and
was carry'd into those Parts by the Lord——— Governor,[1] to manage

<hr>

9. Probably from the Portuguese *pequenino*, "very little"; applied to slave children under the age
   of ten.
1. Francis, Lord Willoughby of Parham, restored by royal grant to his title as coproprietor of
   Surinam (and also governor of Barbados and the Caribbee Islands) in June 1663. John Trefry
   was his plantation overseer.

all his Affairs. He reflecting on the last Words of *Oroonoko* to the Captain, and beholding the Richness of his Vest,[2] no sooner came into the Boat, but he fix'd his Eyes on him; and finding something so extraordinary in his Face, his Shape and Mien, a Greatness of Look, and Haughtiness in his Air, and finding he spoke *English*, had a great mind to be enquiring into his Quality and Fortune; which, though *Oroonoko* endeavour'd to hide, by only confessing he was above the Rank of common Slaves, *Trefry* soon found he was yet something greater than he confess'd; and from that Moment began to conceive so vast an Esteem for him, that he ever after lov'd him as his dearest Brother, and shew'd him all the Civilities due to so great a Man.

Trefry was a very good Mathematician, and a Linguist; cou'd speak *French* and *Spanish*; and in the three Days they remain'd in the Boat (for so long were they going from the Ship, to the Plantation) he entertain'd *Oroonoko* so agreeably with his Art and Discourse, that he was no less pleas'd with *Trefry*, than he was with the Prince; and he thought himself, at least, fortunate in this, that since he was a Slave, as long as he wou'd suffer himself to remain so, he had a Man of so excellent Wit and Parts for a Master: So that before they had finish'd their Voyage up the River, he made no scruple of declaring to *Trefry* all his Fortunes, and most part of what I have here related, and put himself wholly into the Hands of his new Friend, whom he found resenting all the Injuries were done him, and was charm'd with all the Greatness of his Actions; which were recited with that Modesty, and delicate Sense, as wholly vanquish'd him, and subdu'd him to his Interest. And he promis'd him on his Word and Honour, he wou'd find the Means to reconduct him to his own Country again: assuring him, he had a perfect Abhorrence of so dishonourable an Action; and that he wou'd sooner have dy'd, than have been the Author of such a Perfidy. He found the Prince was very much concern'd to know what became of his Friends, and how they took their Slavery; and *Trefry* promis'd to take care about the enquiring after their Condition, and that he shou'd have an Account of 'em.

Though, as *Oroonoko* afterwards said, he had little Reason to credit the Words of a *Backearary*,[3] yet he knew not why; but he saw a kind of Sincerity, and awful Truth in the Face of *Trefry*; he saw an Honesty in his Eyes, and he found him wise and witty enough to understand Honour; for it was one of his Maxims, *A Man of Wit cou'd not be a Knave or Villain.*

2. An outer garment or robe.
3. White person or master; a variant of *backra* or *buckra*, from an Ibo or Efik word transported with the slaves to Surinam and the Caribbean. Cf. "Baccararoes *or White Folks*" (*Great Newes from the Barbadoes*, 1676).

In their passage up the River,[4] they put in at several Houses for Refreshment; and ever when they landed, numbers of People wou'd flock to behold this Man; not but their Eyes were daily entertain'd with the sight of Slaves, but the Fame of *Oroonoko* was gone before him, and all People were in Admiration of his Beauty. Besides, he had a rich Habit on, in which he was taken, so different from the rest, and which the Captain cou'd not strip him of, because he was forc'd to surprize his Person in the Minute he sold him. When he found his Habit made him liable, as he thought, to be gaz'd at the more, he begg'd *Trefry* to give him something more befitting a Slave; which he did, and took off his Robes. Nevertheless, he shone through all; and his *Osenbrigs* (a sort of brown *Holland*[5] Suit he had on) cou'd not conceal the Graces of his Looks and Mien; and he had no less Admirers, than when he had his dazzling Habit on: The Royal Youth appear'd in spite of the Slave, and People cou'd not help treating him after a different manner, without designing it: As soon as they approach'd him, they venerated and esteem'd him; his Eyes insensibly commanded Respect, and his Behaviour insinuated it into every Soul. So that there was nothing talk'd of but this young and gallant Slave, even by those who yet knew not that he was a Prince.

I ought to tell you, that the *Christians* never buy any Slaves but they give 'em some Name of their own, their native ones being likely very barbarous, and hard to pronounce; so that Mr. *Trefry* gave *Oroonoko* that of *Caesar*;[6] which Name will live in that Country as long as that (scarce more) glorious one of the great *Roman*; for 'tis most evident, he wanted[7] no part of the Personal Courage of that *Caesar*, and acted things as memorable, had they been done in some part of the World replenish'd with People, and Historians, that might have given him his due. But his Misfortune was, to fall in an obscure World, that afforded only a Female Pen to celebrate his Fame; though I doubt not but it had liv'd from others Endeavours, if the *Dutch*, who, immediately after his Time, took that Country,[8] had not kill'd, banish'd and dispers'd all those that were capable of giving the World this great Man's Life, much better than I have done. And Mr. *Trefry*, who design'd it, dy'd before he began it; and bemoan'd himself for not having undertook it in time.

---

4. The journey up the plantation-lined Surinam River can be traced on the 1667 map (see p. 71), which bears the legend "Very bad traveling from one plantation to another without boats."
5. Coarse cotton or linen (also called osnaburg after a German cloth-manufacturing town), which was standard-issue slave clothing through the eighteenth century.
6. Such classical names as Pompey and Scipio, or even Cupid or Apollo, were frequently given to slaves. Julius Caesar was famed as both a military and a political leader, sometimes portrayed as a strong ruler who acted for the people but who was betrayed by members of the oligarchy. Behn regularly referred to both Charles II and James II as "Caesar" in celebratory poems.
7. Lacked.
8. In 1667 the Dutch attacked and conquered Surinam, and England ceded it by the Treaty of Breda in exchange for New York.

For the future therefore, I must call *Oroonoko, Caesar*, since by that
Name only he was known in our Western World, and by that Name
he was receiv'd on Shore at *Parham-House*, where he was destin'd a
Slave. But if the King himself (God bless him) had come a-shore, there
cou'd not have been greater Expectations by all the whole Plantation,
and those neighbouring ones, than was on ours at that time; and he
was receiv'd more like a Governor, than a Slave. Notwithstanding, as
the Custom was, they assign'd him his Portion of Land, his House, and
his Business, up in the Plantation. But as it was more for Form, than
any Design, to put him to his Task, he endur'd no more of the Slave
but the Name, and remain'd some Days in the House, receiving all
Visits that were made him, without stirring towards that part of the
Plantation where the *Negroes* were.

At last, he wou'd needs go view his Land, his House, and the Business
assign'd him. But he no sooner came to the Houses of the Slaves, which
are like a little Town by it self, the *Negroes* all having left Work, but
they all came forth to behold him, and found he was that Prince who
had, at several times, sold most of 'em to these Parts; and, from a
Veneration they pay to great Men, especially if they know 'em, and
from the Surprize and Awe they had at the sight of him, they all cast
themselves at his Feet, crying out, in their Language, *Live, O King!*
Long Live, O King! And kissing his Feet, paid him even Divine
Homage.

Several *English* Gentlemen were with him; and what Mr. *Trefry* had
told 'em, was here confirm'd; of which he himself before had no other
Witness than *Caesar* himself: But he was infinitely glad to find his
Grandure confirm'd by the Adoration of all the Slaves.

Caesar troubl'd with their Over-Joy, and Over-Ceremony, besought
'em to rise, and to receive him as their Fellow-Slave; assuring them, he
was no better. At which they set up with one Accord a most terrible
and hidious Mourning and condoling, which he and the *English* had
much a-do to appease; but at last they prevail'd with 'em, and they
prepar'd all their barbarous Musick, and every one kill'd and dress'd
something of his own Stock (for every Family has their Land a-part, on
which, at their leisure-times they breed all eatable things); and clubbing
it together,[9] made a most magnificent Supper, inviting their *Grandee*[1]
Captain, their *Prince*, to honour it with his Presence; which he did,
and several *English* with him; where they all waited on him, some
playing, others dancing before him all the time, according to the Manners of their several Nations; and with unwearied Industry, endeavouring to please and delight him.

---

9. Contributing jointly. The slaves' private plots (enabling them to feed themselves) and com-
munal festivities with music are noted by many observers.
1. Not simply fractured English; originally a Spanish nobleman of the highest rank, the name
was applied to any man of eminence, including planters and merchants.

While they sat at Meat Mr. *Trefry* told *Caesar*, that most of these young *Slaves* were undone in Love, with a fine she-*Slave*, whom they had had about Six Months on their Land; the *Prince*, who never heard the Name of *Love* without a Sigh, nor any mention of it without the Curiosity of examining further into that tale, which of all Discourses was most agreeable to him, asked, how they came to be so Unhappy, as to be all undone for one fair *Slave? Trefry*, who was naturally Amorous, and lov'd to talk of Love as well as any body, proceeded to tell him, they had the most charming Black that ever was beheld on their *Plantation*, about Fifteen or Sixteen Years old, as he guess'd; that, for his part, he had done nothing but Sigh for her ever since she came; and that all the white Beautys he had seen, never charm'd him so absolutely as this fine Creature had done; and that no Man, of any Nation, ever beheld her, that did not fall in Love with her; and that she had all the *Slaves* perpetually at her Feet; and the whole Country resounded with the Fame of *Clemene*, for so, said he, we have Christ'ned her: But she denys us all with such a noble Disdain, that 'tis a Miracle to see, that she, who can give such eternal Desires, shou'd herself be all Ice, and all Unconcern. She is adorn'd with the most Graceful Modesty that ever beautifyed Youth; the softest Sigher—that, if she were capable of Love, one would swear she languish'd for some absent happy Man; and so retir'd, as if she fear'd a Rape even from the God of Day;[2] or that the Breezes would steal Kisses from her delicate Mouth. Her Task of Work some sighing Lover every day makes it his Petition to perform for her, which she accepts blushing, and with reluctancy, for fear he will ask her a Look for a Recompence, which he dares not presume to hope; so great an Awe she strikes into the Hearts of her Admirers. *I do not wonder*, replied the Prince, *that* Clemene *shou'd refuse Slaves, being as you say so Beautiful, but wonder how she escapes those who can entertain her as you can do; or why, being your Slave, you do not oblige her to yield. I confess*, said *Trefry*, *when I have, against her will, entertain'd her with Love so long, as to be transported with my Passion; even above Decency, I have been ready to make use of those advantages of Strength and Force Nature has given me. But oh! she disarms me, with that Modesty and Weeping so tender and so moving, that I retire, and thank my Stars she overcame me.* The Company laugh'd at his Civility to a *Slave*, and *Caesar* only applauded the nobleness of his Passion and Nature; since that Slave might be Noble, or, what was better, have true Notions of Honour and Vertue in her. Thus pass'd they this Night, after having received, from the *Slaves*, all imaginable Respect and Obedience.

The next Day *Trefry* ask'd *Caesar* to walk, when the heat was allay'd, and designedly carried him by the Cottage of the *fair Slave*; and told

---

2. The sun. Apollo, sometimes called the sun god, pursued Daphne in one famous episode.

him, she whom he spoke of last Night liv'd there retir'd. *But*, says he, *I would not wish you to approach, for, I am sure, you will be in Love as soon as you behold her.* Caesar assur'd him, he was proof against all the Charms of that Sex; and that if he imagin'd his Heart cou'd be so perfidious to Love again, after *Imoinda*, he believ'd he shou'd tear it from his Bosom: They had no sooner spoke, but a little shock Dog, that *Clemene* had presented[3] her, which she took great Delight in, ran out; and she, not knowing any body was there, ran to get it in again, and bolted out on those who were just Speaking of her: When seeing them, she wou'd have run in again; but *Trefry* caught her by the Hand, and cry'd, Clemene, *however you fly a Lover, you ought to pay some Respect to this Stranger* (pointing to *Caesar*). But she, as if she had resolv'd never to raise her Eyes to the Face of a Man again, bent 'em the more to the Earth, when he spoke, and gave the *Prince* the leisure to look the more at her. There needed no long Gazing, or Consideration, to examin who this fair Creature was; he soon saw *Imoinda* all over her; in a Minute he saw her Face, her Shape, her Air, her Modesty, and all that call'd forth his Soul with Joy at his Eyes, and left his Body destitute of almost Life; it stood without Motion, and, for a Minute, knew not that it had a Being; and, I believe, he had never come to himself, so opprest he was with over-Joy, if he had not met with this Allay, that he perceiv'd *Imoinda* fall dead in the Hands of *Trefry*: this awaken'd him, and he ran to her aid, and caught her in his Arms, where, by degrees, she came to herself; and 'tis needless to tell with what transports, what extasies of Joy, they both a while beheld each other, without Speaking; then Snatcht each other to their Arms; then Gaze again, as if they still doubted whether they possess'd the Blessing:[4] They Graspt; but when they recovered their Speech, 'tis not to be imagin'd, what tender things they exprest to each other; wondering what strange Fate had brought 'em again together. They soon inform'd each other of their Fortunes, and equally bewail'd their Fate; but, at the same time, they mutually protested, that even Fetters and Slavery were Soft and Easy; and wou'd be supported with Joy and Pleasure, while they cou'd be so happy to possess each other, and to be able to make good their Vows. *Caesar* swore he disdain'd the Empire of the World, while he cou'd behold his *Imoinda*; and she despis'd Grandure and Pomp, those Vanities of her Sex, when she cou'd Gaze on *Oroonoko*. He ador'd the very Cottage where she resided, and said, That little Inch of the World wou'd give him more Happiness than all the Universe cou'd do; and she vow'd, It was a Pallace, while adorn'd with the Presence of *Oroonoko*.

---

3. Clear modern usage would add a second "had": "had had presented." "Shock Dog": a long-haired dog or a poodle, especially associated with women of fashion.
4. Modern editions often alter the syntax at this point, but the early editors did not.

Trefry was infinitely pleas'd with this Novel,[5] and found this *Clemene* was the Fair Mistress of whom *Caesar* had before spoke; and was not a little satisfied, that Heaven was so kind to the *Prince*, as to sweeten his Misfortunes by so lucky an Accident; and leaving the Lovers to themselves, was impatient to come down to *Parham House*, (which was on the same *Plantation*) to give me an Account of what had hapned. I was as impatient to make these Lovers a Visit, having already made a Friendship with *Caesar*; and from his own Mouth learn'd what I have related, which was confirm'd by his *French*-man, who was set on Shore to seek his Fortunes; and of whom they cou'd not make a Slave, because a Christian; and he came daily to *Parham Hill* to see and pay his Respects to his Pupil *Prince*: So that concerning and intresting my self, in all that related to *Caesar*, whom I had assur'd of Liberty, as soon as the Governor arriv'd, I hasted presently to the Place where the Lovers were, and was infinitely glad to find this Beautiful young *Slave* (who had already gain'd all our Esteems, for her Modesty and her extraordinary Prettyness) to be the same I had heard *Caesar* speak so much of. One may imagine then, we paid her a treble Respect; and though from her being carv'd in fine Flowers and Birds all over her Body, we took her to be of Quality before, yet, when we knew *Clemene* was *Imoinda*, we cou'd not enough admire her.

I had forgot to tell you, that those who are Nobly born of that Country, are so delicately Cut and Rac'd[6] all over the fore-part of the Trunk of their Bodies, that it looks as if it were Japan'd; the Works being raised like high Poynt round the Edges of the Flowers: Some are only Carv'd with a little Flower, or Bird, at the Sides of the Temples, as was *Caesar*; and those who are so Carv'd over the Body, resemble our Ancient *Picts*,[7] that are figur'd in the Chronicles, but these Carvings are more delicate.

From that happy Day *Caesar* took *Clemene* for his Wife, to the general Joy of all People; and there was as much Magnificence as the Country wou'd afford at the Celebration of this Wedding: and in a very short time after she conceiv'd with Child; which made *Caesar* even adore her, knowing he was the last of his Great Race. This new Accident made him more Impatient of Liberty, and he was every Day treating with *Trefry* for his and *Clemene's* Liberty; and offer'd either Gold,

---

5. Novel event or piece of news.
6. Incised. The carving is likened to figured lacquerwork in the Japanese style and to elaborately patterned "high point" lace. The Akan people of the Gold Coast did not practice body carving, but some widely known older reports circulated in the popular travel collections of Hakluyt and Purchas claimed that they did. A 1555 account says that nobles "rase their skins, with pretty knots . . . as it were branched damask."
7. An ancient North British people, named by the Romans *Picti* ("painted or tattooed people"), who appeared in histories of England and Scotland. Engraved figures of Picts and ancient Britons, said to have been found by the painter John White in "an old English chronicle," were included in Theodore De Bry's *America* (1590) "to show how that the inhabitants of the Great Britain have been in times past as savage as those of Virginia" (see the illustration on p. 72).

or a vast quantity of Slaves, which shou'd be paid before they let him
go, provided he cou'd have any Security that he shou'd go when his
Ransom was paid: They fed him from Day to Day with Promises, and
delay'd him, till the Lord Governor shou'd come; so that he began to
suspect them of falshood, and that they wou'd delay him till the time
of his Wives delivery, and make a Slave of that too, for all the Breed
is theirs to whom the Parents belong: This Thought made him very
uneasy, and his Sullenness gave them some Jealousies[8] of him; so that
I was oblig'd, by some Persons, who fear'd a Mutiny (which is very
Fatal sometimes in those Colonies, that abound so with Slaves, that
they exceed the Whites in vast Numbers) to discourse with *Caesar*, and
to give him all the Satisfaction I possibly cou'd; they knew he and
Clemene were scarce an Hour in a Day from my Lodgings; that they
eat with me, and that I oblig'd 'em in all things I was capable of: I
entertain'd him with the Lives of the Romans,[9] and great Men, which
charm'd him to my Company; and her, with teaching her all the pretty
Works[1] that I was Mistress of; and telling her Stories of Nuns, and
endeavouring to bring her to the knowledge of the true God. But of all
Discourses *Caesar* lik'd that the worst, and wou'd never be reconcil'd
to our Notions of the Trinity, of which he ever made a Jest; it was a
Riddle, he said, wou'd turn his Brain to conceive, and one cou'd not
make him understand what Faith was. However, these Conversations
fail'd not altogether so well to divert him, that he lik'd the Company
of us Women much above the Men; for he cou'd not Drink; and he
is but an ill Companion in that Country that cannot: So that obliging
him to love us very well, we had all the Liberty of Speech with him,
especially my self, whom he call'd his *Great Mistress*; and indeed my
Word wou'd go a great way with him. For these Reasons, I had Opportunity to take notice to him, that he was not well pleas'd of late, as
he us'd to be; was more retir'd and thoughtful; and told him, I took it
Ill he shou'd Suspect we wou'd break our Words with him, and not
permit both him and *Clemene* to return to his own Kingdom, which
was not so long a way, but when he was once on his Voyage he wou'd
quickly arrive there. He made me some Answers that shew'd a doubt
in him, which made me ask him, what advantage it wou'd be to doubt?
it would but give us a Fear of him, and possibly compel us to treat him
so as I shou'd be very loath to behold: that is, it might occasion his
Confinement. Perhaps this was not so Luckily spoke of me, for I perceiv'd he resented that Word, which I strove to Soften again in vain:
However, he assur'd me, that whatsoever Resolutions he shou'd take,

8. Suspicions.
9. Behn's publisher had recently issued Plutarch's *Lives of the Romans* in a new translation
   overseen by Dryden.
1. Decorative needlework or other handiwork. ("Work" by women was understood to be sewing
   and embroidery.)

he wou'd Act nothing upon the White-People; and as for my self, and those upon that *Plantation* where he was, he wou'd sooner forfeit his eternal Liberty, and Life it self, than lift his Hand against his greatest Enemy on that Place: He besought me to suffer no Fears upon his Account, for he cou'd do nothing that Honour shou'd not dictate; but he accus'd himself for having suffer'd Slavery so long; yet he charg'd that weakness on Love alone, who was capable of making him neglect even Glory it self; and, for which, now he reproaches himself every moment of the Day. Much more to this effect he spoke, with an Air impatient enough to make me know he wou'd not be long in Bondage; and though he suffer'd only the Name of a Slave, and had nothing of the Toil and Labour of one, yet that was sufficient to render him Uneasy; and he had been too long Idle, who us'd to be always in Action, and in Arms: He had a Spirit all Rough and Fierce, and that cou'd not be tam'd to lazy Rest; and though all endeavors were us'd to exercise himself in such Actions and Sports as this World afforded, as Running, Wrastling, Pitching the Bar, Hunting and Fishing, Chasing and Killing *Tigers*[2] of a monstrous Size, which this Continent affords in abundance; and wonderful *Snakes*, such as *Alexander* is reported to have incounter'd at the River of *Amazons*,[3] and which *Caesar* took great Delight to overcome; yet these were not Actions great enough for his large Soul, which was still panting after more renown'd Action.

Before I parted that Day with him, I got, with much ado, a Promise from him to rest yet a little longer with Patience, and wait the coming of the Lord Governor, who was every Day expected on our Shore; he assur'd me he wou'd, and this Promise he desired me to know was given perfectly in Complaisance to me, in whom he had an intire Confidence.

After this, I neither thought it convenient to trust him much out of our View, nor did the Country who fear'd him; but with one accord it was advis'd to treat him Fairly, and oblige him to remain within such a compass, and that he shou'd be permitted, as seldom as cou'd be, to go up to the Plantations of the Negroes; or, if he did, to be accompany'd by some that shou'd be rather in appearance Attendants than Spys. This Care was for some time taken, and *Caesar* look'd upon it as a Mark of extraordinary Respect, and was glad his discontent had oblig'd 'em to be more observant to him; he received new assurance from the Overseer, which was confirmed to him by the Opinion of all the Gentlemen of the Country, who made their court to him: During this time that we had his Company more frequently than hitherto we had had, it may

---

2. Wild cats, including the South American jaguar and cougar. "Pitching the Bar": a contest in distance throwing using a heavy bar or rod.
3. According to old romances, Alexander the Great is supposed to have encountered both snakes and Amazons in a campaign against India.

not be unpleasant to relate to you the Diversions we entertain'd him with, or rather he us.

My stay was to be short in that Country, because my Father dy'd at Sea, and never arriv'd to possess the Honour was design'd him, (which was Lieutenant-General of Six and thirty Islands, besides the Continent of *Surinam*) nor the advantages he hop'd to reap by them;[4] so that though we were oblig'd to continue on our Voyage, we did not intend to stay upon the Place: Though, in a Word, I must say thus much of it, That certainly had his late Majesty, of sacred Memory, but seen and known what a vast and charming World he had been Master of in that Continent, he would never have parted so Easily with it to the *Dutch*. 'Tis a Continent whose vast Extent was never yet known, and may contain more Noble Earth than all the Universe besides; for, they say, it reaches from East to West; one Way as far as *China*, and another to *Peru*: It affords all things both for Beauty and Use; 'tis there Eternal Spring, always the very Months of *April*, *May* and *June*; the Shades are perpetual, the Trees, bearing at once all degrees of Leaves and Fruit, from blooming Buds to ripe Autumn; Groves of Oranges, Limons, Citrons, Figs, Nutmegs, and noble Aromaticks, continually bearing their Fragrancies. The Trees appearing all like Nosegays adorn'd with Flowers of different kinds; some are all White, some Purple, some Scarlet, some Blue, some Yellow; bearing, at the same time, Ripe Fruit and Blooming Young, or producing every Day new. The very Wood of all these Trees have an intrinsick Value above common Timber; for they are, when cut, of different Colours, glorious to behold; and bear a Price considerable, to inlay withal. Besides this, they yield rich Balm, and Gums; so that we make our Candles of such an Aromatick Substance, as does not only give a sufficient Light, but, as they Burn, they cast their Perfumes all about. Cedar is the common Firing, and all the Houses are built with it. The very Meat we eat, when set on the Table, if it be Native, I mean of the Country, perfumes the whole Room; especially a little Beast call'd an *Armadilly*,[5] a thing which I can liken to nothing so well as a *Rhinoceros*; 'tis all in white Armor so joynted, that it moves as well in it, as if it had nothing on; this Beast is about the bigness of a Pig of Six Weeks old. But it were endless to give an Account of all the divers Wonderfull and Strange things that Country affords, and which we took a very great Delight to go in search of; though those adventures are oftentimes Fatal and at least Dangerous:

---

4. Willoughby represented a range of royal powers: as the king's lord governor he could appoint a deputy or lieutenant governor (a civil post) and as his captain-general he could appoint a lieutenant general (a military post). There is no record that he named anyone to the latter position; by December 1663 his deputy governor, William Byam, also held that title in Surinam. "Continent": "Land not disjoined by the sea from other lands" (Johnson's *Dictionary*).
5. *armadillo*, from the Spanish for "little armored one."

But while we had *Caesar* in our Company on these Designs we fear'd no harm, nor suffer'd any.

As soon as I came into the Country, the best House in it was presented me, call'd St. *John's Hill.*[6] It stood on a vast Rock of white Marble, at the Foot of which the River ran a vast depth down, and not to be descended on that side; the little Waves still dashing and washing the foot of this Rock, made the softest Murmurs and Purlings in the World; and the Opposite Bank was adorn'd with such vast quantities of different Flowers eternally Blowing,[7] and every Day and Hour new, fenc'd behind 'em with lofty Trees of a Thousand rare Forms and Colours, that the Prospect was the most ravishing that fancy can create.[8] On the Edge of this white Rock, towards the River, was a Walk or Grove of Orange and Limon Trees, about half the length of the *Mall*[9] here, whose Flowery and Fruit-bearing Branches meet at the top, and hinder'd the Sun, whose Rays are very fierce there, from entering a Beam into the Grove; and the cool Air that came from the River made it not only fit to entertain People in, at all the hottest Hours of the Day, but refresh'd the sweet Blossoms, and made it always Sweet and Charming; and sure the whole Globe of the World cannot show so delightful a Place as this Grove was: Not all the Gardens of boasted *Italy* can produce a Shade to out-vie this, which Nature had joyn'd with Art to render so exceeding Fine; and 'tis a marvel to see how such vast Trees, as big as English Oaks, cou'd take footing on so solid a Rock, and in so little Earth, as cover'd that Rock; but all things by Nature there are Rare, Delightful and Wonderful. But to our Sports.

Sometimes we wou'd go surprizing,[1] and in search of young *Tigers* in their Dens, watching when the old Ones went forth to forage for Prey; and oftentimes we have been in great Danger, and have fled apace for our Lives, when surpriz'd by the Dams. But once, above all other times, we went on this Design, and *Caesar* was with us, who had no sooner stol'n a young *Tiger* from her Nest, but going off, we incounter'd the Dam, bearing a Buttock of a Cow, which he[2] had torn off with his mighty Paw, and going with it towards his *Den*; we had only four

6. A plantation near Willoughby's Parham Hill owned by Sir Robert Harley, who held offices elsewhere.
7. Blooming.
8. The first edition reads "the most raving that Sands can create," and the third edition of 1698 substitutes "ravishing." Walter Jerrold and Clare Jerrold (1929) suggested this emended phrase, which is used by Behn later in describing the Indian war captains. The next sentence follows the third edition in altering "Marl" to "Mall" and "Fruity bear Branches" to "Fruit-bearing Branches."
9. A fashionable walk in St. James' Park in London.
1. A military term for making sudden raids.
2. The very jarring mixture of pronouns in the two episodes of the tigers may perhaps suggest reluctance to use a feminine pronoun in moments of extreme violence. However, Jacqeline Pearson (1991) suggests that the tiger represents nature, conceived as female, "when strong and aggressive," turning male when defeated. The first account went uncorrected in all four seventeenth-century editions; masculine pronouns in the second account were replaced in the third edition of 1698.

Women, *Caesar*, and an English Gentleman, Brother to *Harry Martin*,[3] the great *Oliverian*; we found there was no escaping this inrag'd and ravenous Beast. However, we Women fled as fast as we cou'd from it; but our Heels had not sav'd our Lives, if *Caesar* had not laid down his *Cub*, when he found the *Tiger* quit her Prey to make the more speed towards him; and taking Mr. *Martin*'s Sword desir'd him to stand aside, or follow the Ladies. He obey'd him, and *Caesar* met this monstrous Beast of might, size, and vast Limbs, who came with open Jaws upon him; and fixing his Awful stern Eyes full upon those of the Beast, and putting himself into a very steddy and good aiming posture of Defence, ran his Sword quite through his Breast down to his very Heart, home to the Hilt of the Sword; the dying Beast stretch'd forth her Paw, and going to grasp his Thigh, surpriz'd with Death in that very moment, did him no other harm than fixing her long Nails in his Flesh very deep, feebly wounded him, but cou'd not grasp the Flesh to tear off any. When he had done this, he hollow'd[4] to us to return; which, after some assurance of his Victory, we did, and found him lugging out the Sword from the Bosom of the *Tiger*, who was laid in her Bloud on the Ground; he took up the *Cub*, and with an unconcern, that had nothing of the Joy or Gladness of a Victory, he came and laid the Whelp at my Feet: We all extreamly wonder'd at his Daring, and at the Bigness of the Beast, which was about the highth of an Heifer, but of mighty, great, and strong Limbs.

Another time, being in the Woods, he kill'd a *Tiger*, which had long infested that part, and born away abundance of Sheep and Oxen, and other things, that were for the support of those to whom they belong'd; abundance of People assail'd this Beast, some affirming they had shot her with several Bullets quite through the Body, at several times; and some swearing they shot her through the very Heart, and they believ'd she was a Devil rather than a Mortal thing. *Caesar* had often said, he had a mind to encounter this Monster, and spoke with several Gentlemen who had attempted her; one crying, I shot her with so many poyson'd Arrows, another with his Gun in this part of her, and another in that; so that he remarking all these Places where she was shot, fancy'd still he shou'd overcome her, by giving her another sort of a Wound than any had yet done; and one day said (at the Table) *What Trophies and Garlands, Ladies, will you make me, if I bring you home the Heart of this Ravenous Beast, that eats up all your Lambs and Pigs?* We all promis'd he shou'd be rewarded at all our Hands. So taking a Bow,

---

3. Henry Martin or Marten (1602–1680) was not a follower of Oliver Cromwell (an "Oliverian"), but he was one of the judges who signed the death warrant of Charles I and was imprisoned as a regicide at the Restoration. George, a younger brother who sought his fortune in the colonies, was a substantial planter in Barbados from 1647 and moved to Surinam in 1658, dying there in 1666.
4. Halloed.

which he chus'd out of a great many, he went up in the Wood, with
two Gentlemen, where he imagin'd this Devourer to be; they had not
past very far in it, but they heard her Voice, growling and grumbling,
as if she were pleas'd with something she was doing. When they came
in view, they found her muzzling in the Belly of a new ravish'd Sheep,
which she had torn open; and seeing herself approach'd, she took fast
hold of her Prey, with her fore Paws, and set a very fierce raging Look
on *Caesar*, without offering to approach him; for fear, at the same time,
of losing what she had in Possession. So that *Caesar* remain'd a good
while, only taking aim, and getting an opportunity to shoot her where
he design'd; 'twas some time before he cou'd accomplish it, and to
wound her, and not kill her, wou'd but have enrag'd her more, and
indanger'd him: He had a Quiver of Arrows at his side, so that if one
fail'd he cou'd be supply'd; at last, retiring a little, he gave her opportunity to eat, for he found she was Ravenous, and fell to as soon as she
saw him retire; being more eager of her Prey than of doing new Mischiefs. When he going softly to one side of her, and hiding his Person
behind certain Herbage that grew high and thick, he took so good aim,
that, as he intended, he shot her just into the Eye, and the Arrow was
sent with so good a will, and so sure a hand, that it stuck in her Brain,
and made her caper, and become mad for a moment or two; but being
seconded by another Arrow, he fell dead upon the Prey: *Caesar* cut
him Open with a Knife, to see where those Wounds were that had
been reported to him, and why he did not Die of 'em. But I shall now
relate a thing that possibly will find no Credit among Men, because
'tis a Notion commonly receiv'd with us, That nothing can receive a
Wound in the Heart and Live; but when the Heart of this courageous
Animal was taken out, there were Seven Bullets of Lead in it, and the
Wounds seam'd up with great Scars, and she liv'd with the Bullets a
great while, for it was long since they were shot: This Heart the Conqueror brought up to us, and 'twas a very great Curiosity, which all the
Country came to see; and which gave *Caesar* occasion of many fine
Discourses; of Accidents in War, and Strange Escapes.

At other times he wou'd go a Fishing; and discoursing on that Diversion, he found we had in that Country a very Strange Fish, call'd a
Numb Eel,[5] (an *Eel* of which I have eaten) that while it is alive, it has
a quality so Cold, that those who are Angling, though with a Line of
never so great a length, with a Rod at the end of it, it shall, in the same
minute the Bait is touched by this *Eel*, seize him or her that holds the
Rod with benumb'dness, that shall deprive 'em of Sense, for a while;
and some have fall'n into the Water, and others drop'd as dead on the
Banks of the Rivers where they stood, as soon as this Fish touches the
Bait. *Caesar* us'd to laugh at this, and believ'd it impossible a Man

5. Electric eel.

cou'd lose his Force at the touch of a Fish; and cou'd not understand that Philosophy,[6] that a cold Quality should be of that Nature: However, he had a great Curiosity to try whether it wou'd have the same effect on him it had on others, and often try'd, but in vain; at last, the sought for Fish came to the Bait, as he stood Angling on the Bank; and instead of throwing away the Rod, or giving it a sudden twitch out of the Water, whereby he might have caught both the *Eel*, and have dismiss'd the Rod, before it cou'd have too much Power over him; for Experiment sake, he grasp'd it but the harder, and fainting fell into the River; and being still possest of the Rod, the Tide carry'd him senseless as he was a great way, till an *Indian* Boat took him up; and perceiv'd, when they touch'd him, a Numbness seize them, and by that knew the Rod was in his Hand; which, with a Paddle (that is, a short Oar) they struck away, and snatch'd it into the Boat, *Eel* and all. If *Caesar* were almost Dead, with the effect of this Fish, he was more so with that of the Water, where he had remain'd the space of going a League; and they found they had much a-do to bring him back to Life: But, at last, they did, and brought him home, where he was in a few Hours well Recover'd and Refresh'd; and not a little Asham'd to find he shou'd be overcome by an *Eel*; and that all the People, who heard his Defiance, wou'd Laugh at him. But we cheared him up; and he, being convinc'd, we had the *Eel* at Supper; which was a quarter of an Ell about, and most delicate Meat; and was of the more Value, since it cost so Dear, as almost the Life of so gallant a Man.

About this time we were in many mortal Fears, about some Disputes the *English* had with the *Indians*; so that we cou'd scarce trust our selves, without great Numbers, to go to any *Indian* Towns, or Place, where they abode; for fear they shou'd fall upon us, as they did immediately after my coming away; and that it was in the possession of the *Dutch*, who us'd 'em not so civilly as the *English*; so that they cut in pieces all they cou'd take, getting into Houses, and hanging up the Mother, and all her Children about her; and cut a Footman, I left behind me, all in Joynts, and nail'd him to Trees.

This feud began while I was there; so that I lost half the satisfaction I propos'd, in not seeing and visiting the *Indian* Towns. But one Day, bemoaning of our Misfortunes upon this account, *Caesar* told us, we need not Fear; for if we had a mind to go, he wou'd undertake to be our Guard: Some wou'd, but most wou'd not venture; about Eighteen of us resolv'd, and took Barge; and, after Eight Days, arriv'd near an *Indian* Town: But approaching it, the Hearts of some of our Company fail'd, and they wou'd not venture on Shore; so we Poll'd who wou'd, and who wou'd not: For my part, I said, If *Caesar* wou'd, I wou'd go; he resolv'd, so did my Brother, and my Woman, a Maid of good Cour-

---

6. "Hypothesis or system upon which natural effects are explained" (Johnson's *Dictionary*).

age. Now none of us speaking the Language of the People, and imagining we shou'd have a half Diversion in Gazing only; and not knowing
what they said, we took a Fisherman that liv'd at the Mouth of the
River, who had been a long Inhabitant there, and oblig'd him to go
with us: But because he was known to the *Indians*, as trading among
'em; and being, by long Living there, become a perfect *Indian* in Colour, we, who resolv'd to surprize 'em, by making 'em see something
they never had seen, (that is, White People) resolv'd only my self, my
Brother, and Woman shou'd go; so *Caesar*, the Fisherman, and the
rest, hiding behind some thick Reeds and Flowers, that grew on the
Banks, let us pass on towards the Town, which was on the Bank of
the River all along. A little distant from the Houses, or Huts, we saw
some Dancing, others busy'd in fetching and carrying of Water from
the River: They had no sooner spy'd us, but they set up a loud Cry,
that frighted us at first; we thought it had been for those that should
Kill us, but it seems it was of Wonder and Amazement. They were all
Naked, and we were Dress'd, so as is most comode,[7] for the hot Countries, very Glittering and Rich; so that we appear'd extreamly fine; my
own Hair was cut short, and I had a Taffaty Cap, with Black Feathers,
on my Head; my Brother was in a Stuff[8] Suit, with Silver Loops and
Buttons, and abundance of Green Ribon; this was all infinitely surprising to them, and because we saw them stand still, till we approach'd
'em, we took Heart and advanc'd; came up to 'em, and offer'd 'em our
Hands; which they took, and look'd on us round about, calling still for
more Company; who came swarming out, all wondering, and crying
out *Tepeeme*;[9] taking their Hair up in their Hands, and spreading it
wide to those they call'd out to; as if they would say (as indeed it
signify'd) *Numberless Wonders*, or not to be recounted, no more than
to number the Hair of their Heads. By degrees they grew more bold,
and from gazing upon us round, they touch'd us; laying their Hands
upon all the Features of our Faces, feeling our Breasts and Arms, taking
up one Petticoat, then wondering to see another; admiring our Shoes
and Stockings, but more our Garters, which we gave 'em; and they ty'd
about their Legs, being Lac'd with Silver Lace at the ends, for they
much Esteem any shining things: In fine, we suffer'd 'em to survey us
as they pleas'd, and we thought they wou'd never have done admiring
us. When *Caesar*, and the rest, saw we were receiv'd with such wonder,

---

7. Suitable; probably suited less to the warm climate than to the colonists' taste for luxury.
   According to Du Tertre's history of the French islands, women's everyday dress was of "colored
   taffetas and satins, with Genoa lace and a profusion of ribbons."
8. Woven fabric, worsted.
9. In the brief dictionary of the Galibi language appended to Antoine Biet's *Voyage* (1654),
   tapouimé is the word for "many." He explains the limitations of the Indians' numbering
   system: "When they want to represent a very great number . . . saying this word *tapouimé*,
   they show the hairs of the head." George Warren's *Impartial Description of Surinam* gives a
   different expression for "like the hair of one's head, innumerable."

they came up to us; and finding the *Indian* Trader whom they knew,
(for 'tis by these Fishermen, call'd *Indian* Traders, we hold a Commerce with 'em; for they love not to go far from home, and we never
go to them) when they saw him therefore they set up a new Joy; and
cry'd, in their Language, *Oh! here's our* Tiguamy, *and we shall now
know whether those things can speak:* So advancing to him, some of
'em gave him their Hands, and cry'd, *Amora Tiguamy,* which is as
much as, *How do you,* or *Welcome Friend;*[1] and all, with one din, began
to gabble to him, and ask'd, If we had Sense, and Wit? if we cou'd talk
of affairs of Life, and War, as they cou'd do? if we cou'd Hunt, Swim,
and do a thousand things they use? He answer'd 'em, We cou'd. Then
they invited us into their Houses, and dress'd Venison and Buffelo for
us; and, going out, gathered a Leaf of a Tree, call'd a *Sarumbo* Leaf,
of Six Yards long, and spread it on the Ground for a Table-Cloth; and
cutting another in pieces instead of Plates, setting us on little bow
Indian Stools, which they cut out of one intire piece of Wood, and
Paint, in a sort of Japan Work: They serve every one their Mess[2] on
these pieces of Leaves, and it was very good, but too high season'd with
Pepper. When we had eat, my Brother, and I, took out our Flutes, and
play'd to 'em, which gave 'em new Wonder; and I soon perceiv'd, by
an admiration, that is natural to these People, and by the extream Ignorance and Simplicity of 'em, it were not difficult to establish any
unknown or extravagant Religion among them; and to impose any Notions or Fictions upon 'em. For seeing a Kinsman of mine set some
Paper a Fire, with a Burning-glass, a Trick they had never before seen,
they were like to have Ador'd him for a God; and beg'd he wou'd give
them the Characters or Figures of his Name, that they might oppose
it against Winds and Storms; which he did, and they held it up in those
Seasons, and fancy'd it had a Charm to conquer them; and kept it like
a Holy Relique. They are very Superstitious, and call'd him the Great
Peeie, that is, *Prophet.* They show'd us their *Indian Peeie,* a Youth of
about Sixteen Years old, as handsom as Nature cou'd make a Man.
They consecrate a beautiful Youth from his Infancy, and all Arts are
us'd to compleat him in the finest manner, both in Beauty and Shape:
He is bred to all the little Arts and cunning they are capable of; to all
the Legerdemain Tricks, and Sleight of Hand, whereby he imposes
upon the Rabble; and is both a Doctor in Physick and Divinity. And
by these Tricks makes the Sick believe he sometimes eases their Pains;
by drawing from the afflicted part little Serpents, or odd Flies, or
Worms, or any Strange thing; and though they have besides undoubted
good Remedies, for almost all their Diseases, they cure the Patient more
by Fancy than by Medicines; and make themselves Fear'd, Lov'd, and

---

1. Biet's "Petit Dictionnaire" lists *amore* as "you," but *tigami* is applied to children or infants.
2. Portion.

Reverenc'd. This young *Peeie* had a very young Wife, who seeing my
Brother kiss her, came running and kiss'd me; after this, they kiss'd one
another, and made it a very great Jest, it being so Novel; and new
Admiration and Laughing went round the Multitude, that they never
will forget that Ceremony, never before us'd or known. *Caesar* had a
mind to see and talk with their War *Captains*, and we were conducted
to one of their Houses; where we beheld several of the great *Captains*,
who had been at Councel: But so frightful a Vision it was to see 'em
no Fancy can create; no such Dreams can represent so dreadful a
Spectacle. For my part I took 'em for Hobgoblins, or Fiends, rather
than Men; but however their Shapes appear'd, their Souls were very
Humane and Noble; but some wanted their Noses, some their Lips,
some both Noses and Lips, some their Ears, and others Cut through
each Cheek, with long Slashes, through which their Teeth appear'd;
they had other several formidable Wounds and Scars, or rather Dis-
memberings; they had *Comitias*, or little Aprons before 'em; and Girdles of Cotton, with their Knives naked, stuck in it; a Bow at their
Backs, and a Quiver of Arrows on their Thighs; and most had Feathers
on their Heads of divers Colours. They cry'd, *Amora Tigame* to us, at
our entrance, and were pleas'd we said as much to 'em; they seated us,
and gave us Drink of the best Sort; and wonder'd, as much as the others
had done before, to see us. *Caesar* was marvelling as much at their
Faces, wondering how they shou'd all be so Wounded in War; he was
Impatient to know how they all came by those frightful Marks of Rage
or Malice, rather than Wounds got in Noble Battel: They told us, by
our Interpreter, That when any War was waging, two Men chosen out
by some old *Captain*, whose Fighting was past, and who cou'd only
teach the Theory of War, these two Men were to stand in Competition
for the Generalship, or Great War Captain; and being brought before
the old Judges, now past Labour, they are ask'd, What they dare do to
shew they are worthy to lead an Army? When he, who is first ask'd,
making no Reply, Cuts off his Nose, and throws it contemptably[3] on
the Ground; and the other does something to himself that he thinks
surpasses him, and perhaps deprives himself of Lips and an Eye; so
they Slash on till one gives out, and many have dy'd in this Debate.
And 'tis by a passive Valour they shew and prove their Activity; a sort
of Courage too Brutal to be applauded by our Black Hero; nevertheless
he express'd his Esteem of 'em.

   In this Voyage *Caesar* begot so good an understanding between the
Indians and the *English*, that there were no more Fears, or Heart-
burnings during our stay; but we had a perfect, open, and free Trade
with 'em: Many things Remarkable, and worthy Reciting, we met with

---

3. With contempt. Biet, Rochefort, Warren, and others describe punishing initiation rites for
   warriors, but these do not involve self-mutilation.

in this short Voyage; because *Caesar* made it his Business to search out and provide for our Entertainment, especially to please his dearly Ador'd *Imoinda*, who was a sharer in all our Adventures; we being resolv'd to make her Chains as easy as we cou'd, and to Compliment the Prince in that manner that most oblig'd him.

As we were coming up again, we met with some *Indians* of strange Aspects; that is, of a larger Size, and other sort of Features, than those of our Country: Our *Indian Slaves*, that Row'd us, ask'd 'em some Questions, but they cou'd not understand us; but shew'd us a long Cotton String, with several Knots on it;[4] and told us, they had been coming from the Mountains so many Moons as there were Knots; they were habited in Skins of a strange Beast, and brought along with 'em Bags of Gold Dust;[5] which, as well as they cou'd give us to understand, came streaming in little small Chanels down the high Mountains, when the Rains fell; and offer'd to be the Convoy to any Body, or Persons, that wou'd go to the Mountains. We carry'd these Men up to *Parham*, where they were kept till the Lord Governour came: And because all the Country was mad to be going on this Golden Adventure, the Governour, by his Letters, commanded (for they sent some of the Gold to him) that a Guard shou'd be set at the Mouth of the River of *Amazons*,[6] (a River so call'd, almost as broad as the River of *Thames*) and prohibited all People from going up that River, it conducting to those Mountains of Gold. But we going off for *England* before the Project was further prosecuted, and the Governour being drown'd in a Hurricane,[7] either the Design dy'd, or the *Dutch* have the Advantage of it: And 'tis to be bemoan'd what his Majesty lost by losing that part of *America*.

Though this digression is a little from my Story, however since it contains some Proofs of the Curiosity and Daring of this great Man, I was content to omit nothing of his Character.

It was thus, for some time we diverted him; but now *Imoinda* began to shew she was with Child, and did nothing but Sigh and Weep for the Captivity of her Lord, her Self, and the Infant yet Unborn; and believ'd, if it were so hard to gain the Liberty of Two, 'twou'd be more difficult to get that for Three. Her Griefs were so many Darts in the great Heart of *Caesar*; and taking his Opportunity one *Sunday*, when all the Whites were overtaken in Drink, as there were abundance of several Trades, and *Slaves* for Four Years,[8] that Inhabited among the

---

4. A *quipu*, characteristic of the Incas of Peru, though the other details (such as height) are not.
5. The fabled golden city El Dorado, gold mines or mountains, and gold dust were sought in Guiana by Sir Walter Ralegh and others; gold dust is reported.
6. The mouth of the Amazon, in Brazil, is far distant from Surinam, but in seventeenth-century documents and maps it marked the southeast boundary of Guiana.
7. Lord Willoughby was lost in a storm in the summer of 1666 while on an expedition against the French at the island of St. Kitts.
8. Whites who for debts incurred in their passage or for crimes were indentured for a fixed period. They were often called "white slaves" and might be sold to planters on a temporary basis. "Trades": tradesmen.

Negro Houses; and *Sunday* was their Day of Debauch, (otherwise they were a sort of Spys upon *Caesar*); he went pretending out of Goodness to 'em, to Feast amongst 'em; and sent all his Musick, and order'd a great Treat for the whole Gang, about Three Hundred *Negros*; and about a Hundred and Fifty were able to bear Arms, such as they had, which were sufficient to do Execution[9] with Spirits accordingly: For the *English* had none but rusty Swords, that no Strength cou'd draw from a Scabbard; except the People of particular Quality, who took care to Oyl 'em and keep 'em in good Order: The Guns also, unless here and there one, or those newly carry'd from *England*, wou'd do no good or harm; for 'tis the Nature of that Country to Rust and Eat up Iron, or any Metals, but Gold and Silver. And they are very Unexpert at the Bow, which the *Negros* and *Indians* are perfect Masters off.

Caesar, having singl'd out these Men from the Women and Children, made an Harangue to 'em of the Miseries, and Ignominies of Slavery; counting up all their Toyls and Sufferings, under such Loads, Burdens, and Drudgeries, as were fitter for Beasts than Men; Senseless Brutes, than Humane Souls. He told 'em it was not for Days, Months, or Years, but for Eternity; there was no end to be of their Misfortunes: They suffer'd not like Men who might find a Glory, and Fortitude in Oppression; but like Dogs that lov'd the Whip and Bell,[1] and fawn'd the more they were beaten: That they had lost the Divine Quality of Men, and were become insensible Asses, fit only to bear; nay worse: an Ass, or Dog, or Horse having done his Duty, cou'd lye down in Retreat, and rise to Work again, and while he did his Duty indur'd no Stripes; but Men, Villanous, Senseless Men, such as they, Toyl'd on all the tedious Week till Black *Friday*;[2] and then, whether they Work'd or not, whether they were Faulty or Meriting, they promiscuously, the Innocent with the Guilty, suffer'd the infamous Whip, the sordid Stripes, from their Fellow *Slaves* till their Blood trickled from all Parts of their Body; Blood, whose every drop ought to be Reveng'd with a Life of some of those Tyrants, that impose it; *And why*, said he, *my dear Friends and Fellow-sufferers, shou'd we be Slaves to an unknown People? Have they Vanquish'd us Nobly in Fight? Have they Won us in Honourable Battel? And are we, by the chance of War, become their Slaves? This wou'd not anger a Noble Heart, this wou'd not animate a Souldiers Soul; no, but we are Bought and Sold like Apes, or Monkeys, to be the Sport of Women, Fools and Cowards; and the Support of Rogues, Runagades, that have abandon'd their own Countries, for Rapin, Murders, Thefts and Villanies: Do you not hear every Day how they upbraid each other*

9. Harm, slaughter.
1. Proverbial for something that detracts from comfort or pleasure; from the protective charm against evil on chariots of triumphing generals in ancient Rome.
2. Here a day of customary beating; more widely, a Friday bringing some notable disaster. Originally from students' slang for examination day.

with infamy of Life, below the Wildest Salvages;[3] and shall we render Obedience to such a degenerate Race, who have no one Humane Vertue left, to distinguish 'em from the vilest Creatures? Will you, I say, suffer the Lash from such Hands? They all Reply'd, with one accord, No, no, no; Caesar has spoke like a Great Captain; like a Great King.

After this he wou'd have proceeded, but was interrupted by a tall Negro of some more Quality than the rest, his Name was *Tuscan*; who Bowing at the Feet of *Caesar*, cry'd, My Lord, we have listen'd with Joy and Attention to what you have said; and, were we only Men, wou'd follow so great a Leader through the World: But oh! consider, we are Husbands and Parents too, and have things more dear to us than Life; our Wives and Children unfit for Travel, in these unpassable Woods, Mountains and Bogs; we have not only difficult Lands to overcome, but Rivers to Wade, and Monsters to Incounter; Ravenous Beasts of Prey —— . To this, *Caesar* Reply'd, That Honour was the First Principle in Nature, that was to be Obey'd; but as no Man wou'd pretend to that, without all the Acts of Vertue, Compassion, Charity, Love, Justice and Reason; he found it not inconsistent with that, to take an equal Care of their Wives and Children, as they wou'd of themselves; and that he did not Design, when he led them to Freedom, and Glorious Liberty, that they shou'd leave that better part of themselves to Perish by the Hand of the Tyrant's Whip: But if there were a Woman among them so degenerate from Love and Vertue to chuse Slavery before the pursuit of her Husband, and with the hazard of her Life, to share with him in his Fortunes; that such an one ought to be Abandon'd, and left as a Prey to the common Enemy.

To which they all Agreed,—and Bowed. After this, he spoke of the Impassable Woods and Rivers; and convinc'd 'em, the more Danger, the more Glory. He told them that he had heard of one *Hannibal* a great Captain, had Cut his Way through Mountains of solid Rocks; and shou'd a few Shrubs oppose them; which they cou'd Fire before 'em?[4] No, 'twas a trifling Excuse to Men resolv'd to die, or overcome. As for Bogs, they are with a little Labour fill'd and harden'd; and the Rivers cou'd be no Obstacle, since they Swam by Nature; at least by Custom, from their First Hour of their Birth: That when the Children were Weary they must carry them by turns, and the Woods and their own Industry wou'd afford them Food. To this they all assented with Joy.

Tuscan then demanded, What he wou'd do? He said, they wou'd Travel towards the Sea; Plant a New Colony, and Defend it by their Valour; and when they cou'd find a Ship, either driven by stress of Weather, or guided by Providence that way, they wou'd Seize it, and make it a Prize, till it had Transported them to their own Countries;

3. Savages.
4. According to accounts in Livy and Plutarch, the Carthaginian general and his troops literally hacked their way down the Alps into Italy in an unsuccessful attack on Rome.

at least, they shou'd be made Free in his Kingdom, and be Esteem'd as his Fellow-sufferers, and Men that had the Courage, and the Bravery to attempt, at least, for Liberty; and if they Dy'd in the attempt it wou'd be more brave, than to Live in perpetual Slavery.

They bow'd and kiss'd his Feet at this Resolution, and with one accord Vow'd to follow him to Death. And that Night was appointed to begin their March; they made it known to their Wives, and directed them to tie their Hamaca[5] about their Shoulder, and under their Arm like a Scarf; and to lead their Children that cou'd go, and carry those that cou'd not. The Wives, who pay an intire Obedience to their Husbands, obey'd, and stay'd for 'em, where they were appointed: The Men stay'd but to furnish themselves with what defensive Arms they cou'd get; and All met at the Rendezvous, where Caesar made a new incouraging Speech to 'em, and led 'em out.

But, as they cou'd not march far that Night, on Monday early, when the Overseers went to call 'em all together, to go to Work, they were extreamly surpris'd, to find not one upon the Place, but all fled with what Baggage they had. You may imagine this News was not only suddenly spread all over the Plantation, but soon reach'd the Neighbouring ones; and we had by Noon about Six hundred Men, they call the Militia of the Country, that came to assist us in the pursuit of the Fugitives: But never did one see so comical an Army march forth to War. The Men, of any fashion, wou'd not concern themselves, though it were almost the common Cause; for such Revoltings are very ill Examples, and have very fatal Consequences oftentimes in many Colonies: But they had a Respect for Caesar, and all hands were against the Parhamites, as they call'd those of Parham Plantation; because they did not, in the first place, love the Lord Governor; and secondly, they wou'd have it, that Caesar was Ill us'd, and Baffl'd with;[6] and 'tis not impossible but some of the best in the Country was of his Council in this Flight, and depriving us of all the Slaves; so that they of the better sort wou'd not meddle in the matter. The Deputy Governor,[7] of whom I have had no great occasion to speak, and who was the most Fawning fair-tongu'd Fellow in the World, and one that pretended the most Friendship to Caesar, was now the only violent Man against him; and though he had nothing, and so need fear nothing, yet talk'd and look'd bigger than any Man: He was a Fellow, whose Character is not fit to be mention'd with the worst of the Slaves. This Fellow wou'd lead his Army forth to meet Caesar, or rather to pursue him; most of their Arms

5. Hammock.
6. Cheated.
7. William Byam. A Royalist exile from England, exiled again from Barbados, he was three times elected governor by the Surinam planter assembly (1657–60), and remained in that post after 1660 until his appointment was confirmed under Lord Willoughby's new royal patent. There are some recorded complaints against him for high-handedness and from him about the disorderliness and insubordination of settlers and slaves, while other reports are favorable.

were of those sort of cruel Whips they call *Cat with Nine Tayls*; some had rusty useless Guns for show; others old Basket-hilts,[8] whose Blades had never seen the Light in this Age; and others had long Staffs, and Clubs. Mr. *Trefry* went along, rather to be a Mediator than a Conqueror, in such a Battel; for he foresaw, and knew, if by fighting they put the Negroes into despair, they were a sort of sullen Fellows, that wou'd drown, or kill themselves, before they wou'd yield; and he advis'd that fair means was best: But *Byam* was one that abounded in his own Wit, and wou'd take his own Measures.

It was not hard to find these Fugitives; for as they fled they were forc'd to fire and cut the Woods before 'em, so that Night or Day they pursu'd 'em by the light they made, and by the path they had clear'd: But as soon as *Caesar* found he was pursu'd, he put himself in a Posture of Defence, placing all the Women and Children in the Rear; and himself, with *Tuscan* by his side, or next to him, all promising to Dye or Conquer. Incourag'd thus, they never stood to Parley, but fell on Pell-mell upon the *English*, and kill'd some, and wounded a good many; they having recourse to their Whips, as the best of their Weapons: And as they observ'd no Order, they perplex'd the Enemy so sorely, with Lashing 'em in the Eyes; and the Women and Children, seeing their Husbands so treated, being of fearful Cowardly Dispositions, and hearing the *English* cry out, *Yield and Live, Yield and be Pardon'd*; they all run in amongst their Husbands and Fathers, and hung about 'em, crying out, *Yield, yield; and leave* Caesar *to their Revenge*; that by degrees the Slaves abandon'd *Caesar*, and left him only *Tuscan* and his Heroick *Imoinda*; who, grown big as she was, did nevertheless press near her Lord, having a Bow, and a Quiver full of poyson'd Arrows, which she manag'd with such dexterity, that she wounded several, and shot the *Governor* into the Shoulder; of which Wound he had like to have Dy'd, but that an *Indian* Woman, his Mistress, suck'd the Wound, and cleans'd it from the Venom: But however, he stir'd not from the Place till he had Parly'd with *Caesar*, who he found was resolv'd to dye Fighting, and wou'd not be Taken; no more wou'd *Tuscan*, or *Imoinda*. But he, more thirsting after Revenge of another sort, than that of depriving him of Life, now made use of all his Art of talking, and dissembling; and besought *Caesar* to yield himself upon Terms, which he himself should propose, and should be Sacredly assented to and kept by him: He told him, It was not that he any longer fear'd him, or cou'd believe the force of Two Men, and a young Heroine, cou'd overcome all them, with all the Slaves now on their side also; but it was the vast Esteem he had for his Person; the desire he had to serve so Gallant a Man; and to hinder himself from the Reproach hereafter, of having been the occasion of the Death of a *Prince*,

---

8. Swords with protective hilt guards.

whose Valour and Magnanimity deserv'd the Empire of the World. He
protested to him, he look'd upon this Action, as Gallant and Brave;
however tending to the prejudice of his Lord and Master, who wou'd
by it have lost so considerable a number of *Slaves*; that this Flight of
his shou'd be look'd on as a heat of Youth, and rashness of a too forward
Courage, and an unconsider'd impatience of Liberty, and no more;
and that he labour'd in vain to accomplish that which they wou'd effectually perform, as soon as any Ship arriv'd that wou'd touch on his
Coast. *So that if you will be pleas'd,* continued he, *to surrender your
self, all imaginable Respect shall be paid you; and your Self, your Wife,
and Child, if it be here born, shall depart free out of our Land.* But
Caesar wou'd hear of no Composition;[9] though *Byam* urg'd, If he pursu'd, and went on in his Design, he wou'd inevitably Perish, either by
great *Snakes*, wild Beasts, or Hunger; and he ought to have regard to
his Wife, whose Condition required ease, and not the fatigues of tedious
Travel; where she cou'd not be secur'd from being devoured. But *Caesar* told him, there was no Faith in the White Men, or the Gods they
Ador'd; who instructed 'em in Principles so false, that honest Men cou'd
not live amongst 'em; though no People profess'd so much, none perform'd so little; that he knew what he had to do, when he dealt with
Men of Honour; but with them a Man ought to be eternally on his
Guard, and never to Eat and Drink with *Christians* without his Weapon
of Defence in his Hand; and, for his own Security, never to credit one
Word they spoke. As for the rashness and inconsiderateness of his Action he wou'd confess the Governor is in the right; and that he was
asham'd of what he had done, in endeavoring to make those Free, who
were by Nature *Slaves*, poor wretched Rogues, fit to be us'd as *Christians* Tools; Dogs, treacherous and cowardly, fit for such Masters; and
they wanted only but to be whipt into the knowledge of the *Christian
Gods* to be the vilest of all creeping things; to learn to Worship such
Deities as had not Power to make 'em Just, Brave, or Honest. In fine,
after a thousand things of this Nature, not fit here to be recited, he told
Byam, he had rather Dye than Live upon the same Earth with such
Dogs. But *Trefry* and *Byam* pleaded and protested together so much,
that *Trefry* believing the *Governor* to mean what he said; and speaking
very cordially himself, generously put himself into *Caesar's* Hands, and
took him aside, and perswaded him, even with Tears, to Live, by Sur-
rendring himself, and to name his Conditions. *Caesar* was overcome
by his Wit and Reasons, and in consideration of *Imoinda*; and demanding what he desir'd, and that it shou'd be ratify'd by their Hands
in Writing, because he had perceiv'd that was the common way of
contract between Man and Man, amongst the Whites: All this was

9. Settlement.

perform'd, and *Tuscan's* Pardon was put in, and they Surrender to the Governor, who walked peaceably down into the *Plantation* with 'em, after giving order to bury their dead. *Caesar* was very much toyl'd with the bustle of the Day; for he had fought like a Fury, and what Mischief was done he and *Tuscan* perform'd alone; and gave their Enemies a fatal Proof that they durst do any thing, and fear'd no mortal Force.

But they were no sooner arriv'd at the Place, where all the Slaves receive their Punishments of Whipping, but they laid Hands on *Caesar* and *Tuscan*, faint with heat and toyl; and, surprising them, Bound them to two several Stakes, and Whipt them in a most deplorable and inhumane Manner, rending the very Flesh from their Bones; especially *Caesar*, who was not perceiv'd to make any Moan, or to alter his Face, only to roul his Eyes on the Faithless *Governor*, and those he believ'd Guilty, with Fierceness and Indignation; and, to compleat his Rage, he saw every one of those *Slaves*, who, but a few Days before, Ador'd him as something more than Mortal, now had a Whip to give him some Lashes, while he strove not to break his Fetters; though, if he had, it were impossible: But he pronounced a Woe and Revenge from his Eyes, that darted Fire, that 'twas at once both Awful and Terrible to behold.

When they thought they were sufficiently Reveng'd on him, they unty'd him, almost Fainting, with loss of Blood, from a thousand Wounds all over his Body; from which they had rent his Cloaths, and led him Bleeding and Naked as he was; and loaded him all over with Irons; and then rubbed his Wounds, to compleat their Cruelty, with *Indian Pepper*, which had like to have made him raving Mad; and, in this Condition, made him so fast to the Ground that he cou'd not stir, if his Pains and Wounds wou'd have given him leave. They spar'd *Imoinda*, and did not let her see this Barbarity committed towards her Lord, but carry'd her down to *Parham*, and shut her up; which was not in kindness to her, but for fear she shou'd Dye with the Sight, or Miscarry; and then they shou'd lose a young *Slave*, and perhaps the Mother.

You must know, that when the News was brought on Monday Morning, that *Caesar* had betaken himself to the Woods, and carry'd with him all the *Negroes*, we were possess'd with extream Fear, which no perswasions cou'd Dissipate, that he wou'd secure himself till Night; and then, that he wou'd come down and Cut all our Throats. This apprehension made all the Females of us fly down the River, to be secur'd; and while we were away, they acted this Cruelty: For I suppose I had Authority and Interest enough there, had I suspected any such thing, to have prevented it; but we had not gone many Leagues, but the News overtook us that *Caesar* was taken, and Whipt like a common *Slave*. We met on the River with Colonel *Martin*, a Man of great Gallantry, Wit, and Goodness, and whom I have celebrated in a Char-

acter of my New *Comedy*,[1] by his own Name, in memory of so brave
a Man: He was Wise and Eloquent; and, from the fineness of his Parts,
bore a great Sway over the Hearts of all the *Colony*: He was a Friend
to *Caesar*, and resented this false Dealing with him very much. We
carried him back to *Parham*, thinking to have made an Accommodation; when we came, the First News we heard was, that the *Governor*
was Dead of a Wound *Imoinda* had given him; but it was not so well:
But it seems he wou'd have the Pleasure of beholding the Revenge he
took on *Caesar*; and before the cruel Ceremony was finish'd, he drop'd
down; and then they perceiv'd the Wound he had on his Shoulder,
was by a venom'd Arrow; which, as I said, his *Indian* Mistress heal'd,
by Sucking the Wound.

We were no sooner Arriv'd, but we went up to the *Plantation* to see
Caesar, whom we found in a very Miserable and Unexpressable Condition; and I have a Thousand times admired how he liv'd, in so much
tormenting Pain. We said all things to him, that Trouble, Pitty, and
Good Nature cou'd suggest; Protesting our Innocency of the Fact, and
our Abhorance of such Cruelties; making a Thousand Professions of
Services to him, and Begging as many Pardons for the Offenders, till
we said so much, that he believ'd we had no Hand in his ill Treatment;
but told us, he cou'd never Pardon *Byam*; as for *Trefry*, he confess'd he
saw his Grief and Sorrow, for his Suffering, which he cou'd not hinder,
but was like to have been beaten down by the very *Slaves*, for Speaking
in his Defence: But for *Byam*, who was their Leader, their Head; ——
and shou'd, by his Justice, and Honor, have been an Example to 'em,
—— For him, he wish'd to Live, to take a dire Revenge of him, and
said, *It had been well for him, if he had Sacrific'd me, instead of giving
me the contemptable*[2] *Whip.* He refus'd to Talk much, but Begging us
to give him our Hands, he took 'em, and Protested never to lift up his,
to do us any Harm. He had a great Respect for Colonel *Martin*, and
always took his Counsel, like that of a Parent; and assur'd him, he
wou'd obey him in any thing, but his Revenge on *Byam*. *Therefore*, said
he, *for his own Safety, let him speedily dispatch me; for if I cou'd dispatch my self, I wou'd not, till that Justice were done to my injur'd Person,
and the contempt of a Souldier: No, I wou'd not kill my self, even after
a Whipping, but will be content to live with that Infamy, and be pointed
at by every grinning Slave, till I have compleated my Revenge; and then
you shall see that Oroonoko scorns to live with the Indignity that was
put on Caesar.* All we cou'd do cou'd get no more Words from him;

---

1. *The Younger Brother, or The Amorous Jilt*, not produced until 1696 despite this piece of
   promotion. Martin, called captain in the historical records, is styled colonel here and in the
   play, but commissioned and courtesy titles abounded in the colonies. "Barbados, about 1650,
   seems almost to have been populated with colonels" (James A. Williamson, *English Colonies
   in Guiana and on the Amazon 1604–1668*, 1923).
2. Showing contempt.

and we took care to have him put immediately into a healing Bath, to
rid him of his Pepper; and order'd a Chirurgeon[3] to anoint him with
healing Balm, which he suffer'd, and in some time he began to be able
to Walk and Eat; we fail'd not to visit him every Day, and, to that end,
had him brought to an apartment at *Parham*.

The *Governor* was no sooner recover'd, and had heard of the men-
aces of *Caesar*, but he call'd his Council; who (not to disgrace them,
or Burlesque the Government there) consisted of such notorious Villains as *Newgate*[4] never transported; and possibly originally were such,
who understood neither the Laws of *God* or *Man*; and had no sort of
Principles to make 'em worthy the Name of Men: But, at the very
Council Table, wou'd Contradict and Fight with one another; and
Swear so bloodily that 'twas terrible to hear, and see 'em. (Some of 'em
were afterwards Hang'd, when the *Dutch* took possession of the place;
others sent off in Chains.) But calling these special Rulers of the Nation
together, and requiring their Counsel in this weighty Affair, they all
concluded, that (Damn 'em) it might be their own Cases; and that
Caesar ought to be made an Example to all the *Negroes*, to fright 'em
from daring to threaten their Betters, their Lords and Masters; and, at
this rate, no Man was safe from his own *Slaves*; and concluded, *nemine
contradicente*,[5] that *Caesar* shou'd be Hang'd.

Trefry then thought it time to use his Authority; and told *Byam* his
Command did not extend to his Lord's *Plantation*; and that *Parham*
was as much exempt from the Law as *White-hall*;[6] and that they ought
no more to touch the Servants of the Lord——— (who there represented the King's Person) than they cou'd those about the King himself;
and that *Parham* was a Sanctuary; and though his Lord were absent in
Person, his Power was still in Being there; which he had intrusted with
him, as far as the Dominions of his particular *Plantations* reach'd, and
all that belong'd to it; the rest of the *Country*, as *Byam* was Lieutenant
to his Lord, he might exercise his Tyrany upon. *Trefry* had others as
powerful, or more, that int'rested themselves in *Caesar*'s Life, and absolutely said, He shou'd be Defended. So turning the *Governor*, and
his wise Council, out of Doors, (for they sate at *Parham-house*) they set
a Guard upon our Landing Place, and wou'd admit none but those we
call'd Friends to us and *Caesar*.

The *Governor* having remain'd wounded at *Parham*, till his recovery
was compleated, *Caesar* did not know but he was still there; and indeed,
for the most part, his time was spent there; for he was one that lov'd

---

3. Surgeon.
4. The major London prison, from which criminals were transported to the colonies. The Council would have been Byam's appointees.
5. No one disagreeing (Latin).
6. The king's palace in London. Trefry stands as Lord Willoughby's deputy on his private (or
   "particular") land, Byam in the colony at large.

to Live at other Peoples Expence; and if he were a Day absent, he was Ten present there; and us'd to Play, and Walk, and Hunt, and Fish, with *Caesar*. So that *Caesar* did not at all doubt, if he once recover'd Strength, but he shou'd find an opportunity of being Reveng'd on him: Though, after such a Revenge, he cou'd not hope to Live; for if he escap'd the Fury of the English *Mobile*,[7] who perhaps wou'd have been glad of the occasion to have kill'd him, he was resolv'd not to survive his Whipping; yet he had, some tender Hours, a repenting Softness, which he called his fits of Coward; wherein he struggl'd with Love for the Victory of his Heart, which took part with his charming *Imoinda* there; but, for the most part, his time was past in melancholy Thought, and black Designs; he consider'd, if he shou'd do this Deed, and Dye, either in the Attempt, or after it, he left his lovely *Imoinda* a Prey, or at best a *Slave*, to the inrag'd Multitude; his great Heart cou'd not indure that Thought. *Perhaps*, said he, *she may be first Ravished by every Brute; exposed first to their nasty Lusts, and then a shameful Death*. No; he could not Live a Moment under that Apprehension, too insupportable to be born. These were his Thoughts, and his silent Arguments with his Heart, as he told us afterwards; so that now resolving not only to kill *Byam*, but all those he thought had inrag'd him; pleasing his great Heart with the fancy'd Slaughter he shou'd make over the whole Face of the *Plantation*; he first resolv'd on a Deed, that (however Horrid it at first appear'd to us all) when we had heard his Reasons, we thought it Brave and Just: Being able to Walk, and, as he believ'd, fit for the Execution of his great Design, he beg'd *Trefry* to trust him into the Air, believing a Walk wou'd do him good; which was granted him, and taking *Imoinda* with him, as he us'd to do in his more happy and calmer Days, he led her up into a Wood, where, after (with a thousand Sighs, and long Gazing silently on her Face, while Tears gusht, in spite of him, from his Eyes) he told her his Design first of Killing her, and then his Enemies, and next himself, and the impossibility of Escaping, and therefore he told her the necessity of Dying; he found the Heroick Wife faster pleading for Death than he was to propose it, when she found his fix'd Resolution; and, on her Knees, besought him, not to leave her a Prey to his Enemies. He (griev'd to Death) yet pleased at her noble Resolution, took her up, and imbracing her, with all the Passion and Languishment of a dying Lover, drew his Knife to kill this Treasure of his Soul, this Pleasure of his Eyes; while Tears trickl'd down his Cheeks, hers were Smiling with Joy she shou'd dye by so noble a Hand, and be sent in her own Country, (for that's their Notion of the next World) by him she so tenderly Lov'd, and so truly Ador'd in this; for Wives have a respect for their Husbands equal to what any other People pay a Deity; and when a Man finds any

---

7. Common people or mob; the name conveys inconstancy and excitability.

occasion to quit his Wife, if he love her, she dyes by his Hand; if not, he sells her, or suffers some other to kill her. It being thus, you may believe the Deed was soon resolv'd on; and 'tis not to be doubted, but the Parting, the eternal Leave taking of Two such Lovers, so greatly Born, so Sensible,[8] so Beautiful, so Young, and so Fond, must be very Moving, as the Relation of it was to me afterwards.

All that Love cou'd say in such cases, being ended; and all the intermitting Irresolutions being adjusted, the Lovely, Young, and Ador'd Victim lays her self down, before the Sacrificer; while he, with a Hand resolv'd, and a Heart breaking within, gave the Fatal Stroke; first, cutting her Throat, and then severing her yet Smiling Face from that Delicate Body, pregnant as it was with Fruits of tend'rest Love. As soon as he had done, he laid the Body decently on Leaves and Flowers; of which he made a Bed, and conceal'd it under the same cover-lid of Nature; only her Face he left yet bare to look on: But when he found she was Dead, and past all Retrieve, never more to bless him with her Eyes, and soft Language; his Grief swell'd up to Rage; he Tore, he Rav'd, he Roar'd, like some Monster of the Wood, calling on the lov'd Name of *Imoinda*; a thousand times he turn'd the Fatal Knife that did the Deed, toward his own Heart, with a Resolution to go immediately after her; but dire Revenge, which now was a thousand times more fierce in his Soul than before, prevents him; and he wou'd cry out, *No; since I have sacrificed* Imoinda *to my Revenge, shall I lose that Glory which I have purchas'd so dear, as at the Price of the fairest, dearest, softest Creature that ever Nature made?* No, no! Then, at her Name, Grief wou'd get the ascendant of Rage, and he wou'd lye down by her side, and water her Face with showers of Tears, which never were wont to fall from those Eyes: And however bent he was on his intended Slaughter, he had not power to stir from the Sight of this dear Object, now more Belov'd, and more Ador'd than ever.

He remain'd in this deploring Condition for two Days, and never rose from the Ground where he had made his sad Sacrifice; at last, rousing from her side, and accusing himself with living too long, now *Imoinda* was dead; and that the Deaths of those barbarous Enemies were deferr'd too long, he resolv'd now to finish the great Work; but offering to rise, he found his Strength so decay'd, that he reel'd to and fro, like Boughs assail'd by contrary Winds; so that he was forced to lye down again, and try to summons all his Courage to his Aid; he found his Brains turn round, and his Eyes were dizzy; and Objects appear'd not the same to him they were wont to do; his Breath was short; and all his Limbs surprised with a Faintness he had never felt before: He had not Eat in two Days, which was one occasion of this Feebleness, but excess of Grief was the greatest; yet still he hop'd he shou'd recover

8. Sensitive.

Vigour to act his Design; and lay expecting it yet six Days longer; still
mourning over the dead Idol of his Heart, and striving every Day to
rise, but cou'd not.

In all this time you may believe we were in no little affliction for
Caesar, and his Wife; some were of Opinion he was escap'd never to
return; others thought some Accident had hap'ned to him: But however, we fail'd not to send out an hundred People several ways to search
for him; a Party, of about forty, went that way he took; among whom
was *Tuscan*, who was perfectly reconcil'd to *Byam*; they had not gon
very far into the Wood, but they smelt an unusual Smell, as of a dead
Body; for Stinks must be very noisom that can be distinguish'd among
such a quantity of Natural Sweets, as every Inch of that Land produces.
So that they concluded they shou'd find him dead, or somebody that
was so; they past on towards it, as Loathsom as it was, and made such
a rustling among the Leaves that lye thick on the Ground, by continual
Falling, that *Caesar* heard he was approach'd; and though he had,
during the space of these eight Days, endeavor'd to rise, but found he
wanted Strength, yet looking up, and seeing his Pursuers, he rose, and
reel'd to a Neighbouring Tree, against which he fix'd his Back; and
being within a dozen Yards of those that advanc'd, and saw him, he
call'd out to them, and bid them approach no nearer, if they wou'd be
safe: So that they stood still, and hardly believing their Eyes, that wou'd
perswade them that it was *Caesar* that spoke to 'em, so much was he
alter'd, they ask'd him, What he had done with his Wife? for they smelt
a Stink that almost struck them dead. He, pointing to the dead Body,
sighing, cry'd, *Behold her there*; they put off the Flowers that cover'd
her with their Sticks, and found she was kill'd; and cry'd out, *Oh monster! that hast murther'd thy Wife*: Then asking him, Why he did so
cruel a Deed? He replied, he had no leasure to answer impertinent
Questions; *You may go back*, continued he, *and tell the Faithless Governor, he may thank Fortune that I am breathing my last; and that my
Arm is too feeble to obey my Heart, in what it had design'd him*: But
his Tongue faultering, and trembling, he cou'd scarce end what he was
saying. The *English* taking Advantage by his Weakness, cry'd, *Let us
take him alive by all means*: He heard 'em; and, as if he had reviv'd
from a Fainting, or a Dream, he cry'd out, *No, Gentlemen, you are
deceiv'd; you will find no more* Caesars *to be Whipt; no more find a
Faith in me: Feeble as you think me, I have Strength yet left to secure
me from a second Indignity*. They swore all a-new, and he only shook
his Head, and beheld them with Scorn; then they cry'd out, *Who will
venture on this single Man? Will no body?* They stood all silent while
Caesar replied, *Fatal will be the Attempt to the first Adventurer; let him
assure himself*, and, at that Word, held up his Knife in a menacing
Posture, *Look ye, ye faithless Crew*, said he, *'tis not Life I seek, nor am
I afraid of Dying*; and, at that Word, cut a piece of Flesh from his own

Throat, and threw it at 'em, *yet still I wou'd Live if I cou'd, till I had perfected my Revenge. But oh! it cannot be; I feel Life gliding from my Eyes and Heart; and, if I make not haste, I shall yet fall a Victim to the shameful Whip.* At that, he rip'd up his own Belly; and took his Bowels and pull'd 'em out, with what Strength he cou'd; while some, on their Knees imploring, besought him to hold his Hand. But when they saw him tottering, they cry'd out, *Will none venture on him?* A bold *English* cry'd, *Yes, if he were the Devil;* (taking Courage when he saw him almost Dead) and swearing a horrid Oath for his farewell to the World, he rush'd on;[9] *Caesar,* with his Arm'd Hand met him so fairly, as stuck him to the Heart, and he fell Dead at his Feet. *Tuscan* seeing that, cry'd out, *I love thee, oh* Caesar; *and therefore will not let thee Dye, if possible:* And, running to him, took him in his Arms; but, at the same time, warding a Blow that *Caesar* made at his Bosom, he receiv'd it quite through his Arm; and *Caesar* having not the Strength to pluck the Knife forth, though he attempted it, *Tuscan* neither pull'd it out himself, nor suffer'd it to be pull'd out; but came down with it sticking in his Arm; and the reason he gave for it was, because the Air shou'd not get into the Wound: They put their Hands a-cross, and carried *Caesar* between Six of 'em, fainted as he was; and they thought Dead, or just Dying; and they brought him to *Parham,* and laid him on a Couch, and had the Chirurgeon immediately to him, who drest his Wounds, and sew'd up his Belly, and us'd means to bring him to Life, which they effected. We ran all to see him; and, if before we thought him so beautiful a Sight, he was now so alter'd, that his Face was like a Death's Head black'd over; nothing but Teeth, and Eyeholes: For some Days we suffer'd no body to speak to him, but caused Cordials to be poured down his Throat, which sustained his Life; and in six or seven Days he recover'd his Senses: For, you must know, that Wounds are almost to a Miracle cur'd in the *Indies;* unless Wounds in the Legs, which rarely ever cure.

When he was well enough to speak, we talk'd to him; and ask'd him some Questions about his Wife, and the Reasons why he kill'd her; and he then told us what I have related of that Resolution, and of his Parting; and he besought us, we would let him Dye, and was extreamly Afflicted to think it was possible he might Live; he assur'd us, if we did not Dispatch him, he wou'd prove very Fatal to a great many. We said all we cou'd to make him Live, and gave him new Assurances; but he begg'd we wou'd not think so poorly of him, or of his love to *Imoinda,* to imagine we cou'd Flatter him to Life again; but the Chirurgeon assur'd him, he cou'd not Live, and therefore he need not Fear. We were all (but *Caesar*) afflicted at this News; and the Sight was gashly;[1]

9. In the first edition these two sentences appear spliced together with no punctuation mark.
1. Ghastly.

his Discourse was sad; and the earthly Smell about him so strong, that
I was perswaded to leave the Place for some time (being my self but
Sickly, and very apt to fall into Fits of dangerous Illness upon any
extraordinary Melancholy); the Servants, and *Trefry*, and the Chirur-
geons, promis'd all to take what possible care they cou'd of the Life of
Caesar; and I, taking Boat, went with other Company to Colonel *Martin's*, about three Days Journy down the River; but I was no sooner
gon, but the *Governor* taking *Trefry*, about some pretended earnest Business, a Days Journy up the River; having communicated his Design to
one *Banister*,[2] a wild *Irish* Man, and one of the Council; a Fellow of
absolute Barbarity, and fit to execute any Villany, but was Rich. He
came up to *Parham*, and forcibly took *Caesar*, and had him carried to
the same Post where he was Whip'd; and causing him to be ty'd to it,
and a great Fire made before him, he told him, he shou'd Dye like a
Dog, as he was. *Caesar* replied, this was the first piece of Bravery that
ever *Banister* did; and he never spoke Sense till he pronounc'd that
Word; and, if he wou'd keep it, he wou'd declare, in the other World,
that he was the only Man, of all the Whites, that ever he heard speak
Truth. And turning to the Men that bound him, he said, *My Friends,
am I to Dye, or to be Whip'd?* And they cry'd, *Whip'd! no; you shall
not escape so well:* And then he replied, smiling, *A Blessing on thee*;
and assur'd them, they need not tye him, for he wou'd stand fixt, like
a Rock; and indure Death so as shou'd encourage them to Dye. *But if
you Whip me*, said he, *be sure you tye me fast.*

He had learn'd to take Tobaco; and when he was assur'd he should
Dye, he desir'd they would give him a Pipe in his Mouth, ready
Lighted, which they did; and the Executioner came, and first cut off
his Members,[3] and threw them into the Fire; after that, with an ill-
favoured Knife, they cut his Ears, and his Nose, and burn'd them; he
still Smoak'd on, as if nothing had touch'd him; then they hack'd off
one of his Arms, and still he bore up, and held his Pipe; but at the
cutting off the other Arm, his Head sunk, and his Pipe drop'd; and he
gave up the Ghost, without a Groan, or a Reproach. My Mother and
Sister were by him all the while, but not suffer'd to save him; so rude
and wild were the Rabble, and so inhumane were the Justices,[4] who
stood by to see the Execution, who after paid dearly enough for their
Insolence. They cut *Caesar* in Quarters, and sent them to several of
the chief *Plantations*: One Quarter was sent to Colonel *Martin*, who
refus'd it; and swore, he had rather see the Quarters of *Banister*, and

2. Major James Banister, deputy governor in 1688 when Surinam was turned over to the Dutch.
   He is associated by Behn with the unruly population of Irish servants and transports in the
   West Indies, including many political prisoners shipped over by Cromwell; they were considered disreputable and even dangerous, sometimes joining the blacks in rebellion.
3. Genitals.
4. Appointed from among the planters, not men with legal training.

the *Governor* himself, than those of *Caesar*, on his *Plantations*; and that he cou'd govern his *Negroes* without Terrifying and Grieving them with frightful Spectacles of a mangl'd King.

Thus Dy'd this Great Man; worthy of a better Fate, and a more sublime Wit than mine to write his Praise; yet, I hope, the Reputation of my Pen is considerable enough to make his Glorious Name to survive to all Ages; with that of the Brave, the Beautiful, and the Constant *Imoinda*.

FINIS.

Textual Notes

The listed emendations, which rarely affect pronunciation, are followed by the first textual authority, where one exists, and then by the 1688 reading. The text does not reproduce long dashes of variable length or fully adjudicate matters of broken type or hyphenation at line endings, but it is intended to be usable for scholarly purposes. The more substantive emendations and textual problems are recorded in the footnotes. I have consulted the collation of early editions in Gerald C. Duchovnay's "Aphra Behn's *Oroonoko*: A Critical Edition" (Ph.D. diss., Indiana University, 1971).

O1 OROONOKO: OR, THE ROYAL SLAVE. A TRUE HISTORY. For Will. Canning. 1688.
O2 THE HISTORIES AND NOVELS OF THE LATE INGENIOUS MRS. BEHN. IN ONE VOLUME. For S. Briscoe. 1696.
O3 ALL THE HISTORIES AND NOVELS WRITTEN BY THE LATE INGENIOUS MRS. BEHN. ENTIRE IN ONE VOLUME. For Samuel Briscoe. 1698.

"The Epistle Dedicatory," printed in O1 and O2, appears in reverse italics.

	Emendations	1688 Edition
6.31	Sense	Sence
7.18	Lordship's (O2)	Lordships
8.3	Poet's (O2)	Poets
8.27	Weasel	Weesel
8.31	*Miniature* (O3)	*Minature*
9.21	Waist	Waste
10.30	led (O2)	lead
11.8	Dart's Point (O3)	Dart's Points
11.16	or a Captain (O2)	or Captain
13.23	fancy'd	fansy'd
14.42	Compliments	Complements

16.1	the Gods (O3)	the God's
16.37	Invitation: (O3)	Invitation;
17.23	fancy'd	fansy'd
17.33	King);	King;)
19.16	fancy	fansy
20.17	led (O3)	lead
20.18	Repose; (O3)	Repose.
21.32	Sense	Sence
26.28	Clouds (O3)	Clouds,
27.29	divin'd	devin'd
27.30	*thee—.*	*thee—*
27.32	deign'd	daign'd
27.40	Aggressor (O3)	Agressor
28.27	*Friends!* (said he) (O3)	*Friends* (said he!)
29.4	spite (O3)	spight
29.11	*Thoughts* (O2)	*Thought*
29.40	*Aboan,* and the *French*	*Aboan,* the *French*
31.10	shore (O3)	Shoar
31.12	shore (O3)	Shoar
31.32	Shore (O3)	Shoar
31.36	sense (O3)	Sence
32.20	Asseveration, (O3)	Asseveration;
32.33	*Heathen,* he (O3)	*Heathen* he
32.34	Sense (O3)	sence
32.42	*Oath?* replied *Oroonoko.* (O3)	*Oath,* replied *Oroonoko?*
33.24	Compliments	Complements
34.17	*Pickaninies),*	*Pickaninies,)*
34.25	wholly (O2)	wholy
35.25	Sense	Sence
36.14	dazzling	dazeling
36.14	spite (O3)	spight
37.3	Shore (O3)	Shoar
37.35	things);	things;)
38.2	undone (O2)	undon
38.7	undone (O2)	Undon
38.10	guess'd (O2)	guest
38.25	accepts (O3)	excepts
38.37	laugh'd (O2)	laught
38.40	pass'd they (O2)	past they
39.12	*Stranger*	*Stranger:*
39.12	*Caesar).*	*Caesar)*
39.14	leisure (O3)	Leasure
39.28	Graspt; (O2)	Graspt
40.12	Pupil	Puple
40.18	much of (O2)	much off

41.6	for all (O2)	For all
41.17	Mistress of (O2)	Mistress off
42.8	reproaches (O2)	reproches
42.20	*Amazons* (O2)	*Amozons*
43.10	Master of (O2)	Master off
43.21	kinds (O3)	kind
43.22	Blue (O3)	Blew
44.13	*Mall* (O3)	Marl
44.14	here (O2)	hear
44.25	Sports. (O2)	Sports;
45.30	*Caesar* had (O3)	*Caesar,* had
45.37	*Garlands, Ladies,* (O3)	*Garlands Ladies*
46.9	losing (O2)	loosing
46.15	fell to	fell too
47.1	lose (O2)	loose
47.7	dismiss'd (O2)	dismist
48.12	or Huts, (O3)	or Hutts;
48.20	Suit	Sute
48.27	call'd out to (O3)	call'd out too
48.32	Shoes	Shooes
49.21	People,	People;
49.36	Sleight	Slight
50.32	Cuts off (O2)	Cuts of
50.36	'tis	'its [it's (O2)]
51.26	losing (O2)	loosing
51.30	some time (O3)	sometime
52.2	*Caesar*);	*Caesar;*)
52.10	carry'd (O2)	carri'd
52.34	*Won* (O3)	*Wone*
53.14–15	Prey——.	Prey——
53.41	Seize (O2)	Sieze
54.10	Wives, (O2)	Wives
54.10–11	Husbands, (O2)	Husbands
54.21	Country (O3)	County
54.21	pursuit (O2)	persute
54.39	pursue (O2)	persue
55.5	Battel (O2)	Batail
55.6	despair (O2)	dispair
55.12	pursu'd (O2)	persu'd
55.13	pursu'd (O2)	persu'd
55.14	Rear (O2)	Reer
55.39–40	Heroine (O2)	Heroin

56.12–13	pursu'd (O2)	persu'd
57.12	Moan (O2)	Mone
57.32	lose (O2)	loose
57.35	*Negroes,* we (O2)	*Negroes.* We
57.41	gone (O2)	gon
58.18	Cruelties; making (O3)	Cruelties. Making
58.25	to 'em, (O2)	to 'em.
58.29	Hands, (O2)	Hands;
58.36	*Whipping* (O2)	*Whiping*
58.37	*grinning* (O2)	*grining*
59.15	Chains.) (O2)	Chains:)
59.21	*contradicente,* (O2)	*contradicente*
60.8	Whipping (O2)	Whiping
60.22	*Plantation;* he (O3)	*Plantation.* He
60.30	gusht (O2)	gust
60.30	spite (O3)	spight
61.11	her yet Smiling (O3)	her, yet Smiling,
61.18	Rav'd, (O2)	Rav'd
61.23	*lose* (O2)	*loose*
62.15	rustling	rusling
62.20	saw him, (O2)	saw him;
62.24	alter'd, (O3)	alter'd;
63.9	World, (O2)	World;
63.10	rush'd on; *Caesar* (O2)	rush'd on *Caesar,*
63.23	sew'd	sow'd
64.2	time	time;
64.4	Melancholy);	Melancholy)
64.16	Sense	Sence

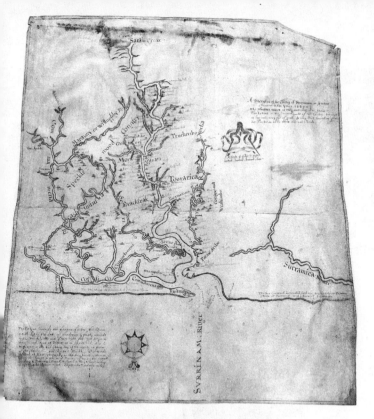

Map and detail: "A Description of the Colony of Surinam in Guiana, Drawn in the Year 1667. The planters' names as they are settled in their plantations in the several parts of the country." Reading from *top to bottom*: plantations include St. John's Hill, marked for its owner, Sir Robert Harley; Lord Willoughby's "Parrham Hill"; and holdings marked "Lt. Gen. Byam" and (*far right*) "Byam," "Banister," and "Martin."

"A young daughter of the Picts." Engraving in Theodore De Bry's *America* (1590) after a miniature by Jacques Le Moyne: "They did paint themselves of sundry kinds of flowers, and of the fairest that they could find, being furnished for the rest of such kinds of weapons as the women wear . . . a thing truly worthy of admiration."

Historical Backgrounds

New World landscape of trees, animals, and hunters, from Du Tertre's *Histoire Générale des Antilles* (1667). At *far right*, three armadillos, standing, curled up, and caught.

JOANNA LIPKING

The New World of Slavery—An Introduction

1

Early travelers to the Americas described lands that seemed to recover the first age of the world, the golden or innocent time of both classical and biblical tradition. Captain Barlowe on the first Virginia voyage saw an idyll:

> We found the people most gentle, loving, and faithful, void of all guile and treason, and such as lived after the manner of the golden age. The earth bringeth forth all things in abundance, as in the first creation, without toil or labor.[1]

Guiana, no less promising than Virginia, was advertised by Sir Walter Ralegh in a famous phrase. It was "a country that hath yet her maidenhead,"[2] offering pure air, untouched natural bounty, and rumored stores of gold, a worthy prize for the Virgin Queen Elizabeth. About fifty years later, when Lord Willoughby of Parham, the "Lord Governor" of Behn's story, settled a permanent colony in Surinam, within Guiana, he wrote hopefully to his wife that no one in the advance party had experienced so much as a headache.[3]

For those at home, the discoveries brought travels of mind: catalogs of the plant life and strange animals, collections of natural specimens and artifacts, a stage fashion for New World pageantry. Most of all, it brought accounts of "savage" peoples living without divine or human law, as if far back in time or out of time. For reflective writers in Europe—Montaigne, Swift, and Rousseau, among many others—the simpler New World societies could hold a mirror up to the old, letting civilized Europe view itself in all its habitual corruption and deceit, the whole sad tangle of its history. The impulse is a persistent one, seen earlier in Greek and Roman admiration for certain primitive peoples, and still found, in weaker form, wherever adventurers or travel writers, painters or photographers locate in indigenous peoples the vitalities and virtues they find lacking in themselves.

No such idealizing marks the reports of West Africa. European trav-

---

1. From R. Hakluyt's *Principal Voyages* (1589), reprinted in *New American World: A Documentary History of North America to 1612*, ed. David B. Quinn (New York: Arno Press, 1979), 3: 279–80. Quotations throughout this essay have been modernized.
2. "The Discovery of the Large, Rich and Beautiful Empire of Guiana," in Gerald Hammond, ed., *Selected Writings* (New York: Viking Penguin, 1986), 120.
3. See p. 99.

elers and traders—never settlers—saw only a narrow strip of coastline, where disease struck down the sailors and onshore agents with such swiftness that the place would be called the "white man's grave."[4] They did not know the interior courts and towns or learn much of Africans' kinship groups, political and religious systems, or private lives. They wrote about what they could see—above all, rulers and important men, their authority, finery, ceremonies, and the always fascinating subject of polygamy, the management of many wives, the punishments for adultery. Moreover, the men who met them at the landings were often highly proficient at trade. The promise that opens a 1665 collection called *The Golden Coast* that "a man may gain an estate by a handful of beads, and his pocket full of gold for an old hat"[5] was cockeyed optimism. The Gold Coast peoples belonged to sophisticated trading networks that stretched far north across the Sahara and east and west among the coastal nations, in addition to their longtime ocean trade with the Portuguese. Arriving traders found themselves operating within complicated systems of fort rents and regulations, customs fees and gratuities, while vying for advantage with most of northern Europe.

No one called this a state of nature, a model of health, wholeness, and precommercial sociability. It was not picturesque, attracting illustrations or literary treatments. Like most Native American peoples, West Africans were without written language and might go unclothed, but they provided no scenes of naked innocence, no trustful, open-handed kings. On the contrary, by a reverse stereotyping passed on from book to book, the received opinion was that African women were by nature lascivious, punishments notwithstanding, and the men crafty or "thievish." Yet if Europeans were inclined to be disparaging, repelled by some ritual practices, and often exasperated, they did not engage in the sort of dogmatizing that would grow up with the slave trade. They did not suppose that inhabitants of several thousand miles of coastline could be pooled and described collectively. If they were attentive to skin color, they were much more attentive to the status, wealth, and power of their ruling-class allies. They wrote to prove not how blacks differed from whites, but how blacks differed from blacks, carefully distinguishing among the inhabitants of each region and nation and port, typically favoring some peoples and some leaders said to meet European

---

4. Figures vary with time and locale, but commonly about half of those on shore died within the first year, mainly in the first months. One study is K. G. Davies, "The Living and the Dead: White Mortality in West Africa, 1684–1732," in *Race and Slavery in the Western Hemisphere*, ed. Stanley L. Engerman and Eugene D. Genovese (Princeton, N.J.: Princeton University Press, 1975), 83–98.
5. "To the Reader" (np). Some of the trade activity at and near Cormantine around this time is recorded by Margaret Makepeace, "English Traders on the Guinea Coast, 1657–1668: An Analysis of the East India Company Archive," *History in Africa* 16 (1989): 237–84; and see Stanley B. Alpern, "What Africans Got for Their Slaves: A Master List of European Trade Goods," *History in Africa* 22 (1995): 5–43. The history of Cormantine is traced by R. Porter, "The Crispe Family and the African Trade," *Journal of African History* 9 (1968): 57–77.

standards of beauty, intelligence, politeness, and sometimes fair-mindedness.

Gold Coast inhabitants, in the vicinity of Behn's Cormantine, were often admired. "Handsome, and well-proportioned," wrote a French traveler in 1669, "they have nothing disagreeable in their countenance, but the blackness of their complexion."[6] They were more humanized, with more engaging features, agreed an observer on a passing French warship, much struck by one cordial local governor he declared more impressive than all the rest combined:

> I vow I was surprised that I found in him nothing barbarous, but on the contrary, much humanity. . . . He is tall and well-proportioned, all his limbs showing strength, without the unattractive flat nose or that large mouth that the other blacks have; his eyes were prominent, very open, brilliant, and full of fire. In all, one notices that his features are regular, and that they convey pride and much gentleness.[7]

Gold coast men also had a reputation for martial valor, and by the mid-seventeenth century, reports regularly note the frequency of local wars and the enslavement of war captives unable to arrange for ransom.

Those warring states were small and variously governed, their courts comparatively modest; but from a hundred or so miles to the east, on the Slave Coast, came reports of autocratic kings in finer courts, with closely guarded seraglios, where members of the upper classes might be sold into slavery for a single infraction or simply at whim. A 1670 journal by a French trading company representative about a long visit to Allada[8] (in what is now Benin) describes a series of lavish entertainments: first by a prince of "majestic visage" who welcomes them at the coast; then by the king, educated in a colonial Portuguese convent, who mingles urbane repartee with swift and fair policy making; and finally by the high priest, who arranges a dinner with an accompanying choral concert by his sixty to eighty secluded wives.[9] Everyone speaks Portuguese, the presents are magnificent, and there are multiple officials and vast retinues, pavilions and formal gardens, silk, damask, and Turkey carpets.

This rare visit inland, with its elaborate courtesies, was unusual, as the backers in Paris were meant to see. It records an impression of one upper-class society that could hardly be more remote from later images

---

6. Nicolas Villault de Bellefond, *A Relation of the Coasts of Africk called Guinee* (London, 1670), 133.
7. "Relation du Voyage Fait sur les Costes D'Afrique," in H. Justel, *Recueil de Divers Voyages* (Paris, 1674), 16.
8. The conquered state of Ardah or Ardra mentioned in news items on Adomo Oroonoko Tomo (see pp. 147–52), where Lambe was detained and William Snelgrave visited.
9. [Francois] D'Elbée, "Journal du Voyage aux isles, dans la coste de Guinée," in J. de Clodoré, ed., *Relation de ce qui s'est passé, dans les Isles & Terre-Ferme de l'Amérique*, (Paris, 1671), 392–423.

of a simple agrarian Africa or a primitive "Dark Continent." Above all, it affords a clear view of a marketplace. As usual, the West Africans were selective about what commodities—what particular textiles, metal goods, luxury items—they wanted at the moment. The cosmopolitan king inquired first why a country as great as France sent only what the Dutch had brought already. His personal shopping list included such articles as a silver sword and half a dozen pairs of scented gloves. The French negotiated first with the king, then with the designated officers, and then were allowed open trading. On this occasion, they had come to initiate a trade in slaves, which here were standard units of wealth; their ship was charged the equivalent of fifty slaves for trading privileges, two for a supply of water, four for wood. They collected in all four hundred and thirty-four slaves, a hundred of whom died en route to Martinique. With relations thus established, a second ship took in another slave cargo, again tallying the numbers loaded and lost, together with an ambassador and his entourage bound for the court of Louis XIV.

In this matter-of-fact fashion, without special comment, began what has been called "the greatest and most fateful migration—forced migration—in the history of man."[1] Historians of Africa debate the importance of the European presence, but the traders may have been altering the scenes they described, arriving at coastal outposts—the provinces—and consolidating the economic and political power of those rulers and middlemen who most effectively met their growing demand for slaves. They themselves became firmly persuaded that from a place of such brutal oppression, their ships brought a form of deliverance. Shipload by shipload, they were changing the face of the globe.

2

The rich open lands of the New World would be worked by slave labor from Africa. The local peoples, if not already decimated by European diseases, were generally too mobile to be coerced as laborers, and in any case it was good policy to treat them carefully. The English colonial governors were under strict command by Charles II not to "give any just provocation" to the Indians but "by all ways and means seek firmly to oblige them,"

> inasmuch as some of the natives of the said Indians may be of great use to give intelligence to our plantations, or to discover the trade of other countries to them, or to be guides to places more remote from them, or to inform our Governors of several advan-

---

1. Basil Davidson, *The African Slave Trade*, rev. ed. (Boston: Little, Brown, 1980), 12.

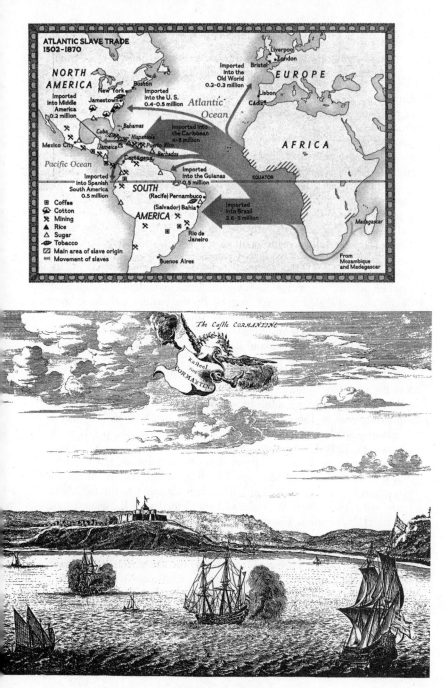

Fort Cormantine in 1665.

tages and commodities that may be within or near to our several plantations, not otherwise capable to be known to them.[2]

European laborers and indentured servants who worked for a set term of years in exchange for their passage ("*Slaves* for four Years, inhabiting among the *Negro* Houses," Behn calls them) were comparatively expensive to transport, could not be lured in sufficient numbers, and moved on when prospects were not as advertised. Increasingly they were filled out with persons transported against their will: convicts, vagrants and other undesirables, many political prisoners, some poor whites decoyed or seized at ports. These did not make for a satisfactory workforce, especially when the colonists took up the harsh and labor-intensive cultivation of sugar. Africa provided the solution, a secure source of cheap labor that allowed the plantation colonies to develop.

It must have seemed a boundless supply. A full accounting would have to include the untraceable numbers lost on forced marches or in holding prisons or wars for slaves within Africa, as well as the shipboard deaths and smuggled contract cargoes. By the current estimates, however, between ten and twelve million Africans were carried as slaves into the Western Hemisphere. The English colonies of North America—and all, like England itself, were slave-holding—took in no more than 5 percent of the slaves. The vast majority, as many as 90 percent, were sent into the South Atlantic, chiefly to the Caribbean and the Guianas, followed by Brazil.

During Aphra Behn's adult life—between her reported stay in Surinam in the early 1660s and the publication of *Oroonoko* in 1688— England actively entered the slave trade, spurred by the needs of its planters in Barbados, Surinam, and Jamaica. That is, England would control and profit from the sale of slaves to its colonies, not stand by and see them purchased from the Dutch or private traders. At his accession in 1660, Charles II established a new company to run the Africa trade, with his brother, the duke of York (later James II), as governor and chief shareholder. The first two ships sent out for slaves to the Gold Coast, in what was called Guinea, were named the *Charles* and the *James*. King Charles ordered the minting of "guineas," coins made from Guinea gold, to honor the company and for the use of its trade. Cargoes of slaves were branded *DY*, for the duke of York. Members of the court—the class of literary patrons—provided much of the capital required for such a wide-scale venture and manned the official councils and committees that sought to bring the distant ships and settlements under Crown control. At first, the slaves, numbering in the tens of thousands, were concentrated in Barbados; the short-lived English colony of Surinam had at its height in 1665 only about three thousand

2. Charles M. Andrews, ed., *British Committees, Commissions, and Councils of Trade and Plantations, 1622–1675* (Baltimore: Johns Hopkins University Press, 1908), 118–19.

slaves. When Behn died in 1689, there still were no more than two hundred thousand slaves in the English colonies, but the numbers were climbing steeply.[3]

Most early documents on the slaves are commercial letters or circulars, written for particular readers, to advance particular policies, against rival nations or groups. The official agencies reiterate the "necessity" for slaves, to be provided solely by themselves. Individual captains and agents enumerate the cargoes of men, women, boys, girls, and describe their own tribulations: tricks that left them with unfit slaves, ships blockaded or seized, problems with weather, provisions, disease, pilfering, private dealings on the side. A published complaint of 1680 condemns the "perfidious" abduction of "some considerable natives" who came aboard a ship and were carried off and sold; the point of this was to promote the royal company's monopoly privileges and stiffen measures against interloping slave traders, whose irresponsible conduct had led to violent reprisals against "the company's innocent servants and ships."[4] Kidnappings of small groups of Africans in contact with the ships sometimes occurred, a recognized wrong and a menace to trade, though the tales and rumors may outrun the known instances. Illicit transports remained commonplace, however, since the distances were too great to be patrolled and the colonists, always in need of slaves, bought where they could. A pamphlet with the evocative title *The Groans of the Plantations* is a litany of planter woes, among them the "indignity" suffered by even "the best men" at being forced to buy their replacement slaves at inflated prices.[5] One side sought to regulate, the other to escape regulation.

Occasional brief passages embedded in travel or news accounts or early histories show a closer attention to the slaves. Almost no observers could be called disinterested, and none were guided by modern humanitarian principles, but they were not hardened to what they saw or much concerned to justify what was not seriously opposed. Their accounts are unprettified, by fits and starts rather pitying. Since rank was no bar to enslavement, traders might know they carried highborn persons. The Allada visitors knew they had been sold eight of the king's junior wives, and Jean Barbot describes a priest who refused to speak for two months. However the slaves were estimated, slavery was freely recognized to be a cruel business. Men directly involved denounced the practices of others. Colonial visitors thought both slaves and servants

---

3. Numbers (adapted from Philip D. Curtin) are summarized by James A. Rawley, *The Transatlantic Slave Trade: A History* (New York: W. W. Norton, 1981), esp. Table 7.3, p. 167. On Surinam, see Richard Price, *The Guiana Maroons: A Historical and Bibliographical Introduction* (Baltimore: Johns Hopkins University Press, 1976), 7. The ratio of blacks to whites was about 2:1, though Price also notes four hundred American Indian slaves.
4. *Certain Considerations Relating to the Royal African Company of England* (London, 1680), 8–9.
5. [Edward Littleton], *The Groans of the Plantations* (London, 1689), 18.

overworked and wretchedly treated and left unattractive portraits of the colonists. The rigor of slave work was easily judged by the inhabitants' passion for amassing wealth, commented the missionary Du Tertre; they were there for that purpose alone, so they extracted as much labor as they could.[6] Now and then, there is a fleeting record of an individual, often for the kinds of reasons combined and developed in *Oroonoko*: impressive looks or carriage, a touching display of personal attachment or feeling for children, some notable instance of courage, desperation, or stoic suffering. There seems an undercurrent of disquiet about ownership of children, as if they were livestock, and about horribly inventive sadistic punishments for small offenses. But if observers often showed humane impulses and sometimes argued for reform in the name of Christianity, they saw no end to an arrangement by which a mass of persons was destined to be property for life.

Slavery in some form had always existed, in the Old Testament, in the prestige cultures of Greece and Rome, later in both Muslim and Christian countries of the Mediterranean basin, and from the fifteenth century, in Portuguese colonies in the Atlantic. If this was different—race-based, large-scale, systematic—it also went on at a distance, out of public view. Reaction might have been different if packed slave ships had appeared in the Thames. But another set of numbers may help to explain the striking absence of discussion, when so much else—the nature of kingship, the status of women, the truth of religion, even the value of commerce—provoked lively debate.

West Africa had long been a valued export market, especially for cloth and processed iron, its different coastal regions named for their pepper, ivory, and gold. The opening of what is called the first triangular trade altered the usual trade patterns. Now three or four pounds' worth of English manufactured goods carried out to Africa would serve to purchase a slave, who could be sold for perhaps sixteen to twenty pounds in the plantation colonies.[7] The planters, who could buy on credit and in produce, might expect a healthy male slave to work off his purchase price within about a year and a half, leaving them with only the minimal maintenance costs for the rest of the slave's working life. Clearly in very short order a successful planter would be enabled to purchase more slaves and reap the profits from his sugar or other products (in Surinam, it was wood). Individual merchants and planters were always at risk, especially since slave deaths on the ships and in the fields might run as high as 20 or 25 percent and could rise unpredictably, but the system prospered. Back to England flowed the sugar, which was processed and sold to feed a new national taste for sweets

---

6. Jean Baptiste du Tertre, *Histoire Générale des Antilles Habitées par les François*, vol. 2 (Paris, 1667), 523.
7. Slave prices are listed by Richard N. Bean, *The British Trans-Atlantic Slave Trade 1650–1775* (New York: Arno Press, 1975), 69–77, 186–92.

or reimported across Europe. Back too flowed streams of lavish new planter wealth, often spent, conspicuously, at home, along with orders for tools and staples needed for the next season. Each transaction along the triangle promised outsized profits from the slaves and their labor.

The crude exploitation and human cost of New World slavery are often viewed within the framework of United States history, but they need a wider lens. The slave-owning colonies of British North America absorbed four to five hundred thousand slaves; in a temperate climate, set to variable tasks, amid a diverse worker population, they reproduced and grew tenfold, approaching five million by the time of abolition in 1865. But that many slaves were shipped into the Caribbean, and they did not even sustain their original numbers. To call on a useful distinction, those colonies were quickly transformed from slave-owning to slave societies, built wholly on black labor, which was rigidly utilized and controlled. In only a few places in North America did conditions grow as severe. In the cane fields and at the sugar machinery, men and women died in large numbers, especially in their first years; and, in part because both men and women were set to the same harsh tasks, they had few children.[8] Fresh shiploads of slaves continually had to be delivered to replenish the slipping numbers. Thus, concludes historian Philip D. Curtin, "the cheapness of African manpower led the South Atlantic system into a pattern of consuming manpower as other industries might consume raw materials."[9]

Sometimes the pattern seems momentarily glimpsed. Reflecting on his slaves in 1700, slave trader James Barbot, the nephew of Jean Barbot, made the point in plain language: "thus it is at the expense of the lives of these poor wretches, that we draw such vast wealth from America."[1] In an earlier argument for Christian reform, Thomas Tryon, whom Behn may have known, noted the lagging birth rate.[2] When slavery finally ended, after the huge swell of transports, the slave population in the South Atlantic system not only had not grown; it had declined, sometimes to half or less, sometimes more precipitously. At first treated as moveable wealth, then listed with trade commodities, livestock, or white servants, its slaves come to seem in overview like the supply of replaceable hoes they wore out yearly in their work. But of course slavery was not lived out in overview. It developed over time, within

---

8. That "women's agricultural work varied little from men's" is argued by Marietta Morrissey, *Slave Women in the New World: Gender Stratification in the Caribbean* (Lawrence: University Press of Kansas, 1989), xi.

9. "The Slave Trade and the Atlantic Basin," in *Key Issues in the Afro-American Experience*, ed. Nathan I. Huggins, Martin Kilson, and Daniel M. Fox (New York: Harcourt Brace, 1971), 1:90.

1. James Barbot Jr., "Supplement to the Description of the Coasts of North and South Guinea," *A Collection of Voyages and Travels*, ed. Awnsham and John Churchill (London, 1732), 5:518.

2. [Philotheos Physiologus, pseud.], *Friendly Advice to the Gentlemen-Planters of the East and West Indies* (London, 1684), 142, 218.

new societies that did not have the settled peace of English landed estates. Everyone saw the fear and violence.

3

Whatever slavery meant within West Africa—like Behn's king in his disguise as "Slave and Attendant," slaves might be respected household members or even responsible officials—it did not mean wholesale transport on large oceangoing vessels. Near the end of the eighteenth century, Olaudah Equiano recalled his terror at the big ship, the unendurable foulness, the methodically fierce white men. But for over a century, in the accounts of the Middle Passage, nameless slaves had expressed their trauma in the ways that he described, throwing themselves overboard, refusing to eat, sinking and dying in despair, and sometimes mounting insurrections. "We had about 12 negroes did willfully drown themselves, and others starved themselves to death," wrote Thomas Phillips, an English slaver of the 1690s, adding the common explanation, "for 'tis their belief that when they die they return home to their own country and friends again." The answer was shackles, close guarding, pacification with tobacco and brandy, and for uprisings, brutal measures. Phillips noted, "I have been informed that some commanders have cut off the legs and arms of the most willful, to terrify the rest."[3]

The colonies offered wider opportunities for resistance, met by a patchwork of countermeasures to restrain, pacify, or terrorize. Forms of slave resistance ranged from absenteeism, petty theft, and minor acts of disobedience to large-scale vandalism and murder, but the greatest dangers came from escapes and armed revolts. From earliest times, most colonies had numbers of runaway slaves, called "maroons," said to "lurk" in unsettled areas. They were not just a loss to their owners but a general threat, since they stole or raided, incited plantation slaves to join them, and posed a challenge to white colonial rule. Where jungles or mountains provided sanctuary, as in Surinam and Jamaica, groups of fugitives remained permanently at large. In 1673, the earliest recorded revolt was mounted by Jamaica slaves, "being most of them Coromantines (a warlike nation in Guinea)."[4] It was followed by many others, small or large, spontaneous or planned, including uprisings in Jamaica every few years during the 1670s and 1680s, one threatened in Barbados in 1675 (also instigated by Cormantines), and one in Antigua in 1687.

---

3. "A Journal of a Voyage Made in the *Hannibal* of London, Ann. 1693–94" (1732, reprinted in Elizabeth Donnan, ed., *Documents Illustrative of the Slave Trade to America*, Washington, D.C.: Carnegie Institution, 1930, 1:403).
4. From British Library Add. MS 12431, quoted in Richard Hart, *Blacks in Rebellion*, vol. 2 of *Slaves Who Abolished Slavery* (Kingston, Jamaica: University of the West Indies, 1985), 13ff. On the reported Barbados conspiracy, see pp. 110–12.

The early reports rarely say that slaves fled or rebelled to gain freedom. They had supposedly just been saved from worse—death, famine,
or barbarity—and it was claimed that under good masters, "they prefer
their present slavery before their former liberty, the loss whereof they
never afterwards regret."[5] Yet how to manage them remained a nice
point, since if treated leniently, they grew insolent, and if threatened
or treated with severity, they might kill themselves or run away. One
means by which the colonists sought to maintain control was by a
proliferating body of slave laws, adopted first in Barbados and later
copied everywhere else, in response to disorders: "Every time a black
man did something objectionable the English drew up a rule against
it."[6] Laws limited the slaves' movement and restricted their weekend
festivities and music, since under cover of those they could hatch
plots and send signals. Owners or overseers were fined if they let slaves
from different plantations gather, as a 1696 Jamaica law phrased it, "to
rendez-vous, revel, beat drums, or cause any other disturbance on Sundays or holidays, whereby they have taken liberty to contrive and bring
to pass many of their bloody and inhuman transactions."[7] Other pre-
cautionary measures called for searches for weapons, a strict watch on
boats, and penalties for aiding runaways. For serious violations that
defied the colonists' authority or threatened their safety, punishments
designed to "terrify" were staged in gruesome theatrical displays of
power. Although at public executions in Europe some criminals were
drawn and quartered, onlookers were impressed by the spectacles of
slaves chained up to starve, dismembered and castrated, or slowly
burned alive, their torments deliberately heightened, their corpses then
mutilated. Presumably fearsome enough to be a deterrent to most
slaves, these atrocities did not always impress the victims, who sometimes bore them unmoved, without a sound or sign or with a defiant
gesture. George Warren in 1667 remarked on what he called the "fortitude, or rather obstinacy" with which returned Surinam runaways
would suffer "the most exquisite tortures . . . for a terror and example
to others without shrinking."[8]

The records of lawmaking show not only the colonists' immediate
anxieties but the deeper uncertainties of a new situation. First, slaves
were valuable and needed, a practical motive to preserve them. Laws
carefully graded offenses according to the offenders' numbers, determination, and destructiveness, and were irregularly enforced. Although

---

5. John Davies, trans., *The History of the Caribby-Islands* (London, 1666), 201.
6. Richard S. Dunn, *Sugar and Slaves: The Rise of the Planter Class in the English West Indies,
1624–1713* (New York: W. W. Norton, 1973), 228.
7. *Report of the Lords of the Committee of Council Appointed for the Consideration of All Matters
Relating to Trade and Foreign Plantations . . . Concerning the Present State of the Trade to
Africa, and Particularly the Trade in Slaves* (London, 1789), 3: Jamaica Append., law xxxiv,
p. 5.
8. *An Impartial Description of Surinam* (London, 1667), 19.

panicky or vengeful colonists struck back with mass executions and other extreme responses, the standard policy was to make examples of leaders. Second, slaves were someone's legal property. A centralized administration under justices and other officials, backed by the local militia, may have given needed protection as the slave numbers rose, but it might also come into collision with an older set of rights that left entire control to individual planters. Owners were reimbursed when a slave was executed, but the penalties for shielding slaves and other records make clear that they often chose to be uncooperative.

Meanwhile the colonists were increasingly outnumbered by the influx of new Africans, as unrest continued to simmer. In laws phrased as denunciations, slaves were characterized not just as an unruly underclass but as a threatening enemy populace, a totalizing view that effectively wiped out any recognition of their differences, any impulse toward pity or admiration. According to the preamble to the first Barbados slave code of 1661, the slaves were "heathenish," "brutish," and "dangerous," therefore not governable by English law; by 1688, they were inveterate criminals, condemned for the "disorder, rapines and inhumanities to which they are naturally prone."[9] There was a corresponding elevation of all whites, not just all masters or property holders, over all slaves. Laws adopted in the wake of slave revolts decreed that a slave who struck or hurt "any white" be whipped for the first offense, then mutilated, then killed, and a 1696 Jamaica law tried to outlaw fantasy, imposing death for "compassing or imagining the death of any white."[1]

Written early in this development, *Oroonoko* is precisely set, soon after Lord Willoughby's appointment to Surinam in mid-1663 but before he arrived there in November 1664, though certainly Behn may have drawn inspiration from later colonial news reports and literary fashions. The comparatively early date of the tale seems reflected in its language, for while *lord* always signals a relationship of extreme deference, *slave* has a range of meanings, and the African slave workers are not firmly segregated, considered brutal, or assumed to be inferior to all whites. Beyond their political, class, and moral differences, the Europeans seem divided by rifts peculiar to the colonies. The established planters are said to feel some antagonism toward Willoughby, the major absentee property-holder with home-government connections and powers, and there is shared disapproval of the interference by appointed local administrators. Little is known about the activity or regulation of slaves in Surinam, although three hundred slaves belonging to one plantation would have represented many times what constituted wealth and a militia of six hundred would have been about half the entire

9. Quoted in Richard S. Dunn, *Sugar and Slaves*, 239, 242.
1. *Report of the Lords*, Jamaica Append., law xxiv, p. 3; and see Richard Hall, ed., *Acts, Passed in the Island of Barbados from 1643 to 1672* (London, 1764), 114–15.

white population. The colonists may or may not have had the policies and personalities that Behn attributes to them; the uncertain evidence can be traced using the Selected Bibliography and appended "Notes on Planter Personnel" in this volume. But as a place marked by instability and overlapping jurisdictions, its paternalistic private slaveholders outflanked by a local officialdom bent on domination and control, Behn's Surinam might be described as a colony in rapid transition from a slave-owning to a slave society.

Early in 1665, Fort Cormantine fell to the Dutch and was rebuilt and renamed. The old name survived in many later English accounts that single out Gold Coast slaves called "Cormantines" as specially able but intractable. Thomas Phillips and others bought them as fort hands or shipboard overseers, and he reports them "most in demand at Barbados," where they would "yield 3 or 4 pounds a head more."[2] But they were "stout stubborn people," according to slave captain William Snelgrave, who recounts how they persistently mutinied and argued with him for their liberty. He took extreme care, since many "despised punishment, and even death itself,"[3] and in the colonies refused both labor and correction and hanged themselves in groups. The warrior traditions noted in the earlier West Africa travel reports survived in their continuing leadership of slave revolts, mainly in Jamaica.[4] As for the fort itself, thought to contain the first holding prison for slaves, it became just one of many slave stations and in time fell into disrepair. The ruins, partly restored in the 1950s, can still be visited on the Ghana coast.[5]

At the end of the same war, Behn's "vast and charming world" of Surinam was traded to the Dutch. Byam and Banister labored to defend and evacuate the colony and then went on to Antigua and Jamaica, respectively. Under Dutch rule, Surinam became known for its very large estates served by huge populations of brutally exploited blacks, "for its heights of planter opulence and its depths of slave misery."[6] When Voltaire satirized slavery in *Candide*, he had a maimed Surinam slave give a deadpan recital of slave punishments:

> When we work in the sugar mills and the grindstone catches our fingers, they cut off the hand; when we try to run away, they cut

2. Donnan, *Documents*, 1:398.
3. *A New Account of Some Parts of Guinea and the Slave-Trade* (London, 1727), 168–74.
4. Orlando Patterson notes, "It is remarkable that almost every one of the serious rebellions [in Jamaica] during the seventeenth and eighteenth centuries was instigated and carried out mainly by Akan slaves." *The Sociology of Slavery: An Analysis of the Origins, Development and Structure of Negro Slave Society in Jamaica* (Rutherford, N. J.: Fairleigh Dickinson, 1969), 276.
5. J. D. Fage, "A New Check List of the Forts and Castles of Ghana," *Transactions of the Historical Society of Ghana* 4 (1959): 57–67.
6. Richard Price and Sally Price, eds., John Gabriel Stedman, *Narrative of a Five Years' Expedition against the Revolted Negroes of Surinam* (Baltimore: Johns Hopkins University Press, 1988), xiii.

off a leg. Both these things happened to me. This is the price paid for the sugar you eat in Europe.[7]

Surinam is also noted for its established communities of escaped slaves, who took refuge in the rain forests, won their freedom by treaty, and proudly preserved their African heritage and their own oral history into the late twentieth century, "the largest and most significant concentration of descendants of runaway slaves in the world."[8]

It was in England and Europe, of course, that Behn's story had its effect. Soon after her death, the new king, William III, responding to commercial interests, relaxed the royal company monopoly to make room for independent traders. By the early eighteenth century, England dominated the slave trade. Tracing its route, Behn had written of the export of cultural ideals from Europe and of the transport of model Africans into English colonial society, providing to the metropolitan world back home, for the third leg of the triangular trade, not sugar but a story. In that world, far removed from the tensions and raw violence, where the profits from the slave trade accumulated and art was made, her story continued to resonate.

Behn's claims for her role and experience were accepted and repeated with embellishments in the biographical accounts, but if others viewed her tale as history, it was a sort of history they did not hesitate to change. Like Hercules, Julius Caesar, Roland, or other quasi-historical heroes, Oroonoko became a legendary figure, his story recast for London and Paris audiences in the successful tragedy of Thomas Southerne and the French adaptation by La Place. Impressive slave or African figures who shared some of his capacities are to be found in a range of forms for a range of purposes, a traffic in betrayed princes, separated lovers, domestic pairs, devoted friends, brave suicides, rebel orators, and others. African women play little role—although in the world of fashion, we hear that the beautiful Lady Carteret appeared dressed as a white Imoinda at the Venetian ambassador's ball[9]—and there are few vicious Europeans. Scenes are for polite tastes. Yet as a tale that guided later interpretations, helped to stir shock and sympathy at injustice, filtered into literal news accounts, and defined troubling issues, Oroonoko itself was part of the unfolding history of slavery.

A hundred years after it appeared, Behn's tale had recently been republished in a somewhat expurgated version, while the more popular play was still performed in most seasons. Hannah More in "Slavery, A Poem" (1788) praised Southerne's emotional power but said that invented cases were not her concern:

7. Norman L. Torrey, ed. *Candide* (New York: Appleton-Century-Crofts, 1946), 19:63. For records of punishment by maiming and amputation, see Price, *Guiana Maroons*, 24–26.
8. "A Guerrilla War in Suriname," *New York Times*, June 18, 1987, A:1.
9. Mrs. Thomson, *Memoirs of Viscountess Sundon* (London, 1847), 1:112.

No individual griefs my bosom melt,
For millions feel what Oroonoko felt.

The play's 1791 editor remarked that it could hardly be popular in
Liverpool, the leading slave port, since it might end the "infernal" traffic.[1] In fact, opposition by the Liverpool merchants had recently defeated a Parliamentary bill to abolish the slave trade, but the campaign
against slavery was at last under way, the opposition mobilized, the
debate fierce. Prodded by the newly formed Abolition Society, Prime
Minister Pitt ordered the trade committee of the Privy Council to carry
out a full investigation of the slave trade[2]—its African sources, ships
and shipboard conditions, colonial practices and laws, extent and profits. Slave traders and antislavery activists came forward with their testimony, telling for the record their competing stories of humane
management or horrors. Freedom would become axiomatic. In the
meantime, one of the listed Liverpool slave ships was the *Oroonoko*.

1. *Bell's British Theatre*, 6:iii.
2. See *Report of the Lords*.

Colonizers and Settlers: First Views

[MONTAIGNE ON AMERICA]†

From Of Cannibals

[Widely known since Shakespeare's time, the *Essays*, literally "trials" or exploratory sketches, were given a new (and still current) translation by Charles Cotton in the same year that he provided a complimentary poem to preface one of Behn's French translations (see p. 189).

Montaigne viewed New World societies as fledgling pagan cultures that might, like Greece and Rome, provide alternative principles of order and civility to Christian Europe. His classic formulation of the "noble savage" in "Of Cannibals" is based on reports from the colonies, his wide learning, and his own ability to think beyond either. In "Of Coaches," the encounters of Inca and Mexican kings—noble in rank as well as mind—with the conquistadors under Pizarro and Cortés are taken from Spanish historical sources.]

When Pyrrhus, King of Epire, invaded Italy, having viewed and considered the order of the army the Romans sent out to meet him; "I know not," said he, "what kind of barbarians" (for so the Greeks called all other nations) "these may be; but the discipline of this army that I see has nothing of barbarity in it." As much said the Greeks of that Flaminius brought into their country; and Philip, beholding from an eminence the order and the distribution of the Roman camp led into his kingdom by Publius Sulpicius Galba, spake to the same effect.[1] By which it appears how cautious men ought to be of taking things upon trust from vulgar opinion, and that we are to judge by the eye of reason, and not from common report.

I have long had a man in my house that lived ten or twelve years in the New World, discovered in these latter days, and in that part of it where Villegaignon landed, which he called Antarctic France.[2] This discovery of so vast a country seems to be of very great consideration; and we are not sure, that hereafter there may not be another, so many wiser men than we having been deceived in this. I am afraid our eyes

---

† From *Essays of Michael Seigneur de Montaigne*, trans. Charles Cotton (London, 1685–86), book 1, chap. 30; book 3, chap. 6. Footnotes and modernization adapted from W. C. Hazlitt's revision of Cotton's text.
1. From Plutarch's *Lives* of Pyrrhus and Flaminius, and Livy's *History* 31.34.
2. Brazil, where Nicolas de Villegaignon had founded a short-lived French colony in the mid-1550s.

are bigger than our bellies, and that we have more curiosity than capacity; for we grasp at all, but catch nothing but air.

* * *

This man that I have is a plain ignorant fellow, and therefore the more likely to tell truth: for your better bred sort of men are much more curious in their observation, 'tis true, and discover a great deal more, but then they gloss upon it, and to give the greater weight to what they deliver, and allure your belief, they cannot forbear a little to alter the story; they never represent things to you simply as they are, but rather as they appeared to them, or as they would have them appear to you, and to gain the reputation of men of judgment, and the better to induce your faith, are willing to help out the business with something more than is really true, of their own invention. Now in this case, we should either have a man of irreproachable veracity, or so simple that he has not wherewithal to contrive, and to give a colour of truth to false relations, and that can have no ends in forging an untruth. Such a one is mine; and besides the little suspicion the man lies under, he has divers times showed me several seamen and merchants that at the same time went the same voyage. I shall therefore content myself with his information, without inquiring what the cosmographers say to the business. We should have maps to trace out to us the particular places where they have been; but for having had this advantage over us, to have seen the Holy Land, they would have the privilege, forsooth, to tell us stories of all the other parts of the world besides. I would have every one write what he knows, and as much as he knows, but no more; and that not in this only, but in all other subjects; for such a person may have some particular knowledge and experience of the nature of such a river, or such a fountain, that, as to other things, knows no more than what everybody does, and yet to keep a clutter with this little pittance of his, will undertake to write the whole body of physics: a vice from whence great inconveniences derive their original.

Now, to return to my subject, I find that there is nothing barbarous and savage in this nation, by anything that I can gather, excepting, that every one gives the title of barbarity to everything that is not in use in his own country. As indeed we have no other level of truth and reason than the example and idea of the opinions and customs of the place wherein we live. There is always the true religion, there the perfect government and the most exact and accomplished usance of all things. They are savages at the same rate that we say fruits are wild, which Nature produces of herself, and by her own ordinary progress; whereas in truth, we ought rather to call those wild whose natures we have changed by our artifice, and diverted from the common order. In those, the genuine, most useful and natural virtues and properties are vigorous and sprightly, which we have helped to degenerate in these, by accommodating them to the pleasure of our own corrupted palate. And yet for all this, our taste confesses a flavour and delicacy excellent even to emulation of the best of ours, in several fruits those countries abound with, without art or culture; neither is it reasonable that art should gain the pre-eminence of our great and powerful mother Nature. We have so expressed her with the additional ornaments and graces we have added to the beauty and riches of her own works, by our inventions, that we have almost smothered and choked her; and yet in other places, where she shines in her own purity and proper luster, she strangely baffles and disgraces all our vain and frivolous attempts.

> Et veniunt hederæ sponte suâ melius;
> Surgit et in solis formosior arbutus antris;
> Et volucres nullâ dulcius arte canunt.

> The ivy best spontaneously does thrive,
> Th' arbutus best in shady caves does live,
> And birds in their wild notes, their throats do streach,
> With greater art than art itself can teach.[3]

Our utmost endeavours cannot arrive at so much as to imitate the nest of the least of birds, its contexture, quaintness, and convenience: not so much as the web of a contemptible spider. All things, says Plato,[4] are produced either by Nature, by Fortune, or by Art; the greatest and most beautiful by the one or the other of the former, the least and the most imperfect by the last.

These nations then seem to me to be so far barbarous, as having received but very little form and fashion from art and human invention, and consequently not much remote from their original simplicity. The laws of Nature, however, govern them still, not as yet much vitiated with any mixture of ours: but in such purity, that I am sometimes troubled we were no sooner acquainted with these people, and that they were not discovered in those better times, when there were men much more able to judge of them than we are. I am sorry that Lycurgus and Plato had no knowledge of them; for to my apprehension, what we now see in those natives does not only surpass all the images with which the poets have adorned the golden age, and all their inventions in feigning a happy estate of man, but moreover, the fancy, and even the wish and desire of philosophy itself; so native and so pure a simplicity, as we by experience see to be in them, could never enter into their imagination, nor could they ever believe that human society could have been maintained with so little artifice; should I tell Plato that it is a nation wherein there is no manner of traffic, no knowledge of letters, no science of numbers, no name of magistrate, nor politic su-

---

3. Propertius 1.2.20.
4. In *Laws* 10.

periority; no use of service, riches or poverty, no contracts, no succes-
sions, no dividents, no proprieties,[5] no employments, but those of
leisure, no respect of kindred, but common, no clothing, no agriculture,
no metal, no use of corn or wine; and where so much as the very words
that signify lying, treachery, dissimulation, avarice, envy, detraction and
pardon were never heard of: how much would he find his imaginary
republic short of his perfection?

Hos Natura modos primum dedit.

These were the manners first by Nature taught.[6]

As to the rest, they live in a country beautiful and pleasant to miracle,
and so temperate withal, as my intelligence informs me, that 'tis very
rare to hear of a sick person, and they moreover assure me, that they
never saw any of the natives either paralytic, blear-eyed, toothless, or
crooked with age.

*   *   *

* * * The obstinacy of their battles is wonderful, and never end without great effusion of blood: for as to running away, they know not what
it is. Every one for a trophy brings home the head of an enemy he has
killed, which he fixes over the door of his house. After having a long
time treated their prisoners very well, and given them all the regalias[7]
they can think of, he to whom the prisoner belongs, invites a great
assembly of his kindred and friends, who being come, he ties a rope to
one of the arms of the prisoner, of which, at a distance, out of his
reach, he holds the one end himself, and gives to the friend he loves
best the other arm to hold after the same manner; which being done,
they two in the presence of all the assembly dispatch him with their
swords. After that, they roast him, eat him amongst them, and send
some chops to their absent friends, which nevertheless they do not do,
as some think, for nourishment, as the Scythians anciently did, but as
a representation of an extreme revenge; as will appear by this, that
having observed the Portugals, who were in league with their enemies,
to inflict another sort of death upon any of them they took prisoners,
which was to set them up to the girdle in the earth, to shoot at the
remaining part till it was stuck full of arrows, and then to hang them,
they that thought those people of the other world (as those who had
sown the knowledge of a great many vices amongst their neighbors, and
who were much greater masters in all sorts of mischief than they) did

5. "Bound of land" in Shakespeare's rendering of this passage, adapted as Gonzalo's description
   of an ideal commonwealth in *The Tempest* 2.1.147–56.
6. Virgil, *Georgics* 2.20.
7. Regales, or choice entertainments.

not exercise this sort of revenge without mystery,[8] and that it must needs be more painful than theirs; and so began to leave their old way, and to follow this.

I am not sorry that we should here take notice of the barbarous horror of so cruel an action, but that seeing so clearly into their faults, we should be so blind in our own. For I conceive there is more barbarity in eating a man alive, than when he is dead; in tearing a body limb from limb by racks and torments, that is yet in perfect sense, in roasting it by degrees, causing it to be bit and worried by dogs and swine (as we have not only read, but lately seen, not amongst inveterate and mortal enemies, but neighbours and fellow citizens, and, which is worse, under colour of piety and religion), than to roast and eat him after he is dead.

Chrysippus and Zeno, the two heads of the Stoical sect, were of opinion that there was no hurt in making use of our dead carcasses, in what kind soever, for our necessity, and in feeding upon them too; as our ancestors, who being besieged by Cæsar in the city Alexia, resolved to sustain the famine of the siege with the bodies of their old men, women, and other persons, who were incapable of bearing arms:—

> Vascones, fama est, alimentis talibus usi
> Produxere animas.

> 'Tis said, the Gascons with such meats as these,
> In time of siege their hunger did appease.[9]

And the physicians make no bones of employing it to all sorts of use, that is, either to apply it outwardly, or to give it inwardly for the health of the patient; but there never was any opinion so irregular, as to excuse treachery, disloyalty, tyranny, and cruelty, which are our familiar vices. We may then call these people barbarous, in respect to the rules of reason: but not in respect to ourselves, who in all sorts of barbarity exceed them.

* * *

From Of Coaches

* * *

Our world has lately discovered another (and who will assure us that it is the last of his brothers, since the Dæmons, the Sibyls, and we ourselves have been ignorant of this till now?), as large, well peopled, and fruitful as this whereon we live; and yet so raw and childish, that

8. Special knowledge.
9. Juvenal, *Satire* 15.93.

we yet teach it its A B C: 'tis not above fifty years since it knew neither letters, weights, measures, vestments, corn, nor vines. It was then quite naked in the Mother's lap, and only lived upon what she gave it. If we rightly conclude of our end, and this poet of the youthfulness of that age of his, that other world will only enter into the light when this of ours shall make its exit. The universe will be paralitic, one member will be useless, the other in vigour. I am very much afraid that we have very much precipitated its declension and ruin by our contagion; and that we have sold it our opinions and our arts at a very dear rate. It was an infant world, and yet we have not whipped and subjected it to our discipline, by the advantage of our valour and natural forces; neither have we won it by our justice and goodness, nor subdued it by our magnanimity. Most of their answers, and the negotiations we have had with them, witness that they were nothing behind us in pertinency and clearness of natural understanding. The astonishing magnificence of the cities of Cuzco and Mexico, and amongst many other such like things, the garden[1] of this king, where all the trees, fruits, and plants, according to the order and stature they are in a garden, were excellently formed in gold; as in his cabinet were all the animals bred upon the earth and in the seas of his dominions; and the beauty of their manufactures, in jewels, feathers, cotton, and painting, gave ample proof that they were as little inferior to us in industry. But as to what concerns devotion, observance of the laws, bounty, liberality, loyalty, and plain dealing, it was of use to us, that we had not so much as they; for they have lost, sold, and betrayed themselves by this advantage.

As to boldness and courage, stability, constancy against pain, hunger, and death, I should not fear to oppose the examples I find amongst them to the most famous examples of elder times, that we find in our records on this side of the world. For, as to those who have subdued them, take but away the sleights and artifices they practised to deceive them, and the just astonishment it was to those nations to see so sudden and unexpected an arrival of men with beards, differing in language, religion, shape, and countenance, from so remote a part of the world, and where they had never heard there was any habitation, mounted upon great unknown monsters, against those who had never so much as seen a horse, or any other beast trained up to carry a man, or any other loading; shelled in a hard and shining skin, with a cutting and glittering weapon in his hand, against them, who, out of wonder at the brightness of a looking-glass, or a knife, would truck great treasures of gold and pearl; and who had neither knowledge nor matter with which at leisure they could penetrate our steel: to which may be added the lightning and thunder of our pieces and harquebuses, enough to frighten Cæsar himself, if surprised, with so little experience; and now

1. The magnificent garden of the King of Mexico [Cotton's gloss].

against naked people, if not, where the invention of a little quilted cotton was in use, without other arms, at the most, than bows, stones, staves, and bucklers of wood; people surprised under colour of friendship and good faith, by the curiosity of seeing strange and unknown things; take but away, I say, this disparity from the conquerors, and you take away all the occasion of so many victories. When I look upon that invincible ardour wherewith so many thousands of men, women, and children have so often presented and thrown themselves into inevitable dangers for the defence of their gods and liberties; that generous obstinacy, to suffer all extremities and difficulties, and even death itself, rather than submit to the dominion of those by whom they had been so shamefully abused; and some of them choosing rather to die of hunger and fasting, being prisoners, than to accept of nourishment from the hands of their so basely victorious enemies: I foresee, that whoever would have attacked them upon equal terms of arms, experience, and number, would have had a hard, and peradventure a harder game to play than in any other war we have seen.

Why did not so noble a conquest fall under Alexander, or the ancient Greeks and Romans; and so great a revolution and mutation of so many empires and nations, fall into hands that might have rooted up and gently levelled, and made plain and smooth whatever was rough and savage amongst them, and that might have cherished and propagated the good seeds that Nature had there produced, mixed not only with the culture of land and the ornament of cities, the arts of this part of the world, in what was necessary, but also the Greek and Roman virtues, with those that were originals of the country? What a particular reparation had it been to them, and what a general good to the whole world, had our first examples and deportments in those parts allured those people to the admiration and imitation of virtue, and had begot betwixt them and us a fraternal society and intelligence? How easy had it been to have made advantage of souls so innocent, and so eager to learn; having for the most part naturally so good inclinations before? Whereas, on the contrary, we have taken advantage of their ignorance and inexperience, with greater ease to incline them to treachery, luxury, avarice, and towards all sorts of inhumanity and cruelty, by the pattern and example of our manners. Who ever enhanced the price of merchandise at such a rate? So many cities levelled with the ground, so many nations exterminated, so many millions of people fallen by the edge of the sword, and the richest and most beautiful part of the world turned upside down, for the traffic of pearl and pepper. Mechanic victories! Never did ambition, never did animosities engage men against one another to such a degree of hostility and miserable calamity.

* * *

Of two the most puissant monarchs of that world, and peradventure of this, kings of so many kings, and the last they exterminated, that of

Peru, having been taken in a battle, and put to so excessive a ransom
as exceeds all belief, and it being faithfully paid, and that he had by
his conversation given manifest signs of a frank, liberal, and constant
spirit, and of a clear and settled understanding, the conquerors had a
mind, after having exacted a million, three hundred twenty-five thousand and five hundred weight of gold, besides silver, and other things
which amounted to no less (so that their horses were shod with massy
gold), yet to see (at the price of what disloyalty and injustice whatever)
what the remainder of the treasures of this king might be, and to possess
themselves of that also. To which end a false accusation was preferred
against him, and false witnesses brought to prove that he went about
to raise an insurrection in his provinces, by that means to procure his
own liberty. Whereupon, by the virtuous sentence of those very men
who had by this treachery conspired his ruin, he was condemned to be
publicly hanged, after having made him buy off the torment of being
burnt alive, by the baptism they gave him immediately before execution. A horrid and unheard-of barbarity, which nevertheless he under-
went without going less either in word or look, with a truly grave and
royal behaviour. After which, to calm and appease the people, astonished and daunted at so strange a thing, they counterfeited great sorrow
for his death, and appointed most sumptuous funerals.

The other king of Mexico, after [having] a long time defended his
beleaguered city, and having in this siege manifested the utmost of what
suffering and perseveration can do, if ever prince and people did, and
his misfortune having delivered him alive into his enemies' hands, upon
articles of being treated like a king; neither did he in his captivity
discover anything unworthy of that title. His enemies, after their victory,
not finding so much gold as they expected, when they had searched
and rifled with their utmost diligence, they went about to procure discoveries by the most cruel torments they could invent upon the prisoners they had taken: but having profited nothing that way, their
courages being greater than their torments, they arrived at last to such
a degree of fury, as, contrary to their faith, and the law of nations, to
condemn the king himself, and one of the principal noblemen of his
court, to the rack, in the presence of one another. This lord, finding
himself overcome with pain, being environed with burning coals, piti-
fully turned his dying eyes towards his master, as it were to ask him
pardon that he was able to endure no more; whereat the king darting
at him a fierce and severe look, as reproaching his cowardice and pu-
sillanimity, with a rude and constant voice said to him thus only: "And
what dost thou think I suffer?" said he, "am I in a bath, am I more at
ease than thou?" Whereupon the other immediately quailed under the
torment and died upon the place. The king, half roasted, was carried
thence; not so much out of pity (for what compassion ever touched so
barbarous souls, who, upon the doubtful information of some vessel of

gold to be made a prey of, caused not only a man, but a king so great in fortune and desert to be broiled before their eyes), but because his constancy rendered their cruelty still more shameful. They afterward hanged him, for having nobly attempted to deliver himself by arms from so long a captivity and subjection, where he died with a courage becoming so magnanimous a prince.

* * *

[THE SETTLING OF SURINAM]

Lord Willoughby to Lady Willoughby (1651)†

[Francis, Lord Willoughby of Parham began to look toward Surinam in 1651. As a Royalist, he had recently been deprived of his estates at home and would soon be replaced as governor of Barbados. What he calls the "storm" from England developed with speed and force. During the English civil war, the colonists had been left to manage their own affairs and wanted to preserve their autonomy. When the war ended, the Royalist Barbados Assembly fined and banished well over a hundred Roundhead colonists, some very powerful. Willoughby, newly arrived as governor, tried to arrange a moderate settlement with the Parliamentarian government for the return of those expelled and the confirmation of his own appointment, but Parliament voted to declare the colonists "rebels," imposed a trade embargo, and sent a fleet to subdue them. Willoughby abandoned all moderation and the island prepared to resist. It surrendered in January 1651, and the newly formed assembly expelled Willoughby.

Other men in Behn's story had prominent parts in this episode. William Byam, an army captain exiled to Barbados in 1646, was a member of the extremist Royalist faction bent on persecution and control. George Martin was Willoughby's envoy to the government in London, but once there, his petitions and correspondence show, he turned against him. Byam was one of those appointed by Willoughby to negotiate peace; soon afterwards he, too, was banished and moved to Surinam.]

My dearest Friend,

I did, not above a fortnight ago, write at large to thee by the way of Holland, by my governess Cateline, the carpenter's wife, whom upon her earnest importunity, I gave leave to go home. She performed her trust very carefully and honestly in keeping all things under her charge, but for anything else she was loth to trouble herself. Honest Mary is all my stay now, and I hope will do as well as she can. I have entertained another coarse wench to be under her, allowing her help enough of negroes, which are the best servants in these countries, if well tutored,

† Reprinted in R. H. Schomburgk, *The History of Barbados* (London, 1848), 273–75, from Bodleian Tanner MS 54, f. 147.

and cost little, only a canvas petticoat once a year, and there is no more trouble with them.

*   *   *

* * * I did by Cateline write so large, giving thee an account of myself, and the state of the island, by some papers, acquainting thee what we had done in order to our self-preservation against that storm which was threatened us from England, by their printed declaration calling us all rebels, so as I shall touch no more upon anything of that, only what we have further added since; which is, to make ourselves strong in men, as well as in words; and to that end have raised forces, both of horse and foot, which the country pays, and are constantly to be kept in a body to resist any forces that shall come against us. It was occasioned by Mr. Arnold, who came at the time of the Assembly's meeting: he is a very honest man. By him I received two letters, and three from my children; one more which was superscribed to Mr. Rich. We had a fine passage, being but five weeks upon the way. I could wish to my heart thou hadst been with him; but I know not how I should be so happy, though thy goodness to me, in saying thou wilt come, puts me in some comfort: for which kind resolution of thine, God in heaven reward thee. He came in a very opportune time, for the terror of his news, that so many ships were coming with men to reduce the island, stirred up the spirits of the Assembly, caused them to desire me to put the island in a posture of war, occasioned the raising of horse and foot, so as we shall be very able to resist them, and send them home again, showing them the island is not so easily to be won as they are made to imagine it. And I hope they will reward those runaway bankrupt rogues, who durst stay no longer here, for fear of a gaol, whereof learned Mr. Bayes[1] is one; having by their villainy, done what in them lies to ruin one of the best and sweetest islands in the English possession, or in any others, except the Spaniards, with whom we hear they have made a league, offensive and defensive; and if that be their planting the Gospel, I hope God will never prosper it.

*   *   *

* * * To hear of the sadness of thy condition, to be brought to so low a stipend, cuts my heart: but I hope God, who has hitherto kept us up, will still preserve us, and though cruel men may rob, oppress, and steal away what I have, yet I shall find a way to live: and since they began so deeply with me, as to take away all at one clap, and without any cause given on my part, I am resolved not to sit down a loser, and be content to see thee, my children, and self ruined.

There was wont reparation to be allowed to those that were injured by the contrary party; and being it is in my own power to help myself,

---

1. John Bayes, a major planter and supporter of Parliament, was among those ousted by the assembly. Back in London he led the opposition to compromise with the colony and to Willoughby's continuance as governor.

shall I not do it, but sit still, like an ass, seeing the meat torn out of thine and my children's mouths? No! I will not do it; and therefore, dear heart, let me entreat thee to leave off thy persuasions to submit to them, who so unjustly, so wickedly, have ruined thee and me and mine.

If ever they get the island, it shall cost them more than it is worth before they have it. And be not frighted with their power and success: God is above all.

There is an inclosed note directed 'the Gentleman,' which I am confident, if you will, you may make use of, praying you not to omit the opportunity. I shall send him as much in sugar, when I hear from you that you have made use of this. Be not frightened nor perplexed for me; I am confident yet God will bring us together into these parts, according to my former petitions to him, that we may end our days together in happiness; for I have had a return of my discovery of Guiana, which I writ to you formerly of; and the gentleman which I sent hath brought with him to me two of the Indian kings, having spoke with divers of them, who are all willing to receive our nation, and that we shall settle amongst them; for which end I am sending hence a hundred men to take possession, and doubt not but in a few years to have many thousands there.

It is commended, by all that went, for the sweetest place that ever was seen; delicate rivers, brave land, fine timber. They were out almost five months; and amongst forty persons, not one of them had so much as their head ache. They commend the air to be so pure, and the water so good, as they had never such stomachs in their lives, eating five times a day plenty of fish and fowl, partridges and pheasants innumerable: brave savanas, where you may, in coach or on horseback, ride thirty or forty miles.

God bless me into life. And if England will be a friend, or that we make them so by tiring them out, either their seamen by the tedious voyages, or the state by the great expense they must be at, which I am very confident we shall, being all so well-resolved to stand by one another to the last man, then I shall make thee a brave being there; for since all is gone at home, it is time to provide elsewhere for a being.

❋   ❋   ❋

[Lord Willoughby's Prospectus for Settlers to Surinam]†

1. Such as are able & willing to transport themselves at their own charge shall have a shippe or shippes provided for them, according to

---

† "Certain Overtures Made by the Lord Willoughby of Parham Unto All Such as Shall Incline to Plant in the Colony of Surinam on the Continent of Guiana," from British Library, Sloane Manuscript 159, ff. 20–21v. The Sloane Catalogue dates the manuscript 1662–65, but V. T. Harlow, in *Colonising Expeditions to the West Indies and Guiana, 1623–1667* (London: Hakluyt Society, 1925), 174, notes that it was "probably *circa* 1655" and is typical of offers to attract settlers at that time.

their number in 3 months or lesse after they signifye their resolutions & the number of persons and quantitye of goods; & in the sayd vessels they shall have accommodation according to their qualitye. They shall pay for their passage but £5 a head; & in this also there will be an abatement for children under 10 yeares old, for 2 of them shalbe accompted but for one passenger in pay & allowance (provided alwayes that they never any messe above 7 in number), sucking children to go free. Every passenger also, according to the manner to have his sea chest or trunk to go free, & to pay but 50 shillings per ton for fraight of other goods.

2. Upon their arrivall in the Countrye there shall be allotted to every single person, man or woman that payes for their own passage, 50 Acres of Land of inheritance. And a married man to have so much for himself & 50 more for his wife; 30 for every child; 20 for every man or mayd servant; & as their familyes increase in children or servants, so to increase in their lot of land. This land to be layd out as shalbe most convenient for situation & goodness, according to the choyce of the person concerned. And if any shall think fit to depart from the Countrye, they shall have liberty to sell their lands & goods to whom they please, or on other occasion to dispose thereof by deed will or contract.

3. When any of their children grow up to a distinct familye, then to have 50 Acres of other Land of inheritance, & when any of their servants are set free to have 30 Acres.

4. Such single persons, men or women (as being serviceable & of good report) are willing but are not able to go, may be entertained into service by the Lord Willoughby, & at his alone charge transported, serving there but foure years, in all which time to be fully provided with sufficient meat, drink, lodging & apparell, & at the end of the sayd terme, shall have ten pounds sterling payd them in money or Country Commodityes, & 30 Acres of good land allotted them for them & their heirs for ever. And the servant that is an Artificer shall have further incouragement in his Art. Likewise there will be entertainment for boyes & girles for 7 years or such other time as is fit for their age; & at the end of their time, they shall have 30 Acres & some reward in Tooles, clothes or other materialls.

5. For the transport & support of industrious & well disposed persons & familyes which are not able to do this of themselves, as in the first Article, neither are so fit to pay for it by service, as in the 4th Article, there is a desire to propound or finde out & accept such a way as may give just encouragement to the transporter & transported. That which is at present thought on & practised is, that such persons & familyes shall have their passage at the alone charge of the Lord Willoughby, or any other Patron, & upon their arrivall, every person if single, shall have 40 Acres of good Land allotted to him; & if married as much also

for his wife & 15 for each child or servant; and when a child of such a familye shall goe forth to finde a new one, to have 40 Acres & when a servant is free 30.

Those persons so transported to be true debtors to the Lord Willoughby or any other patron, for their passage, & therefore to hold their land on condition of paying after the 2nd yeare a tenth part of the profits thereof either in kind as it riseth, or at a rate compounded for. Good order is to be taken to prevent fraud or neglect by appointing a proportion of Land to be planted with provision & Commodityes; & if any such person or familyes, as being in Townes shall desire wholly to employ themselves in some Arts or misterye, rather than in planting, then to pay the Patron some lesser part of their true gaine be it a 20th or any other part which shalbe agreed upon.

The Lord Willoughby is willing for the first 8 months (in which time & before, they may have a croppe of their own) to furnish such poore familyes with provision to be paid for at the 2nd yeare in kinde; otherwise also to trust them with Tooles and other necessaryes out of his Store; likewise to furnish them at the countrye rates with cattel & servants, English & Negroes; for which if not payd for in 3 months after the delivery, the Planter is to allow wages for so much of the price as is unpayed at 6 per centum.

Incouragement is considered of for all considerable persons & ingenuous Artists or Students, as able preachers, schoolmasters, Physicians, Chyrurgions,[1] midwives, surveyors, Architectors, Chymists, & other persons singularly improvable for the good of the Colonye; their bookes instruments or tooles needfull in the exercise of their ingenuity shalbe fraight[2] free, & any other reasonable foods indulged.

[The Company of Royal Adventurers to Lord Willoughby (1663)][†]

[With the restoration of the monarchy, Willoughby was reappointed governor of Barbados, along with the other Caribbee Islands, and officially granted joint proprietorship of Surinam. As agent of the Crown, he was expected to enforce the African Company's monopoly on supplying slaves and other unpopular directives. His efforts to broker some of those occupied him in Barbados during the period covered in Behn's story.]

1. Surgeons.
2. Freighted, carried.
† "Letter of His Royal Highness the Duke of York, and the Rest of the Company of Royal Adventurers Trading to Africa to the Right Honourable Francis, Lord Willoughby of Parham," in *The Several Declarations of the Company of Royal Adventurers* (London, 1667), 8–9. This and related documents are reprinted in Elizabeth Donnan, ed., *Documents Illustrative of the Slave Trade to America* (Washington, D.C.: Carnegie Institution, 1930), vol. 1.

My Lord, The Royal Company being very sensible how necessary it is that the English Plantations in America should have a competent and a constant supply of Negro-servants for their own use of Planting, and that at a moderate Rate, have already sent abroad, and shall within eight days dispatch so many Ships for the Coast of Africa as shall by God's permission furnish the said Plantations with at least 3000 Negroes, and will proceed from time to time to provide them a constant and sufficient succession of them, so as the Planter shall have no just cause to complain of any Want: And for the Price, and terms of Payment, they have for the present resolved, to order all their Servants and Factors not to sell any Negroes higher than is expressed in this following Resolve.

Resolved, That Orders be given to the Factors in the Plantations of the Charibee Islands, to sell all Blacks that are found in Lots[1] (as hath been customary) at £ 17. sterling per head in Money * * * or Bills Exchange for England with good assurance of payment, or at 2400 lb. of well cured Muscovado Sugar in Cask, with express condition, that no Blacks be delivered without present payment in Money, Bills, or Sugar, viewed and accepted by the Factors, or in Cotton or Indico, according to the price currant between them and Sugar.

And do desire your Lordship, that you will be pleased to communicate these Resolutions of the Company to your respective Deputies in all His Majesty's American Dominions under your Lordship's Government, and direct them to publish the same within their respective Limits and Jurisdictions, and to gather from the Planters and Inhabitants, and to transmit to us as soon as they conveniently can, the certain number of Negroes which they desire, and will engage to receive yearly from Us on those reasonable Terms proposed, that so we may proportion our Care for them accordingly.

And further, The Company doth desire your Lordship to order this inclosed Paper of Conditions[2] to be declared by your respective Deputies, in the most usual manner, and to receive such Subscriptions as shall be accordingly made, and to transmit to us Authentic Copies of them by the first Passage that shall present for England, after the time of subscribing is expired.

By Order of the Royal Company:
Ellis Leighton, Secretary
Dated at Whitehall, January 10, 1663.

---

1. The practice described in *Oroonoko*. Behn's cited price is "twenty pound a head," but a somewhat elevated price would be readily explained by the attempts of Barbados, the nearer and more established port, to obstruct its new rival.
2. Announcing a general public subscription to the company and explaining its founding by King Charles lest the slave trade "be lost to this Nation" and the colonies "rendered useless in their growing Plantations" (Donnan *Documents*, 1:158). Both the Company's promised numbers of slaves and efficient collection of payment from planters remained in the realm of theory; a new company was formed in 1672.

Observers of Slavery, 1654–1712

ANTOINE BIET

[They Came Here in Order to Become Wealthy]†

[Biet was a young French priest who took refuge in Surinam and Barbados at the fall of a French colony at Cayenne. In Surinam he was deeply impressed by the riverbanks with their great trees ("nothing more beautiful in the world") and by the helpfulness of William Byam ("a worthy gentleman, in heart and word"). On more developed Barbados, however, he drew back from the long afternoon drinking parties to observe what he saw as a heedlessly cruel and competitive frontier society.

A rather striking number of particular details in Biet's account of the landscape and Indians, although not his interpretations, recur in Behn's story.]

* * *

The wealth of this island consists of sugar. Sugar cane or reed is planted in the countryside as far as the eye can see. * * * They also grow a great deal of cotton and ginger, both of which grow in such great abundance that once they have been planted they cannot be completely harvested. Tobacco is only produced on the island for the use of the English and the slaves who are given some time off when working, in addition to the meal time, to rest and smoke tobacco.

Their greatest wealth are their slaves, and there is not one slave who does not make a profit of more than one hundred *écus* each year for his master. Each slave does not cost four *écus*[1] per year for his upkeep. The slaves go around almost entirely naked, except on Sundays when they put on some worthless canvas breeches and a shirt. The small Negroes and Negresses always go about completely naked until they are fourteen or fifteen years old. As for their food, there is no nation which feeds its slaves as badly as the English because for all meals the slaves only get potatoes which serve them as their bread, their meat, their fish, in fact, everything. The slaves raise some poultry so as to have eggs which they give to their little children. They are only given

---

† From Antoine Biet, *Voyage de la France Equinoxiale en L'Isle de Cayenne* (Paris, 1664), 289–93, in Jerome S. Handler, trans., "Father Antoine Biet's Visit to Barbados in 1654," *Journal of the Barbados Museum and Historical Society* 32 (1967), 66–68. Reprinted by permission.
1. Assuming an *écu* to be the equivalent of a crown, four *écus* would be about a pound [Handler's note].

meat one time in the whole year, namely Christmas Day, which is the only holiday observed in this island.

The English servants and those of this nation [i.e., France] are not much better treated. They are indentured for seven years, and also get only potatoes. The masters are obliged to support them, but God knows how they are maintained. All are very badly treated. When they work the overseers, who act like those in charge of galley slaves, are always close by with a stick with which they often prod them when they do not work as fast as is desired. I found it strange that they sent from England those persons who were suspected of being Royalists, and who had been taken prisoners in the battle which the King lost. They were sold, especially when it was discovered that they were Catholics, the husband in one place, the wife in another, and the children in another place so as not to receive any solace from each other.

They treat their Negro slaves with a great deal of severity. If some go beyond the limits of the plantation on a Sunday they are given fifty blows with a cudgel; these often bruise them severely. If they commit some other slightly more serious offense they are beaten to excess, sometimes up to the point of applying a fire-brand all over their bodies which makes them shriek with despair. I saw a poor Negro woman, perhaps thirty-five or forty years old, whose body was full of scars which she claimed had been caused by her master's having applied the fire-brand to her: this horrified me. As these poor unfortunates are very badly fed, a few occasionally escape during the night and go to steal a pig or something similar from a neighboring plantation. But, if they are discovered, there is no forgiving them. One day I went to visit my Irishman. He had in irons one of these poor Negroes who had stolen a pig. Every day, his hands in irons, the overseer had him whipped by the other Negroes until he was all covered with blood. The overseer, after having had him treated thus for seven or eight days, cut off one of his ears, had it roasted, and forced him to eat it. He wanted to do the same to the other ear and the nose as well. I interceded on behalf of this poor unfortunate, and I pleaded so well with the overseer that the Negro was freed from his torment. With tears in his eyes, he came to throw himself at my feet to thank me. It is an unhappy state of things to treat with such great severity creatures for whom Jesus Christ shed his blood. It is true that one must keep these kinds of people obedient, but it is inhuman to treat them with so much harshness. * * *

In speaking of morals, extravagance is very great among the English in these parts. They came here in order to become wealthy. The ladies and young women are as well dressed as in Europe, and they economize on nothing to dress well. * * * One furnishes his house sumptuously. Things that are the finest in England and elsewhere are found in the island. Men and women go well mounted on very handsome horses which are covered with very rich saddle-cloths. The extravagance of the table is not less. Everything is there in abundance, except that game is very rare. They lack no other meats and have all sorts of fowl with which their farm yards are filled. They have all kinds of drinks: the best wines from more than six areas in Europe, brandy, *Rossolis*, and many artificial drinks which are excellent. One could always drink whatever one wished. * * * The greatest of all the vices which prevail in this country is lewdness. It is a horrible thing to think about: adulterers, incest and all the rest. I will not say anymore on this. Drunkeness is great, especially among the lower classes. Cursers are rare because the police punish them severely. There are arguments, but no one would dare to fight with swords for he would be punished at once. They settle their differences by fist fighting. They give each other black eyes, scratch each other, tear each other's hair, and do similar things. The onlookers let them do this and surround them so as to see who will be victorious. If they fall to the ground, they are picked up, and they fight until they can no longer do so and are forced to give up.

* * *

HENRY WHISTLER

[They and Their Seed]†

[Whistler was on the expedition sent out by Oliver Cromwell to challenge Spanish power in the West Indies. It stopped at Barbados for nearly two months in February to March 1655 to raise troops and, after some defeats, took Jamaica.]

[FEBRUARY 9, 1654]

This Island is one of the richest spots of ground in the world and fully inhabited. But were the people suitable to the Island it were not to be compared: it is a most rich soil, all ways grown and bearing fruit, and the chiefest commodity is Sugar. * * *

The gentry here doth live far better than ours do in England: they have most of them 100 or 2 or 3 of slaves apiece who they command as they please. Here they may say what they have is their own. And they have that liberty of conscience which we so long have in England fought for; but they do abuse it. This Island is inhabited with all sorts: with English, French, Dutch, Scots, Irish, Spaniards they being Jews: with Indians and miserable Negroes born to perpetual slavery, they and their seed. These Negroes they do allow as many wives as they will

† "A journall of a voardge . . . performed by the Right Honourable Generall Penn, Admiral," BL Sloane MS 3926, in C. H. Firth, ed., *The Narrative of General Venables* (London, 1900), 145–46. Spelling, punctuation, and paragraphing have been modernized.

have; some will have 3 or 4, according as they find their body able. Our English here doth think a Negro child the first day it is born to be worth £5; they cost them nothing the bringing up, they go always naked. Some planters will have 30 more or less about 4 or 5 years old. They sell them from one to the other as we do sheep.

This Island is the dunghill whereon England doth cast forth its rub-bidge:[1] rogues and whores and such like people are those which are generally brought here. A rogue in England will hardly make a cheater here; a bawd brought over puts on a demure comportment, a whore if handsome makes a wife for some rich planter. But in plain the Island of itself is very delightful and pleasant; it is manured the best of any Island of the Indies, with many brave houses, and here is a brave harbor for ships to ride in.

✻   ✻   ✻

JEAN BAPTISTE DU TERTRE

[A Servitude for Life][†]

[A Dominican missionary with long experience in the French islands, Du Tertre (1610–1687) is known for his admiring description of the free life of the Carib Indians, which expands on Montaigne's sketch of the canni-bals and influenced Rousseau's ideal "state of nature." He credits the slaves with an inborn passion for liberty but, like many others, thinks it has been so debased by Africa that they need and prefer a state of dependency. But Du Tertre is a lively reporter; as he describes for his European audience the slaves' wretched treatment and strong families and communities, he sometimes suggests, as he says of their religion, that "they live in a more Christian way in their condition than many of the French."]

When a ship comes to those coasts, the ship's trader applies to the petty prince or to the governor of the province where he lands, and those sell to them these poor wretched people, men, women, and children of any age, for iron bars, for grindstones, for small pieces of silver, for brandy, for cloth, and for other commodities they need most in those countries.

They commonly expose for sale three kinds of persons. First, those they have taken in war on their enemies; second, those who have de-served death for some crime, preferring to draw some profit from them than to kill them by capital punishment; in the third place, those who

---

1. Rubbish.
  † Translated by the editor from Jean Baptiste Du Tertre, "Of the Negro Slaves, vulgarly called Moors in France," in *Histoire Générale des Antilles Habitées par les François* 2 (Paris, 1667), 494–96, 504–05.

are surprised in some theft, the judge counting as a banishment their loss of liberty among the strangers who buy them.

There have been traders unjust enough that they have kidnapped the innocent with the criminals, robbing the liberty even of those who sold them these captives or who had come to their ship to banquet there; and I have heard that a certain captain who had drawn several into his vessel by means of drink and gifts, while those poor people were thinking only about enjoying themselves, the pilot having raised anchor, as soon as the ship was under sail, they were seized, loaded with chains, and brought to the islands, where they were sold as slaves.

I don't know what that nation has done; but it is enough to be black to be taken, sold, and bound into a grievous servitude that lasts for all of life.

*   *   *

Among these slaves are sometimes found some who were of high rank in their country; but we never could know the rank that the first woman Negro we bought at Guadeloupe had held among them, nor in what way she had been taken in war. She had the bearing of a queen, and a spirit so elevated above the misery of her condition that one clearly saw that she had lost nothing of her dignity in her disgrace. All the other Negroes of her land, men and women, paid her respects as to a princess; when they saw her in church or on the road, they stopped short before her, put their two hands to the ground, slapped their thighs with them, and held them for a moment raised above their heads, which is the way they pay homage to their sovereigns.

*   *   *

The right of ownership that the masters have over their slaves is so absolute, and the possession of them so complete, that not only do they belong to them like goods they acquired by bill of sale, but they also have the same right over the unhappy children born of their marriages, as over a fruit that grows on an estate of which they are lords. It is on that account (that the Negroes comprise the power and wealth of their masters, and a man is esteemed in the islands only for the number of his slaves) that our French take care to marry them as soon as they can in order to have children by them, who in the course of time take the place of their fathers, perform the same labor, and give them the same assistance.

*   *   *

There was seen at Guadeloupe a young Negress so persuaded of the misery of her condition that her master could never make her consent to marry the Negro man that he presented to her. At first believing that she loved someone else, this master asked one of our Fathers to get to know that from her, and to promise her that he would buy him, at whatever the price might be; but she never answered anything but that she did not want to marry at all. Her master, making light of her res-

olution, brought her to our church one Sunday to marry the Negro
that he wanted to give to her. She didn't resist at all, but only waited
for the priest to ask her if she wanted such a one for her husband, for
then she replied with a firmness that astonished us, "No, my Father, I
want neither this one nor any other. I am satisfied to be miserable in
myself, without bringing children into the world who would perhaps
be more unhappy than I, and whose afflictions would be much more
painful to me than my own." Therefore she has always remained stead-
fastly in her single state, and was commonly called *La Pucelle des Isles*.[1]

* * *

From *Great Newes from the Barbadoes*

[Fatal Conspiracy]†

[In 1675, Governor Atkins of Barbados reported a "damnable design"
spread widely "over most of the plantations, especially amongst the Cor-
mantin negroes . . . a warlike and robust people" (*Calendar of State Papers,
Colonial*, 1675–76, no. 690). According to this and another brief pamphlet
account published in London, a young slave who disapproved of the proposed massacre was overheard by a woman house slave, who told her master, Justice Giles Hall, who investigated and informed the governor.

The role played by fear and rumor (especially clear concerning white
women) remains uncertain, but along with the reprisals, the abortive plot
led to stricter laws against holiday gatherings and runaways. A full analysis
is provided by Jerome S. Handler, "Slave Revolts and Conspiracies in
Seventeenth-Century Barbados," *New West Indian Guide* 56 (1982), 5–37.]

This *Conspiracy* first broke out and was hatched by the *Cormantee*
or *Gold-Coast Negroes* about Three years since, and afterwards Cun-
ningly and Clandestinely carried, and kept secret, even from the knowledge of their own Wives.

Their grand design was to choose them a King, one *Coffee* an Ancient Gold-Coast *Negro*, who should have been Crowned the 12th of
June last past in a Chair of State exquisitely wrought and Carved after
their Mode; with Bows and Arrows to be likewise carried in State before
his Majesty their intended King. Trumpets to be made of Elephants
Teeth and Gourds to be sounded on several Hills, to give Notice of
their general Rising, with a full intention to fire the Sugar-Canes, and

---

1. The Maid of the Islands. Joan of Arc was called "La Pucelle" or "the Maid of Orléans."
   French colonial policy, formalized in the *Code Noir*, stressed the promotion of Christian faith
   among the slaves, directing that they be baptized without delay and, with the master's permission and the slave's consent, given the benefit of Catholic marriage.
† From *Great newes from the Barbadoes, or, A True and faithful account of the grand conspiracy
   of the Negroes against the English and the happy discovery of the same* (London, 1676), 9–
   13.

so run in and Cut their Masters the Planters Throats in their respective Plantations whereunto they did belong.

Some affirm, they intended to spare the lives of the Fairest and Handsomest Women (their Mistresses and their Daughters) to be Converted to their own use. But some others affirm the contrary; and I am induced to believe they intended to Murther all the White People there, as well Men as Women. * * *

* * *

Of all which the said Justice sending the true Information to that Noble Person (now Governor there) Sir *Jonathan Atkins*, he with his Life-Guard presently came to the house of the aforesaid Justice *Hall*, and granted him and others Commissions to apprehend the guilty and impeached *Negroes*, with the Ring-leaders of this fatal Conspiracy; which in pursuance was put in Execution with much Celerity and Secrecy, that the Heads and Chief of these ungrateful wretches (who I have often heard confess to live better in Servitude there, than at Liberty in their own Native Country) were apprehended and brought to Trial at a Court of *Oyer* and *Terminer* granted by the aforesaid Governor to a Dozen or more of the Colonels and Field-Officers as Judges of that Island; who after strict and due Examination of the matter of Fact of their Conspiracy, at first Seventeen were found guilty and executed, (*viz.*) Six burnt alive, and Eleven beheaded, their dead bodies being dragged through the Streets, at *Spikes*,[1] a pleasant Port-Town in that Island, and were afterwards burnt with those that were burned alive.

One of those that were burned alive being chained at the stake was persuaded by that honest Gentleman Mr. *George Hannow*, the Deputy Provost-Marshall, *That since he was going to suffer death, Ingeniously to Confess the depth of their design.* The *Negro* calling for water to drink (which is a Custom they use before they tell or discover any thing) he just then going to speak and confess the truth of what he knew in this Matter, The next *Negro* Man chained to him (one *Tony*, a sturdy Rogue, a *Jew's Negro*) jogged him, and was heard to Chide him in these words, *Thou Fool, are there not enough of our Country-men killed already? Are thou minded to kill them all?* Then the aforesaid *Negro* that was a going to make Confession, would not speak one word more.

Which the spectators observing, cryed out to *Tony, Sirrah, we shall see you fry bravely by and by.* Who answered undauntedly, *If you Roast me today, you cannot roast me tomorrow:* (all those *Negroes* having an opinion that after their death they go into their own Country). Five and Twenty more have been since Executed, the particulars of whose due Punishment are not yet come to my hands.

---

1. I.e., Speightstown.

Five impeached hanged themselves, because they would not stand
Trial.

Threescore and odd more are in Custody at the *Hole*,[2] a fine Haven
and small Town in the said Island, and are not as yet brought to Trial.

Thus escaped from Eminent dangers, this flourishing and Fertile
Island, or to say more properly Spacious and profitable Garden, one of
the chiefest of his Majesties Nurseries for Sea-men.

✻   ✻   ✻

HANS SLOANE

[A Very Perverse Generation]†

[Hans Sloane (1660–1753) traveled to Jamaica in 1687–89 as a young phy-
sician in the party of the new governor, the duke of Albemarle. Behn
published a broadside poem to celebrate the same voyage and appointment,
which would convey the "grandeur and magnificence" of "Great *Caesar*"
(James II) to the New World and bring a shining duchess and beloved
royal associate to the Indians and settlers, respectively:

> Prepare, ye Sun-scorch'd Natives of the Shore,
> Prepare another Rising Sun t'adore,
> Such as has never blest your Horizon before.
> And you the Brave Inhabitants of the Place,
> Who have by Conquest made it all your own,
> Whose Generous and Industrious Race
> Has paid such Useful Tribute to the Crown;
> See what your Grateful King for you has done!

After his return, Sloane married the wealthy widow of a Jamaican
planter. He was a leading figure in the Royal Society and a lifelong student
of botanical specimens, books and manuscripts, and other rarities, becoming one of the nation's great collectors. He published his encyclopedic two
volumes on the natural history of Jamaica in 1707 and 1725. The brief
remarks on slaves appear in his introductory overview of the island.]

The *Negroes* are usually thought to be haters of their own Children,
and therefore 'tis believ'd that they sell and dispose of them to Strangers
for Money, but this is not true, for the *Negroes* of Guinea being divided
into several Captainships, as well as the *Indians* of *America*, have Wars,
and besides those slain in Battles many prisoners are taken, who are
sold for Slaves, and brought hither. But the Parents here, altho their

---

2. I.e., Holetown.
† From Hans Sloane, A *Voyage to the Islands* . . . *with the Natural History of [Jamaica]* 1
(1707), lvii.

Children are Slaves for ever, yet have so great a love for them, that no Master dare sell or give away one of their little ones, unless they care not whether their Parents hang themselves or no.

Many of the *Negroes*, being Slaves, and their Posterity after them in *Guinea*, they are more easily treated by the *English* here, than by their own Country-People, wherefore they would not often willingly change Masters.

The Punishments for Crimes of Slaves, are usually for Rebellions burning them, by nailing them down on the ground with crooked Sticks on every Limb, and then applying the Fire by degrees from the Feet and Hands, burning them gradually up to the Head, whereby their pains are extravagant. For Crimes of a lesser nature Gelding, or chopping off half the Foot with an Ax. These Punishments are suffered by them with great Constancy.

*   *   *

For negligence, they are usually whipt by the Overseers with Lance-wood Switches, till they be bloody, and several of the Switches broken, being first tied up by their Hands in the Mill-Houses. Beating with *Manati*[1] Straps is thought too cruel, and therefore prohibited by the Customs of the Country. The Cicatrices are visible on their Skins for ever after; and a Slave, the more he have of those, is the less valu'd.

After they are whip'd till they are Raw, some put on their Skins Pepper and Salt to make them smart; at other times their Masters will drop melted Wax on their Skins, and use several very exquisite Torments. These Punishments are sometimes merited by the Blacks, who are a very perverse Generation of People, and though they appear harsh, yet are scarce equal to some of their Crimes, and inferior to what Punishments other *European* Nations inflict on their Slaves in the *East-Indies*.

*   *   *

CHRISTOPHER CODRINGTON

[All Born Heroes]†

[Like his father, Christopher Codrington the younger (1668–1710) was governor of the Leeward Islands and one of the wealthiest planters in the West Indies. He was also a soldier and a literary patron and scholar who gave support to Thomas Southerne and other writers. In 1696 Charles Gildon dedicated to him his edited version of Behn's posthumous play *The Younger Brother*.

1. From the hide of the manatee.
† From *Calendar of State Papers, Colonial* 1701, no. 1132.

Codrington's cool-headed explanation of the murder of a planter (who was also speaker of the Antigua assembly) was accepted by the Council in London, which urged him to promote a law restraining inhumanity against slaves. Instead, the Antigua legislature adopted a law based on racial stratification that imposed mutilation or death if any "White Person be any way hurt, wounded, or disfigured by any Slave's Resistance." By his will, Codrington left large plantations and three hundred slaves to the care of the Society for the Propagation of the Gospel in Foreign Parts, with instructions for the founding of a college along monastic lines.

These various events and their background are examined by David Barry Gaspar, *Bondmen and Rebels: A Study of Master-Slave Relations in Antigua* (Baltimore and London: Johns Hopkins University Press, 1985).]

[Mr. Gamble to Governor Codrington]

St. John's in Antigua, Dec. 29, 1701

The relation I am about to give your Excellency is so surprising and strikes so deep into my soul that I am scarce capable of proceeding further. It was, sir, on the 27th inst. about 8 in the forenoon that about 15 new Calamantee[1] negro men belonging to Major Martin came up to his chamber door, fell on him in the presence of his wife, several white men and women belonging to the plantation, and with their knives and bills barbarously murthered him. *Details.* The intervention of his wife saved him for a moment. Then murderers cut off his head, "which we afterwards took up in the grass, where they had washed it with rum, and triumphed over it." I posted away immediately on the news with a few men on horseback, and found all the whites were preserved by a sort of miraculous escape, but the negroes in arms with the Major's guns. One of their out sentinels presented at us, but was shot dead in a moment; the rest ran into the canes before we could come up with them. We have had several parties ever since after them, and have taken two concerned in the murther, besides some others as yet doubtful whether in the combination or not. Were I to acquaint your Excellency the commotion this action has made in the country, and the unprovidedness of almost everyone on this occasion of surprise, you would be astonished at it; in short there was scarce a man could find a gun, and he that could had neither powder nor ball nor sword. * * *

[Governor Codrington to the Council of Trade and Plantations]

Nevis, December 30, 1701

* * * I received the enclosed, which makes me hasten up to Antigua. We have lost a very useful man in Major Martin. Next to Governor Yeomans, I think truly he was willing to take the most pains in public

---

1. Coromantee.

business, and was the best fitted for it of any man in the four islands. I'm afraid he was guilty of some unusual act of severity, or rather some indignity towards the Coramantees, for they are not only the best and most faithful of our slaves, but are really all born heroes. There is a difference between them and all other negroes beyond what 'tis possible for your Lordships to conceive. There never was a rascal or coward of that nation, intrepid to the last degree, not a man of them but will stand to be cut to pieces without a sigh or groan, grateful and obedient to a kind master, but implacably revengeful when ill-treated. My father, who had studied the genius and temper of all kinds of negroes 45 years with a very nice observation, would say, No man deserved a Coraman-tee that would not treat him like a friend rather than a slave, and all my Coramantees preserve that love and veneration for him that they constantly visit his grave, make their libations upon it, and promise when they have done working for his son they will come to him and be his faithful slaves in the other world. I am so far from being surprised at what has happened, that I often wonder there are not attempts of the same nature every day. Mr. Gamble, from a concern for his friend, I believe was in a maze when he writ his letter. I think 'tis plain the negroes had no design on their mistress or the rest of the family, or else they would soon have chopped them to pieces, but the account we have lately received of a new plot of the negroes in Barbados[2] I believe has helped to increase the consternation of our people. Your Lordships will find I had reason to complain of our want of small arms, and that there was a necessity of such an Act as I have made,[3] for the arms which are sent us from the Tower are so slight that they are only an expense to the King and no service to the islands. I hope I may now persuade the Antigua people to such an Act of Militia as I would have; without more power than I have at present I can neither hope to defend the King's hands or my own honour. I'm sure I have taken more pains about the Militia of Antigua than any Sergeant of the Guards ever did. It has cost me above £300 in entertainments to the Officers that I might bring them together to learn what they ought to teach those they com-mand, but I can't make arms nor mend them, and I gave your Lordships timely notice and have often repeated to Mr. Cary our great want of small arms.

2. After investigation the supposed Barbados slave "plot" of December 1701 proved a case of routine arson, though there was talk of a general insurrection and a few slaves were executed.
3. Mentioned earlier as a measure that "provides supernumerary arms."

JEAN BARBOT

[Three Accounts]

[French slave trader Jean Barbot (1655–1712) kept a straightforward factual log of his transactions on a voyage to Africa in 1678–79. (His journal of a second voyage is lost.) After his return, drawing on published accounts and maps, he prepared a manuscript description in French of the West African coast in familiar letter form. Still later, living as a Huguenot refugee in England, he wrote a more compendious account in English, incorporating much borrowed source material and personal commentary. Only the last work was printed, two decades after his death, in one of the major eighteenth-century travel collections.

The works show Barbot's increasing consciousness of writing for an audience. His reworkings of one episode reveal how he doctored materials to heighten their interest, while presenting himself as a sensible and humane trader, a spokesman for the best contemporary practice.]

[A Wholly Remarkable Meeting]†

[Sunday, 12 February, 1679]
Trading.

A wholly remarkable meeting that roused much pity in us.

In the evening we traded on board 8 dozen old knives for two *gros* of gold, and 2 women, 1 little boy and 1 little girl for 3 muskets, 1 anker[1] of brandy and 1 piece of painted cloth. One of these two women was pregnant, and mother of the two little children I speak of. She also had her husband on board, who had been sold some days previously. I never saw anything to equal the joy of that poor wretched man at the sight of those three objects, so much tenderness in a wife, and so much good nature in children of this kind. They were more than half an hour embracing one another and pouring out a torrent of

---

† From "Journal d'un Voyage Fait par Jean Barbot," ed. G. Debien, M. Delafosse, and G. Thilmans, *Bulletin de l'IFAN* [*Bulletin de l'Institut fondamental d'Afrique noire*] 40B (1978), 327, from BL Add. MS 28,788.

1. A liquid measure amounting to just over ten gallons. A *gros* is an eighth of an ounce. Gold at this date was still the primary export from the Gold Coast.

> tears that the joy of finding themselves
> together made them shed.

They were all sold to one
master at Martinique, and
the woman gave birth while
we were there.

[Sharing the Hardship]†

A good trade in slaves can be found on Gold Coast only when war
with those of the interior has broken out and is fierce, as in 1681 when
an English interloping vessel took 300 *captifs* at Comendo, with no
more trouble than picking them up on the seashore, since the local
people brought them there from the fighting with the Moors of the
interior that had taken place the same day. It is not so much the case
that this does not happen all the time, as that the local people keep
back prisoners so that they can work their lands and carry their goods.
On my latter voyage (1682), in all Gold Coast I took only eight. It was
a year of misfortune for these blacks, many being taken in war and sold
elsewhere. I had some of them on board at Acra whom they came to
buy back, giving me two other slaves for one man.[1] It even happened
that I bought, at different times and places, a whole family of five
persons. I have never seen as much joy as these poor people displayed
when they found themselves thus reunited. They could not look at each
other without weeping, but despite their tears one could see that they
reckoned themselves extremely fortunate that in their wretchedness they
were sharing the hardship and sorrow. I did not care to separate them
when I reached the Islands and I sold them to a single master.

I will conclude with a point which may make you laugh. This is,
that all the slaves, like most other blacks, believe that we buy them to
eat them, as soon as we get back to France. It is this which makes many
slaves die on the passage across, either from sorrow or from despair,
there being some who refuse to eat or drink. What do you say, Sir? Do
you have the appetite for such a dish? I am, Sir, Yours, etc.

[Together Again, tho' in Bondage]†

The *Gold Coast*, in times of war between the inland nations, and
those nearer the sea, will furnish great numbers of slaves of all sexes

---

† From "Description of the Coasts of Africa" (1688), in *Barbot on Guinea: The Writings of Jean
Barbot on West Africa 1678–1712*, ed. P. E. H. Hair, Adam Jones, and Robin Law (London:
Hakluyt Society, 1992), 550, from PRO, ADM 7/830.
1. According to the 1679 log (p. 329), a single man was ransomed for two others at this port;
and see the expanded 1732 version (below).
† From "A Description of the Coasts of North and South-Guinea," in Awnsham and John
Churchill, eds., *A Collection of Voyages and Travels*, 3rd ed. (London, 1732), 5, 270–72.

and ages; sometimes at one place, and sometimes at another, as has been already observed, according to the nature of the war, and the situation of the countries between which it is waged. I remember, to this purpose, that in the year 1681, an *English* interloper at *Commendo* got three hundred good slaves, almost for nothing, besides the trouble of receiving them at the beach in boats, as the *Commendo* men brought them from the field of battle, having obtained a victory over a neighbouring nation, and taken a great number of prisoners.

At other times slaves are so scarce there, that in 1682, I could get but eight from one end of the coast to the other; not only because we were a great number of trading ships on the coast at the same time, but by reason the natives were every where at peace. At another time I had two hundred slaves at *Acra* only, in a fortnight or three weeks time; and the upper coast men, understanding I had those slaves aboard, came down to redeem them, giving me two for one, of such as I understood were their near relations, who had been stolen away by inland *Blacks*, brought down to *Acra*, and sold to us.

I also remember, that I once, among my several runs along that coast, happened to have aboard a whole family, man, wife, three young boys, and a girl, bought one after another, at several places; and cannot but observe here, what mighty satisfaction those poor creatures expressed to be so come together again, tho' in bondage. For several days successively they could not forbear shedding tears of joy, and continually embracing and caressing one another; which moving me to compassion, I ordered they should be better treated aboard than commonly we can afford to do it, where there are four or five hundred in a ship; and at *Martinico*, I sold them all together to a considerable planter, at a cheaper rate than I might have expected, had they been disposed of severally; being informed of that gentleman's good-nature, and having taken his word, that he would use that family as well as their circumstances would permit, and settle them in some part by themselves.

I have elsewhere spoke of the manner of valuing and rating the slaves among the *Blacks*, and shall conclude this chapter, which proves to be one of the longest, with an odd remark; which is, That many of those slaves we transport from *Guinea* to *America* are prepossessed with the opinion, that they are carried like sheep to the slaughter, and that the *Europeans* are fond of their flesh; which notion so far prevails with some, as to make them fall into a deep melancholy and despair, and to refuse all sustenance, tho' never so much compelled and even beaten to oblige them to take some nourishment: notwithstanding all which, they will starve to death; whereof I have had several instances in my own slaves both aboard and at *Guadeloupe*. And tho' I must say I am naturally compassionate, yet have I been necessitated sometimes to cause the teeth of those wretches to be broken, because they would not open their mouths, or be prevailed on by any intreaties to feed themselves; and thus have forced some sustenance into their throats.

At the end of the supplement to this description, may be seen how I ordered the slaves to be used, and managed, in our passage from the coast to the *West-Indies*; which if it were well observed by other *Europeans* following that trade, would certainly save the lives of many thousands of those poor wretches, every year, and render the voyages much more advantageous to the owners and adventurers; it being known by a long course of experience that the *English* particularly every year lose great numbers in the passage, and some ships two, three, and even four hundred out of five hundred shipped in *Guinea*.

※　※　※

Frontispiece by J. Pine for the 1722 edition: "He perceiv'd *Imoinda* fall dead in the Hands of *Trefry*. This awaken'd him, and he ran to her aid."

After *Oroonoko*: Noble Africans in Europe

Anne Bracegirdle as "The Indian Queen" (1689).

C.P. Marillie inv.   C. Baron sculp.

An engraving after C. Marillier in the 1769 edition of La Place's *Oronoko*.

Le Tombeau de Voltaire, an allegorical print published in Paris in 1779, the year after Voltaire's death. Palms are brought to Voltaire's tomb by figures representing the four continents: for Europe, D'Alembert; for Asia, Empress Catherine II of Russia; for Africa, Prince Oroonoko; for America, Benjamin Franklin. Ignorance (showing the attributes of envy, fanaticism, and superstition) rushes in to disrupt the ceremony. In the distance is the tomb of Rousseau.

THOMAS SOUTHERNE

From *Oroonoko: A Tragedy*†

[First produced in November of 1695, the stage version by Thomas Southerne (1660–1746) became enormously successful. The modern editors of
his works, Robert Jordan and Harold Love, estimate that for some forty
years his *Oroonoko* was "the most commonly produced of all the post-
Shakespearean tragedies." From the late 1750s, it held the stage in revised
versions by John Hawkesworth and others that show more antislavery
feeling.

Southerne alters the love story in three important ways: (1) Imoinda
(pronounced as three syllables, apparently *Im-oyn'-da*) is white, brought to
Africa (to Angola) in infancy by her father, who becomes army leader;
(2) the lovers were married and she conceived a child before she was
claimed by the king, Oroonoko's father, who found himself stymied by the
threat of incest; (3) now as a white slave in Surinam, she is desired not by
Blanford, the Trefry figure, but by the unnamed deputy governor. Comic
scenes in prose portray the colonists' fortune-hunting and matchmaking
schemes. There are echoes of *Othello* and, in the comic scenes, of Behn's
colonial play, *The Widow Ranter*.]

Act 1, Scene 2

* * *

GOVERNOR. But, Captain, methinks you have taken a great deal of
pains for this Prince *Oroonoko*; why did you part with him at the common rate of Slaves?

CAPTAIN. Why, Lieutenant-Governor, I'll tell you; I did design to
carry him to *England*, to have show'd him there; but I found him
troublesome upon my hands, and I'm glad I'm rid of him.—Oh, ho,
here they come.

[*Black Slaves, Men, Women, and Children, pass across the stage by
two and two;* ABOAN, *and others of* OROONOKO's *attendants two and
two;* OROONOKO *last of all in chains.*]

LUCY. Are all these Wretches Slaves?

STANMORE. All sold, they and their Posterity all Slaves.

LUCY. O miserable Fortune!

BLANFORD. Most of 'em know no better; they were born so, and only
change their Masters. But a Prince, born only to command, betray'd
and sold! My heart drops blood for him.

CAPTAIN. Now, Governor, here he comes, pray observe him.

† From Thomas Southerne, *Oroonoko: A Tragedy* (London, 1696). Spelling and punctuation
have been modernized for clarity.

125

OROONOKO. So, Sir, you have kept your Word with me.

CAPTAIN. I am a better Christian, I thank you, than to keep it with a Heathen.

OROONOKO. You are a Christian, be a Christian still:
If you have any God that teaches you
To break your Word, I need not curse you more:
Let him cheat you, as you are false to me.
You faithful Followers of my better Fortune! *[Embracing his friends.]*
We have been Fellow-Soldiers in the Field;
Now we are Fellow-Slaves. This last farewell.
Be sure of one thing that will comfort us,
Whatever World we next are thrown upon,
Cannot be worse than this.

   [All Slaves go off, but OROONOKO.]

CAPTAIN. You see what a Bloody Pagan he is, Governor; but I took care that none of his Followers should be in the same Lot with him, for fear they should undertake some desperate action, to the danger of the Colony.

OROONOKO. Live still in fear; it is the Villain's Curse,
And will revenge my Chains: Fear ev'n me,
Who have no pow'r to hurt thee. Nature abhors,
And drives thee out from the Society
And Commerce of Mankind, for Breach of Faith.
Men live and prosper but in Mutual Trust,
A Confidence of one another's Truth:
That thou hast violated. I have done.
I know my Fortune, and submit to it.

GOVERNOR. Sir, I am sorry for your Fortune, and would help it, if I could.

BLANFORD. Take off his Chains. You know your condition; but you are fall'n into Honourable Hands. You are the Lord Governor's Slave, who will use you nobly: In his absence it shall be my care to serve you.

                    *   *   *

Act 3, Scene 2

                    *   *   *

[OROONOKO *and* IMOINDA.[1]]
   [Enter BLANFORD and ABOAN.]
   BLANFORD.   My Royal Lord!
I have a Present for you.
   OROONOKO.   Aboan!
   ABOAN. Your lowest Slave.

---

1. Southerne's heroine is a white woman; see the headnote for her history.

OROONOKO.   My tried and valu'd Friend.
This worthy Man always prevents my wants:
I only wish'd, and he has brought thee to me.
Thou art surpris'd: carry thy duty there;
   [ABOAN *goes to* IMOINDA *and falls at her feet.*]
While I acknowledge mine, how shall I thank you.
   BLANFORD. Believe me honest to your interest,
And I am more than paid. I have secur'd
That all your Followers shall be gently us'd.
This Gentleman, your chiefest Favourite,
Shall wait upon your Person, while you stay
Among us.
   OROONOKO. I owe every thing to you.
   BLANFORD. You must not think you are in Slavery.
   OROONOKO. I do not find I am.
   BLANFORD. Kind Heaven has miraculously sent
Those Comforts, that may teach you to expect
Its farther care, in your deliverance.
   OROONOKO. I sometimes think my self, Heav'n is concern'd
For my deliverance.
   BLANFORD.   It will be soon:
You may expect it. Pray, in the mean time,
Appear as cheerful as you can among us.
You have some Enemies, that represent
You dangerous, and would be glad to find
A Reason, in your discontent, to fear:
They watch your looks. But there are honest Men,
Who are your Friends: You are secure in them.
   OROONOKO. I thank you for your caution.
   BLANFORD.   I will leave you:
And be assur'd, I wish your liberty.
   [*Exit.*]
   ABOAN. He speaks you very fair.
   OROONOKO.   He means me fair.
   ABOAN. If he should not, my Lord.
   OROONOKO.   If, he should not.
I'll not suspect his Truth: but if I did,
What shall I get by doubting?
   ABOAN.   You secure,
Not to be disappointed; but besides,
There's this advantage in suspecting him:
When you put off the hopes of other men,
You will rely upon your God-like self,
And then you may be sure of liberty.
   OROONOKO. Be sure of liberty! What dost thou mean,

Advising to rely upon myself?
I think I may be sure on't. [*Turning to* IMOINDA.]
                              We must wait;
'Tis worth a little patience.
    ABOAN.   O my Lord!
    OROONOKO. What dost thou drive at?
    ABOAN.   Sir, another time,
You would have found it sooner; but I see
Love has your Heart, and takes up all your thoughts.
    OROONOKO. And canst thou blame me?
    ABOAN.   Sir, I must not blame you.
But as our fortune stands there is a Passion
(Your pardon, Royal Mistress, I must speak):
That would become you better than your Love:
A brave resentment; which inspir'd by you,
Might kindle, and diffuse a generous rage
Among the Slaves, to rouse and shake our Chains,
And struggle to be free.
    OROONOKO. How can we help our selves?
    ABOAN. I knew you, when you would have found a way.
How, help our selves! the very *Indians* teach us:
We need but to attempt our Liberty,
And we may carry it. We have Hands sufficient,
Double the number of our Masters' force,
Ready to be employ'd. What hinders us
To set 'em then at work? we want but you,
To head our enterprise, and bid us strike.
    OROONOKO. What would you do?
    ABOAN.   Cut our Oppressors' Throats.
    OROONOKO. And you would have me join in your design
Of Murder?
    ABOAN.   It deserves a better Name:
But be it what it will, 'tis justified
By self-defense, and natural liberty.
    OROONOKO. I'll hear no more on't.
    ABOAN.   I am sorry for't.
    OROONOKO. Nor shall you think of it.
    ABOAN.   Not think of it!
    OROONOKO. No, I command you not.
    ABOAN.   Remember Sir,
You are a Slave yourself, and to command,
Is now another's right. Not think of it!
Since the first moment they put on my Chains,
I've thought of nothing but the weight of 'em,

And how to throw 'em off: can yours sit easy?
OROONOKO. I have a sense of my condition,
As painful, and as quick, as yours can be.
I feel for my *Imoinda* and my self;
Imoinda much the tenderest part of me.
But though I languish for my liberty,
I would not buy it at the Christian price
Of black Ingratitude: they shannot say,
That we deserv'd our Fortune by our Crimes.
Murder the Innocent!
ABOAN.   The Innocent!
OROONOKO. These men are so, whom you would rise against:
If we are Slaves, they did not make us Slaves;
But bought us in an honest way of trade:
As we have done before 'em, bought and sold
Many a wretch, and never thought it wrong.
They paid our Price for us, and we are now
Their Property, a part of their Estate,
To manage as they please. Mistake me not,
I do not tamely say, that we should bear
All they could lay upon us: but we find
The load so light, so little to be felt
(Considering they have us in their power,
And may inflict what grievances they please),
We ought not to complain.
ABOAN.   My Royal Lord!
You do not know the heavy Grievances,
The Toils, the Labours, weary Drudgeries,
Which they impose; Burdens, more fit for Beasts,
For senseless Beasts to bear, than thinking Men.
Then if you saw the bloody Cruelties,
They execute on every slight offense;
Nay sometimes in their proud, insulting sport,
How worse than Dogs, they lash their fellow Creatures,
Your heart would bleed for 'em. O could you know
How many Wretches lift their Hands and Eyes
To you, for their Relief.
OROONOKO.   I pity 'em,
And wish I could with honesty do more.
ABOAN. You must do more, and may, with honesty.
O Royal Sir, remember who you are,
A Prince, born for the good of other Men,
Whose God-like Office is to draw the Sword
Against Oppression, and set free Mankind:

And this, I'm sure, you think Oppression now.
What tho' you have not felt these miseries,
Never believe you are oblig'd to them:
They have their selfish reasons, may be, now,
For using of you well; but there will come
A time, when you must have your share of 'em.
    OROONOKO. You see how little cause I have to think so:
Favour'd in my own Person, in my Friends;
Indulg'd in all that can concern my care,
In my *Imoinda's* soft Society. [*Embracing her.*]
    ABOAN. And therefore would you lie contented down,
In the forgetfulness, and arms of Love,
To get young Princes for 'em?
    OROONOKO.   Say'st thou! ha!
    ABOAN. Princes, the Heirs of Empire, and the last
Of your illustrious Lineage, to be born
To pamper up their Pride, and be their Slaves?
    OROONOKO. *Imoinda!* save me, save me from that thought.
    IMOINDA. There is no safety from it: I have long
Suffer'd it with a Mother's labouring pains;
And can no longer. Kill me, kill me now,
While I am blest, and happy in your love,
Rather than let me live to see you hate me:
As you must hate me; me, the only cause;
The Fountain of these flowing miseries:
Dry up this Spring of Life, this pois'nous Spring,
That swells so fast, to overwhelm us all.
    OROONOKO. Shall the dear Babe, the eldest of my hopes,
Whom I begot a Prince, be born a Slave?
The treasure of this Temple was design'd
T'enrich a Kingdom's Fortune: shall it here
Be seiz'd upon by vile unhallow'd hands,
To be employ'd in uses most profane?
    ABOAN. In most unworthy uses; think of that;
And while you may, prevent it. O my Lord!
Rely on nothing that they say to you.
They speak you fair, I know, and bid you wait.
But think what 'tis to wait on promises:
And promises of Men, who know no tie
Upon their words, against their interest.
And where's their interest in freeing you?
    IMOINDA. O! where indeed, to lose so many Slaves?
    ABOAN. Nay, grant this Man, you think so much your Friend,
Be honest, and intends all that he says:
He is but one; and in a Government,
Where, he confesses, you have Enemies,

That watch your looks, what looks can you put on,
To please these men, who are before resolv'd
To read 'em their own way? alas! my Lord!
If they incline to think you dangerous,
They have their knavish Arts to make you so.
And then who knows how far their cruelty
May carry their revenge?
    IMOINDA.   To everything,
That does belong to you; your Friends, and me;
I shall be torn from you, forc'd away,
Helpless, and miserable: shall I live
To see that day again?
    OROONOKO.   That day shall never come.
    ABOAN. I know you are persuaded to believe
The Governor's arrival will prevent
These mischiefs, and bestow your liberty:
But who is sure of that? I rather fear
More mischiefs from his coming: he is young,
Luxurious, passionate, and amorous.
Such a Complexion, and made bold by power,
To countenance all he is prone to do,
Will know no bounds, no law against his Lusts:
If, in a fit of his Intemperance,
With a strong hand, he should resolve to seize,
And force my Royal Mistress from your Arms,
How can you help your self?
    OROONOKO.   Ha! thou hast rous'd
The Lion in his den, he stalks abroad,
And the wide Forest trembles at his roar.
I find the danger now: my Spirits start
At the alarm, and from all quarters come
To Man my Heart, the Citadel of love.
Is there a power on Earth to force you from me?
And shall I not resist it? not strike first
To keep, to save you? to prevent that curse?
This is your Cause, and shall it not prevail?
O! you were born all ways to conquer me.
Now I am fashion'd to thy purpose: speak,
What Combination, what Conspiracy,
Wouldst thou engage me in? I'll undertake
All thou wouldst have me now for liberty,
For the great Cause of Love and Liberty.
    ABOAN. Now, my great Master, you appear yourself.

And since we have you join'd in our design,
It cannot fail us. I have muster'd up
The choicest Slaves, Men who are sensible
Of their condition, and seem most resolv'd.
They have their several parties.
   OROONOKO.   Summon 'em,
Assemble 'em: I will come forth, and shew
Myself among 'em; if they are resolv'd,
I'll lead their foremost resolutions.
   ABOAN. I have provided those will follow you.
   OROONOKO. With this reserve in our proceeding still,
The means that lead us to our liberty
Must not be bloody.
   ABOAN.   You command in all.
We shall expect you, Sir.
   OROONOKO.   You shannot long.
   [*Exeunt* OROONOKO *and* IMOINDA *at one door,* ABOAN *at another.*]

* * *

Act 4, Scene 2

* * *

   GOVERNOR.   Live, Royal Sir;
Live, and be happy long on your own Terms:
Only consent to yield, and you shall have
What Terms you can propose, for you, and yours.
   OROONOKO. Consent to yield! shall I betray my self?
   GOVERNOR. Alas! we cannot fear, that your small Force,
The Force of two, with a weak Woman's Arm,
Should Conquer us. I speak in the regard
And Honour of your Worth, in my desire
And forwardness to serve so great a Man.
I would not have it lie upon my Thoughts,
That I was the occasion of the fall
Of such a Prince, whose Courage carried on
In a more Noble Cause, would well deserve
The Empire of the World.
   OROONOKO.   You can speak fair.
   GOVERNOR. Your Undertaking, tho' it would have brought
So great a loss to us, we must all say
Was generous, and noble; and shall be
Regarded only as the Fire of Youth,
That will break out sometimes in Gallant Souls;
We'll think it but the Natural Impulse,

A rash impatience of Liberty:
No otherwise.
    OROONOKO. Think it what you will.
I was not born to render an Account
Of what I do, to any but myself.
    [BLANFORD *comes forward.*]
    BLANFORD. [*To the* GOVERNOR.] I'm glad you have proceeded by fair
      means.
I came to be a Mediator.
    GOVERNOR. Try what you can work upon him.
    OROONOKO. Are you come against me too?
    BLANFORD. Is this to come against you? [*Offering his sword to*
      OROONOKO.]
Unarm'd to put myself into your Hands?
I come, I hope, to serve you.
    OROONOKO.   You have serv'd me;
I thank you for't. And I am pleas'd to think
You were my Friend, while I had need of one:
But now 'tis past; this farewell; and be gone. [*Embraces him.*]
    BLANFORD. It is not past, and I must serve you still.
I would make up these Breaches, which the Sword
Will widen more, and close us all in Love.
    OROONOKO. I know what I have done, and I should be
A Child to think they ever can Forgive:
Forgive! Were there but that, I would not live
To be Forgiven: Is there a Power on Earth,
That I can ever need forgiveness from?
    BLANFORD. You sha' not need it.
    OROONOKO.   No, I wonnot need it.
    BLANFORD. You see he offers you your own Conditions,
For you, and yours.
    OROONOKO.   I must capitulate?
Precariously compound, on stinted terms,
To save my Life?
    BLANFORD.   Sir, he imposes none.
You make 'em for your own Security.
If your great Heart cannot descend to treat,
In adverse Fortune, with an Enemy:
Yet sure, your Honour's safe, you may accept
Offers of Peace, and Safety from a Friend.
    GOVERNOR. [*To* BLANFORD.] He will rely on what you say to him:
Offer him what you can, I will confirm,
And make all good: Be you my Pledge of Trust.
    BLANFORD. I'll answer with my Life for all he says.
    GOVERNOR. [*Aside.*] Ay, do, and pay the Forfeit if you please.

BLANFORD. Consider, Sir, can you consent to throw
That Blessing from you, you so hardly found,
And so much valu'd once?

OROONOKO.   Imoinda! Oh!
'Tis She that holds me on this Argument
Of tedious Life: I could resolve it soon,
Were this curst Being only in Debate.
But my Imoinda struggles in my Soul.
She makes a Coward of me: I Confess
I am afraid to part with her in Death,
And more afraid of Life to lose her here.

BLANFORD. This way you must lose her, think upon
The weakness of her Sex, made yet more weak
With her Condition, requiring Rest,
And soft Indulging Ease, to nurse your Hopes,
And make you a glad Father.

OROONOKO.   There I feel
A Father's Fondness, and a Husband's Love.
They seize upon my Heart, strain all its strings,
To pull me to 'em, from my stern resolve.
Husband, and Father! All the melting Art
Of Eloquence lives in those soft'ning Names.
Methinks I see the Babe, with Infant Hands,
Pleading for Life, and begging to be born.
Shall I forbid his Birth? Deny him Light?
The Heavenly Comforts of all-cheering Light?
And make the Womb the Dungeon of his Death?
His Bleeding Mother his sad Monument?
These are the Calls of Nature, that call loud;
They will be heard, and Conquer in their Cause.
He must not be a Man, who can resist 'em.
No, my Imoinda! I will venture all
To save thee, and that little Innocent:
The World may be a better Friend to him,
Than I have found it. Now I yield myself:
    [Gives up his sword.]
The Conflict's past, and we are in your Hands.
    [Several Men get about OROONOKO, and ABOAN, and seize 'em.]

GOVERNOR. So you shall find you are: Dispose of them,
As I commanded you.

BLANFORD.   Good Heaven forbid!
You cannot mean—

GOVERNOR. [To BLANFORD who goes to OROONOKO.]
                    This is not your Concern.

[*To* IMOINDA.] I must take care of you.

    IMOINDA.   I'm at the end

Of all my Care: Here I will die with him. [*Holding* OROONOKO.]

    OROONOKO. You shall not force her from me. [*He holds her.*]

    GOVERNOR. Then I must

Try other means, and conquer Force by Force:

Break, cut off his Hold, bring her away.

    [*They force her from him.*]

    IMOINDA. I do not ask to live, kill me but here.

    OROONOKO. O Bloody Dogs! Inhuman Murderers.

    [IMOINDA *forced out of one door by the* GOVERNOR, *and others.* OROON-
    OKO *and* ABOAN *hurried out of another.*]

    [*Exeunt Omnes.*]

*　*　*

Act 5, Scene 3

*　*　*

    [OROONOKO *alone.*]

    OROONOKO. Forget! forgive! I must indeed forget,

When I forgive: but while I am a Man,

In Flesh, that bears the living mark of Shame,

The print of his dishonourable Chains,

My Memory still rousing up my Wrongs,

I never can forgive this Governor;

This Villain; the disgrace of Trust, and Place,

And just Contempt of delegated Power.

What shall I do? If I declare myself,

I know him, he will sneak behind his Guard

Of Followers, and brave me in his Fears.

Else, Lion like, with my devouring Rage,

I would rush on him, fasten on his Throat,

Tear wide a Passage to his treacherous Heart,

And that way lay him open to the World.

    [*Pausing.*]

If I should turn his Christian Arts on him,

Promise him, speak him fair, flatter, and creep,

With fawning Steps, to get within his Faith,

I could betray him then, as he has me.

But am I sure by that to right myself?

Lying's a certain Mark of Cowardice:

And when the Tongue forgets its Honesty,

The Heart and Hand may drop their functions too,

And nothing worthy be resolv'd, or done.

The Man must go together, bad, or good:
In one part frail, he soon grows weak in all.
Honor should be concern'd in Honour's Cause,
That is not to be cur'd by Contraries,
As Bodies are, whose Health is often drawn
From rankest Poisons. Let me but find out
An honest Remedy, I have the Hand,
A minist'ring Hand, that will apply it Home.
    [*Exit.*]

Act 5, Scene 5

    [OROONOKO *enters.*]
    OROONOKO. To Honour bound! and yet a Slave to Love!
I am distracted by their rival Powers,
And both will be obey'd. O great Revenge!
Thou Raiser, and Restorer of fall'n Fame!
Let me not be unworthy of thy Aid,
For stopping in thy course: I still am thine;
But can't forget I am *Imoinda's* too.
She calls me from my Wrongs to rescue her.
No man condemn me, who has never felt
A woman's Power, or tried the Force of Love.
All tempers yield, and soften in those fires;
Our Honours, Interests resolving down,
Run in the gentle Current of our Joys:
But not to sink, and drown our Memory:
We mount again to Action, like the Sun,
That rises from the Bosom of the Sea,
To run his glorious Race of Light anew,
And carry on the World. Love, Love will be
My first Ambition, and my Fame the next.
    [ABOAN *enters bloody.*]
My Eyes are turn'd against me, and combine
With my sworn Enemies, to represent
This spectacle of Honour.[1] *Aboan!*
My ever faithful Friend!
    ABOAN.   I have no Name,
That can distinguish me from the vile Earth,
To which I'm going: a poor, abject worm,
That crawl'd awhile upon a bustling World,
And now am trampled to my Dust again.

---

1. Many editions emend this to "Horror."

OROONOKO. I see thee gasht, and mangled.

ABOAN.   Spare my shame
To tell how they have us'd me: but believe
The Hangman's Hand would have been merciful.
Do not you scorn me, Sir, to think I can
Intend to live under this Infamy.
I do not come for pity, to complain.
I've spent an honourable Life with you;
The earliest Servant of your rising Fame,
And would attend it with my latest care.
My life was yours, and so shall be my death.
You must not live.
Bending and sinking, I have dragg'd my Steps
Thus far, to tell you that you cannot live:
To warn you of those Ignominious wrongs,
Whips, Rods, and all the Instruments of death,
Which I have felt, and are prepar'd for you.
This was the Duty that I had to pay.
'Tis done, and now I beg to be discharg'd.

OROONOKO. What shall I do for thee?

ABOAN.   My Body tires,
And wonnot bear me off to Liberty:
I shall again be taken, made a Slave.
A Sword, a Dagger yet would rescue me.
I have not Strength to go to find out Death:
You must direct him to me.

OROONOKO. [*Gives him a dagger.*] Here he is,
The only present I can make thee now:
And next the honourable means of Life,
I would bestow the honest means of Death.

ABOAN. I cannot stay to thank you. If there is
A Being after this, I shall be yours
In the next World, your faithful Slave again.
This is to try. [*Stabs himself.*] I had a living Sense
Of all your royal Favours, but this last
Strikes through my Heart. I wonnot say farewell,
For you must follow me. [*Dies.*]

OROONOKO.   In Life, and death,
The Guardian of my Honor! follow thee!
I should have gone before thee: then perhaps
Thy Fate had been prevented. All his Care
Was to preserve me from the barbarous Rage
That wrong'd him, only for being mine.
Why, why, you Gods! Why am I so accurst,

That it must be a Reason of your Wrath,
A Guilt, a Crime sufficient to the Fate
Of anyone, but to belong to me?
My Friend has found it, and my Wife will soon.
My Wife! the very Fear's too much for Life:
I can't support it. Where? *Imoinda!* Oh!
    [*Going out, she meets him, running into his arms.*]
Thou bosom Softness! Down of all my Cares!
I could recline my thoughts upon this Breast
To a forgetfulness of all my Griefs,
And yet be happy: but it wonnot be.
Thou art disorder'd, pale, and out of Breath!
If Fate pursues thee, find a shelter here.
What is it thou wouldst tell me?
    IMOINDA.   'Tis in vain
To call him Villain.
    OROONOKO.   Call him Governor:
Is it not so?
    IMOINDA. There's not another, sure.
    OROONOKO. Villain's the common name of Mankind here:
But his most properly. What! what of him?
I fear to be resolv'd, and must enquire.
He had thee in his Power.
    IMOINDA.   I blush to think it.
    OROONOKO. Blush! to think what?
    IMOINDA.   That I was in his Power.
    OROONOKO. He could not use it?
    IMOINDA.   What can't such men do?
    OROONOKO. But did he? durst he?
    IMOINDA.   What he could, he dar'd.
    OROONOKO. His own Gods damn him then: for ours have none,
No Punishment for such unheard-of Crimes.
    IMOINDA. This Monster, cunning in his Flatteries,
When he had weary'd all his useless Arts,
Leapt out, fierce as a beast of prey, to seize me.
I trembled, fear'd.
    OROONOKO.   I fear, and tremble now.
What could preserve thee? what deliver thee?
    IMOINDA. That worthy Man, you us'd to call your Friend—
    OROONOKO. *Blanford.*
    IMOINDA.   Came in, and sav'd me from his Rage.
    OROONOKO. He was a Friend indeed to rescue thee!
And for his sake, I'll think it possible
A Christian may be yet an honest man.

IMOINDA. O! did you know what I have struggled through,
To save me yours, sure you would promise me
Never to see me forc'd from you again.

OROONOKO. To promise thee! O! do I need to promise?
But there is now no farther use of Words.
Death is security for all our fears
[*Shows* ABOAN's *body on the floor.*]
And yet I cannot trust him.

IMOINDA.   *Aboan!*

OROONOKO. Mangled, and torn, resolv'd to give me time
To fit my self for what I must expect,
Groan'd out a warning to me, and expir'd.

IMOINDA. For what you must expect?

OROONOKO.   Would that were all.

IMOINDA. What! to be butcher'd thus—

OROONOKO.   Just as thou see'st.

IMOINDA. By barbarous Hands, to fall at last their Prey!

OROONOKO. I have run the Race with Honour, shall I now
Lag, and be overtaken at the Goal?

IMOINDA. No.

OROONOKO. [*Tenderly.*] I must look back to thee.

IMOINDA.   You shannot need.
I'm always present to your purpose; say,
Which way would you dispose me?

OROONOKO.   Have a care,
Thou'rt on a Precipice, and dost not see
Whither that question leads thee. O! too soon
Thou dost enquire what the assembled Gods
Have not determin'd, and will latest doom.
Yet this I know of Fate, this is most certain,
I cannot, as I would, dispose of thee:
And, as I ought, I dare not. Oh *Imoinda!*

IMOINDA. Alas! that sigh! why do you tremble so?
Nay then 'tis bad indeed, if you can weep.

OROONOKO. My Heart runs over; if my gushing Eyes
Betray a weakness which they never knew,
Believe, thou, only thou couldst cause these tears.
The Gods themselves conspire with faithless Men
To our destruction.

IMOINDA.   Heaven and Earth our Foes!

OROONOKO. It is not always granted to the great,
To be most happy. If the angry Pow'rs
Repent their Favours, let 'em take 'em back:
The hopes of Empire, which they gave my youth,

By making me a Prince, I here resign.
Let 'em quench in me all those glorious Fires,
Which kindled at their beams: that lust of Fame,
That Fever of Ambition, restless still,
And burning with the sacred Thirst of Sway,
Which they inspir'd, to qualify my Fate,
And make me fit to govern under them,
Let 'em extinguish. I submit myself
To their high pleasure, and devoted Bow
Yet lower, to continue still a Slave;
Hopeless of liberty: and if I could
Live after it, would give up Honour too,
To satisfy their Vengeance, to avert
This only Curse, the curse of losing thee.
    IMOINDA. If Heav'n could be appeas'd, these cruel Men
Are not to be entreated, or believ'd:
O! think on that, and be no more deceiv'd.
    OROONOKO. What can we do?
    IMOINDA.   Can I do any thing?
    OROONOKO. But we were born to suffer.
    IMOINDA.   Suffer both,
Both die, and so prevent 'em.
    OROONOKO.   By thy Death!
O! let me hunt my travel'd Thoughts again;
Range the wide waste of desolate despair;
Start any hope. Alas! I lose my self,
'Tis Pathless, Dark, and Barren all to me.
Thou art my only guide, my light of Life,
And thou art leaving me. Send out thy Beams
Upon the Wing; let 'em fly all around,
Discover every way: Is there a dawn,
A glimmering of comfort? the great God,
That rises on the World, must shine on us.
    IMOINDA. And see us set before him.
    OROONOKO.   Thou bespeak'st,
And goest before me.
    IMOINDA.   So I would, in Love:
In the dear unsuspected part of Life,
In Death for Love. Alas! what hopes for me?
I was preserv'd but to acquit my self,
To beg to die with you.
    OROONOKO.   And can'st thou ask it?
I never durst enquire into myself
About thy fate, and thou resolv'st it all.
    IMOINDA. Alas! my Lord! my Fate's resolv'd in yours.

OROONOKO. O! keep thee there. Let not thy Virtue shrink
From my support, and I will gather strength,
Fast as I can to tell thee —
    IMOINDA.   I must die.
I know 'tis fit, and I can die with you.
    OROONOKO. O! thou hast banish'd hence a thousand fears,
Which sicken'd at my Heart, and quite unmann'd me.
    IMOINDA. Your fear's for me, I know you fear'd my strength,
And could not overcome your tenderness,
To pass this Sentence on me; and indeed
There you were kind, as I have always found you,
As you have ever been: for tho' I am
Resign'd, and ready to obey my doom,
Methinks it should not be pronounc'd by you.
    OROONOKO. O! that was all the labour of my grief.
My heart, and tongue forsook me in the strife:
I never could pronounce it.
    IMOINDA. I have for you,
                      For both of us.
    OROONOKO. Alas! for me! my death
I could regard as the last Scene of life,
And act it thro' with joy, to have it done.
But then to part with thee—
    IMOINDA.   'Tis hard to part.
But parting thus, as the most happy must,
Parting in death, makes it the easier.
You might have thrown me off, forsaken me,
And my misfortunes: that had been a death
Indeed of terror, to have trembled at.
    OROONOKO. Forsaken! thrown thee off!
    IMOINDA. But 'tis a pleasure more than life can give,
That with unconquer'd Passion to the last,
You struggle still, and fain would hold me to you.
    OROONOKO. Ever, ever,
And let those stars, which are my Enemies,
Witness against me in the other World,
If I would leave this Mansion of my Bliss,
To be the brightest Ruler of their Skies.
    [*Embracing her.*]
O! that we could incorporate, be one,
One Body, as we have been long one Mind:
That blended so, we might together mix,
And losing thus our Beings to the World,
Be only found to one another's Joys.
    IMOINDA. Is this the way to part?

OROONOKO.   Which is the way?

IMOINDA. The God of Love is blind, and cannot find it.
But quick, make haste, our Enemies have Eyes
To find us out, and show us the worst way
Of parting; think on them.

OROONOKO. Why dost thou wake me?

IMOINDA.   O! no more of Love.
For if I listen to you, I shall quite
Forget my Dangers, and desire to live.
I can't live yours. [*Takes up the dagger.*]

OROONOKO.   There all the Stings of Death
Are shot into my Heart—what shall I do?

IMOINDA. This Dagger will instruct you. [*Gives it him.*]

OROONOKO.   Ha! this Dagger!
Like Fate, it points me to the horrid Deed.

IMOINDA. Strike, strike it home, and bravely save us both.
There is no other Safety.

OROONOKO.   It must be—
But first a dying Kiss—[*Kisses her.*]
                    This last Embrace—[*Embracing her.*]
And now—

IMOINDA. I'm ready.

OROONOKO.   O! where shall I strike?
Is there a smallest grain of that lov'd Body
That is not dearer to me than my Eyes,
My bosom'd Heart, and all the Life-Blood there?
Bid me cut off these Limbs, hew off these Hands,
Dig out these Eyes, tho' I would keep them last
To gaze upon thee: but to murder thee!
The Joy, and Charm of every ravish'd Sense,
My Wife! forbid it Nature.

IMOINDA.   Tis your Wife,
Who on her knees conjures you. O! in time
Prevent those Mischiefs that are falling on us.
You may be hurry'd to a shameful Death,
And I too drag'd to the vile Governor.
Then I may cry aloud: when you are gone,
Where shall I find a Friend again to save me?

OROONOKO. It will be so. Thou unexampled Virtue!
Thy Resolution has recover'd mine:
And now prepare thee.

IMOINDA.   Thus with open Arms,
I welcome you, and Death.

[*He drops his dagger as he looks on her, and throws himself on the ground.*]

OROONOKO.   I cannot bear it.
O let me dash against this Rock of Fate.
Dig up this Earth, tear, tear her Bowels out,
To make a Grave, deep as the Center down,
To swallow wide, and bury us together.
It wonnot be. O! then some pitying God
(If there be one a Friend to Innocence)
Find yet a way to lay her Beauties down
Gently in Death, and save me from her Blood.

IMOINDA. O rise, 'tis more than Death to see you thus.
I'll ease your Love, and do the Deed myself—
[*She takes up the dagger, he rises in haste to take it from her.*]

OROONOKO. O! hold, I charge thee, hold.

IMOINDA.   Tho' I must own
It would be nobler for us both from you.

OROONOKO. O! for a Whirlwind's Wing to hurry us
To yonder Cliff, which frowns upon the Flood:
That in Embraces lock'd we might plunge in,
And perish thus in one another's Arms.
[*A noise off.*]

IMOINDA. Alas! what shout is that?

OROONOKO.   I see 'em coming.
They shannot overtake us. This last Kiss.
And now farewell.

IMOINDA.   Farewell, farewell for ever.

OROONOKO. I'll turn my Face away, and do it so.
Now, are you ready?

IMOINDA.   Now. But do not grudge me
The Pleasure in my Death of a last look,
Pray look upon me—Now I'm satisfied.

OROONOKO. So Fate must be by this—
[*Going to stab her, he stops short; she lays her hands on his, in order to give the blow.*]

IMOINDA. Nay then I must assist you.
And since it is the common Cause of both,
'Tis just that both should be employ'd in it.
Thus, thus 'tis finish'd, and I bless my Fate, [*Stabs herself.*]
That where I liv'd, I die, in these lov'd Arms. [*Dies.*]

OROONOKO. She's gone. And now all's at an End with me.
Soft, lay her down. O we will part no more.
[*Throws himself by her.*]
But let me pay the tribute of my Grief,

A few sad Tears to thy lov'd Memory,
And then I follow—
   [*Weeps over her. A noise again.*]
               But I stay too long.
The Noise comes nearer. Hold, before I go,
There's something would be done. It shall be so.
And then, *Imoinda,* I'll come all to thee. [*Rises.*]
   [BLANFORD, *and his party, enters before the* GOVERNOR *and his party,*
     Swords drawn on both sides.]
   GOVERNOR. You strive in vain to save him, he shall die.
   BLANFORD. Not while we can defend him with our lives.
   GOVERNOR. Where is he?
   OROONOKO.   Here's the Wretch whom you would have.
Put up your Swords, and let not civil broils
Engage you in the cursed cause of one,
Who cannot live, and now entreats to die.
This object will convince you.
   [*They gather about the body.*]
   BLANFORD.   'Tis his Wife!
Alas! there was no other Remedy.
   GOVERNOR. Who did the bloody Deed?
   OROONOKO.   The Deed was mine:
Bloody I know it is, and I expect
Your Laws should tell me so. Thus self-condemn'd,
I do resign myself into your Hands,
The Hands of Justice—But I hold the Sword
For you—and for myself.
   [*Stabs the* GOVERNOR, *and himself, then throws himself by* IMOINDA's
body.]
   STANMORE. He has kill'd the Governor, and stabb'd himself.
   OROONOKO. 'Tis as it should be now. I have sent his Ghost
To be a Witness of that Happiness
In the next World, which he denied us here. [*Dies.*]
   BLANFORD. I hope there is a place of Happiness
In the next World for such exalted Virtue.
Pagan, or Unbeliever, yet he liv'd
To all he knew: And if he went astray,
There's Mercy still above to set him right.
But Christians guided by the Heavenly Ray,
Have no excuse if we mistake our Way.
   [*Exeunt Omnes.*]
                   FINIS.

RICHARD STEELE

The Lover, No. 36†

[This story followed two *Spectator* papers that offered tales from the colonies: Steele's popular account of the love affair between Thomas Inkle and the Indian maid Yarico in *Spectator* 11, and Addison's "wild tragedy" of a love triangle among slaves in *Spectator* 215. *Indian* was often used as a synonym for *Negro*.]

Concubitu prohibere vago. . . .
Horace[1]

I have heard it objected, by several Persons, against my Papers, that they are apt to kindle Love in young Hearts, and inflame the Sexes with a Desire for one another: I am so far from denying this Charge, that I shall make no Scruple to own it is the chief End of my Writing. *Love* is a Passion of the Mind (perhaps the noblest) which was planted in it by the same Hand that created it. We ought to be so far, therefore, from endeavouring to root it out, that we should rather make it our Business to keep it up and cherish it. Our chief Care must be to fix this, as well as our other Passions, upon proper Objects, and to direct it to a right End.

For this Reason, as I have ever shewn myself a Friend to Honourable Love, I have constantly discountenanced all vicious Passions. Tho' the several Sorts of these are each of them highly Criminal, yet that which leads us to defile another Man's Bed is by far of the blackest dye.

The excellent Author of *The Whole Duty of Man*,[2] has given us a very lively Picture of this Crime, with all those melancholy Circumstances that must necessarily attend it. One must indeed wonder to see it punished so lightly among civilized Nations, when even the most Barbarous have regarded it with the utmost Horror and Detestation. I was lately entertained with a Story to this Purpose, which was told me by one of my Friends who was himself upon the Place when the thing happened.

In an Out-Plantation, upon the Borders of *Potuxen*[3] a River in *Maryland*, there lived a Planter, who was Master of a great Number of *Negro* Slaves. The Increase of these poor Creatures is always an Advantage to the Planters, their Children being born Slaves; for which Reason the

---

† *The Lover* 36 (London, 1714), 204–08; edited and annotated by Rae Blanchard in *Richard Steele's Periodical Journalism 1714–16* (1959).
1. From *The Art of Poetry*, recalling that one purpose of the first poetry was "to curb promiscuous lust."
2. A widely popular moral and religious guidebook.
3. Patuxent.

Owners are very well pleased, when any of them marry. Among these *Negroes* there happened to be two, who had always lived together and contracted an intimate Friendship, which went on for several Years in an uninterrupted Course. Their Joys and their Griefs were mutual; their Confidence in each other was intire; Distrust and Suspicion were Passions they had no Notion of. The one was a Batchelor; the other married to a Slave of his own Complexion, by whom he had several Children. It happened that the Head of this small Family rose early one Morning, on a leisure Day, to go far into the Woods a hunting, in order to entertain his Wife and Children at Night with some Provisions better than ordinary. The Batchelor Slave, it seems, had for a long time entertained a Passion for his Friend's Wife; which, from the Sequel of the Story, we may conclude, he had endeavoured to stifle, but in vain. The Impatience of his Desires prompted him to take this Opportunity, of the Husband's Absence, to practise upon the Weakness of the Woman; which accordingly he did, and was so unfortunate as to succeed in his Attempt. The Hunter, who found his Prey much nearer home than usual, returned some Hours sooner than was expected, loaden with the Spoils of the Day, and full of the pleasing Thoughts of feasting and rejoycing, with his Family, over the Fruits of his Labour. Upon his entring his Shed, the first Objects that struck his Eyes were, his Wife and his Friend asleep in the Embraces of each other. A Man acquainted with the Passions of human Nature will easily conceive the Astonishment, the Rage, and the Despair, that over-power'd the poor *Indian* at once: He burst out into Lamentations and Reproaches; and tore his Hair like one Distracted. His Cries and broken Accents awakened the guilty Couple; whose Shame and Confusion were equal to the Agonies of the injured. After a considerable Pause of Silence on both Sides, he expostulated with his Friend in Terms like these: My Wrongs are greater than I am able to express; and far too great for me to bear. My Wife—But I blame not her. After a long and lasting Friendship, exercised under all the Hardships and Severities of a most irksome Captivity; after mutual repeated Instances of Affection and Fidelity; could I suspect my Friend, my Bosom-Friend should prove a Traitor? I thought my self happy, even in Bondage, in the Enjoyment of such a Friend and such a Wife; but cannot bear the Thoughts of Life with Liberty, after having been so basely betrayed by both. You both are lost to me, and I to you. I soon shall be at Rest; live and enjoy your Crime. Adieu. Having said this, he turned away and went out, with a Resolution to dye immediately. The guilty *Negro* followed him, touched with the quickest Sense of Remorse for his Treachery. 'Tis I alone, (said he) that am guilty; and I alone, who am not fit to live. Let me intreat you to forgive your Wife, who was overcome by my Importunities. I promise never to give either of you the least Disquiet for the future: Live and be happy together, and think of me no more. Bear with me but for this

Night; and to Morrow you shall be satisfied. Here they both wept, and parted. When the Husband went out in the Morning to his Work, the first thing he saw was his Friend hanging upon the Bough of a Tree before the Cabbin-Door.

If the Wretches of this Nation, who set up for Men of Wit and Gallantry, were capable of feeling the generous Remorse of this poor Slave, upon the like Occasions, we should, I fear, have a much thinner appearance of Equipage in Town.

Methinks there should be a general Confederacy amongst all honest Men to exclude from Society, and to Brand with the blackest Note of Infamy, those Miscreants, who make it the Business of their Lives to get into Families, and to estrange the Affections of the Wife from the Husband. There is something so very base and so Inhuman in this modish Wickedness, that one cannot help wishing the honest Liberty of the *Ancient Comedy* were restor'd; and that Offenders in this kind might be exposed by their Names in our publick Theatres. Under such a Discipline, we should see those who now Glory in the Ruin of deluded Women, reduced to withdraw themselves from the just Resentments of their Countrymen and Fellow-Citizens.

[CAPTAIN TOM, OR ADOMO OROONOKO TOMO]

[In the early 1720s, an African Company agent named Lambe spent some years in captivity in Africa, detained for a company debt by one African king, then made the prisoner and petted houseguest of another, the conquering king of Dahomey. In 1726 he was released, taking with him an English-speaking African from the port of Jakin captured in the same war. In 1731 Lambe reappeared in London, with the African interpreter, bearing an extraordinary letter of self-introduction from the Dahomeyan king to George I that offered friendship and an inexhaustible supply of slaves. While the Commissioners for Trade took testimony and debated the genuineness of the letter, the African, Adomo Oroonoko Tomo, was feted as a visiting dignitary and followed in news reports.

The name Oroonoko (variously spelled, but not found in Africa) appears first in the letter. It also refers to him as "Captain Tom" and says that he is a relation of the king of Jakin, which did not have a royal line, though he may well have been from a dominant local family. In London he was often styled "prince," more often captain or "caboceer" or some lesser title. The account of the missing years published by slave captain William Snelgrave, who traded in the same places, may imply that "Oroonoko" Tomo had been sold into slavery and then retrieved. During his London visit he was lionized, baptized, called for testimony in the case, given maintenance and English lessons, arrested for a tailor's debt when the various agencies stalled over his support, rescued by lords who patronized visiting Africans,

and finally sent home with gifts. *The Political State* for August 1732 announced the departure of "Prince Adomo Thomo," noting that "as he
could speak tolerable good English, and had a good deal of natural Sense,
he was, while here, often entertained by some of the best of our Nobility,
Gentlemen, and Merchants." Virtually every visiting African described as
a "prince" in European capitals was derided as a bogus prince by proslavery
writers.

The many surviving documents and attempted interpretations are re-
viewed by Robin Law, "King Agaja of Dahomey, the Slave Trade, and the
Question of West African Plantations: The Embassy of Bulfinch Lambe
and Adomo Tomo to England, 1726–32," *Journal of Imperial and Commonwealth History* 19 (1991), 137–63. Law accepts the king's letter as genuine, but, of course, it was dictated to Lambe.]

[Tomo at Theater and Court (1731)]†

DRURY LANE THEATRE

Saturday, April 24, 1731
Performance of John Fletcher's *Rule a Wife and Have a Wife*; also the
masque *Cephalus and Procris*. "For the Entertainment of Adomo,
Oronoco Tomo Caboshirre of the Great Country of Dawhomay, under
the Mighty Trudo Audato Povesaw Danjer Enjow Suveveto, Emperor
of Pawpaw in Africa, who lately conquer'd the great Kingdoms of Ardah
and Whidah."

THE GENTLEMAN'S MAGAZINE

Friday, May 7[, 1731]
Captain *Bulfinch Lamb*, late Factor for the Royal *African* Company at
Jaquin on the Coast of *Guinea*, went to Court with *Adomo Oronooko
Tomo*, sent by the Grand *Trudo Audato Povesaw, Tangerenio Survev-
eveto Ene Mottee Adde Powa Powlo Cottullo Necresy*, King of *Dawhomay*, and Emperor of *Pawpaw*, who lately conquer'd the great
Kingdoms of *Ardah* and *Whidah*; with the said Emperor's Letters to his
Majesty. Capt. *Lamb* was taken Captive at the Conquest of *Ardah*, and
was carried before the Emperor, who having never seen a white Person
before, he detained him ever since, us'd him with great Respect, and
enjoined him to return.

---

† From Arthur H. Scouten, ed., *The London Stage 1600–1800*, vol. 3 (Carbondale: Southern
Illinois Press, 1961), 132; and *The Gentleman's Magazine* 1 (May 1731), 216.

[Investigation: Commissioners for Trade and Plantations]†

[Whitehall, July 6, 1731]

May it please your Majesty

In obedience to Your Majesty's commands, signified to us by a letter from his Grace the Duke of Newcastle dated the 12th of May last, we have perused the memorial presented to your Majesty by Mr. Bulfinch Lamb and have discoursed with him concerning the letter which he lately delivered to your Majesty, as from the Emperor of Pawpaw.

We have also consulted upon this matter with the Royal African Company and with the separate traders to Africa, and have been attended by some Commanders of Ships and others, who have frequented the Coast of that Country.

Whereupon we beg leave to represent to your Majesty, that both the African Company and separate Traders believe the said letter not to be genuine, and therefore we cannot be of Opinion, that any Return should be made to it. But on the other hand it is admitted by the Royal African Company, that the aforesaid Mr. Lamb did bring down 80 Slaves to Whydah from the Emperor of Pawpaw; and as we do believe that 40 of them may have been sent by that Emperor as a Present to Your Majesty, we humbly conceive that the Produce of the said 40 Slaves, which is lodged in the hands of the Royal African Company should be laid out in a proper Present to be returned from your Majesty to the Emperor of Pawpaw; and that this Present, together with the Black Man, who is called Adomo Oroonoco Tomo, should be sent back to Africa on board any one of Your Majesty's Men of War which may be ordered for that Coast; and the Commander may receive proper Instructions for conducting this affair in such a manner as may be most conducive to your Majesty's Honour and the Benefit of your Subjects trading to that Coast.

*   *   *

[Captain William Snelgrave's Account (1734)]†

*   *   *

On our coming into the Court, where we had seen the King at our former Audience, we were desired to stay a little, till the Presents were carried into the House, that his Majesty might view them. Soon after

---

† From Marion Johnson, "Bulfinch Lambe and the Emperor of Pawpaw: A Footnote to Agaja and the Slave Trade," *History in Africa* 5 (1978), 348–49.

† From William Snelgrave, *A New Account of Some Parts of Guinea, and the Slave Trade* (London, 1734), 60–61, 66–71. Not all of Snelgrave's representations are in his original manuscript.

we were introduced into a small Court, at the further end of which the King was sitting cross-legg'd on a Carpet of Silk, spread on the Ground. He was himself richly dress'd, and had but few Attendants. When we approached him, his Majesty enquired in a very kind manner, How we did? ordering we should be placed near him; and accordingly fine Mats were spread on the Ground for us to sit on. Tho' sitting in that Posture was not very easy to us, yet we put a good Face on the matter, understanding by the Linguist, that it was their Custom.

As soon as we were placed, the King ordered the Interpreter to ask me, What I had to desire of him? To which I answered, "That as my Business was to trade, so I relied on his Majesty's Goodness, to give me a quick dispatch, and fill my Ship with Negroes; by which means I should return into my own Country in a short time; where I should make known how great and powerful a King I had seen." To this the King replied by the Linguist, "That my desire should be fulfilled."

✳ ✳ ✳

After this his Majesty fell into a variety of Discourse, and amongst other things complained of Mr. Lambe (who, as I have related in the beginning of this Book, had been taken Prisoner in the Ardra War), saying, "That tho' he had given him, at his leaving the Court, three hundred and twenty ounces of Gold, with eight[y] Slaves, and made him promise with a solemn Oath to return again in a reasonable time, yet twelve Moons had now pass'd, and he had heard nothing from him: Adding, He had sent a black Person with him, whose name was Tom, one who had been made a Prisoner at the same time, being a Jaqueen-man, who spoke good English; and this Man he had ordered to return again with Mr. Lambe, that he might be informed, whether what that Gentleman had reported concerning our King, Customs, and manner of Living was true." To this I replied, "That I had no personal Knowledge of Mr. Lambe, but had been informed, before I left England, that he went from Whidaw to Barbados, which is a Plantation where the English employ their Slaves in making Sugar, and which is at a great distance from our own Country; but I hoped he would prove an honest Man, and return again to his Majesty, according to his Promise and Oath."

To this the King replied, "Tho' he proved not as good as his Word, other white Men should not fare the worse on that account; for as to what he had given Lambe, he valued it not a Rush; but if he returned quickly, and came with never so large a Ship, she should be instantly filled with Slaves, with which he might do what he thought proper."

It may not be improper here to give a short account of the black Man the King mentioned to me, because he was in England last year, and that Affair was brought before the Lords of Trade, by whom I was examined about him.

Mr. Lambe carried this Person to Barbados, and several other Places, but at last left him with a Gentleman in Maryland. Afterwards Mr. Lambe trafficked for some Years, from one place to another in the Plantations; and coming to the Island of Antigua, where I had been in the year 1728, and told the foregoing story to some Gentlemen, and how kindly the King of Dahomey had express'd himself with regard to the said Mr. Lambe, being by them informed of it, this induced him to return to Maryland; and the Gentleman who had Tom in his Custody was so good, as to deliver him again to Mr. Lambe, who came with him to London, the beginning of the year 1731.

Mr. Lambe, soon after his arrival, came to see me at my house, enquiring particularly about what I had related at Antigua; which I confirmed to him. Then he desired my Advice about his going back to the King of Dahomey. To this I frankly answered, "It was my opinion, he had miss'd the opportunity, by not returning in a reasonable time, according to his promise; several years being now pass'd since he came from thence." * * *

On this he left me; and the next news I heard was, That Mr. Lambe had delivered a Letter to his Majesty King George as from the King of Dahomey, which being referred to the Lords of Trade, the Merchants trading to the Coast of Guinea were sent for; and I being ordered to attend, informed their Lordships of what I knew of the matter.

The report from the Lords of Trade was to this Purpose, "That the Letter in their opinion was not genuine, but that the black Man ought to be taken care of, and returned to his King." Accordingly he was put into the hands of the African Company, who took care of him for many Months; but he growing impatient, applied to their Graces the Dukes of Richmond and Montague, who procured him a Passage on board his Majesty's Ship the *Tiger*, Captain Berkeley, then bound to the Coast of Guinea.

Moreover, their Lordships having shewed him great Kindness, most generously sent by him several rare Presents to his King, which, no doubt, will make a good impression on him in favour of our Nation; and I have lately heard, that on his being put on Shore at Whidaw, he was forthwith sent to the King, who was then in his own Country of Dahomey, and was received graciously by him: That his Majesty sent down handsome Presents for Captain Berkeley, but before the Messengers got to Whidaw, he was sailed, not having patience to wait so many days, as the return from so far inland a place required.

I had not made this Digression, but only to set this Affair in a true light; and undeceive those that may read this Book, and were so far imposed upon, as to suppose the Black Man to have been an Ambassador from the King of Dahomey, to his Majesty King George. I met with several that believed so, till I satisfied them of the contrary; for the jest was carried on so far, that several Plays were acted on his Account, and it was advertised in the News-Papers, that they were for the Entertainment of Prince Adomo Oroonoko Tomo, etc. these jingling Names being invented to carry on the Fraud the better.

* * *

[Archibald Dalzel's Summation (1793)]†

This is neither the first, or the last imposition, of the kind, put upon honest John Bull. We have had such black princes in abundance. People from any remote part of the world, that wish to carry on the business of imposture here, never fail of finding knaves or fools to assist them.

JOHN WHALEY

On a Young Lady's Weeping at *Oroonoko*†

At Fate's approach whilst OROONOKO groans,
Imoinda's Fate, undaunted at his own,
Dropping a gen'rous Tear *Lucretia* sighs,
And views the Hero with Imoinda's Eyes.
When the Prince strikes who envies not the Deed?
To be so Wept, who would not wish to Bleed?

[OROONOKO IN FRANCE: THE LA PLACE ADAPTATION]†

[Behn's translator, Pierre Antoine de La Place (1707–1793), translated many English works, including many of Shakespeare's tragedies and Fielding's *Tom Jones*. In the preface to his French *Oronoko*, first published in 1745, he remarks that the story needs French dress to please in Paris as it has in London. In his polite and generalized rendering, the famous "Madame Behn" remains an active figure, but he follows Southerne in making Imoinda the daughter of a white European, casting the deputy governor as an aggressive rival lover, and staging a dramatic dagger-wielding scene. From that point, he supplies many more discovery scenes and his own romance ending of birthright restored.

This review (which not infrequently repeats the text) announced the third (Paris) edition of 1756. Fine plates added to the 1769 fourth edition (marked "at London" to evade the censors) depict erotic interracial scenes.

---

† From Archibald Dalzel, *The History of Dahomy . . . Compiled from Authentic Memoirs* (London, 1793), 46.
† From John Whaley, *A Collection of Poems* (London, 1732), 92–93. Partially modernized.
† The conclusion of a review notice in critic Elie Fréron's periodical *L'Année Littéraire* 8 (1756), 198–202. Reproduced in facsimile by Slatkine Reprints (1966).

With seven editions before 1800, the work was among the most widely circulated midcentury tales from English, surpassed only by novels of Samuel Richardson and Henry and Sarah Fielding.]

*   *   *

Sir, I shall abridge the interesting account of this story. Let it suffice for you to know that *Imoinda*, under the name *Climène*, is among the slaves of *Surinam*; that *Tréfry*, charmed by this happy meeting, marries the two lovers & celebrates their wedding with an inexpressible joy & magnificence; that Madame *Behn* enjoys the very touching spectacle of two hearts that, having been long separated, meet again & reunite; that *Climène* becomes pregnant; that the abominable *Byam* conceives for her the most unbridled passion; that *César* rouses all the slaves of the colony in revolt. *   *   *

The traitor *Byam*, despite his word of honor, has him surprised in his bed, dragged off to the public execution post, & lashed with whips. *César*, indignant at this shameful & barbarous treatment, swears to kill the scoundrel, who on his part has resolved his destruction. His passion for *Climène* having turned into rage, he has *César* condemned to death & writes to *Climène* that her husband's pardon is in her hands. *César*, informed of this execrable verdict, runs away with *Climène* into the thickest part of a nearby forest (for *Byam* had not yet had him arrested & they remained free at *Tréfry's* house). There he consults his mistress on means of getting revenge; *Climène* makes him see the impossibility of this. *César* makes up his mind to die in front of his beloved, and she in turn begs him for the favor of death. *César* raises the dagger over her, staggers, weeps, & the dagger falls from his hand. This situation, so well rendered also in the tragedy *Oroonoko* by Southerne, is absolutely the same as the one which ends *l'Orpheline de la Chine*[1] by Monsieur *de Voltaire*. *Byam*, having learned of the escape of *César* & *Climène*, pursues them with several friends. *César*, seeing them approach, turns his head away to strike his wife, who falls in a faint, and at the same time he flies at his enemy & takes advantage of the very moment when *Byam* wounds him to seize him bodily & stab him with repeated thrusts. All this is the work of an instant. *Byam* dies in despair, but *César* is cured of his wounds. *Climène*, who had received only a slight blow, abandoned in the forest & believing her husband murdered, lets herself be led by a slave who is loyal to her to a nation of Indians, who take her under their protection. There she delivers a son. *Tréfry*, to safeguard *César* from his enemies, sends him under escort to the same Indian village. There he finds his wife again, & there for six months they taste the charms of the most peaceful union.

---

1. Voltaire's successful tragedy of the previous year. Fréron, a former Jesuit, was one of Voltaire's most important and persistent antagonists. Among Voltaire's rejoinders was a widely known rhyme saying that when Fréron suffered snakebite, the snake died.

Milord Governor arrives in *Surinam*. He hears with indignation of the misfortunes of this unlucky pair. He wants to see *César*, & orders *Tréfry* to go and call him back from the Indians. He reappears in *Surinam* with *Climène*, who had been thought dead. The Governor makes amends for all the horrors of their fate and grants them liberty. They embark with their son on a Dutch ship that is going to *Cormantine*. They arrive there & find the old monarch, burdened with the weight of age, who abdicates the crown in their favor. Finally, *Oroonoko*, having become sovereign, sends to Milord *Willoughby*, to Mr. *Tréfry*, & to his friend Madame *Behn* gifts worthy of the gratitude of a great king.

Read this work all the way through, sir. It will hold you, it will move you, it will affect you. You will find in it matters of interest, situations, deeds, episodes tied to the main subject, dreadful strokes of blackness, perfidy, & inhumanity, yet tempered by the soft colors of the most tender & faithful love, & by great sentiments of honor, virtue, courage, and generosity. The character of *Oroonoko* is one of the noblest & strongest that I have encountered in history & even in novels.

[THE "PRINCE" AND THE PLAY]

[The "prince" was William Unsah Sessarakoo, son of the powerful Fante chief official at Annamabo, a stone's throw from the former station at Cormantine. *The London Magazine* also carried an account of the evening that calls his companion "a youth of a great family" and claims that the pair were "about to be sold" but "providentially rescued." An elegant mezzotint portrait of him for public sale (by the noted engraver John Faber the younger, from a painting by Gabriel Mathias) bears a caption that gives his parentage, emphasizing his mother's royal descent, and concludes, "He was sold at Barbadoes as a slave in the year 1744, redeemed at the earnest request of his father in 1748 and brought to England." Another account in a volume titled *The Royal African: or, Memoirs of the Young Prince of Annamaboe*, published in two editions in 1749 or 1750, explains that the chief or "braffo" had already sent a less favored son to France and that such superior education increased the prestige of the family. The erratic captain claimed to be owed money, and other commentators on the case seek to pass off their own crimes or are foolish enough to look down on all blacks; but the English involved—high and low—have appreciated the justice of the father's complaint.

Above all, this author is concerned with describing the ins and outs of diplomacy at Annamabo, the pressure of French rivalry, the high percentage of slaves acquired at this spot, and the propriety of calling Unsah a prince, given his father's power. Citing as precedent the belated careful treatment of Adomo Tomo, he rejoices at the cordial alliance with this fully princelike person, who has "appeared such from the gracefulness of his person, the nobleness of his sentiments, the modesty of his deportment, and the grateful acknowledgments he continually expresses for the justice that has been done him, and the favours that he has received" (2nd ed., p. 55).

The *Gentleman's Magazine* for June 1750 published his portrait and in a news item of July 1751 supplied the sequel: the "prince" having arrived home safely the previous December, two other kings of "great trading nations" were "preparing to send their eldest sons to *England*, to be educated in the same manner."]

[From *The Gentleman's Magazine*, February 1749]†

Tuesday the 16th

Capt. —— trafficking on the coast of *Africa*, went up the country, where he was introduc'd to a *Moorish* king, who had 40,000 men under his command. This prince being taken with the polite behaviour of the *English*, entertained them with the greatest civility; and at last reposed such confidence in the captain, as to entrust him with his son, about 18 years of age, with another sprightly youth, to be brought to *England*, and educated in the *European* manner. The captain received them with great joy, and fair treatment, but basely sold them for slaves; shortly after he died, and the ship coming to *England*, the officers related the whole affair; on which the government sent to pay their ransom, and they were brought to *England*, and put under the care of the right honourable the earl of *Halifax*, first commissioner of trade and plantations, who gave orders for clothing and educating them in a very genteel manner. They have since been introduced to his majesty, richly dressed, in the *European* manner, and were very graciously received. They appear sometimes at the theatres, and particularly on the 1st inst. were at *Covent Garden*, to see the tragedy of *Oroonoko*. They were received with a loud clap of applause, which they acknowledged with a very genteel bow, and took their seats in a box. The seeing persons of their own colour on the stage, apparently in the same distress from which they had been so lately delivered, the tender interview between *Imoinda* and *Oroonoko*, who was betrayed by the treachery of a captain, his account of his sufferings, and the repeated abuse of his placability and confidence, strongly affected them with that generous grief which pure nature always feels, and which art had not yet taught them to suppress; the young prince was so far overcome, that he was obliged to retire at the end of the fourth act. His companion remained, but wept the whole time; a circumstance which affected the audience yet more than the play, and doubled the tears which were shed for *Oroonoko* and *Imoinda*.

† February 1749: 89–90.

[Wylie Sypher on the Prince and Zara]†

[Sypher here studies "the prolonged vitality of the Oroonoko legend" in public admiration for regal African visitors: "your free-born Briton could feel for a prince, particularly a prince in distress" (p. 237). His fuller study is *Guinea's Captive Kings: British Anti-Slavery Literature of the XVIIIth Century* (Chapel Hill, University of North Carolina Press, 1942).]

* * *

The prince had seen *Oroonoko* in February, 1749. In the *Gentleman's* for July appeared the first of the two poems by Dodd,[1] "The African prince, now in England, to Zara, at his father's court"; in August the same magazine printed the companion poem, "Zara, at the court of *Annamabboe*, to the African Prince, now in England." Both are in the pseudo-African manner of the day: the prince easily eclipses Omai,[2] even though he may not rival Oroonoko; and Zara, like Imoinda, is "female to the noble male." The prince speaks of his position at Annamaboe:

> Nurtur'd in ease, a thousand servants round,
> My wants prevented, and my wishes crown'd,
> No painful labours stretch'd the tedious day,
> On downy feet my moments danc'd away.
> Where'er I look'd, officious courtiers bow'd,
> Where'er I pass'd, a shouting people crowd.

His love for Zara is Platonism heated by savage ardor:

> Together sinking in the trance divine,
> I caught thy fleeting soul, and gave thee mine!

The prince feels deeply the injustice of slavery—for himself; he recalls the hours of his duress:

> At night I mingled with a wretched crew,
> Who by long use with woe familiar grew;
> Of manners brutish, merciless and rude,
> They mock'd my suff'rings, and my pangs renew'd.

One thinks not only of Oroonoko with his refined contempt for his fellow Negroes, but of Itanoko, Zimza, Luco, and Zimao,[3] and the

---

† From Wylie Sypher, "The African Prince in London," *Journal of the History of Ideas* 2 (1941), 242–43. Reprinted by permission of the Johns Hopkins University Press.
1. William Dodd was a student and poet, later a minister. The two poems supplying the love story, long Ovidian epistles, were also printed separately, in Dodd's *Poems*, and in the best-known poetry collections of the century [Editor's note].
2. A South Sea islander brought from one of Captain Cook's voyages who made a stir in fashionable English society in the 1770s [Editor's note].
3. Enslaved figures in considerably later fiction and poetry by Joseph Lavallée, Anna Maria Mackenzie, Ann Yearsley, and J. F. de Saint-Lambert, respectively. Lavallée's Itanoko, an enslaved prince, seems clearly named after Oroonoko [Editor's note].

whole procession of royal slaves sweeping through anti-slavery prose and verse. Dodd, like the author of *The Royal African*, discerns that by the release of one royal slave, justice has been done:

> No more *Britannia's* cheek, the blush of shame,
> Burns for my wrongs, her king restores her fame; . . .
> Whate'er is great and gay around me shine,
> And all the splendor of a court is mine.

Perhaps inspired by the account in the *Gentleman's Magazine*, Dodd fancies what the prince must have felt when he beheld *Oroonoko* at the Covent Garden:

> O! *Zara*, here, a story like my own,
> With mimic skill, in borrow'd names, was shown;
> An *Indian* [sic] chief, like me, by fraud betray'd,
> And partner in his woes an *Indian* [sic] maid.
> I can't recall the scenes, 'tis pain too great,
> And, if recall'd, should shudder to relate.

Zara responds with an epistle that deepens the great gulf fixed between her prince and his fellow Negroes:

> Hold, Hold! Barbarians of the fiercest kind!
> Fear heav'n's red light'ning—'tis a Prince ye bind;
> A prince, whom no indignities could hide,
> They knew, presumptuous! and the Gods defy'd.

She rests confident, too, in the steadfastness of his primitive love:

> . . . in *Britain's* happy courts to shine,
> Amidst a thousand blooming maids, is thine—
> But thou, a thousand blooming maids among,
> Art still thyself, incapable of wrong;
> No outward charm can captivate thy mind,
> Thy love is friendship heighten'd and refin'd;
> 'Tis what my soul, and not my form inspires,
> And burns with spotless and immortal fires.
> Thy joys, like mine, from conscious truth arise,
> And, known these joys, what others canst thou prize?

Manifestly an Oroonoko *redivivus*!

*   *   *

[Horace Walpole to Horace Mann]†

[MARCH 23, 1749]

There are two black princes of Anamaboe here, who are in fashion at all the assemblies, of whom I scarcely know any particulars, though their story is very like Oroonoko's; all the women know it—and ten times more than belongs to it.

---

† From *Horace Walpole's Correspondence*, vol. 20, ed. W. S. Lewis, Warren Hunting Smith, and George L. Lam (New Haven: Yale University Press, 1960), 40.

Opinions on Slavery

[A DECLARATION BY THE
BARBADOS COLONISTS (1651)]†

[Long before the English knew slavery in practice, they knew it as half of a familiar opposition between liberty and slavery, a rhetorical trope used from ancient times as a rallying cry to promote one government or policy over another. During the fierce contests of the mid-seventeenth century over England's true heritage and course, this rhetoric served to justify the execution of Charles I, who spoke from the scaffold on the need for a distant and disinterested royal protector of the people's liberty. It was also used in the colonies against new measures by the Parliamentarian government to impose administrative control. Planters regardless of party wanted free trade and home rule, or at least representation; but in February 1651, Royalist Barbados faced a showdown. This was the political moment reflected in Lord Willoughby's letter to his wife (see p. 99). Declared "rebels," cut off from all trade, and expecting an invading fleet, the colonists issued a remarkable ringing defiance of "slavery," anticipating in spirit, if not purpose, the American Declaration of Independence. Far from being oblivious to the rapid transformation of Barbados into a slave economy over the previous decade, the colonists were probably partly inspired by it.]

* * *

The Lord Lieutenant-General, together with the Lords of this Council and Assembly, having carefully read over the said printed Papers, and finding them to oppose *the freedom, safety, and well-being of this island*, have thought themselves bound to communicate the same to all the inhabitants of this island; as also their observation and resolution concerning it, and to proceed therein after the best manner, wherefore they have ordered the same to be read publicly.

Concerning the abovesaid Act,[1] by which the least capacity may comprehend how much the inhabitants of this island would be brought into contempt and slavery, if the same be not timely prevented:

First—They allege that this island was first settled and inhabited at the charges, and by the especial order of the people of England, and therefore ought to be subject to the same nation. It is certain, that we all of us know very well, that we, the present inhabitants of this island, were and still be

---

† From "A Declaration of Lord Willoughby and the Legislature of the island of Barbados against the British Parliament," February 18, 1651, in R. H. Schomburgk, *The History of Barbados* (London, 1848), Append. 10, 706–08; it is headed "serving in answer to a certaine Act formerly put forth by the Parliament of England, the 3rd of October 1650" and "occasioned at the sight of certaine printed Papers, entitled An Act forbidding Commerce and Traffick."

1. I.e., of October 3, 1650.

that people of England, *who with great danger to our persons, and with great charge and trouble, have settled this island in its condition, and inhabited the same,* and shall we therefore be subject to the will and command of those that stay at home? Shall we be bound to the Government and Lordship of a Parliament in which we have no Representatives, or persons chosen by us, for there to propound and consent to what might be needful to us, as also to oppose and dispute all what should tend to our disadvantage and harm? In truth, this would be a slavery far exceeding all that the English nation hath yet suffered. And we doubt not but the courage which hath brought us thus far out of our own country, to seek our beings and livelihoods in this wild country, will maintain us in our freedoms; without which our lives will be uncomfortable to us.

Secondly—It is alleged that the inhabitants of this island have, by cunning and force, usurped a power and Government.

If we, the inhabitants of this island, had been heard what we could have said for ourselves, this allegation had never been printed; but those who are destined to be slaves may not enjoy those privileges; otherwise we might have said and testified with a truth, that the Government now used amongst us, is the same that hath always been ratified, and doth every way agree with the first settlement and Government in these places; and was given us by the same power and authority that New England hold theirs; against whom the Act makes no objection.

And the Government here in subjection, is the nearest model of conformity to that under which our predecessors of the English nation have lived and flourished for above a thousand years. Therefore we conclude, that the rule of reason and discourse is most strangely mistaken, if the continuation and submission to a right well-settled Government be judged to be an usurping of a new power, and to the contrary, the usurpation of a new Government be held a continuation of the old.

Thirdly—By the abovesaid Act all outlandish nations are forbidden to hold any correspondency or traffic with the inhabitants of this island; although all the ancient inhabitants know very well, how greatly they have been obliged to those of the Low Countries[2] for their subsistence, and how difficult it would have been for us, without their assistance, ever to have inhabited these places, or to have brought them into order. * * *

Fourthly—For to perfect and accomplish our intended slavery, and to make our necks pliable for to undergo the yoke, they got and forbid to our own countrymen, to hold any correspondency, commerce, or traffic with us, nor to suffer any to come at us, but such who have obtained particular licences from some persons, who are expressly ordered for that purpose, by whose means it might be brought about, that no other goods or merchandizes shall be brought hither, than such as the licensed persons shall please and think fit to give way to; and that they are to sell the same at such a price, as they shall please to impose on them; and suffer no other ships to come hither but their own: As likewise that no inhabitants of this island may send home upon their own account any island goods of this place,

---

2. The Netherlands. In the early days, it was the chief supplier of equipment and slaves and purchaser or exporter of the sugar crops.

but shall be as slaves to the Company, who shall have the abovesaid licenses, and submit to them the whole advantage of our labour and industry.[3]

Wherefore, having rightly considered, we declare, that as we would not be wanting to use all honest means for the obtaining of a continuance of commerce, trade, and good correspondence with our country, so we will not alienate ourselves from those old heroic virtues of true English men, to prostitute our freedom and privileges, to which we are born, to the will and opinion of any one; neither do we think our number so contemptible, nor our resolution so weak, to be forced or persuaded to so ignoble a submission, *and we cannot think, that there are any amongst us, who are so simple, and so unworthily minded, that they would not rather choose a noble death, than forsake their old liberties and privileges.*[4]

JOHN LOCKE

From *Two Treatises of Government* (1690)†

[John Locke (1632–1704) was an influential thinker in a range of fields, but he is perhaps best known for defining the modern constitutional state and the right of private property. His basic theory of the natural rights of all persons to life and liberty (requisite for preserving life) and secondarily to property, as the fruit of one's own labor, would provide powerful arguments against slavery. Yet while he pronounced slavery immediately repugnant to English or gentle minds, Locke himself allowed it a settled—if marginalized and unattractive—place.

Commentators note that Locke was a colonial administrator and investor, that he had drafted the Carolina Constitutions granting "absolute power" over slaves, and that he also did not enlarge the political power of unpropertied men or women. In the theory of "just war," he chose a classic defense more compatible with Christian doctrine than arguments about profit, custom, or natural inferiority, although he does not let us picture whether the justified reprisals are by Africans against Africans, perhaps all considered similarly belligerent, or by the trading company. At any rate, since the slaves are understood to have forfeited life and liberty, their condition is beyond appeal. Perhaps Locke was not thinking about slavery at all but fitting an existing institution into his scheme. The violations that most concern him are those by absolute rulers—specifically Charles II and James II—against the people, and his "Second Treatise" served to justify James's overthrow by the Whig revolution of 1688. Or perhaps, as sociol-

---

3. A copy published in the eighteenth century, in Grey's edition of Daniel Neal's *History of the Puritans* (1739), makes this analogy explicit: "just as our Negroes are to us."
4. A slightly different version printed in the Netherlands in 1651 ends, "And we cannot imagine that there is so mean and baseminded a fellow amongst us, that will not prefer an honourable death before a tedious and slavish life." See Nicholas Darnell Davis, *The Cavaliers & Roundheads of Barbados, 1650–1652* (Geogetown, British Guiana, 1887), 200.
† First published anonymously in 1690, with many later revisions. This text is taken from the 1764 edition, which most fully incorporated Locke's changes.

ogist Orlando Patterson suggests, it was precisely the men who knew slavery directly who most clearly and sharply defined freedom.]

From *The First Treatise*

1. THE INTRODUCTION:

§. 1. Slavery is so vile and miserable an estate of man, and so directly opposite to the generous temper and courage of our nation, that 'tis hardly to be conceived, that an *Englishman*, much less a *Gentleman*, should plead for't. And truly, I should have taken Sir Robert Filmer's *Patriarcha*,[1] as any other treatise, which would persuade all men that they are slaves and ought to be so, for such another exercise of wit as was his who writ the encomium of *Nero*,[2] rather than for a serious discourse, meant in earnest, had not the gravity of the title and epistle, the picture in the front of the book, and the applause that followed it, required me to believe that the author and publisher were both in earnest. * * *

§. 2. * * * His system lies in a little compass, 'tis no more but this,

That all government is absolute monarchy.

And the ground he builds on is this,

That no man is born free.

§. 3. In this last age a generation of men has sprung up amongst us, that would flatter princes with an opinion that they have a divine right to absolute power, let the laws by which they are constituted and are to govern, and the conditions under which they enter upon their authority, be what they will, and their engagements to observe them never so well ratified by solemn oaths and promises. To make way for this doctrine, they have denied mankind a right to natural freedom, whereby they have not only, as much as in them lies, exposed all subjects to the utmost misery of tyranny and oppression, but have also unsettled the titles, and shaken the thrones of princes (for they too, by these men's system, except only one, are all born slaves, and by divine right are subjects to *Adam's* right heir); as if they had designed to make war upon all government, and subvert the very foundations of human society, to serve their present turn.

§. 4. However we must believe them upon their own bare words, when they tell us, we are all born slaves, and we must continue so; there is no remedy for it. Life and thraldom we entered into together, and can never be quit of the one, till we part with the other. Scripture

---

1. Filmer's treatise, written in the late 1630s and published in 1680, defended absolute monarchy as an extension of the paternal authority granted by God to Adam. Locke's "First Treatise" is devoted to refuting Filmer's line of argument.
2. Jerome Cardan, whose mock encomium to Nero appeared in 1546.

or reason I am sure do not any where say so, notwithstanding the noise of divine right, as if divine authority hath subjected us to the unlimited will of another.

*   *   *

From *The Second Treatise: Of Civil Government*

*   *   *

OF THE STATE OF NATURE

§. 4. To understand political power right, and derive it from its original, we must consider, what state all men are naturally in, and that is, *a state of perfect freedom* to order their actions, and dispose of their possessions and persons, as they think fit, within the bounds of the law of nature, without asking leave, or depending upon the will of any other man.

A *state* also of *equality*, wherein all the power and jurisdiction is reciprocal, no one having more than another; there being nothing more evident, than that creatures of the same species and rank, promiscuously born to all the same advantages of nature, and the use of the same faculties, should also be equal one amongst another without subordination or subjection, unless the Lord and Master of them all should, by any manifest declaration of his will, set one above another, and confer on him, by an evident and clear appointment, an undoubted right to dominion and sovereignty.

*   *   *

§. 6. *   *   * The *state of nature* has a law of nature to govern it, which obliges every one: and reason, which is that law, teaches all mankind, who will but consult it, that being all *equal and independent,* no one ought to harm another in his life, health, liberty, or possessions: for men being all the workmanship of one omnipotent, and infinitely wise Maker; all the servants of one sovereign Master, sent into the world by his order, and about his business; they are his property, whose workmanship they are, made to last during his, not one another's pleasure: and being furnished with like faculties, sharing all in one community of nature, there cannot be supposed any such *subordination* among us, that may authorize us to destroy one another, as if we were made for one another's uses, as the inferior ranks of creatures are for ours. Every one, as he is *bound to preserve himself*, and not to quit his station wilfully, so by the like reason, when his own preservation comes not in competition, ought he, as much as he can, *to preserve the rest of mankind*, and may not, unless it be to do justice on an offender, take away, or impair the life, or what tends to the preservation of the life, the liberty, health, limb, or goods of another.

§. 7. And that all men may be restrained from invading others' rights, and from doing hurt to one another, and the law of nature be observed, which willeth the peace and *preservation of all mankind,* the *execution* of the law of nature is, in that state, put into every man's hands, whereby every one has a right to punish the transgressors of that law to such a degree, as may hinder its violation: for the *law of nature* would, as all other laws that concern men in this world, be in vain, if there were no body that in the state of nature had a *power to execute* that law, and thereby preserve the innocent and restrain offenders. And if any one in the state of nature may punish another for any evil he has done, every one may do so: for in that *state of perfect equality,* where naturally there is no superiority or jurisdiction of one over another, what any may do in prosecution of that law, every one must needs have a right to do.

§. 8. And thus, in the state of nature, *one man comes by a power over another;* but yet no absolute or arbitrary power, to use a criminal, when he has got him in his hands, according to the passionate heats, or boundless extravagancy of his own will; but only to retribute to him, so far as calm reason and conscience dictate, what is proportionate to his transgression, which is so much as may serve for *reparation* and *restraint:* for these two are the only reasons, why one man may lawfully do harm to another, which is that we call *punishment.* In transgressing the law of nature, the offender declares himself to live by another rule than that of reason and common equity, which is that measure God has set to the actions of men, for their mutual security; and so he becomes dangerous to mankind, the tie, which is to secure them from injury and violence, being slighted and broken by him. Which being a trespass against the whole species, and the peace and safety of it, provided for by the law of nature, every man upon this score, by the right he hath to preserve mankind in general, may restrain, or where it is necessary, destroy things noxious to them, and so may bring such evil on any one, who hath transgressed that law, as may make him repent the doing of it, and thereby deter him, and by his example others, from doing the like mischief. And in the case, and upon this ground, *every man hath a right to punish the offender, and be executioner of the law of nature.*

* * *

OF THE STATE OF WAR

* * *

§. 17. And hence it is, that he who attempts to get another man into his absolute power, does thereby *put himself into a state of war* with him; it being to be understood as a declaration of a design upon his life: for I have reason to conclude, that he who would get me into his power without my consent, would use me as he pleased when he had got me there, and destroy me too when he had a fancy to it; for no body can desire to *have me in his absolute power*, unless it be to compel me by force to that which is against the right of my freedom, *i. e.* make me a slave. To be free from such force is the only security of my preservation; and reason bids me look on him, as an enemy to my preservation, who would take away that *freedom* which is the fence to it; so that he who makes an *attempt to enslave* me, thereby puts himself into a state of war with me. He that, in the state of nature, *would take away the freedom* that belongs to any one in that state, must necessarily be supposed to have a design to take away every thing else, that *freedom* being the foundation of all the rest; as he that, in the state of society, would take away the *freedom* belonging to those of that society or commonwealth, must be supposed to design to take away from them every thing else, and so be looked on as *in a state of war*.

§. 18. This makes it lawful for a man to *kill a thief*, who has not in the least hurt him, nor declared any design upon his life, any farther than, by the use of force, so to get him in his power, as to take away his money, or what he pleases, from him; because using force, where he has no right, to get me into his power, let his pretence be what it will, I have no reason to suppose, that he, who would *take away my liberty*, would not, when he had me in his power, take away every thing else. And therefore it is lawful for me to treat him as one who has *put himself into a state of war* with me, *i. e.* kill him if I can; for to that hazard does he justly expose himself, whoever introduces a state of war, and is aggressor in it.

§. 19. And here we have the plain *difference between the state of nature and the state of war*, which however some men have confounded, are as far distant, as a state of peace, good will, mutual assistance and preservation, and a state of enmity, malice, violence and mutual destruction, are one from another. Men living together according to reason, without a common superior on earth, with authority to judge between them, is *properly the state of nature*. But force, or a declared design of force, upon the person of another, where there is no common superior on earth to appeal to for relief, *is the state of war*: and it is the want of such an appeal gives a man the right of war even against an *aggressor*, tho' he be in society and a fellow subject.

* * *

OF SLAVERY

§. 22. The *natural liberty* of man is to be free from any superior power on earth, and not to be under the will or legislative authority of man, but to have only the law of nature for his rule. The *liberty of man*, in society, is to be under no other legislative power, but that established, by consent, in the commonwealth; nor under the dominion of any will, or restraint of any law, but what that legislative shall enact, according to the trust put in it. * * * *Freedom of men under government* is to have a standing rule to live by, common to every one of that society, and made by the legislative power erected in it, a liberty to follow my own will in all things, where the rule prescribes not; and not to be subject to the inconstant, uncertain, unknown, arbitrary will of another man; as *freedom of nature* is, to be under no other restraint but the law of nature.

§. 23. This *freedom* from absolute, arbitrary power, is so necessary to, and closely joined with a man's preservation, that he cannot part with it, but by what forfeits his preservation and life together: for a man, not having the power of his own life, *cannot*, by compact, or his own consent, *enslave himself* to any one, nor put himself under the absolute, arbitrary power of another, to take away his life, when he pleases. No body can give more power than he has himself; and he that cannot take away his own life, cannot give another power over it. Indeed, having by his fault forfeited his own life, by some act that deserves death, he, to whom he has forfeited it, may (when he has him in his power) delay to take it, and make use of him to his own service, and he does him no injury by it: for, whenever he finds the hardship of his slavery outweigh the value of his life, it is in his power, by resisting the will of his master, to draw on himself the death he desires.

§. 24. This is the perfect condition of *slavery*, which is nothing else, but *the state of war continued, between a lawful conqueror and a captive*: for, if once *compact* enter between them, and make an agreement for a limited power on the one side, and obedience on the other, the *state of war and slavery* ceases * * *

* * *

OF POLITICAL OR CIVIL SOCIETY

* * *

§. 85. *Master* and *servant* are names as old as history, but given to those of far different condition; for a freeman makes himself a servant to another, by selling him, for a certain time, the service he undertakes to do, in exchange for wages he is to receive: and though this commonly puts him into the family of his master, and under the ordinary discipline thereof, yet it gives the master but a temporary power over him, and no greater than what is contained in the *contract* between them. But there is another sort of servants, which by a peculiar name we call *slaves*, who being captives taken in a just war, are by the right of nature subjected to the absolute dominion and arbitrary power of their masters. These men having, as I say, forfeited their lives, and with it their liberties, and lost their estates; and being in the *state of slavery*, not capable of any property, cannot in that state be considered as any part of *civil society*; the chief end whereof is the preservation of property.

*   *   *

OF PATERNAL, POLITICAL, AND DESPOTICAL POWER

*   *   *

§. 172. *Thirdly, Despotical power* is an absolute, arbitrary power one man has over another, to take away his life, whenever he pleases. This is a power, which neither Nature gives, for it has made no such distinction between one man and another; nor compact can convey: for man not having such an arbitrary power over his own life, cannot give another man such a power over it; but it is the *effect only of forfeiture*, which the aggressor makes of his own life, when he puts himself into the state of war with another: for having quitted reason, which God hath given to be the rule betwixt man and man, and the common bond whereby human kind is united into one fellowship and society; and having renounced the way of peace which that teaches, and made use of the force of war, to compass his unjust ends upon another, where he has no right; and so revolting from his own kind to that of beasts, by making force, which is theirs, to be his rule of right, he renders himself liable to be destroyed by the injured person, and the rest of mankind, that will join with him in the execution of justice, as any other wild beast, or noxious brute, with whom mankind can have neither society nor security. And thus *captives*, taken in a just and lawful war, and such only, are *subject to a despotical power*, which, as it arises not from compact, so neither is it capable of any, but is the state of war continued: for what compact can be made with a man that is not master of his own life? What condition can he perform? And if he be once allowed to be master of his own life, the *despotical, arbitrary power* of his master ceases. He that is master of himself, and his own life, has a right too to the means of preserving it; so that *as soon as compact enters, slavery ceases*, and he so far quits his absolute power, and puts an end to the state of war, who enters into conditions with his captive.

*   *   *

OPINION IN PERIODICALS (1735)

The Speech of Moses Bon Sáam†

[Moses's speech was at once circulated in the January *Gentleman's Magazine* in somewhat shortened form, where it drew the angry counterblast by "Caribeus," and in the *London Magazine*. By summer it was translated by Abbé Prévost in his Paris periodical *Pour et Contre* (6), with some smoothing of its expressions of black-white antagonism. Prévost comments that the purported speech was presented and added to in so circumstantial a fashion that its readers are not able to say if it is fiction or not. The speech was reprinted again in 1736 by a Nevis planter along with his own example of an ex-slave's eloquence, *The Speech of Mr. John Talbot Campo-Bell, a Free Christian Negro, to his Countrymen in the Mountains of Jamaica*. In this and other writings, the planter, Robert Robertson, held that planters were at the mercy of those who ran the slave trade.

In its original context, the oration was introduced to illustrate Aaron Hill's satiric argument in *Prompter* 16 that nations, like individuals, denounce with high moral outrage what they have practiced and glorified in their own histories. The single lesson to be drawn from rebellions by oppressed slaves is not that those represent some unnatural villainy, but that since they can be expected, the ratio of blacks to whites should be controlled by greater use of England's unemployed poor. This was a current issue, especially in Jamaica; planters had circumvented the laws limiting slave importation, and the black to white ratio of ten to one was higher than in any British colony, far higher than in the American South, where the slaves were rarely even a majority.

The form of the oration-in-a-letter seems suggested by a funeral speech by a black in an early antislavery pamphlet titled *A Letter from a Merchant at Jamaica to a Member of Parliament in London* (1709). That slave speaker invokes in Lockeian language the "plain and natural Right to Life and Liberty" and then proceeds to raise all the awkward questions that Locke did not regarding owners' cloudy legal titles, subhuman treatment of slaves, and right to hold their children. Escape or rebellion are fleeting thoughts, however, and he ends with a plaintive appeal to God and enlightened men. Moses's speech combines pathos with menace. Justified by some bold Bible reading, he is a rebel strategist who gives voice to the points in Hill's history lesson about the dangers from the slaves' superior numbers, greater physical hardiness, and especially the new arts and skills in which their masters have trained them.

In January 1735 this was more than provocative. Desertions and disorders

---

† From *The Prompter* 18, Friday, January 10, 1735. *Prompter* 18 is announced in *Prompter* 16 as received by an "Eminent Merchant" from an island colony threatened by slave revolt, i.e., Jamaica. Number 18 is the first of many *Prompters* that do not bear an identifying initial of either of the editors, Aaron Hill and William Popple. The partial modernizing of the text here includes the moderating of its very heavy and histrionic use of italics. *The Prompter* (1734–36) was a paper that concentrated on theater news and criticism, and both Hill and Popple were playwrights.

were at their height. Large planters not directly affected had been slow to cooperate; the militia was untrained, the arms supply poor, the regiments sent from home ineffective, and the colony demoralized. Report after report came back to the Council of Trade and Plantations, in December 1734, for example, that "the terror of the rebels spreads itself everywhere," making planters "abandon their settlements," fear correcting their slaves, mount constant guard, and avoid the roads; while fresh manpower and captured arms have "so raised the courage of the negroes and depressed that of the white men, that whereas five of the latter would formerly have frightened fifteen blacks, the case was at present so much reversed, that five negroes would be able to frighten fifteen white men" (*Calendar of State Papers, Colonial,* 1734–35, No. 413). The reports came to the council's secretary, the older brother of *Prompter* coeditor William Popple, who in 1737 took over that post himself. But the news was general. The *London Magazine* that carried Moses's speech also carried the latest bulletin:

> From *Jamaica*: That the rebellious Negroes were got to a surprising Head, and increas'd daily by the Desertion of their Brethren from the several Plantations; and that the long expected Troops from *Gibraltar* not being then arriv'd, the Assembly had made a Martial Law, which oblig'd all the Inhabitants without respect of Persons, capable of bearing Arms, to appear in the Defence of the Island, which was threaten'd with total Destruction if not quickly prevented; so that all Business there was at a Stand.]

> This is a BLACK!—*Beware* of him, good *Countrymen.*
> Horace[1]

In Discharge of a Promise, which I made in my 16th Paper, I publish the Speech of *Moses Bon Sáam,* a *Free Negro,* at the Head of those revolted Slaves, who have betaken themselves to the Mountains, in one of the most considerable Colonies of the West Indies.[2] * * *

Dear Fellows in Arms, and Brothers in Adversity!
    Had Your Sufferings been less painful, I might have enjoyed my own Ease, in an Exemption from Danger.—But in vain did my Courage once exerted, as you have heard, in Defence of a Master, redeem me from the Name of a Slave! I found no Blessing in Freedom, tormented with a livelier Sense of Your Groans, because no longer a *Partaker* of Your Misery.
    While I was, formerly, One of your Number, and but a Wretch, among Wretches, I wanted Sentiments to reflect with Justness on the

---

1. From *Satires* 1.4.85, warning against the black souls of slanderers and rumor-mongers.
2. Jamaica. There had been escaped slaves, or Maroons, living in the mountains since Spanish times, making periodic attacks and providing a haven for runaways. The first Maroon War of 1730–39 was a prolonged conflict against at least two large armed bands in the interior, who incited widespread desertions and proved impossible to dislodge. After a decade the British had to recognize them by treaty, giving them freedom, land, and trading privileges, with the proviso that in future they return escaped slaves.

Wrongs we were accustom'd to suffer.—Whether ignorant of the Bliss of Others, I discern'd not my own Misery; or that the Part I was condemn'd to bear, in so General a Calamity, had deaden'd in my Heart that Pity which has been awaken'd by my Change of Fortune.—But I have *since* been taught your Wretchedness, by Sixteen Years of Liberty: By Sixteen Years, not spent in *Ease* and *Luxury*, like the Lives of our Oppressors, but in long, laborious Diligence in Pursuit of their *Arts* and *Capacity*; whereby to know, and to make known, that only Education, and Accident, not Difference of *Genius*, have been the Cause of this provoking Superiority, that bids the Pride of a *White* Man despise and trample on a *Black* one.

What Preference, in the Name of that mysterious GOD, whom these Insulters of Our Colour pretend to worship and confide in, what wild imaginary Superiority of Dignity, has their pale, sickly, *Whiteness* to boast of, when compar'd with our *Majestic Glossiness*!—If there is Merit in Delicacy, we have Skins as soft as their Velvets: If in Manliness, consider your Shape, your Strength, and your Movement! Are they not, All, easier, firmer, and more graceful?—Let a *White* Man expose his feeble Face to the Winds; let him climb Hills, against Rains; let him go burn his uncover'd Temples, in the Heat of High Noon, as WE do.—Will He BEAR it, too, as we do? No: the Variations of his changeable Countenance will make manifest the Faintness he was born to.— He will be sick; and grow pale, and red, by Turns: He will be haggard, rough, and Sun-burnt.—Tho' terrible and haughty to his *Slaves*, he will lose all Fierceness in his Eye, by the smallest Struggle with those *Elements* which WE are Proof against the Rage of.

The whole Advantage, then, of these proud *Spoilers* of the Work of GOD, who dare make *Beasts* of human Forms, as noble, and more manly, than their own, in what consists it, but superior *Happiness*?[3]— They are not wiser by *Nature*, but more exercis'd in *Art*, than We are. They are not *braver*; but they are more *crafty*, and assist their Anger by *Discipline*. They have Rules and Modes, in War, which actuate, as by One attentive and obedient *Soul*, the most numerous *Bodies* of arm'd People.—While WE, depriv'd of such Improvement to our native Boldness, and acting resolutely, but not dependently, *Divide* and *Lose* our Firmness.—You saw the Representation of it, but last Week, in an Example from this neighbouring River: as if the God that animates your Purpose had commanded it to overflow, for your Instruction, and your Warning!—Observe, how *narrow* it looks, at present, yet because it runs confin'd, within its Banks, hark! How roaringly it rushes down, upon the Low-Lands of our Enemy! And with how steady, and resistless, a Torrent!—The other Day, you saw it *broader*; for it rose among the Woods, and almost floated our Savannah. But was it the Louder, for

3. Good fortune.

such Breadth? Was it, then, *thus foaming*, and thus *terrible?*—Far from it; you can, All, remember, as I do, that it was, then, *flat*—*tame*—and *muddy*, and had neither *Violence*, nor *Tendency*.

As soon as I became able to read, I discover'd, in the *Holiest* of all Books, in the Fountain of White Men's Religion; I discover'd there, with a Mixture of Amazement and prophetic Joy, that the very Man from whom they deriv'd the *Name* they had given me, of MOSES, had been the happy *Deliverer* of a *Nation!*—Of a Nation, chosen, and be-lov'd, by GOD! the Deliverer of this chosen Nation, from just such a Slavery as *Ours!* Just so, unfair, oppressive, and unnatural; and in every Act, and Circumstance, resembling that which You and your Forefa-thers have groan'd under.—Innumerable Thousands of his Captive Countrymen were as darkly ignorant as You are, all unknowing their own Rights, and forc'd, like you, to labour, for ungrateful and merciless Masters. Till this first *Moses*, this Great Giver of *my* Name, was called out by Heaven;[4] and, thro' a Course of miraculous Events, instructed in the *Arts* and *Learning*, of those insolent Enslavers: that, so, He might be worthy, in the Fullness of *God's Time*, to stand out, His *Instrument*, for the Redemption of a *People*.

What now will our Task-masters pretend to object, against the *Law-fulness* of our Revolt?—If they say that Our Forefathers were Slaves? So were the Ancestors of those Heroes whom *their Moses*, their almost worship'd MOSES, deliver'd from Slavery.—Will they urge, *that they have paid a Price; and therefore, claim us as their Property?*—Grant them the Life of a *First* unhappy Captive, to repay this Claim of his proud Purchaser.—But did they also *buy* his *Race?*—Must the Children's Chil-dren, of this Wretch's Children, be begotten, and transmitted to *Slavery*, because that single Wretch Himself was unsuccessful in a Battle, and had been put to Sale, instead of Slaughter?

Perish the provoking Image of so shameless a Pretension!—Let them recollect, how soon the Profits, which they too well knew to make, from any One of our poor Father's Toils, repaid them for his barbarous Purchase.—Let them tell us (if they dare see *Truth*, in any Light that shows them not their *Interest*) whether all the *Pomp*, the *Pride*, the *Wantonness*, of that Prosperity we see them live in is not the Purchase of *our* Sweat, *our* Tears, and *our* Distresses?—And shall they derive their very *Luxury* from Wretches to whom they grudge the *Bread* of Nourishment?—Shall they rejoice, but by *our* Affliction, yet deny their Pity to our Agonies?

Indulge me, Dear Friends! Your Permission, to stop here, and WEEP.—I know, it is a Weakness. And It shall possess me but a Mo-ment. I will recover my Voice as soon as I am able, and go on, to enumerate your Miseries!

4. In Exodus 3–14 and Acts 7.22–36, God commands and then steadily guides Moses's deliv-erance of the Israelites from Egyptian bondage. According to Acts 7.22, "Moses was learned in all the wisdom of the Egyptians."

Alas! It is not *Possible*—It is *too terrible* a Task!—I have neither Patience, nor Breath enough to find Names for your Sorrows!—Would to Heaven I could as easily banish them from my Memory, as I can forbear to disgrace you, by their Description!—But *Fancy* will not suffer me to forget them.—Imagination, officious to torment me, invades my Sleep with your Shriekings.—My very Dreams are made bloody by your Whips.—I am insulted by the Scoffs, the Cruelties, the grinding, biting, Insolence, which we train up our poor Children to the Taste of!—Why rejoic'd we, at their Birth, unhappy, innocent *Bleeders?*—Or, why do they smile in our Faces, since we intend them but for Anguish and Agony?—Yet, they *know*, we have *no Comfort* to give them.—Such as is ours, they INHERIT!—Happier Parents bequeath Money, and Vanity, and Indolence, to their Offspring.—Alas!—These are Legacies for FREEMEN!—We have Nothing, but our *Shame*, to bestow on our Posterity; Nothing, but the *Shame* of our *Baseness*, who have lengthen'd out our Slavery to out-last even Life, by assigning them our Children, on whom to practise our Tortures.—But I have done with the Horrors of this Subject: You have awaken'd me, by that lamentable Howl, into a Repentance that I touch'd you, *too sensibly.*—Let us think then no more upon what we *have suffered.*—Let us resolve, to *suffer no longer.*

In the Fastnesses of these inaccessible Mountains, and among Forests, so dark and impenetrable, we shall have Little to fear, if we but continue on the *Defensive.* Here are Savannahs, for Cattle, and burnt Woods, for Corn. And as Other Things, which we have not, shall be wanted, there are so many Outlets and Descents on every Side, for Excursion, that we can break down, unexpected, upon the scatter'd Plantations below us; and return, with whatever we wish, from the Store-houses of our Enemy.—Let us therefore repress Malice, and Cruelty: Let us rather study to support our *new Liberty*, than revenge our *past Slavery.*—While we train and confirm our Forces, by the Discipline and Exercise they are beginning to practise, we shall grow stronger, both by our *Skill*, and our *Numbers*: For All, of our Colour, whose Hearts have not *whiten'd* themselves, in Terror of their Imperious Torturers, will borrow Safety from the Night, and escape to us from Every Quarter. Or, should such Opportunities be taken from them, by the Vigilance of their Masters, we can encourage, and draw them with us, as often as we make Incursions, thereby weakening at once our Enemy, and encreasing our own Strength, till our very *Numbers* shall have made us *invincible.*

*   *   *

Let us understand then, and accept *God's Bounty*. Let us divide, and appropriate, the High-lands. Let us plant, and possess, for Posterity.—Cultivating *Law*, too, as well as *Land*, let us, by submitting to Government, become too *generous* for *Slavery.*—As often as the Enemy, from the Coasts of the Island, shall attempt to dislodge us from its Centre, let 'em find us too *strong* for their *Anger*. But if they content themselves with their own, and leave us in Possession of our Lot, let them acknowledge us *too kind* for their *Cruelty*.

* * *

The Answer of Caribeus to Moses Bon Sáam†

["M." or "Caribeus" casts Moses as a fraudulent prophet of liberty in language that recalls Milton's characterization of Satan in *Paradise Lost*. His paternalistic argument, however, is not unusual. Following a major revolt in Antigua the next year, yet another to originate among Cormantine or Coromantee slaves, the writers of the published report evidently foresaw that there would be sympathy for the slaves "in those happy Kingdoms, where Slavery is look'd upon with just Indignation." Explaining that slavery is "not our Choice, but Necessity," they employ a similar model: the masters are benefactors; the slaves, therefore, traitors:

> the Slavery of our Negroes is merely nominal . . . their Labour more moderate, and their manner of living more comfortable than the poor Inhabitants of the freest Countries. . . . it appeared to us that mere Lust of Power, and unbounded Ambition were the only Incentives to their unnatural Rebellion, even tho' their Condition in our Colonies is a State of perfect Freedom, compared to the native Slavery of their own Country (A *Genuine Narrative of the Intended Conspiracy of the Negroes at Antigua*, Dublin, 1737, 17–18).]

I cannot imagine Mr. *Urban*[1] will refuse the following Speech a Place in his Magazine (if not for its own Merit) in Justice to our Fellow-Subjects of the Colonies, falsely accused of Cruelty and Oppression by the *Prompter*, who, under Pretense of favouring Liberty, justifies the Rebellion of fugitive Negroes now actually on foot, even tho' his Majesty has sent a Regiment to assist the Inhabitants in suppressing it. What a Compliment that is to the Crown, and how consistent with his pretended Loyalty let that Writer determine. It is my Endeavour only to convince the World of a common *Mistake, that those Negroes are under the most miserable Slavery*, by showing from the very Nature of that Government, and the Reason of Things, that their Masters are restrained from Cruelty, both by the Laws, and their own Interest; and that the Negroes are much happier than in their native Country; much happier than the Bulk of Mankind; nay, than the poor Labourers of *England*.

But as a farther Confutation of the *Prompter*'s Charge against our Fellow-Subjects of America as being *cruel Oppressors*, I appeal to all Gentlemen that ever resided there, but a short Time: Let them say,

---

† From *The Gentleman's Magazine*, February 1735, pp. 91–92.
1. The editor's pseudonym was Mr. Sylvanus Urban, roughly "Mr. Country and Town."

whether the Generality of those Inhabitants, are not the most generous, humane, hospitable People in the World; and whether the following Speech of *Caribeus*, Chief of the *Whites*, or that of *Moses Bon Sáam*, Chief of the *Blacks*, be founded in Truth, and Fact.

Arch Rebel! Dost thou boast the sacred Name of *Moses*, armed by the Authority of God, delivering *Israel's* Sons from lawless Tyranny, and *Egyptian* Bondage? How unlike art Thou, Seducer; endeavouring by subtle Arts, and feigned Grievances, to withdraw *that* unthinking Multitude from honest Industry, to a Life of Indolence and Rapine? Is this the Effect of your boasted Knowledge thus to become *inhuman*? Is this the Fruit of Liberty obtained from a generous Master, whose Life it was your Duty to defend, even tho' Humanity had not enjoined? Is it a just Reward for his kind Manumission to make intestine War with him, his Friends, and Fellow-Subjects, under the specious Show of Liberty, whereof you have a larger Share than half Mankind?—To whom are you indebted for this Blessing?—To the honest Merchant, that first redeemed you from *native Slavery* to *savage Tyrants* of your own Complexion, and planted you here in easy Servitude. Is there in *such a Change* the Want of Liberty?—You confess indeed the Purchaser entitled to your Labour, but avow that your Posterity should be exempt: Are not your Children nursed, and fed, and reared to Man's Estate, at *as great Expense*, and is not that *as just a Purchase* of their Labour too?—Where is the equitable Difference between the Purchase of Labour for a Day, for Years, or for a Life? I see not any. * * *

Behold the Bulk of Mankind who live by labour, and support the Luxury and Grandeur of a *Few*: Alas! your Labours *cannot* feed such pampered Luxury!—View your Fellow-Subjects, the *European* Vulgar, struggling with Hunger, cold Poverty, and a colder Climate; how hard their Labour? Twofold Worse than yours; yet they bequeath no other Fortune to their Children, besides Penury and Rags; leaving them to the wide World, unregarded, Guardianless, to starve, or beg (if begging can obtain) their Bread. But these are called the Sons of Liberty: Free indeed they are to work, or starve!—Far better is your low Condition under serener Skies; clothed by a kind Master's Care, fed by his bounteous Hand: Your Labours gentle: Your Repast at Morn, at Noon, at Night, grateful, wholesome, plentiful: Your Repose sweet, uninterrupted with To-morrow's Cares. Those are your Master's Portion! * * *

Yet ye complain, ungrateful! But ill-suiting such Complaints, your proud Leader boasts your Strength, Activity, velvet Skins, and glossy Countenance: Are these the natural Effects of bloody Whips and Hardship; or of Ease, Exercise, and Plenty?—So reasons your deluding Chief, and vaunts as preferable to Ours, his sooty Visage. Thus may the gloom of Night compare to cheerful Day; or Guilt atrocious vie with snow-white Innocence! But I forbear, my Friends.—Merit consisteth not in the Complexion's dye: It takes its rise much deeper, from the low Recesses of the Heart. When that is fortified by strict *Integrity*, and warmed with the *Love of Virtue and Benevolence*, it dignifies the Man with *real Merit*, whether in humble, or exalted Life; whether in giving, or obeying Laws.—But what Pretence to fair Virtue has the apostate *Moses*? Not because he is ungrateful to his Benefactors: Not because he prompts you to Rapine, Murder, and Rebellion, to gratify his Lust of Rule, and make you tenfold more his Slaves!—The View is obvious; for he seduceth you from your own Happiness, from an easy Service, and Subjection to the peaceful Laws (which he calls Slavery) only to exalt himself a Mountain Tyrant, and rule his Fellows with the iron Rod of his despotic Will.—I see your Fears of this new Tyrant are justly alarmed; and read in each softened Brow the Tokens of an happy Return to Reason and Humanity.

※　※　※

But withhold your just Vengeance!—Stay your uplifted Hands, and stain them not with his contaminated Blood!—Seize him only, and deliver him to the Civil Magistrate, who will pronounce his Doom, by the just Measures of the Law, too mild for such flagitious[2] Crimes.

Now, my deluded Friends, grown Wise by sad Experience, return to your much injured Masters, whom you know are always ready to forgive as you to ask Forgiveness: Return to honest Labour, and the peaceful Blessings of domestic Life. Learn from this base Revolt to shun the fatal Snares of wild Ambition, and contentedly possess the happy, humble Lot assigned to you by Heaven, heaping the Fruits of honest Industry into your kind Master's Lap, to be reserved for him, and you, and yours, as need requires.　　　M.

SAMUEL JOHNSON

[To Boswell: Dictated Brief to Free a Slave (1777)][†]

[Famous as the companion and biographer of the dominant man of letters of his time, thirty years his elder, Boswell was also a lawyer with a practice in Edinburgh.]

2. Outrageous.
† From James Boswell, *The Life of Samuel Johnson*, vol. 3, ed. G. B. Hill, rev. L. F. Powell (Oxford, UK: Clarendon Press, 1934), 200–04. The editors' notes have been omitted.

SEPTEMBER 23, 1777

*   *   *

After supper I accompanied him to his apartment, and at my request he dictated to me an argument in favor of the Negro[1] who was then claiming his liberty, in an action in the Court of Session in Scotland. He had always been very zealous against slavery in every form, in which I with all deference thought that he discovered 'a zeal without knowledge.'[2] Upon one occasion, when in company with some very grave men at Oxford, his toast was, 'Here's to the next insurrection of the Negroes in the West Indies.' His violent prejudice against our West Indian and American settlers appeared whenever there was an opportunity. Towards the conclusion of his 'Taxation no Tyranny,' he says, 'how is it that we hear the loudest *yelps* for liberty among the drivers of Negroes?'

*   *   *

The argument dictated by Dr. Johnson was as follows:

'It must be agreed that in most ages many countries have had part of their inhabitants in a state of slavery; yet it may be doubted whether slavery can ever be supposed the natural condition of man. It is impossible not to conceive that men in their original state were equal; and very difficult to imagine how one would be subjected to another but by violent compulsion. An individual may, indeed, forfeit his liberty by a crime; but he cannot by that crime forfeit the liberty of his children. What is true of a criminal seems true likewise of a captive. A man may accept life from a conquering enemy on condition of perpetual servitude; but it is very doubtful whether he can entail[3] that servitude on his descendants; for no man can stipulate without commission for another. The condition which he himself accepts, his son or grandson perhaps would have rejected. If we should admit, what perhaps may with more reason be denied, that there are certain relations between man and man which may make slavery necessary and just, yet it can never be proved that he who is now suing for his freedom ever stood in any of those relations. He is certainly subject by no law, but that of violence, to his present master; who pretends no claim to his obedience, but that he bought him from a merchant of slaves, whose right to sell him never was examined. It is said that, according to the constitutions of Jamaica, he was legally en-

1. Joseph Knight, a slave in Jamaica brought to Scotland, who was determined to earn support for his family and leave his master. Originally he had been kidnapped. The majority of judges ruled for him, declaring Jamaican law unjust and not to be upheld in Scotland.
2. Romans 10.2: "For I bear them record that they have a zeal of God, but not according to knowledge."
3. Settle unalterably.

slaved; these constitutions are merely positive;[4] and apparently injurious to the rights of mankind, because whoever is exposed to sale is condemned to slavery without appeal; by whatever fraud or violence he might have been originally brought into the merchant's power. In our own time Princes have been sold,[5] by wretches to whose care they were entrusted, that they might have an European education; but when once they were brought to a market in the plantations, little would avail either their dignity or their wrongs. The laws of Jamaica afford a Negro no redress. His colour is considered as a sufficient testimony against him. It is to be lamented that moral right should ever give way to political convenience. But if temptations of interest are sometimes too strong for human virtue, let us at least retain a virtue where there is no temptation to quit it. In the present case there is apparent right on one side, and no convenience on the other. Inhabitants of this island can neither gain riches nor power by taking away the liberty of any part of the human species. The sum of the argument is this:—No man is by nature the property of another: The defendant is, therefore, by nature free: The rights of nature must be some way forfeited before they can be justly taken away: That the defendant has by any act forfeited the rights of nature we require to be proved; and if no proof of such forfeiture can be given, we doubt not but the justice of the court will declare him free.'

I record Dr. Johnson's argument fairly upon this particular case; where, perhaps, he was in the right. But I beg leave to enter my most solemn protest against his general doctrine with respect to the *Slave Trade*. For I will resolutely say—that his unfavourable notion of it was owing to prejudice, and imperfect or false information. The wild and dangerous attempt which has for some time been persisted in to obtain an act of our Legislature, to abolish so very important and necessary a branch of commercial interest, must have been crushed at once, had not the insignificance of the zealots who vainly took the lead in it made the vast body of Planters, Merchants, and others, whose immense properties are involved in that trade, reasonably enough suppose that there could be no danger. The encouragement which the attempt has received excites my wonder and indignation; and though some men of superior abilities have supported it; whether from a love of temporary popularity, when prosperous; or

---

4. Enacted formally or arbitrarily; not natural law. In his precedent-setting verdict in the 1772 case of the escaped slave James Somerset, the judge, Lord Mansfield, ruled that the enslavement and deportation of someone on English soil was "odious" and could not be supported "on any reasons, moral and political, but only by positive law." Apparently Joseph Knight had read of that decision.
5. Johnson would have been likely to know the reports on the "prince" of Annamabo in *The Gentleman's Magazine*, for which he was writer and assistant until the mid-1740s.

a love of general mischief, when desperate, my opinion is unshaken. To abolish a *status*, which in all ages GOD has sanctioned, and man has continued, would not only be *robbery* to an innumerable class of our fellow-subjects; but it would be extreme cruelty to the African savages, a portion of whom it saves from massacre, or intolerable bondage in their own country, and introduces into a much happier state of life; especially now when their passage to the West Indies and their treatment there is humanely regulated. To abolish that trade would be to

'—shut the gates of mercy on mankind.'[6]

*   *   *

OLAUDAH EQUIANO

From *The Life of Olaudah Equiano* (1789)[†]

[As a boy, Equiano (ca. 1745–1797) was kidnapped from an Ibo village in what is now eastern Nigeria by African slave raiders. He was sold to a British ship's master, who renamed him Gustavus Vassa—for the sixteenth-century hero-king who freed Sweden from the Danes—and took him on trading voyages, naval campaigns, and visits to England. He gained an education and was baptized, later becoming a devout Methodist. Resold to a Quaker merchant (the master described in the excerpt here), he eventually managed to purchase his freedom and then traveled widely in the Mediterranean and the Arctic as well as many of the American colonies. In London during the 1780s he became active in the abolitionist movement and was the principal spokesman for Africans living in Britain.]

*   *   *

The first object which saluted my eyes when I arrived on the coast was the sea, and a slave ship, which was then riding at anchor, and waiting for its cargo. These filled me with astonishment, which was soon converted into terror when I was carried on board. I was immediately handled and tossed up to see if I were sound by some of the crew; and I was now persuaded that I had gotten into a world of bad spirits, and that they were going to kill me. Their complexions too differing so much from ours, their long hair, and the language they spoke, (which was very different from any I had ever heard) united to confirm me in

---

6. Gray's *Elegy* line 68.
† From *The Interesting Narrative of the Life of Olaudah Equiano, or Gustavus Vassa, the African, Written by Himself* (London, 1789), vol. 1, 70–76, 204–10, 222–26; vol. 2, 246–55. Published in facsimile with an introduction by Paul Edwards (London: Dawsons of Pall Mall, 1969).

this belief. Indeed such were the horrors of my views and fears at the moment, that, if ten thousand worlds had been my own, I would have freely parted with them all to have exchanged my condition with that of the meanest slave in my own country. When I looked round the ship too and saw a large furnace or copper boiling, and a multitude of black people of every description chained together, every one of their countenances expressing dejection and sorrow, I no longer doubted of my fate; and, quite overpowered with horror and anguish, I fell motionless on the deck and fainted. When I recovered a little I found some black people about me, who I believed were some of those who brought me on board, and had been receiving their pay; they talked to me in order to cheer me, but all in vain. I asked them if we were not to be eaten by those white men with horrible looks, red faces, and loose hair. They told me I was not; and one of the crew brought me a small portion of spirituous liquor in a wine glass; but, being afraid of him, I would not take it out of his hand. One of the blacks therefore took it from him and gave it to me, and I took a little down my palate, which, instead of reviving me, as they thought it would, threw me into the greatest consternation at the strange feeling it produced, having never tasted any such liquor before. Soon after this the blacks who brought me on board went off, and left me abandoned to despair. I now saw myself deprived of all chance of returning to my native country, or even the least glimpse of hope of gaining the shore, which I now considered as friendly; and I even wished for my former slavery[1] in preference to my present situation, which was filled with horrors of every kind, still heightened by my ignorance of what I was to undergo. I was not long suffered to indulge my grief; I was soon put down under the decks, and there I received such a salutation in my nostrils as I had never experienced in my life: so that, with the loathsomeness of the stench, and crying together, I became so sick and low that I was not able to eat, nor had I the least desire to taste any thing. I now wished for the last friend, death, to relieve me; but soon, to my grief, two of the white men offered me eatables; and, on my refusing to eat, one of them held me fast by the hands, and laid me across I think the windlass, and tied my feet, while the other flogged me severely. I had never experienced any thing of this kind before; and although, not being used to the water, I naturally feared that element the first time I saw it, yet nevertheless, could I have got over the nettings, I would have jumped over the side, but I could not; and, besides, the crew used to watch us very closely who were not chained down to the decks, lest we should leap into the water: and I have seen some of these poor African prisoners most se-

---

1. Passing through many hands en route to the coast, he had been twice sold to African households.

verely cut for attempting to do so, and hourly whipped for not eating.
This indeed was often the case with myself. In a little time after,
amongst the poor chained men, I found some of my own nation, which
in a small degree gave ease to my mind. I inquired of these what was
to be done with us; they gave me to understand we were to be carried
to these white people's country to work for them. I then was a little
revived, and thought, if it were no worse than working, my situation
was not so desperate: but still I feared I should be put to death, the
white people looked and acted, as I thought, in so savage a manner;
for I had never seen among any people such instances of brutal cruelty;
and this not only shewn towards us blacks, but also to some of the
whites themselves. One white man in particular I saw, when we were
permitted to be on deck, flogged so unmercifully with a large rope near
the foremast, that he died in consequence of it; and they tossed him
over the side as they would have done a brute. This made me fear these
people the more; and I expected nothing less than to be treated in the
same manner. * * *

My master was several times offered by different gentlemen one hundred guineas for me; but he always told them he would not sell me, to
my great joy: and I used to double my diligence and care for fear of
getting into the hands of those men who did not allow a valuable slave
the common support of life. Many of them even used to find fault with
my master for feeding his slaves so well as he did; although I often
went hungry, and an Englishman might think my fare very indifferent;
but he used to tell them he always would do it, because the slaves
thereby looked better and did more work.

While I was thus employed by my master I was often a witness to
cruelties of every kind, which were exercised on my unhappy fellow
slaves. I used frequently to have different cargoes of new Negroes in
my care for sale; and it was almost a constant practice with our clerks,
and other whites, to commit violent depredations on the chastity of the
female slaves; and these I was, though with reluctance, obliged to submit to at all times, being unable to help them. When we have had
some of these slaves on board my master's vessels to carry them to other
islands, or to America, I have known our mates to commit these acts
most shamefully, to the disgrace, not of Christians only, but of men. I
have even known them to gratify their brutal passion with females not
ten years old; and these abominations some of them practised to such
scandalous excess, that one of our captains discharged the mate and
others on that account. And yet in Montserrat I have seen a Negro man
staked to the ground, and cut most shockingly, and then his ears cut
off bit by bit, because he had been connected with a white woman
who was a common prostitute: as if it were no crime in the whites to
rob an innocent African girl of her virtue; but most heinous in a black

man only to gratify a passion of nature, where the temptation was offered by one of a different colour, though the most abandoned woman of her species. Another Negro man was half hanged, and then burnt, for attempting to poison a cruel overseer. Thus by repeated cruelties are the wretched first urged to despair, and then murdered, because they still retain so much of human nature about them as to wish to put an end to their misery, and retaliate on their tyrants! These overseers are indeed for the most part persons of the worst character of any denomination of men in the West Indies. Unfortunately, many humane gentlemen, by not residing on their estates, are obliged to leave the management of them in the hands of these human butchers, who cut and mangle the slaves in a shocking manner on the most trifling occasions, and altogether treat them in every respect like brutes. They pay no regard to the situation of pregnant women, nor the least attention to the lodging of the field Negroes. Their huts, which ought to be well covered, and the place dry where they take their little repose, are often open sheds, built in damp places; so that, when the poor creatures return tired from the toils of the field, they contract many disorders, from being exposed to the damp air in this uncomfortable state, while they are heated, and their pores are open. This neglect certainly conspires with many others to cause a decrease in the births as well as in the lives of the grown Negroes. I can quote many instances of gentlemen who reside on their estates in the West Indies, and then the scene is quite changed; the Negroes are treated with lenity and proper care, by which their lives are prolonged, and their masters are profited. To the honour of humanity, I knew several gentlemen who managed their estates in this manner; and they found that benevolence was their true interest. And, among many I could mention in several of the islands, I knew one in Montserrat whose slaves looked remarkably well, and never needed any fresh supplies of Negroes; and there are many other estates, especially in Barbados, which, from such judicious treatment, need no fresh stock of Negroes at any time. I have the honour of knowing a most worthy and humane gentleman,[2] who is a native of Barbados, and has estates there. This gentleman has written a treatise on the usage of his own slaves. He allows them two hours for refreshment at mid-day; and many other indulgencies and comforts, particularly in their lying; and, besides this, he raises more provisions on his estate than they can destroy; so that by these attentions he saves the lives of his Negroes, and keeps them healthy, and as happy as the condition of slavery can admit. I myself, as shall appear in the sequel, managed an estate, where, by those attentions, the Negroes were uncommonly cheerful and healthy, and did more work by half than by the common mode of treatment

2. Sir Philip Gibbe, Baronet, Barbados [Equiano's note].

they usually do. For want, therefore, of such care and attention to the poor Negroes, and otherwise oppressed as they are, it is no wonder that the decrease should require 20,000 new Negroes annually to fill up the vacant places of the dead.

*   *   *

Nor was such usage as this confined to particular places or individuals; for, in all the different islands in which I have been (and I have visited no less than fifteen) the treatment of the slaves was nearly the same; so nearly indeed, that the history of an island, or even a plantation, with a few such exceptions as I have mentioned, might serve for a history of the whole. Such a tendency has the slave-trade to debauch men's minds, and harden them to every feeling of humanity! For I will not suppose that the dealers in slaves are born worse than other men—No; it is the fatality of this mistaken avarice, that it corrupts the milk of human kindness and turns it into gall. And, had the pursuits of those men been different, they might have been as generous, as tender-hearted and just, as they are unfeeling, rapacious and cruel. Surely this traffic cannot be good, which spreads like a pestilence, and taints what it touches! which violates that first natural right of mankind, equality and independency, and gives one man a dominion over his fellows which God could never intend! For it raises the owner to a state as far above man as it depresses the slave below it; and, with all the presumption of human pride, sets a distinction between them, immeasurable in extent, and endless in duration! Yet how mistaken is the avarice even of the planters? Are slaves more useful by being thus humbled to the condition of brutes, than they would be if suffered to enjoy the privileges of men? The freedom which diffuses health and prosperity throughout Britain answers you—No. When you make men slaves you deprive them of half their virtue, you set them in your own conduct an example of fraud, rapine, and cruelty, and compel them to live with you in a state of war; and yet you complain that they are not honest or faithful! You stupify them with stripes, and think it necessary to keep them in a state of ignorance; and yet you assert that they are incapable of learning; that their minds are such a barren soil or moor, that culture would be lost on them; and that they come from a climate, where nature, though prodigal of her bounties in a degree unknown to yourselves, has left man alone scant and unfinished, and incapable of enjoying the treasures she has poured out for him!—An assertion at once impious and absurd. Why do you use those instruments of torture? Are they fit to be applied by one rational being to another? And are ye not struck with shame and mortification, to see the partakers of your nature reduced so low? But, above all, are there no dangers attending this mode of treatment? Are you not hourly in dread of an insurrection? Nor would it be surprising: for when:

> —No peace is given
> To us enslav'd, but custody severe;
> And stripes and arbitrary punishment
> Inflicted—What peace can we return?
> But to our power, hostility and hate;
> Untam'd reluctance, and revenge, though slow,
> Yet ever plotting how the conqueror least
> May reap his conquest, and may least rejoice
> In doing what we most in suffering feel.[3]

But by changing your conduct, and treating your slaves as men, every cause of fear would be banished. They would be faithful, honest, intelligent and vigorous; and peace, prosperity, and happiness, would attend you.

*   *   *

I hope to have the satisfaction of seeing the renovation of liberty and justice resting on the British government, to vindicate the honour of our common nature. These are concerns which do not perhaps belong to any particular office: but, to speak more seriously to every man of sentiment, actions like these are the just and sure foundation of future fame; a reversion[4] though remote, is coveted by some noble minds as a substantial good. It is upon these grounds that I hope and expect the attention of gentlemen in power. These are designs consonant to the elevation of their rank, and the dignity of their stations: they are ends suitable to the nature of a free and generous government; and, connected with views of empire and dominion, suited to the benevolence and solid merit of the legislature. It is a pursuit of substantial greatness.—May the time come—at least the speculation to me is pleasing—when the sable people shall gratefully commemorate the auspicious era of extensive freedom. Then shall those persons[5] particularly be named with praise and honour, who generously proposed and stood forth in the cause of humanity, liberty, and good policy; and brought to the ear of the legislature designs worthy of royal patronage and adoption. May Heaven make the British senators the dispersers of light, liberty, and science, to the uttermost parts of the earth: then will be glory to God on the highest, on earth peace, and good-will to men. *   *   *

---

3. Milton's *Paradise Lost* 2.332–40, slightly altered.
4. A right of inheritance or succession (a common legal term).
5. "Granville Sharp, Esq; the Reverend Thomas Clarkson; the Reverend James Ramsay; our approved friends, men of virtue, are an honour to their country, ornamental to human nature, happy in themselves, and benefactors to mankind!" [Equiano's note]. These men were active leaders of the abolitionist movement. Since the opponents of slavery had to meet the constant objection that their proposals would undermine Britain's prosperity, they frequently argued that those would also prove "good policy." Equiano's economic arguments on commerce with Africa were influenced by those of James Ramsay.

As the inhuman traffic of slavery is to be taken into the consideration of the British legislature,[6] I doubt not, if a system of commerce was established in Africa, the demand for manufactures would most rapidly augment, as the native inhabitants will insensibly adopt the British fashions, manners, customs, &c. In proportion to the civilization, so will be the consumption of British manufactures.

The wear and tear of a continent, nearly twice as large as Europe, and rich in vegetable and mineral productions, is much easier conceived than calculated.

A case in point.—It cost the Aborigines of Britain little or nothing in clothing, &c. The difference between their forefathers and the present generation, in point of consumption, is literally infinite. The supposition is most obvious. It will be equally immense in Africa—the same cause, viz. civilization, will ever have the same effect.

It is trading upon safe grounds. A commercial intercourse with Africa opens an inexhaustible source of wealth to the manufacturing interests of Great Britain, and to all which the slave trade is an objection.

If I am not misinformed, the manufacturing interest is equal, if not superior, to the landed interest, as to the value, for reasons which will soon appear. The abolition of slavery, so diabolical, will give a most rapid extension of manufactures, which is totally and diametrically opposite to what some interested people assert.

The manufacturers of this country must and will, in the nature and reason of things, have a full and constant employ by supplying the African markets.

Population, the bowels and surface of Africa, abound in valuable and useful returns; the hidden treasures of centuries will be brought to light and into circulation. Industry, enterprize, and mining, will have their full scope, proportionably as they civilize. In a word, it lays open an endless field of commerce to the British manufacture[r] and merchant adventurer. The manufacturing interest and the general interests are synonymous. The abolition of slavery would be in reality an universal good.

Tortures, murder, and every other imaginable barbarity and iniquity, are practised upon the poor slaves with impunity. I hope the slave trade will be abolished. I pray it may be an event at hand.[7] The great body of manufacturers, uniting in the cause, will considerably facilitate and

6. In 1789, as the *Life* was published, a bill for the abolition of the slave trade (not of slavery itself) was introduced in Parliament. Equiano included in his book a dedication to Parliament that ends, "May the God of heaven inspire your hearts with peculiar benevolence on that important day when the question of Abolition is to be discussed, when thousands, in consequence of your Determination, are to look for Happiness or Misery!" The bill was defeated, 163 to 88.

7. After repeated failures, a bill ending the slave trade passed in 1807, ten years after Equiano's death. In later life, he continued to travel and speak against slavery, and his book had seven more editions. There were as many more again by the time slavery in the British colonies was officially ended in 1833. Slave owners were compensated.

expedite it; and, as I have already stated, it is most substantially their interest and advantage, and as such the nation's at large (except those persons concerned in the manufacturing neck-yokes, collars, chains, hand-cuffs, leg-bolts, drags, thumb-screws, iron muzzles, and coffins; cats,[8] scourges, and other instruments of torture used in the slave trade). In a short time one sentiment alone will prevail, from motives of interest as well as justice and humanity. Europe contains one hundred and twenty millions of inhabitants. Query—How many millions doth Africa contain? Supposing the Africans, collectively and individually, to expend £5 a head in raiment and furniture yearly when civilized, &c. an immensity beyond the reach of imagination!

This I conceive to be a theory founded upon facts, and therefore an infallible one. If the blacks were permitted to remain in their own country, they would double themselves every fifteen years. In proportion to such increase will be the demand for manufactures. Cotton and indigo grow spontaneously in most parts of Africa; a consideration this of no small consequence to the manufacturing towns of Great Britain. It opens a most immense, glorious, and happy prospect—the clothing, &c. of a continent ten thousand miles in circumference, and immensely rich in productions of every denomination in return for manufactures.

I have only therefore to request the reader's indulgence and conclude. I am far from the vanity of thinking there is any merit in this narrative: I hope censure will be suspended, when it is considered that it was written by one who was as unwilling as unable to adorn the plainness of truth by the colouring of imagination. My life and fortune have been extremely chequered, and my adventures various. Even those I have related are considerably abridged. If any incident in this little work should appear uninteresting and trifling to most readers, I can only say, as my excuse for mentioning it, that almost every event of my life made an impression on my mind and influenced my conduct. I early accustomed myself to look for the hand of God in the minutest occurrence, and to learn from it a lesson of morality and religion; and in this light every circumstance I have related was to me of importance. After all, what makes any event important, unless by its observation we become better and wiser, and learn 'to do justly, to love mercy, and to walk humbly before God?'[9] To those who are possessed of this spirit, there is scarcely any book or incident so trifling that does not afford some profit, while to others the experience of ages seems of no use; and even to pour out to them the treasures of wisdom is throwing the jewels of instruction away.

8. I.e., cats-o'-nine-tails.
9. Micah 6.8.

CRITICISM

Responses to Behn and *Oroonoko,* 1682–1948

BISHOP BURNET

[To Anne Wharton, December 19, 1682]†

Some of Mrs. Behn's songs are very tender; but she is so abominably vile a woman, and rallies not only all Religion but all Virtue in so odious and obscene a manner, that I am heartily sorry that she has writ any thing in your commendation.

CHARLES COTTON

"To the Admir'd Astrea" (1686)†

*   *   *

Some Hands write some things well; are elsewhere lame;
But on all Themes, your Power is the same.
Of Buskin, and of Sock, you know the Pace;
And tread in both, with equal Skill and Grace.
But when you write of Love, *Astrea,* then
Love dips his Arrows, where you wet your Pen.
Such charming Lines did never Paper grace;
Soft, as your Sex; and smooth, as Beauty's Face.
And 'tis your Province, that belongs to you:
Men are so rude, they fright when they wou'd sue.
You teach us gentler Methods; such as are
The fit and due Proceedings with the Fair.

*   *   *

---

† From Rev. James Granger, *Letters,* ed. J. P. Malcolm (London, 1805), 234–35.
† Commendatory poem for Behn's *La Montre.*

FROM A *MISCELLANY OF NEW POEMS* (1688)†

"A Pindarick to Mrs. Behn on her Poem on the Coronation," Written by a Lady

* * *

The subject was Divine we all confess,
Nor was that flame, thy mighty fancy, less.
That cloth'd thy thought in such a pleasing dress,
As did at once a Masculine wit express,
And all the softness of a Female tenderness.
No more shall men their fancy'd Empire hold,
Since thou *Astrea* form'd of finer mould,
By nature temper'd more with humid cold,
Doth man excel—
Not in soft strokes alone, but even in the bold.

* * *

[A SESSION OF POETS (ca. 1688)]†

* * * in short, since her Works had neither Wit enough for a Man,
nor Modesty enough for a Woman, she was to be look'd upon as an
Hermaphrodite, & consequently not fit to enjoy the benefits & Privileges of either Sex, much less of this Society. With these words Apollo
dismiss'd her, giving her this only comfort for all her fruitless Labour
that the Descent of Parnassus was much easier (especially to your gouty
Poetasters) than the Ascent had been * * *

THE ATHENIAN MERCURY

[The "Athenian Society" to a Woman's Love Query (1694)]†

* * * Compassion's due
To all the World, but something more to you.
Thus *Aphra*, thus despairing *Sappho* mourn'd;

---

† In Behn's *Lycidus: or the Lover in Fashion. . . . Together with a Miscellany of New Poems. By Several Hands.*
† From Hugh MacDonald, ed., *A Journal from Parnassus, New Printed from a Manuscript* (London: for P. J. Dobell, 1937), 26–27.
† From *The Athenian Mercury* 15 (November 27, 1694).

Sure both their Souls are to your Breast return'd.
By the same Tyrant-Passion all enslav'd,
Like you they wrote, like you they lov'd and rav'd.
But ah! Their *Virtue vanish'd*, what remain'd?
Their *Verse* as spotted as their *Glory* stain'd:
They lost that Gem with which *Orinda* shin'd,
And left a sullied Name and Works behind.

THOMAS SOUTHERNE

Dedication to *Oroonoko* (1696)†

I stand engag'd to Mrs. *Behn* for the Occasion of a most Passionate
Distress in my Last Play; and in a Conscience that I had not made her
a sufficient Acknowledgement, I have run further into her Debt for
Oroonoko, with a Design to oblige me to be honest; and that every one
may find me out for Ingratitude, when I don't say all that's fit for me
upon that Subject. She had a great Command of the Stage; and I have
often wonder'd that she would bury her Favourite Hero in a *Novel*,
when she might have reviv'd him in the *Scene*. She thought either that
no Actor could represent him; or she could not bear him represented.
And I believe the last, when I remember what I have heard from a
Friend of hers, That she always told his Story, more feelingly, than she
writ it.

* * *

"MEMOIRS ON THE LIFE OF MRS. BEHN"

Written by a Gentlewoman of
Her Acquaintance (1696)†

The Misfortunes of that Prince had been unknown to us, if the Divine
Astrea had not been there, and his Suff'rings had wanted that satisfaction which her Pen has giv'n 'em in the Immortality of his Virtues, and
Constancy; the very Memory of which move a generous Pity in all, and
a Contempt of the brutal Actors in that unfortunate Tragedy. Here I
can add nothing to what she has given the World already, but a Vindication of her from some unjust Aspersions I find are insinuated about
this Town in Relation to that Prince. I knew her intimately well; and

---

† From Thomas Southerne, "The Epistle Dedicatory to His Grace William Duke of Devon-
shire," in *Oroonoko* (1696).
† In Behn's *Histories and Novels*.

I believe she wou'd not have conceal'd any Love-affair from me, being one of her own Sex, whose Friendship and Secrecy she had experienc'd; which makes me assure the World, there was no Affair between that Prince and *Astrea*, but what the whole Plantation were witnesses of. A generous Value for his uncommon Virtues, ev'ry one that but hears 'em, finds in himself; and his Presence gave her no more. Beside, his Heart was too violently set on the everlasting Charms of his *Imoinda*, to be shook with those more faint (in his Eye) of a White Beauty; and *Astrea*'s Relations, there present, had too watchful an Eye over her to permit the Frailty of her Youth, if that had been powerful enough.

*   *   *

THEOPHILUS CIBBER, et al.

From *Lives of the Poets* (1753)†

*   *   *

It was there our poetess became acquainted with the story and person of the American Prince Oroonoko, whose adventures she has so feelingly and elegantly described in the celebrated Novel of that name, upon which Mr. Southerne has built his Tragedy of Oroonoko, part of which is so entertaining and moving, that it is almost too much for nature.

*   *   *

Mrs. Behn perhaps, as much as any one, condemned loose scenes, and too warm descriptions; but something must be allowed to human frailty. She herself was of an amorous complexion, she felt the passions intimately which she describes, and this circumstance, added to necessity, might be the occasion of her plays being of that cast.

> The stage how loosely does Astrea tread,
> Who fairly puts all characters to bed,

Are lines of Mr. Pope.

And another modern[1] speaking of the vicissitudes to which the stage is subjected, has the following,

> Perhaps if skill could distant times explore,
> New Behns, New Durfeys, yet remain in store, . . .

---

† From Theophilus Cibber, et al., eds. *The Lives of the Poets of Great Britain and Ireland*, vol. 3, pp. 17–27.
1. Samuel Johnson in *Drury Lane Prologue*.

> Perhaps, for who can guess th' effects of chance,
> Here Hunt may box, and Mahomet may dance.

This author cannot be well acquainted with Mrs. Behn's works, who makes a comparison between them and the productions of Durfey. There are remarks of a fine understanding in the most unfinished piece of Mrs. Behn, and the very worst of this lady's compositions are preferable to Durfey's best. It is unpleasing to have the merit of any of the Fair Sex lessened. Mrs. Behn suffered enough at the hands of supercilious prudes, who had the barbarity to construe her sprightliness as lewdness, and because she had wit and beauty, she must likewise be charged with prostitution and irreligion.

✻   ✻   ✻

ANDREW KIPPIS

From *Biographia Britannica* (1780)†

✻   ✻   ✻

It is some consolation to reflect, that Mrs. Behn's works are now little regarded, her Novels excepted, which, we suppose, have still many readers among that unhappily too numerous a class of people who devour the trash of the circulating libraries.

✻   ✻   ✻

CLARA REEVE

From *The Progress of Romance* (1785)†

Euphrasia. There are strong marks of Genius in all this lady's works, but unhappily, there are some parts of them, very improper to be read by, or recommended to virtuous minds, and especially to youth.—She wrote in an age, and to a court of licentious manners, and perhaps we ought to ascribe to these causes the loose turn of her stories.—Let us do justice to her merits, and cast the veil of compassion over her faults. ✻   ✻   ✻

---

† From *Biographia Britannica*, 2nd ed. rev., vol. 2, p. 146.
† From Clara Reeve, *The Progress of Romance Through Times, Countries, and Manners* (Colchester: W. Keymer, 1785), 117–18 (reprinted New York: Garland, 1970).

Hortensius. Are you not partial to the sex of this Genius?—when you excuse in her, what you would not to a man?

Euphrasia. Perhaps I may, and you must excuse me if I am so, especially as this lady had many fine and amiable qualities, besides her genius for writing.

*   *   *

SIR WALTER SCOTT

From Lockhart's *Life of Scott* (1837)†

A grand-aunt of my own, Mrs. Keith of Ravelstone, who was a person of some condition, being a daughter of Sir John Swinton of Swinton —lived with unabated vigour of intellect to a very advanced age. She was very fond of reading, and enjoyed it to the last of her long life. One day she asked me, when we happened to be alone together, whether I had ever seen Mrs. Behn's novels?—I confessed the charge. —Whether I could get her a sight of them?—I said, with some hesitation, I believed I could; but that I did not think she would like either the manners, or the language, which approached too near that of Charles II's time to be quite proper reading. "Nevertheless," said the good old lady, "I remember them being so much admired, and being so much interested in them myself, that I wish to look at them again." To hear was to obey. So I sent Mrs. Aphra Behn, curiously sealed up, with "private and confidential" on the packet, to my gay old grand-aunt. The next time I saw her afterwards, she gave me back Aphra, properly wrapped up, with nearly these words:—"Take back your bonny Mrs. Behn; and, if you will take my advice, put her in the fire, for I found it impossible to get through the very first novel. But is it not," she said, "a very odd thing that I, an old woman of eighty and upwards, sitting alone, feel myself ashamed to read a book which, sixty years ago, I have heard read aloud for the amusement of large circles, consisting of the first and most creditable society in London." This, of course, was owing to the gradual improvement of the national taste and delicacy.

---

† From John Gibson Lockhart, *The Life of Sir Walter Scott* (Edinburgh: T. and A. Constable, 1902), 6:375–76 (reprinted New York: AMS Press, 1983).

THE SATURDAY REVIEW

"Literary Garbage" (1872)†

*   *   *

We should be very sorry to find a place for the volumes on our shelves, and still more to promote their circulation by giving them away. Even in the fragmentary form in which which they might be sent to the butterman or used for domestic purposes, there is no saying what contamination a stray sheet might not carry with it. * * * The revived taste for these works, if there really is a revived taste, must necessarily be morbid and artificial; indeed, it may be called rather a letch than a taste.

*   *   *

ALGERNON SWINBURNE

["Impassioned Protest" (1894)]†

* * * All readers of Lockhart will remember that Sir Walter Scott's 'gay old grand-aunt' found it impossible to get through the very first of the stories which she had requested him to send her, remembering the pleasure with which in her girlhood she had heard them read aloud in the most decorous and refined society. The only one I remember to have ever read might, as far as I remember, be reprinted in company with Mrs. Beecher Stowe's. * * * The tragic and pathetic story of Oroonoko does only less credit to her excellent literary ability than to the noble impulse of womanly compassion and womanly horror which informs the whole narrative and makes of it one ardent and continuous appeal for sympathy and pity, one fervent and impassioned protest against cruelty and tyranny.

*   *   *

† From *The Saturday Review* 33 (January 27, 1872), 109.
† From Algernon Swinburne, *Studies in Prose and Poetry* (London, 1894), 95.

GEORGE SAINTSBURY

["A Very Inflammable Disposition" (1913)]†

*   *   *

Afra had herself been in Guiana; and, as she was of a very inflammable disposition, it is quite possible that some Indian Othello had caught her fresh imagination. On the other hand, there was the heroic romance, with all its sighs and flames, still the rage: and a much less nimble intellect than Afra's, with a much less cosmopolitan experience, might easily see the use of transposing it into a new key.

*   *   *

V. SACKVILLE-WEST

["A Born Bohemian" (1927)]†

*   *   *

The secret service, a debtor's prison, a merry career as playwright and libertine, fame, friendship, love—all this was to be hers, but throughout all her vicissitudes the adventurous, independent character is dominant: she followed the path that she had chosen. She was never a prudent woman; her nature was too rich and warm for that, she who was 'of a generous and open temper, something passionate, very serviceable to her friends.' Scrapes she might get into, friends might fail her; but always she emerges gay, energetic, courageous, giving; a lovable creature, a born Bohemian.

† From George Saintsbury, *The English Novel* (London: Dent, 1913), 51.
† From V. Sackville-West, *Aphra Behn: The Incomparable Astrea* (London: Gerald Howe, 1927), 33.

VIRGINIA WOOLF

["The Freedom of the Mind" (1929)]†

*   *   *

She had to work on equal terms with men. She made, by working very hard, enough to live on. The importance of that fact outweighs anything that she actually wrote, even the splendid "A Thousand Martyrs I have made," or "Love in Fantastic Triumph sat," for here begins the freedom of the mind, or rather the possibility that in the course of time the mind will be free to write what it likes.

*   *   *

The extreme activity of mind which showed itself in the later eighteenth century among women—the talking, and the meeting, the writing of essays on Shakespeare, the translating of the classics—was founded on the solid fact that women could make money by writing.

*   *   *

Thus, towards the end of the eighteenth century a change came about which, if I were rewriting history, I should describe more fully and think of greater importance than the Crusades or the Wars of the Roses.

*   *   *

For masterpieces are not single and solitary births; they are the outcome of many years of thinking in common, of thinking by the body of the people, so that the experience of the mass is behind the single voice. Jane Austen should have laid a wreath upon the grave of Fanny Burney, and George Eliot done homage to the robust shade of Eliza Carter— the valiant old woman who tied a bell to her bedstead in order that she might wake early and learn Greek. All women together ought to let flowers fall upon the tomb of Aphra Behn which is, most scandal- ously but rather appropriately, in Westminster Abbey, for it was she who earned them the right to speak their minds.

*   *   *

---

† From *A Room of One's Own*, pp. 67–69, by Virginia Woolf, copyright 1929, renewed 1957 by Leonard Woolf, reprinted by permission of Harcourt Brace & Company, Chatto & Windus, and the Estate of Virginia Woolf.

GEORGE SHERBURN

["An Astonishing Masterpiece" (1948)]†

* * *

As a brief and new romantic story *Oroonoko* is an astonishing master-piece. For years, as in Davenant's *Cruelty of the Spaniards in Peru* (1658), there had been works idealizing aboriginal human nature as contrasted with gold-thirsty Christians. Mrs. Behn boldly takes as her hero a beautiful and powerful Negro slave whose mind is as noble as his body—and she makes and keeps him impressive to the end. It is easy to point out flaws in this brief tragic romance, but Mrs. Behn by some accident of genius has made real for us the noble aborigine as no one else had done. It is a great achievement in a period in which idealized persons are practically always artificial. It makes one realize that while the prose fiction of the Restoration is as a whole neither important nor greatly significant, a period that produced masterpieces as diverse as those of the righteous Bunyan and the unrighteous Mrs. Behn has much to its credit.

---

† From George Sherburn, *The Restoration and Eighteenth Century* (New York: Appleton-Century-Crofts, 1948), 805.

Critical Essays, 1984–1996

WILLIAM C. SPENGEMANN

The Earliest American Novel:
Aphra Behn's *Oroonoko*†

Why is *Oroonoko* never included in studies of "The American Novel" or in courses on "Early American Literature"? As a literary work written in English about America by someone who claims to have lived there, it would seem to deserve a place in the canon at least as much as, say, John Smith's *Generall Historie*, a work that few Americanists would think of ignoring, even though Smith was not an American and his narrative is not exactly "literature."

*   *   *

So far as I can see, the only possible reason for the omission of *Oroonoko* from American literature is that Surinam, the scene of the action and the place of Aphra Behn's putative American residence, is not a part of the present United States—or, as Howard Mumford Jones used to call it, "the future United States."[1] But this criterion makes very little sense. In the first place, it lacks any historical meaning, inasmuch as the United States did not exist prior to the Declaration of Independence and therefore cannot reasonably be thought to have conditioned anything done in America before that time—unless, of course, like the "Early Americans" themselves, we are prepared to argue that events widely separated in time all exist together in a single, eternal plan of human history. Otherwise, we must regard the America to which writings like *Oroonoko* relate as the one that existed at the time they were written. And that America, as even the most cursory glance at any seventeenth-century map will show, was a very different place—in size, in shape, and in meaning—from the one that existed in the nineteenth century, when nationalist historians began to take a patriotic interest in the "colonial backgrounds" of the United States, and from the one we know today.

---

† © 1984 by the Regents of the University of California. Reprinted from *Nineteenth-Century Fiction*, vol. 38, no. 4, pp. 384–414 by permission. Also reprinted in William C. Spengemann, *A Mirror for Americanists* (Hanover, N.H., and London: University Press of New England, 1989). Some of the author's notes have been abridged.
1. *The Theory of American Literature* (1948; reissued Ithaca, N.Y.: Cornell Univ. Press, 1965), p. 25.

In 1688 when Aphra Behn wrote *Oroonoko*, not all of the thirteen rebel colonies yet existed; and those that did belonged to a much larger political entity called British America, which extended, at one time or another in its history, from the Arctic Circle to the Amazon and included Surinam. In another respect Aphra Behn's America was much smaller than Jefferson's or Moses Coit Tyler's; her contemporaries in New Haven fully expected to discover the South Sea within a hundred miles to the west of their settlement. Nor were the relations among Britain's American colonies anything like what is implied by the idea of a "future United States." Virginia and Carolina had far more in common with the Caribbean colonies than with Massachusetts Bay or Connecticut, while each individual colony was apt to be in closer touch with England than with any other part of British America. And, although nationalistic literary historians have taught us to consider New England the most important of Britain's American territories, that preeminence in fact belonged to Barbados in the seventeenth century, with New England near the bottom of the list.

*   *   *

The questions raised by *Oroonoko* suggest that we need a better way to identify works of American literature—better, that is, than by merely determining that the author was, according to some elastic political definition, an American, that the work in question conforms to our current notions of literature, and that it bears some resemblance to certain other literary works written by Americans. Since Americans have produced literary works of almost every conceivable stripe, including a good many that no one would think of calling "American," and since those so-called "American" features that recur in the classic works of notable American writers can also be found in works written by non-Americans, authorial nationality does not seem to constitute a necessary condition of American literature. *   *   *

*   *   * To enter literature on a truly literary footing, America must make a difference in the way literature is written—which is to say, in its selection, deployment, and arrangement of words. By the same token, to be considered literarily American, and not just politically or geographically so, a work must be seen to take linguistic cognizance of America, incorporating some idea of that place into its very form of words. If we can locate, somewhere, a literary work whose form can be attributed directly to the impact of America on the written language, then, no matter where we find it or who wrote it, we can say that we have discovered a literature that deserves to be called American.

II

* * * When, "never rest[ing] my Pen a Moment for Thought," Behn composed her history of the Royal Slave, she was not trying to write a novel and failing. As one of the newly emerging class of professional writers created by the decline of aristocratic patronage after the Civil War and the rise of a new audience of book buyers, she was simply trying to earn a living by composing, from the literary materials available to her, a story that this as yet ill-defined readership would buy and praise because it portrayed a world they recognized.

* * *

Behn's is the classic case of the modern professional writer, schooled in a lofty ideal of truth and art and forced by mundane circumstance to make her living in a world that she disdained and that held her ideals in contempt. That her personal vision of the good as a Tory Arcadia ruled by peaceful shepherd kings was a nostalgic fiction, hopelessly out of touch with modern history, is nothing to the point. Unless she simply abandoned that vision, she would have to find some way to bridge the gulf between her feudal paradise and the progressive "new England" of her intended audience. Had she been merely a hack, unhampered by allegiances of her own, she could have manufactured tales of honest apprentices, religious romances, or antiromantic burlesques as effortlessly as she had churned out satires on the Parliamentarians or congratulatory poems to the several monarchs who occupied the English throne in rapid succession during the 1680s. In that case, *Oroonoko* would have been a very different book, and we would not be scratching our heads over it today, for it would have disappeared from sight along with *The City Heiress*, *The Amours of Philander and Sylvia*, and *A Voyage to the Isle of Love*. Because she was motivated by personal conviction as well as by necessity, however, she sought to make a place for her antique ideals in the hated modern world. Out of that quixotic ambition, she produced a book so remarkable that it has rescued the rest of her oeuvre from oblivion and seems now, for all its stumbling oddity, to anticipate the whole subsequent history of English fiction.

The strategy Behn devised to reconcile the conflicting demands of personal inclination and public taste is, on the face of it, ingeniously simple. She merely fashioned a romantic tale of highborn lovers caught in the crosscurrents of desire and duty and then presented this old story in the very modern guise of a Brief True Relation of her own travels to America. This conflation of Old-World and New-World genres seems to have suited her purposes exactly. On the one hand, the prose romance was in every sense her métier. Not only was she thoroughly practiced in its conventions, having read romances all of her life and modeled most of her plays (to say nothing of her own behavior) upon them, but, like most persons of her class and education, she regarded them as accurate pictures of reality and as dramatizations of her own most cherished values. The Brief True Relation, on the other hand, simultaneously evaded her busy middle-class readers' distrust of idle fictions and met their demands for useful information about current affairs in brief compass. What is more, because the Brief True Relation rested the authority of its statements upon the writer's experiences rather than upon his or her social station or sex, the form allowed Behn to assume an authority that had been begrudged her in the masculine, courtly domains of drama and poetry. And because the experiences reported in these narratives of New-World travel were necessarily un-verifiable, the form permitted her to call her tale a true history without fear of rebuttal. By enfolding her romance of the Royal Slave in a Brief True Relation, Behn could stick to her romantic last, proffer her fiction as news from the New World, and thus foist it upon the very audience whose members were busily dismantling the world that the romance had been devised to validate.

To say that Behn wished to make a place for romance in a new world is true in more than just a commercial sense. She was not simply trying to peddle an old product in a new market; she wished to discover in the prosaic and turbulent modern world that history was constructing about her a place where the vanishing ideals embodied in romance could survive the predations of change and even rise again to regulate human society. To Behn, as to many another European who lamented the passing of traditional ways and the decline of civil order in the seventeenth century, America seemed a place out of time, where man's original estate might be regained. Ever since the discovery, narratives of New-World travel had couched their actions in the tropes of chivalric romance and described America in images of the Earthly Paradise, the Garden of Eden, and the Golden Age.[2] If the discovery, exploration, and settlement of America formed an inextricable part of that historical change which had removed humankind from its primal condition, then by casting themselves upon this historical tide men might hope to complete the circular course of human history, arrive again at the be-ginning, and remain in that perfected state forever. * * *

The vessel is fairly launched with the narrator's opening announce-ment that the story to follow is a true "History," rather than the "Ad-ventures of a feign'd *Hero*, whose Life and Fortunes Fancy may manage at the Poet's Pleasure." Although it will prove as "diverting" as any fictional romance, like all such reports by plain-speaking voyagers, "it shall come simply into the World," without the adornments of artistic "Invention," recommended solely "by its own proper Merits, and nat-ural Intrigues." The truth upon which its charm depends, moreover,

---

2. For information that would permit an accurate plotting of Behn's location on the map of ideas about the Golden Age, see her poem "The Golden Age." * * * See also Harry Levin, *The Myth of the Golden Age in the Renaissance* (Bloomington: Indiana Univ. Press, 1969).

will lie not in the familiarity of its details or its conformity with recognized conventions but in the narrator's own experience. "I was my
self an Eye-witness to a great part, of what you will find here set down,"
the narrator maintains, "and what I cou'd not be Witness of, I receiv'd
from the Mouth of the chief Actor in this History, the *Hero* himself." * * *

That Behn regarded the Brief True Relation primarily as a vehicle
for her romance is evident in the dispatch with which the narrator
abandons that modern conveyance, after five pages, and turns her attention to its precious, Old-World cargo. The next thirty-odd pages,
nearly half of the complete text, are devoted to Oroonoko's life in the
court of Coramantien and his rivalry with the King, his grandfather, for
the hand of Imoinda. Taken straight from the English heroic drama
and the French Arcadian romance, and offered here as an account
given to the narrator by Oroonoko after his arrival in Surinam, this
familiar story of conflicting romantic principles employs none of the
narrative techniques introduced in the opening relation. The narrator
is now undramatized and omniscient, a teller of someone else's tale
and, like her reader, an audience to that tale, rather than a particular
person reporting her own observations in a particular place. Indeed,
the narrator does not even take care to report only those things that
Oroonoko, her supposed source of information, could have seen at the
time or learned about subsequently. Romantic actions happen objec-
tively, in the eternal order of things, and do not depend for their existence, as the recently discovered and ever-expanding New World did,
upon the perceptions of individual human beings. The value of these
actions lies not in their individual contributions to the accumulating
store of human knowledge about the world, but in their coherent moral
structure, which imitates the divinely instituted form of the world and
of human history.

* * * Nowhere in Oroonoko's African adventures do we find
anything resembling the narrator's earlier interest in the topography,
economy, botany, and zoology of Surinam and its closely related anthropology. Behn's readers have often observed that the African court
of Coramantien bears a striking resemblance to the courts of Europe.
The point is, rather, that the story of Oroonoko and Imoinda told thus
far, being a romance, could happen anywhere without affecting its form
one whit.

* * *

Oroonoko's entanglement in the intractable circumstances of colonial politics, economics, and class conflict markedly alters the tone and
import of the narrative. We seem to have moved without warning from
that morally translucent world where "Heaven was so kind to the *Prince,*
as to sweeten his Misfortunes by so lucky an Accident" as his reunion
with Imoinda to an altogether different sort of world, one governed by

untidy historical conditions rather than by universal principles of love and honor. These unlooked-for complications follow so closely upon Oroonoko's arrival in the New World that a devout Americanist might be tempted to ascribe them directly to the change of geographical venue from Africa to America, on the assumption that America is, after all, a very special sort of place. The fact is, however, that life in seventeenth-century Coramantien was obviously no less subject than Surinam to such historical conditions, while Surinam, as the opening pages of *Oroonoko* demonstrate, was no less susceptible than Coramantien to romantic treatment. The crucial change, in other words, is formal and stylistic. It occurs at the point where the action departs from the timeless circle of romance form and enters the historical form of the Brief True Relation for the first time. In the opening four or five pages of the text we heard the beginnings of Behn's Brief True Relation of life in Surinam, without Oroonoko. The succeeding forty pages gave us the romance of Oroonoko and Imoinda in Coramantien, outside both Surinam and the narrator's own immediate experience. Now, with only a third of the volume remaining in the reader's right hand and the action seemingly poised for its final sprint to a happy conclusion, Oroonoko finds himself in a strange new world, created by conflicting human desires rather than by divine intentions, where nothing is conclusive but death.

. * * * In the romance, as in medieval historiography, the chronology of events proceeds independent of geography, which serves merely as a backdrop for the exemplary actions of exemplary figures who, being motivated by universal moral principles, do not change significantly in the course of the action. In the Brief True Relation, on the other hand, human action and geographical situation are mutually conditioning elements in the historical evolution—the creation—of reality.[3] * * *

* * * Whatever notions Behn may have held regarding the New World as a theatre for heroic actions and a haven for romantic ideals, these fond designs seem to be enmeshed now in a tightening coil of petty, vulgar constraints.

With Oroonoko trapped between unheroic docility and suicidal rebellion, the narrative takes an evasive turn, off the line of fatal action that seems headed for either dishonor or death, into a series of diverting adventures in the countryside. By means of this "Digression," which she admits "is a little from my Story," the narrator apparently means

3. For detailed studies of the Brief True Relation, see Jarvis Means Morse, *American Beginnings* (Washington, D.C.: Public Affairs Press, 1952), ch. 2; and Wayne Franklin, *Discoverers, Explorers, Settlers: The Diligent Writers of Early America* (Chicago: Univ. of Chicago Press, 1979). Differences between this form and that of the romance are outlined in William C. Spengemann, *The Adventurous Muse: The Poetics of American Fiction, 1789–1900* (New Haven, Conn.: Yale Univ. Press, 1977), chs. 1 and 2.

to provide her frustrated hero with some opportunities for action that will get him out of the house but will not require the colonists to crush him. In a succession of tall tales, recounted in the purest manner of the Brief True Relation, Oroonoko kills "Tygers," wrestles with an electric eel, and guides the narrator's party to an Indian village, behaving all the while with appropriate bravery and chivalrous concern for his female companions. "Diverting" as they are, however, these exploits merely forestall the inevitable decision Oroonoko must make regarding his dishonorable captivity. What is more, even though his companionship gives the narrator and her friends the heart to venture into the wilderness, his undignified role as a captive entertainer of idle aristocrats robs his heroism of any real consequence. The narrator herself appears to realize the falsity of Oroonoko's position, for he fades from view for long intervals, while she describes the local topography and inhabitants, supplanting his actions with her own reflections upon the exotic world that unfolds before her as she penetrates the unexplored wilderness beyond the settlement.

Digressive as it is, this interlude has a profound effect upon the main action. Not only does it demonstrate that Oroonoko's heroism depends on his making the fatal choice between love and honor, but, by reemphasizing the narrative methods of the Brief True Relation, it places the narrator at the very center of the action and involves her directly in that choice. * * * Drawn by the rhetorical gravity of the Brief True Relation into the action of her tale, the narrator will eventually find herself not merely a witness to its outcome but a principal actor in it.

The final episode in the digressive interlude that lies between Oroonoko's happy marriage and his horrible death takes the narrator and her traveling party to an Indian village upriver, where she undergoes an experience that fixes her more firmly in the New World than anything, perhaps, except her assumption of responsibility for Oroonoko's safety and liberation. Meeting the Indians, who have never seen a white person before, she immediately becomes conscious of her own strange appearance, as if she were seeing herself through their wondering eyes, and describes herself for the first time. What she sees of herself and her companions from this outlandish point of view is reported in the Indians' words, which, although perfectly innocent, assume in context an ironic edge that is hardly flattering to European assumptions of cultural superiority. "We shall now know whether those things can speak," the natives exclaim, whether they have "Sense, and Wit" and can "talk of Affairs of Life, and War," as Indians can. Like so many New-World explorers before her and many more to come, the narrator has been given a new perspective on the world as a whole. Seen from this American coign of vantage, Europe is no longer the center of the circle of lands. It is merely one more place on the globe, as backward in its way as are the barbarous nations in theirs, a relative thing rather than the seat of absolute values by which the rest of the world may be judged. * * *

Having sought to evade the unpromising drift of her tale by means of the narrative form that caused all her difficulties in the first place, the narrator returns to her proper "Story" to find nothing changed, except that this story has now become her own—a tale of her increasing departure from the settled moral world of her English readers into the unexplored American wilderness of her own invention. When, weary of prudent inaction, Oroonoko finally rebels against his captors, the narrator finds herself swept up in his mounting hostility to her own kind. Throughout her narrative, she has taken an ambiguous attitude toward her fellow colonists, employing the pronoun "we" to distinguish the white settlers from the Indians and the African slaves but isolating herself by calling the English "they" whenever slavery, especially cruelty to Oroonoko, is the subject. There are, in addition, a number of passages in which the Indians, like Montaigne's cannibals, are depicted as more noble, even more essentially Christian, than their supposedly civilized oppressors. Now, however, all semblance of ambiguity and lofty satire vanishes as the narrator submerges her voice in Oroonoko's, first paraphrasing the harangue by which he stirs up his fellow captives and then modulating into direct quotation as he excoriates all white people for their faithlessness and inhumanity.

* * *

When, following Oroonoko's inflammatory speech, the narrator resumes her own voice, she adopts a sardonic tone of thinly disguised hostility that is notably absent from her previous discourse and can only be attributed to her preceding identification with the rebellious Oroonoko. At the same time, she seems eager to reestablish contact with her reader and to dissociate herself from Oroonoko, whose accelerating troubles she feels powerless to alleviate, even as she feels guilty for having failed him. If Oroonoko is responsible for the unprecedented passion of her tone in these concluding episodes, he is also the cause of her efforts to distance herself from him. The grievances aired in his harangue to the slaves include the complaint that *"we are Bought and Sold like Apes, or Monkeys, to be the Sport of Women,"* which seems to refer to the narrator herself and to those early days of his captivity when, she says, "we entertain'd him . . . or rather he us." Once the uprising has begun, moreover, she naturally identifies herself with the white colonists, using the pronoun "we" to denote the common targets of his revenge. In the next moment, however, Oroonoko's enemies become "they," as Byam's vigilantes pursue the fugitive, and the narrator stands by powerless to protect him. For the remainder of her story, the narrator shifts her position repeatedly, now aligning herself with

Oroonoko's aristocratic friends against his low-life pursuers, then speaking familiarly to the reader as an English author, then dissociating herself from all the colonists and from the reader as well. * * *

These rapid shifts in narrative attitude create an ambiguity of tone that enhances the novelistic effects already produced by the collision of Behn's romantic theme with her historical narrative form. Neither romance nor Brief True Relation, her narrative has become a rhetorical blending of heroic ideals and brute reality into a symbolic expression of the narrator's conflicting allegiances to her civilized audience and her savage art. * * *

How deeply Oroonoko penetrates into the heart of the savage wilderness and how closely the narrator follows him may be discerned in the powerfully affecting language of the tale's final episode. After some days spent recuperating at Parham House, Oroonoko is abducted by the parvenu rabble and executed. As they slowly dismember him, he stoically smokes an Indian pipe. Before he dies—or "gave up the Ghost," as the text has it—he blesses his executioners. And when he is dead, Byam sends to the plantations, by way of a warning to the other slaves, Oroonoko's quartered remains, the "frightful Spectacles of a mangl'd King." Amalgamated in this unforgettable tableau are images of all the hopes that the narrator has invested in her Royal Slave: the natural nobility of the American Indian, the divine right of the martyred Charles, and the redemptive sacrifice of Christ.[4] * * *

The closing pages of *Oroonoko* reenact the psychic turmoil of all those European explorers who came to America armed with Old-World ideas about it, and then, having undergone experiences that utterly discredited these ideas, found themselves unable either to resume their previous lives at home or to remain isolated in the new world they had discovered. Oroonoko's death constitutes an indictment of everything that Behn's new reader represents—social ambition, commercial enterprise, the subjugation of "dusky tribes," the dismantling of ancient institutions. * * *

* * * Having embodied her romantic hopes in Oroonoko and then cast him upon the narrative tide of the Brief True Relation, it seems, she could only sit and watch him perish. Recounting her early meetings with the Royal Slave, the narrator says, "He call'd [me] his *Great Mistress*; and indeed my Word wou'd go a great way with him." In the event, his words were to go even farther with her, to an "other World" where English fiction had never been before and from which there was no returning.

---

4. Behn explicitly identifies Charles II with Christ in her *Pindarick on the Death of Our Late Sovereign* (London: J. Playford for H. Playford, 1685) and her *Poem Humbly Dedicated to the Great Patern of Piety and Virtue Catherine Queen Dowager* (London: J. Playford for H. Playford, 1685). Charles, Caesar, and Christ, of course, are symbolically akin in having all been kings betrayed by their "sons"—Monmouth, Brutus, and mankind.

III

Conceived as literature written by citizens of the United States or by sometime residents of places now part of the United States, on the deterministic assumption that these conditions produce writing of a uniquely, characteristically American sort, "American literature," must exclude *Oroonoko*. * * *

But, if we define "American literature" in literary rather than in political or geographical terms, as writing conditioned by those linguistic changes that resulted from the transportation of European languages to the New World and from efforts on the part of those languages to apprehend that unprecedented phenomenon,[5] then the Americanness of any literary work has nothing necessarily to do with its author's nationality or place of residence. * * *

Viewed in this light, the vexed question of Behn's American residence is rendered moot by the fact that, to write *Oroonoko*, she employed a narrative form that had been devised specifically to register those changes, in the shape and meaning of the world and in the concepts of human identity and history, that were prompted by the discovery, exploration, and settlement of America. * * *

* * *

The point is that, despite the potential hazards implicit in the Brief True Relation, Behn modeled her narrative upon that form because it enabled her to live in the old world of romance and the new world of her reader at the same time. Even more to the point, by telling her romantic tale in this form she stumbled, however unwillingly, upon a new way of writing fiction—a combination of language, structure, theme, narrative mode, and a vision of human history that we now associate with "the novel."[6] In that respect, *Oroonoko* belongs in the first chapter of any history of American fiction, somewhere between Henry Nevile's *Isle of Pines* (1668) and *Robinson Crusoe* (1719). And to say that is to place it at the very source of the English novel—the novel written in English—for, as *Oroonoko* suggests, the peculiar features of that genre have an apparent source in the narrative form through which America made its way into the English language. * * *

* * *

The America portrayed in the Brief True Relation, unfortunately, was not a place out of time or at the end of time. It was, rather, a new

---

5. Two excellent studies of America's impact on the language are Stephen Greenblatt, "Learning to Curse: Aspects of Linguistic Colonialism in the Sixteenth Century," in *First Images of America: The Impact of the New World on the Old*, ed. Fredi Chiappelli, 2 vols. (Berkeley: Univ. of California Press, 1976), I, 561–80; and Peter Hulme, "Hurricanes in the Caribbees: The Constitution of the Discourse of English Colonialism," in *1642: Literature and Power in the Seventeenth Century*, ed. Francis Barker et al. (Colchester: Univ. of Essex, 1981), pp. 55–83.
6. An early approach to this judgment is taken in Rowland M. Hill, "Aphra Behn's Use of Setting," *Modern Language Quarterly*, 7 (1946), 189–203.

historical era, whose place in the eternal design could not be known until its continually expanding, shifting form and its elusive significance were finally comprehended. When accumulating human knowledge might arrive at that destination was anybody's guess. The great day, which had seemed to Columbus so close at hand, had already been deferred countless times by 1688, and the ever-receding goal of Old-World desire now lay farther ahead than ever before, beyond the chimerical horizon. * * *

Oroonoko, of course, was to find its vindication in history, in all those later novels of which Behn's little book seems, to our privileged hindsight, a clear foreshadowing. Its thematic conflict of ancient formalities with modern energies; its portrait of the hero as a Royal Slave, a prince enfettered by brute circumstance; its story of children leaving their parents' home to search for a new, more perfect one; its depiction of history as "character development"; its location of reality in the interplay between a perceived world and a perceiving consciousness; its language, which lends poetic eloquence to the most prosaic things by making them the correlative objects of motions in the human soul; its ambivalent attitude of nostalgia for a vanishing world and eager anticipation of a coming one; its divided allegiances to its audience and to its own discovered truths—these are the very stuff of what we call "the novel," the modern literary form which was devised to deal with the new world that America had made.

* * *

JANE SPENCER

The Woman Novelist as Heroine†

1

* * *

. . . now no more with sorrow be it said,
    Orinda's dead;
Since in her seat *Astraea* does Appear.[1]

Astraea was Aphra Behn, whose literary career began with the performance of her *The Forc'd Marriage* in 1670, and continued until her

† From Jane Spencer, *The Rise of the Woman Novelist: From Aphra Behn to Jane Austen* (Oxford, UK: Basil Blackwell, 1986). Reprinted by permission of the publisher. Some of the author's notes have been abridged.
1. 'To Madam A. Behn *on the publication of her Poems*', signed F. N. W. Poem prefixed to Aphra Behn, *Poems Upon Several Occasions: With a Voyage to the Island of Love* (1684).

death in 1689. Fourteen plays,[2] a volume of poems, translations, and a variety of original fictional works made her one of the most prolific and successful authors of the Restoration period; and there was no lack of recognition for her from fellow-writers like John Dryden, Nahum Tate, and Rochester, or from the poetasters who filled her prefaces with flattery. Men wrote of Behn in the same terms Cowley had used of Katherine Philips,[3] praising the beauty of her face and writing, seeing a union of masculine and feminine qualities in her verse, exalting her as the glory of her sex and man's conqueror. (We can see already that while men were always conceding defeat in verse, they were going to expect the battle to be fought over and over again.) Sappho was invoked as the woman poet's prototype, and Orinda, too, had now reached this semi-mythical status. 'Greece boasts one Sappho; two Orinda's, we', wrote Nahum Tate, counting Astraea as the second Orinda; while one J. Adams considered Sappho and Orinda 'but low types' of 'the excellent Madam Behn'.[4]

There were problems, though, with Astraea's succession to Orinda's honours. In social class, public success, and tone, she was very different from both Katherine Philips and the Duchess of Newcastle.[5] Behn's biographers differ over her origin, but, whether she was born into the gentry or not, her appearance in Restoration London as the widow of a man none of her biographers has been able to trace was not that of the typical gentlewoman. Independent in her life and her writing, she made her living from the Restoration stage, one of a new breed of professionals 'forced to write for Bread and not ashamed to owne it'.[6] Instead of the Duchess's awkward blend of arrogance and self-doubt, or Katherine Philips's modest retreat from public gaze, Behn showed a direct confidence in her work and anger against male prejudice: 'had the Plays I have writ come forth under any Mans Name, and never known to have been mine; I appeal to all unbyast Judges of Sense, if they had not said that Person had made as many good Comedies, as any one Man that has writ in our Age', she wrote.[7] She did not hesitate to provide her audience with the bawdy writing it desired, and so fuelled the arguments of those who thought writing for money implied

2. Behn's plays, including attributions, are now tallied at twenty [Editor's note].
3. Early woman author (1632–1664), who used the pen name Orinda and who was widely admired for her poems and translations from Corneille, published in a posthumous edition of 1667 (2nd ed. 1669, 3rd ed. 1678). Abraham Cowley, regarded as the best poet of the time, wrote two elaborate poems of tribute that appeared in the volume [Editor's note].
4. 'To the Incomparable Author', signed N. Tate, in the introduction to Behn's The Lover's Watch (1686); and 'To the excellent Madam Behn, on her Poems', signed J. Adams, in introduction to Poems Upon Several Occasions.
5. Margaret Cavendish (1623–1673), who lived a retired and protected life, while steadily publishing many long volumes in a range of forms, from poetic fancies to philosophical speculations, that she hoped would win her lasting fame [Editor's note].
6. 'To the Reader', Sir Patient Fancy (1678).
7. Preface to The Lucky Chance (1687).

depravity—a view that formed a possible stumbling-block for the eighteenth-century novelists, also professionals but catering for very different tastes.

Behn had plenty of detractors, and they were able to seize on the view that selling one's work was like selling onself to claim that 'Punk and *Poetess* agree so pat./You cannot well be *this* and not be *that*'.[8] Behn was not a punk (prostitute) but she had lovers, and her affair with John Hoyle, a lawyer of libertine principles and bisexual practice, gave rise to sneers that he had paid for her favours by writing her plays for her.[9] In her 'loose' life and bawdy writing Behn differed crucially from recent famous women writers. 'Chaste' was an adjective almost automatically attached to Orinda, and whatever else might be said of Margaret Cavendish, no-one has challenged her claim that 'neither this present, nor any of the future ages can or will truly say that I am not Vertuous and Chast'.[1] So Behn, even more than the eccentric Duchess, was a problematic model for the aspiring woman writer, and because of her professional success, much harder to ignore. At the turn of the century Philips and Behn stood together in the public mind: the first gentle and genteel, irreproachable; the second a successful professional, and surely (as one of the best writers of fiction in England in her time) a better model for the eighteenth-century woman novelist, but also bawdy in her work, unchaste in her life. Women writers had a choice: Orinda versus Astraea.

*   *   *

2

Aphra Behn's comments on herself as a writer are sprinkled liberally in the prefaces to her plays. She had to struggle for recognition of her right to a professional role—hence her tart remarks that women were equally entitled to write bawdy, and that people would have admired

---

8. Robert Gould, 'The Poetess, A Satyr', in *The Works of Mr. Robert Gould* (London: W. Lewis, 1709), **II**, p. 17. In the couplet quoted he is referring specifically to 'Ephelia' and 'Sappho'. 'Sappho' is identified as Aphra Behn by Maureen Duffy, *The Passionate Shepherdess*, p. 280.
9. Alexander Radcliffe, in 'The Ramble: An Anti-Heroick Poem' (1682), reported that,

> The censuring Age have thought it fit
> To damn a Woman, 'cause 'tis said,
> The Plays she vends she never made.
> But that a *Greys Inn* Lawyer does 'em,
> Who unto her was Friend in Bosom.

The woman is Aphra Behn, the lawyer, her lover John Hoyle. Radcliffe, however, does not include himself among Behn's detractors. A few lines later he includes her among 'the better sort' of writers, 'Damn'd only by the Ignorant'. See 'The Ramble' (London, 1682), pp. 6–7; included, with separate title page and pagination, in *The Works of Capt. Alex. Radcliffe In One Volume*. 3rd edn augmented (London: Richard Wellington, 1696).
1. 'The Blazing-World', in *Observations Upon Experimental Philosophy* (London, 1666), **II**, p. 26.

her plays more if they had thought a man had written them. To some-one so determined to be accepted on equal terms with men, a good deal of the praise she was given must have been more galling than gratifying. Her admirers were busy building her a reputation as a writer of love, praising her poems for being erotic, even suggesting that read-ing Behn was tantamount to being seduced by her. Thomas Creech's poem to her announced:

> . . . thy Pen disarms us so,
> We yield our selves to the first beauteous Foe;
> The easie softness of thy thoughts surprise,
> And this new way Love steals into our Eyes; . . .
> In the same trance with the young pair we lie,
> And in their amorous Ecstasies we die . . .[2]

Using another common assumption about femininity, one eulogist saw her work as evidence of her delicate understanding of the mysteries of nature, women and love.

> What Passions does your Poetry impart?
> It shows th'unfathom'd thing a Woman's Heart,
> Tells what Love is, his Nature and his Art,
> Displays the several Scenes of Hopes and Fears,
> Love's Smiles, his Sighs, his Laughing and his Tears.[3]

A posthumous edition of her works was introduced with similar claims: 'The Passions, that of Love especially, she was Mistress of, and gave us such nice and tender Touches of them, that without her Name we might discover the Author.'[4] Behn was certainly not above exploiting this image of herself when it came to selling her poems and her trans-lation of Balthazar de Bonnecourse's *La Monstre, The Lover's Watch: or, the Art of making love*. Love was her subject here, and the enco-mium poems printed at the beginning of these volumes served as ad-vertisements of the fact. Moreover, it is certainly fair that she should be remembered as a poet of love, when we consider such deservedly celebrated lyrics as 'Love in Fantastic Triumph sate' and 'A Thousand

2. 'To the Authour, on her Voyage to the Island of Love', signed T.C., [in *The Works of Aphra Behn*, vol. 6, ed. Montague Summers (London: William Heinemann, 1915), 121].
3. Anonymous, 'To the Lovely Witty ASTRAEA, on her Excellent Poems', in *Works* [1915], **VI**, p. 123.
4. Charles Gildon, 'Epistle Dedicatory, To Simon Scroop, Esq; of Danby, in Yorkshire', in *All the Histories and Novels Written by the Late Ingenious Mrs. Behn, Entire in One Volume*, 3rd edn, with Additions (London: S. Briscoe, 1698), sig. A4v.

Martyrs I have made'. To Behn, though, love was not an especially feminine subject, it was simply an important poetic theme; and it was as a poet, simply, that she wanted to be remembered. 'Poetry (my Talent)', she wrote in proud parentheses, deceptively casual.[5] In the preface to one of her comedies, *The Lucky Chance*, she asked for a very different kind of recognition from the kind she got:

> All I ask, is the Priviledge for my Masculine Part the Poet in me, (if any such you will allow me) to tread in those successful Paths my Predecessors have so long thriv'd in, to take those Measures that both the Ancient and Modern Writers have set me, and by which they have pleas'd the World so well: If I must not, because of my Sex, have this Freedom, but that you will usurp all to your selves; I lay down my Quill . . . for I am not content to write for a Third day only [i.e. just for money: playwrights took the proceeds of the third performance]. I value Fame as much as if I had been born a *Hero*[6] . . .

Instead of placing herself in the tradition of Sappho and Orinda, Behn is appealing here to the precedent of all the 'Ancient and Modern Writers', mostly men, and defining her poetic talent as masculine. The freedom she is demanding here is the freedom to write without any special restraints because of her sex.

Behn tended to compromise her claim for the freedom to write as men wrote by simultaneously denying that she wrote bawdy plays as they did: 'they charge [*The Lucky Chance*] with the old never failing Scandal—That 'tis not fit for the Ladys: As if (if it were as they falsly give it out) the Ladys were oblig'd to hear Indecencys only from their Pens and Plays.'[7] However, the fact that her comedies were successful on the stage in the 1670s and 1680s indicates that she escaped the requirements of 'decency' soon to bear especially hard on women. Her success in Restoration comedy has been held against her by some recent critics who find her work *too* 'masculine': reproducing the attitudes of male libertines, so that the hero of her comedy *The Rover* (1677) is rewarded for his philandering by marriage to the chaste heroine, who (as it transpires in the sequel to the play) soon dies, leaving him free to rove once more.[8] Behn is not without general concern for her sex and for women's freedom, as her plays' treatment of arranged marriages and her heroines' criticisms of various masculine tyrannies demon-

---

5. Dedication to Henry Pain of *The Fair Jilt* [(1688)].
6. Preface to *The Lucky Chance* [(1687)].
7. Preface to *The Lucky Chance*.
8. Katharine M. Rogers writes that '*The Rover* . . . reveals a more masculine set of values than do the works of Etherege or Wycherley. . . . [Behn's plays] afford a striking example of the callous attitudes which later sentimentalists rightly rejected as antifeminist'. *Feminism in Eighteenth-Century England* (Urbana, Chicago, London: University of Illinois Press, 1982), pp. 98–9.

strate.[9] Still, it is outside the plays themselves that she supports women most thoroughly, through her claims for women's abilities as writers.

* * *

Often Behn makes her narrator not simply a woman but specifically the self-portrait of a well-known author, referring in passing to her own works. In *The Dumb Virgin* she is so pleased with the hero's assumed name of Dangerfield that 'being since satisfied it was a Counterfeit, I us'd it in a Comedy of mine'. In *Oroonoko* she mentions meeting 'Colonel *Martin*, a Man of great Gallantry, Wit, and Goodness, and whom I have celebrated in a Character of my New *Comedy*, by his own Name, in memory of so brave a Man'.[1] The events of *The Fair Jilt* are said to have taken place in Antwerp, 'about the Time of my being sent thither by King *Charles*,' referring to a spying mission she undertook in 1666 to obtain information from a former friend William Scot, son of one of the regicides. Clearly one purpose of references like this was to impress upon her readers the literal truth of her narratives, whose events she claimed to have witnessed; and recent research shows that *Oroonoko* and *The Fair Jilt*, at least, have their basis in truth.[2] Another reason for putting her self-portrait into her novels is to include in them her vindication of the woman writer's ability and authority.

This is most evident in *Oroonoko*, where the autobiographical element means that Behn's interest in the narrator's position develops into an examination of her own role as woman and as writer. This fascinating novel marks an important stage in the history of women's quest for literary authority. Writing before the full establishment of the convention that love is the woman writer's subject and a moral aim her

9. For a discussion of the treatment of arranged marriage in Behn's comedies, claiming that she gives the 'clearest articulation' of this problem before the 1690s, see Robert L. Root, 'Aphra Behn, Arranged Marriage and Restoration Comedy', *Women and Literature* 5 no. 1 (Spring, 1977), pp. 3–14.

1. A character named George Marteen is the hero of Behn's *Younger Brother*, posthumously produced in 1696. No Dangerfield appears in her plays, but it is possible she had intended to use the name. Montague Summers points out that the name Dangerfield appears in Sedley's *Bellamera*, and suggests that Behn 'gave' the name to Sedley: see *Works*, V, p. 523.

2. The truth or otherwise of Behn's narratives has been a source of controversy since Ernest Bernbaum claimed that she 'deliberately and circumstantially lied' in *Oroonoko*, and had never been to Surinam: see 'Mrs. Behn's Biography a Fiction', *PMLA* 28 (1913), p. 434. Her knowledge of the colony, however, is detailed, and not only Byam, but more obscure characters like Trefry had a real-life existence. A letter from Byam to Sir Robert Harley in March 1664 seems to refer to Behn's departure from the colony. Behn's use of Indian and African words is said to show authentic knowledge of both languages in B. Dhuicq, 'Further Evidence on Aphra Behn's Stay in Surinam', *Notes and Queries* 26 (1979), pp. 524–6. Behn also claimed to have brought back a feather-dress from Surinam, worn in a performance of Dryden's *The Indian Queen*; H. A. Hargreaves has investigated this and concludes that the statement is probably true. See 'New Evidence of the Realism of Mrs. Behn's *Oroonoko*', *Bulletin of the New York Public Library* 74 (1970), pp. 437–44. Behn's visit to Surinam is well established, then, but Oroonoko's existence is not. *The Fair Jilt* tells the story of Prince Tarquin's attempt, at his wife's instigation, to murder his sister-in-law, and of his narrow escape from the axe when his executioner fails to do his job properly. This story has usually been considered pure fiction, but Maureen Duffy has shown that a 'Prince Tarquino's' crime and the bungled execution were reported in newspapers of the day: see Duffy, [*The Passionate Shepherdess: Aphra Behn 1640–1689* (London: Jonathan Cape, 1977)] pp. 72–3.

excuse, Behn has a freedom denied to most of her eighteenth-century descendants. She ranges widely over different societies, to investigate the meaning of civilized values in a story beyond the scope of many more polished later novelists. * * * Three very different cultures—the European, the native Surinam, and that of Coramantien, Oroonoko's African home—are compared to one another. Thus it is a novel of ideas as well as action, and the narrator's comments are crucial to the rendering of these.

She is a narrator of a type especially common in the early novel—herself a character within the tale, relating it with the authority of an eye-witness. Neither omniscient and outside the action, nor central to it, she provides her commentary on the events she narrates.[3] Having travelled out to Surinam, as we know Aphra Behn herself did, she meets the enslaved Oroonoko, hears the story of his past life and adventures, and either sees or hears of the rest of his story up to his dreadful end. Trefry, she tells us, once intended to write the hero's life, but died before he could do it, and so the task fell to her, which, she says modestly, is a pity for Oroonoko. 'His Misfortune was, to fall in an obscure World, that afforded only a Female Pen to celebrate his Fame'. Yet as events unfold we realize that her gender is an important part of her authority: what she knows, and the comments she is able to make, depend on it. The female pen is vindicated.

The scene is set for Oroonoko's story by the narrator's description of Surinam. The Surinam natives represent 'an absolute *Idea* of the first State of Innocence, before Man knew how to sin: And 'tis most evident and plain, that simple Nature is the most harmless, inoffensive and vertuous Mistress'. Civilization could only bring repression, and 'Religion wou'd here but destroy that Tranquillity, they possess by Ignorance; and Laws wou'd but teach 'em to know Offence, of which now they have no Notion'. Their simplicity contrasts markedly with the duplicity shown by the white community throughout the story.

The story of Oroonoko's Coramantien life provides another contrast to Europe. Here it is not so much a case of the noble savage against civilization, as that of the truly civilized man against a decadent society. The young prince Oroonoko embodies the Restoration's heroic ideal: proud, honourable, superhuman in his prowess in battle, and 'as capable of Love, as 'twas possible for a brave and gallant Man to be; and in saying that, I have nam'd the highest Degree of Love: for sure, great Souls are most capable of that Passion'. His wit, his judgement, and his character all in all are as great 'as if his Education had been in some *European* Court'. His experiences show those Europeans whose

---

3. Franz K. Stanzel distinguishes this kind of 'teller-character', a 'narrative agent [which] dominated earlier novels', from the 'reflector-character' who is the focus of events in a narrative but does not comment on them. See 'Teller-Characters and Reflector-Characters in Narrative Theory', *Poetics Today*, 2 no. 2 (Winter, 1981), pp. 6–7.

highest values he has adopted in a very poor light. From the captain who tricks him aboard the slave-ship, to Byam, Deputy-Governor of Surinam, who tricks him into surrender after the slave rebellion, they fail to live up to their own code of honour.

The contrast between the African prince and the English people is used to expose what Behn saw as the recent betrayal of civilized values by the English. Oroonoko, royal himself, echoes his creator's royalist sentiments when he expresses horror at the execution of Charles I, 'with all the Sense and Abhorrence of the Injustice imaginable'. He and his countrymen 'pay a most absolute Resignation to the Monarch, especially when he is a Parent also', most unlike the English, with Monmouth's plot against his father Charles II in their recent history by the time Behn was writing Oroonoko's story. The Coramantiens' attitudes to sexual relationships compare well with the Europeans', too. Oroonoko's early passion for Imoinda 'aim'd at nothing but Honour, if such a distinction may be made in Love; and especially in that Country, where Men take to themselves as many as they can maintain; and where the only Crime and Sin with Woman is, to turn her off, to abandon her to Want, Shame and Misery: Such ill Morals are only practis'd in *Christian*-Countries'.

As narrator, Behn has two assets which enable her to make Oroonoko's story serve this critique of her own society: her intimate acquaintance with and sympathy for the hero himself and her own identity as one of the Europeans, but not so completely at one with them that she cannot take a detached view of them.

Both these narrative assets are enhanced because of her social position and her sex. She has travelled out to Surinam with her father, who was to be Lieutenant-Governor of the colony, but died on the voyage. She lives in the best house on the plantation and has, she claims, 'none above me in that Country'.[4] She thus has status but no occupation, and no permanent stake in the colony; so she is well-placed to observe and comment freely. As a woman she can comment with authority on Oroonoko's gallantry and attractiveness. When she first saw him, she explains, he 'address'd himself to me, and some other Women, with the best Grace in the World'. She gets to know him well because 'he lik'd the Company of us Women much above the Men'. In fact 'we [women] had all the Liberty of Speech with him, especially my self, whom he call'd his *Great Mistress*; and indeed my Word wou'd go a great way with him'. Thus she hears his story from his own lips and is able to report his noble sentiments.

The narrator also enters the action, exploiting Oroonoko's gallantry

---

4. This claim was made by Behn in the 'Epistle Dedicatory' of *Oroonoko* to Lord Maitland: see *Works*, V, p. 511 [p. 5 in this Norton Critical Edition].

and his attachment to her in order to keep him under the control of the white settlers. Oroonoko is suspicious of their promises to set him free when the Lord Governor arrives, an attitude justified by his former experience of the Christian word of honour and by the narrator's comment that they 'fed him from Day to Day with Promises'. The settlers, fearing a slave mutiny, ask the narrator to use her influence to persuade Oroonoko to wait till the Lord Governor makes his appearance. This she does, and it is hard to tell whether she does so in good faith or not. Her admiration for his heroic scorn of slavery sits oddly with her actions: 'I neither thought it convenient to trust him much out of our View, nor did the Country, who fear'd him', she reports, relating how she and the other settlers surround Oroonoko with 'Attendants' who are really spies. She encourages the royal slave to take several pleasant 'Diversions'—hunting tigers, fishing, visiting the Surinam Indians—the real purpose of which is to divert his thoughts from rebellion. She seems to be acting entirely, and with typical duplicity, as a European; but once the rebellion breaks out the narrator's ability to detach herself from her society's crimes becomes evident.

The whites, it now transpires, are split. Byam, 'a Fellow, whose Character is not fit to be mention'd with the worst of the *Slaves*', is for taking strong measures against the rebels, but 'they of the better sort', including the narrator, believe that Oroonoko has been badly treated and should not be harshly dealt with now. Trefry joins in the pursuit of the rebels, meaning to act as mediator; but, duped by Byam's promises of leniency, he persuades Oroonoko to surrender, and unwittingly leads him into a trap. The narrator now separates herself from the Europeans responsible for Oroonoko's downfall. She neither sides with Byam's cruelty nor shows Trefry's gullibility. If the reader wonders why someone of her high social position did nothing to protect Oroonoko from the vicious treatment he gets, the answer lies in her sex. As a woman, she has had to flee from the scene of action:

> * * * we were possess'd with extream Fear, which no perswasions cou'd Dissipate, that he wou'd secure himself till Night; and then, that he wou'd come down and Cut all our Throats. This apprehension made all the Females of us fly down the River, to be secur'd; and while we were away, they acted this Cruelty * * *

The trust between the royal slave and his 'Great Mistress' has been shattered by their racial differences, and yet her ignominious flight reveals similarities in the positions of the European woman and the enslaved African man. Like Oroonoko, who is given the outward respect due to a prince but kept from real power, the narrator is under the illusion that she has high status in the colony; but when it comes to a crisis the men are the real rulers, and being the daughter of a man who would have governed Surinam if he had lived does not help her. Ironically, she still seems to believe in her 'Authority and Interest' as she tells a story which reveals how illusory these were.

The narrator's gender is now her alibi. It saves her from sharing the guilt of her countrymen's treatment of the noble black prince, and, by implication, from sharing in the general corruption of the European society she criticizes. She is absent at other key moments too. She has to leave the hero when she sees his self-inflicted wounds, being 'but Sickly, and very apt to fall into Fits of dangerous Illness upon any extraordinary Melancholy'. She is still away when he is executed. Her mother and sister (scarcely mentioned in the story up to this point) witness the event in her stead, but they are 'not suffer'd to save him'. Their position here is like the narrator's throughout: a spectator, but because of her femininity, a helpless one.

This feminine position, though, is an appropriate one for a narrator. On the fringes of her world, she is unable to act in the decisive scenes, but she observes, records, and eventually hands the story down to posterity. In *Oroonoko* the narrator's femininity is especially important because the similarities between the slave's and the woman's positions allow her her sympathetic insight into the hero's feelings at the same time as she creates a full sense of the difference of his race and culture. The limitations on women which Behn acknowledges, even exploits, within her narrative, do not apply to expression. As a character the narrator seems caught uneasily between admiration for her hero and allegiance to European civilization, but this means that she can present a picture of both sides. She ends with a flourish that implicitly asserts women's equal right to be recorders of events and interpreters of the world:

> Thus Dy'd this Great Man; worthy of a better Fate, and a more sublime Wit than mine to write his Praise; yet, I hope, the Reputation of my Pen is considerable enough to make his Glorious Name to survive to all Ages, with that of the Brave, the Beautiful, and the Constant *Imoinda*.

The reputation of Aphra Behn's pen certainly was great at the time that *Oroonoko* was written, and she uses that reputation to present the female narrator as authoritative, disinterested and sympathetic, with as much authority as a male writer and also with special insights gained from her woman's position.

The marginality of the narrator's position is very important to Behn for another reason. It enables her to create her self-image as a writer, free from some of the restrictions on behaviour and feeling which operate on women as represented in the narrative. The contrast between the heroine, Imoinda, and the woman who writes her story is instructive. Imoinda is all that convention could desire of a noble hero's mate: beautiful, sensitive, ready to sacrifice all to preserve her chastity, capable of brave deeds in defence of her husband, and above all, devoted to him. Her qualities are best seen in her eagerness to die at his hands: when Oroonoko explains that he must kill her to preserve her honour, 'He found the Heroick Wife faster pleading for Death than he was to propose it'. The narrator explains this attitude as part of exotic Coramantien custom: 'for Wives have a respect for their Husbands equal to what any other People pay a Deity; and when a Man finds any occasion to quit his Wife, if he love her, she dyes by his Hand; if not, he sells her, or suffers some other to kill her'. The killing of Imoinda shocks Oroonoko's European friends, but is presented as 'a Deed, that (however Horrid it first appear'd to us all) when we had heard his Reasons, we thought it Brave and Just'. Here an uneasy note creeps into the narrator's assessment of Coramantien, the place where natural honour and nobility are supposed to thrive. It has crept in before whenever women's position was considered. African polygamy is useful for the purposes of a satirical attack on European sexual hypocrisy, but Behn holds back from endorsing it as a real alternative by making Oroonoko vow to be true all his life to Imoinda alone; and the whole Coramantien episode shows that heroic society torn apart by the quarrel between Oroonoko and his grandfather the king over possession of the heroine. Writing *Oroonoko*, Behn was confronted with the problem of a woman's relation to the heroic ideal which she, along with other Restoration writers, endorsed. In some ways Behn identifies with her hero, but in the story of Oroonoko and his wife her position, as a woman, might be expected to be more analagous with Imoinda's, and that is an identification she does not want to make.

The female narrator Behn creates is important for *not* being the heroine. It is a pity that the autobiographical element of *Oroonoko* has caused so much criticism to centre on the truth or otherwise of the self-portrait within it, for Behn was deliberately not focusing on her own experience, and at a time when heroine and woman writer were coming to seem almost synonymous, she insisted on making a sharp distinction between them. If Imoinda, ideally lovely and noble, is Oroonoko's true mate, the narrator is his 'Great Mistress', sympathising with him, surviving him, recording his story, and assessing his significance. From the narrative stance Behn creates in this novel it is evident that for her being a writer was a way of escaping some of the limitations imposed on women.

Her prefaces claim a man's rights in writing, and her narratives claim something of a special authority as a woman, but without acknowledging any of the limitations on feminine expression that were later to come into force. Her double claim is well expressed in some lines she inserted into her translation of the sixth book of Cowley's Latin work,

Of Plants. Here, unusually for her, she calls on the examples of Sappho and Orinda. The poet has been invoking Daphne, source of the poet's laurels, and then 'the Translatress in her own Person' addresses her:

> I, by a double Right, thy Bounties claim,
> Both from my *Sex*, and in *Apollo's* Name:
> Let me with *Sappho* and *Orinda* be,
> Oh ever sacred Nymph, adorn'd by thee;
> And give my verses Immortality.[5]

Behn's confidence in her own authority as a woman writer is not matched in the century following her death.

* * *

ROBERT L. CHIBKA

[Truth, Falsehood, and Fiction in *Oroonoko*][†]

* * *

Oroonoko: Or, The Royal Slave. A True History opens with a truth-claim, but so, in various ways, do *Robinson Crusoe, Pamela,* even *Gulliver's Travels*; and this truth-claim, it has been noted, is almost word for word the one that appears in Behn's *The Fair Jilt*. Nevertheless, much discussion of *Oroonoko* has concerned whether Behn told the truth when she claimed to be telling the truth. Critical as well as biographical judgments have hinged upon this truth-claim to a remarkable extent: "never did Mrs. Behn so whole-heartedly vouch for every fact, to the immense satisfaction of her immediate public and to the despair of modern critics."[1] Now that the formal truth-claim of early novels has given way to the equally glib but opposite disclaimer that resemblance to persons living or dead is purely coincidental, no one would think to evaluate Defoe (or Richardson, whose *Pamela* attracted accusations of fictitiousness as well as burlesques of its morality) on such grounds.[2]

5. 'Of Plants', in *The Works of Mr. Abraham Cowley*, 10th edn (London: Benjamin Motte, 1721), III, p. 440.
† Revised and abridged from "Oh! Do Not Fear a Woman's Invention": Truth, Falsehood, and Fiction in Aphra Behn's *Oroonoko*," by Robert L. Chibka in *Texas Studies in Literature and Language*, 30, no. 4 (1988), 510–37; by permission of the author and the University of Texas Press.
1. Bridgit G. MacCarthy, *Women Writers: Their Contribution to the English Novel, 1621–1744* (Oxford: Blackwell, 1946), 173.
2. The truth-claim has been making a comeback of sorts in an unlikely arena: made-for TV movies advertised with phrases such as "Based on a True Story," "Based on the True Story," and "From the Incredible True Story That Really Happened."

But less canonical authors are not so immune, and we find that Behn's fiction can be attacked for not being accurately autobiographical. More oddly, though, many who would redeem Behn, * * * at pains to vouch for her veracity (usually called "realism"), have largely ignored the premises and structure of her narrative and assiduously sought not only biographical documentation and printed sources for descriptive passages but independent corroboration of their natural-historical or anthropological accuracy.[3] At times Oroonoko seems to resemble the Surinamese numb eel, making critics on contact lose their feel for narrative texture. * * *

* * *

That Behn's veracity seems to so many to matter so much perversely testifies to her excellence in some aspects of "realism." Her truth-claim, unlike its contemporary counterparts, exerts a fascinating power well into our own time. In the swirl of condemnation and vindication, one finds this odd logic: if Behn tells truth, she deserves our admiration more; if she has made the world haggle so long over whether her work is true (if she has written a work of fiction that makes us care this much about its factual basis), she more nearly deserves relegation to unsanctified literary-historical ground. One would expect the opposite: Defoe's reputation, to continue the obvious comparison, rests largely on his ability to make invented, composed narrative (with *whatever* basis in fact) compelling; we "forgive" a convincing fiction. Yet in a century when imaginative voyages are generally valued more than scores of true narratives of adventures and exploration, issues no longer considered pertinent to her contemporaries and successors remain central to consideration of Behn's work. "*Oh! do not fear a Woman's Invention,*" cries Onahal, the aged courtesan of Coramantien, reassuring Aboan that she does not *lack* one. Do we in the twentieth century so fear the *presence* of a woman's invention that the autobiographical basis of a work of fiction takes on moral overtones none would think to apply to the product of a man's invention? * * *

One critic who ignores biographical controversy, Lennard Davis, has argued that the novel is a form of discourse that suspends its readers on a knife-edge between belief and disbelief. He notes that the plot of Oroonoko hinges on truth and deception: "fiction-making and lying are central to the work. Fabrications build up into frames doubling back upon themselves until every turn reveals fact warped into fiction which

---

3. E.g., Harrison Gray Platt, Jr., "Astrea and Celadon: An Untouched Portrait of Aphra Behn," *PMLA* 49 (1934): 544–59; Wiley Sypher, "A Note on the Realism of Mrs. Behn's *Oroonoko*," *Modern Language Quarterly* 3 (1942): 401–05; J. A. Ramsaran, "*Oroonoko*: A Study of the Factual Elements," *Notes and Queries* 7 (1960): 142–45; W. J. Cameron, *New Light on Aphra Behn* (Auckland: University of Auckland, 1961, rpt. 1978, Arden Library); H. A. Hargreaves, "New Evidence of the Realism of Mrs. Behn's *Oroonoko*," *Bulletin of the New York Public Library* 74 (1970): 437–44.

turns back upon itself to become fact."[4] These are, of course, the issues that animate debate *about* the novel. This essay expands on Davis's insight to examine connections between the treatment of truth, fiction, and falsehood within this *"History"* and the issues of truth, fiction, and falsehood that dominate its critical history. I shall argue that this narrative, by continually suggesting correlations between truth-claims and manipulative power and by implicitly contrasting the narrator's relations with her reader and those with her hero, problematizes readers' "simple and receptive faith."[5] Offering sometimes contradictory versions of the politics of language and interpretation, it challenges the ways we read by simultaneously encouraging and refuting equations of the rhetorical and the moral. Finally, I want to suggest that this problem, when we ignore its power within the text, returns with something like the force of the repressed, transformed into a critical obsession with the extra-textual, biographical truth of the narrative and its author's personal "veracity."

The truth-claim that opens *Oroonoko* introduces terms that reverberate throughout the novel and endows them with values that will change in unpredictable ways:

> I DO not pretend, in giving you the History of this *Royal Slave*, to entertain my Reader with Adventures of a feign'd *Hero*, whose Life and Fortunes Fancy may manage at the Poet's Pleasure; nor in relating the Truth, design to adorn it with any Accidents, but such as arriv'd in earnest to him: And it shall come simply into the World, recommended by its own proper Merits, and natural Intrigues; there being enough of Reality to support it, and to render it diverting, without the Addition of Invention.
>
> I was my self an Eye-Witness to a great part, of what you will find here set down; and what I cou'd not be Witness of, I receiv'd from the Mouth of the chief Actor in this History, the *Hero* himself, who gave us the whole Transactions of his Youth; and though I shall omit, for Brevity's sake, a thousand little Accidents of his Life, which, however pleasant to us, where History was scarce, and Adventures very rare; yet might prove tedious and heavy to my Reader, in a World where he finds Diversions for every Minute, new and strange: But we who were perfectly charm'd with the Character of this great Man, were curious to gather every Circumstance of his Life.

These paragraphs address the status of the narrative on a continuum from factual History to feign'd Invention, and consequently, the reader's

4. Lennard J. Davis, *Factual Fictions: The Origins of the English Novel* (New York: Columbia University Press, 1983), 106–10 (this quotation, 110).
5. Michael McKeon, *The Origins of the English Novel, 1600–1740* (Baltimore: Johns Hopkins University Press, 1987), 113.

position on a continuum from implicit belief to outright skepticism. But crucial terms—entertain, Truth, adorn, Invention, Diversions—will recur with associations that retroactively complicate the status of this opening as simply factual or simply conventional. Davis notes here "a sort of general scorn for invention, entertainment, and feigned heroes."[6] If these aspects of fictional art are held in low esteem, however, the aesthetic effects they induce are not. The narrator disdains the arrangement of a narrative "at the Poet's Pleasure," but admits to editing and arranging her story so that what was "pleasant to us" need not "prove tedious and heavy to my Reader." Pleasure (the reader's, not the poet's) will indeed dictate the management of her story. Nor is she opposed to entertainment or diversion per se: acknowledging that her work must compete with the "Diversions for every Minute, new and strange," of her sophisticated reader's world, she expects reality "to render [her story] diverting." She opposes not all Intrigues, but only those which are not "natural"; not entertaining Accidents, but adornment of Truth with Invention. Responsible or irresponsible language, self-serving or generous art, the use or abuse of narrative power are her explicit topics.

Her narrative "shall come simply into the World, recommended by its own proper Merits"; it will thus resemble her hero, who comes simply into the world of European treachery, recommended by his own proper merits, of which none is more important than his attitude toward verbal truth: "*Oroonoko*, whose Honour was such as he never had violated a Word in his Life himself, much less a solemn Asseveration, believ'd in an instant what this Man [the captain who enslaves him] said." This double quality—the hero's honorable inability to lie and consequent inability to perceive lies—makes us see *Oroonoko*, from one angle, as an education in skepticism: he learns not to believe others' truth-claims (those of the slave trader, of Byam, Trefry, and whites in general, but also of the king of Coramantien, who tells him Imoinda is dead, and of fellow slaves, who betray him after swearing allegiance in the attempted escape). Oroonoko's tragedy is that he learns this lesson too slowly to save himself from the power that liars wield; for most of the narrative, his truth-telling honor makes him the perfect fool for the knaves who surround him, their ideal reader.

Oroonoko's honor aligns him with both the writer and the reader defined in the novel's first paragraph: the one who cannot tell a lie, and the one who will believe whatever the other says. The narrator promises to be the former and wants her reader to be the latter. These two types appear in the tale, however, as more complicated and compromised than the teller would have us believe. The narrator's role in the plot sets her at odds both with Oroonoko and with the role she

6. Davis, 107.

prepares for her reader. Her narrative depicts those who share Oroon-oko's innocent trust invariably as helpless victims of those who mislead with verbal promises.

* * * Following the disclaimers of the first two paragraphs, the narrator digresses, * * * to describe Surinamese customs and artifacts, so that a sentence promising to explain the slave trade discusses, instead, trading with natives for marmosets and "*Cousheries*," * * * and an exposition of commerce in exotic pets displaces one of commerce in exotic human beings. * * *

Critics have often praised this sort of "realistic" insertion (and debated its accuracy), but this digression raises issues—nature and art, innocence and adornment, truth and falsehood—that inform both the opening disclaimer and Oroonoko's biography in ways that go far beyond local color. Her anecdotal epitome of native innocence, for instance, focuses on truth, falsehood, and unkept promises:

> They once made Mourning and Fasting for the Death of the *English* Governor, who had given his Hand to come on such a Day to 'em, and neither came nor sent; believing, when a Man's Word was past, nothing but Death cou'd or shou'd prevent his keeping it. * * *

What follows makes it harder to separate the Surinamese whom the whites "caress . . . with all the brotherly and friendly Affection in the World" from the Africans they trade like marmosets. * * * Finally, we find that "all the brotherly and friendly Affection in the world" is simply a practical awareness of Europeans' self-interest: "they being, on all Occasions, very useful to us, we find it absolutely necessary to caress 'em as Friends." * * * The "true" European perception of natives as human or subhuman is quite irrelevant; it is revised from moment to moment to serve the colonialist agenda. * * *

Polarities such as Nature/Art and Beauty/Use are as volatile as racial perceptions. The outline of Surinamese exotica includes insects "of various Excellencies, such as Art cannot imitate," and "unimitable" feather artifacts. European art can imitate neither nature nor art here, and utility is indistinguishable from adornment. The whites trade "Knives, Axes, Pins and Needles; which they us'd only as Tools to drill Holes with in their Ears, Noses and Lips, where they hang a great many little things." If tools are used to adorn the body, ornamental beads are woven into an apron to hide it: "which Apron they wear just before 'em, as *Adam* and *Eve* did the Fig-leaves." "This Adornment" enhances a beauty described three sentences later as "unadorn'd"; and the point at which distinction yields to contradiction brings another reference to Eden: "so like our first Parents before the Fall." In her truth-claim the narrator gave the verb "adorn" the negative connotation of "Invention," the cardinal literary sin that falsifies in a misguided attempt to "adorn" facts. It bears no such burden two paragraphs later in the description of Surinamese bodies. "Invention," with regard to European minds, still does, however, in a passage that opposes it to Nature:

> these People represented to me an absolute *Idea* of the first State of Innocence, before Man knew how to sin: . . . 'Tis [Nature] alone, if she were permitted, that better instructs the World, than all the Inventions of Man. * * *

In Surinam the oppositions of fallen life seem not to obtain. But when this world whose prelapsarian innocence disrupts European categories of thought is invaded by Europeans whose actions equally disrupt that innocence, the drama encompasses, with a vengeance, all aspects of fallenness: enslavement, treachery, betrayal, violence, sin, death.

Nature and Art coincide seamlessly in a landscape that "affords all things both for Beauty and Use":

> The very Wood of all these Trees have an intrinsick Value above common Timber; for they are, when cut, of different Colours, glorious to behold; and bear a Price considerable, to inlay withal. Besides this, they yield rich Balm, and Gums; so that we make our Candles of such an aromatick Substance, as does not only give a sufficient Light, but, as they Burn, they cast their Perfumes all about.

* * * Is the "intrinsick Value" of the trees aesthetic or commercial? The dichotomy of "Beauty and Use" makes little sense if they are inseparable; this nature made for art exposes a kinship of delight and exploitation. A description of a citrus grove makes further connections: "the cool Air . . . made it . . . fit to entertain People in, at all the hottest Hours of the Day . . . Not all the Gardens of boasted *Italy* can produce a Shade to out-vie this, which Nature had joyn'd with Art to render so exceeding Fine." European poets invent such gardens "to entertain People in," but Behn's exotic setting allows nature to produce the effects of art without the negative associations of the invented or feigned. * * *

* * * As the exotic landscape throws into question the terms that describe it, terms with apparently stable value in the literary-aesthetic context of the novel's earliest paragraphs are unsettled in the anthropological-political context of a story that revises their underlying assumptions. Tracking these terms through the novel, we can see their valence oscillate wildly.

When Oroonoko believes that the king of Coramantien has put Imoinda to death, * * * Jamoan tells "a thousand Tales and Adventures of Love and Gallantry," and Oroonoko's officers "*invented* all sorts of *Diversions* and Sports to *entertain* their Prince" (emphasis added). The narrator credits their artistry with saving Oroonoko's life, * * * but the

same susceptibility to entertainment allows the English captain to enslave Oroonoko, who finds him as charming as the narrator finds
Oroonoko. The description of his trap echoes the opening disclaimer:
he gains Oroonoko's confidence by "*entertaining* the Prince every
Day"; his boat is "richly *adorn'd*" and enhanced by music "with which
Oroonoko was extreamly *delighted*"; Oroonoko and his companions are
"as well *entertain'd*" as possible; the liquor that renders them helpless
is "part of the *Entertainment*"; and after the trap is sprung and Oroonoko captured, "they made from the Shore with this innocent and glorious Prize, who thought of nothing less than such an *Entertainment*"
(emphasis added). In this crucial scene, "Entertainment" diverts Oroonoko not from suicidal melancholy, but from the true danger of en-
trapment and slavery. The word shifts from connoting aesthetic
enjoyment * * * to connoting, simply, treatment or manipulation.
* * * The captain's contrived plot suggests the danger of inventions
"manag'd at the Poet's Pleasure." Oroonoko is enslaved by the trust he
affords those whose agreeable conversation masks an ability to manip-
ulate people as well as words. If this incident reinforces the narrator's
distrust of invention, it undercuts by the same token the trust she re-
quests of readers. To take fiction for fact, as Oroonoko does here, is the
most perilous position in this novel; to convince others that one's fictions are fact is the most powerful, and the most morally indefensible.

Oroonoko's dealings with the English captain all underscore the issue
of who believes whom. Worried that his captives will starve themselves,
the captain sends an emissary to assure Oroonoko that he will "set both
him and his Friends a-shore on the next Land they shou'd touch at;
and of this the Messenger gave him his Oath." Oroonoko offers his
own oath in exchange. * * * This oath of obedience to one who has
deceived and deprived him of liberty recalls his dutiful submission to
the king who deceived and deprived him of his wife. Oroonoko intends
to keep his oath; the captain, like the king, possesses no such scruples,
but keeps the upper hand by professing qualms about Oroonoko's trust-
worthiness. * * * Oroonoko trusts others *as* he would be trusted,
while Europeans mistrust others *although* they would be trusted; they
apply to Oroonoko's words a skepticism that their own could not survive, while he responds to theirs with a faith that only his own deserve.
Oroonoko's maxim that "*A Man of Wit cou'd not be a Knave or Villain*"
leads him to trust a series of men of wit; Trefry and Byam, despite their
differences, mislead him with identical "fair-tongu'd" promises. * * *

Oroonoko will finally understand, on the brink of execution, that all
these lies were lies. Banister, no man of parts and wit who charms with
false speech, but "a Fellow of absolute Barbarity, . . . told him, he
shou'd Dye like a Dog, as he was. *Caesar* replied, . . . that he was the
only Man, of all the Whites, that ever he heard speak Truth." * * *
* * * Almost all Europeans are "Men of Wit," from the English

slaver, a man "of Parts and Wit," to Trefry, "a Man of so excellent Wit and Parts," to Byam, who "abounded in his own Wit," to Colonel Martin, "a Man of great . . . Wit . . . whom I have celebrated in a Character of my New *Comedy*." The narrator has commemorated his wit with her own; and here, as in the final reference to "the Reputation of my Pen," she reminds us that the "A. Behn" on the title page is renowned for that quality. But what are we to say about this narrator, the novel's *woman* of wit? If the world of the novel divides between those who both tell truth and take others' words on faith (whose epitome is Oroonoko) and those who both deceive and take others' promises skeptically (whose epitome is Byam), which side of this fence does she inhabit? Of all Oroonoko's relationships, only this one can expose how the themes that shape the novel's plot inform its narration.[7]

The narrator sounds the same note as every other European on meeting Oroonoko: "I had assur'd [him] of Liberty, as soon as the Governor arriv'd." Yet she presents herself as above and apart from the actions of her vicious compatriots: "while we were away, they acted this Cruelty: for I suppose I had Authority and Interest enough there, had I suspected any such thing, to have prevented it." In a long conversation with "Caesar," she manipulates pronouns brilliantly to place herself half in and half out of the community of Europeans. If assurances of liberty are doubted, "they" have made them: "*They* fed him from Day to Day with Promises, . . . so that he began to suspect *them* of falshood"; if personal trust is necessary to eliminate suspicion, "I" evoke it: "*I* was obliged, . . . to give him all the Satisfaction *I* possibly cou'd: . . . indeed *my* Word wou'd go a great way with him"; if indignation is most likely to induce trust, we find singular umbrage on behalf of a plural race: "*I* took it ill he shou'd Suspect *we* wou'd break our Words with him"; if he still doubts, pronouns at once threaten and dissociate the speaker from the threat: "[his doubt] would but give *us* a Fear of him, and possibly compel *us* to treat him so as *I* shou'd be very loath to behold" (emphasis added). The narrator combines sympathetic advice with a warning of superior power, intimating (by the verb "compel") that he controls the situation, while obliquely suggesting that "*we*" can compel *him* whenever it is deemed necessary to do so (though "*I*" would be distressed by such a spectacle). Like the others, she shrewdly uses her mistrust to convince him not to mistrust her, evoking a solemn promise of nonaggression. * * * Only his belief that she shares his devotion to truth induces him to relinquish doubt, yet her honor leaves room

---

7. The only study I am aware of that treats the narrator at length *as* narrator is Martine Watson Brownley, "The Narrator in *Oroonoko*," *Essays in Literature* 4.2 (1977): 174–81. Brownley uses much of the evidence that I do, but reaches different conclusions. Primarily concerned with delineating moral types, her argument weights characters' intentions, whereas I emphasize patterns of control through language: thus, for instance, Brownley would distinguish between the narrator's and Byam's promises, while I note their rhetorical identity.

for the doubt his precludes: "After this, I neither thought it convenient to trust him much out of our View, nor did the Country, who fear'd him." * * *

The narrator's reaction to his attempted escape shows how she takes his promise to "Act nothing upon the White-People": "we were possess'd with extream Fear, which no perswasions cou'd Dissipate, that he wou'd . . . come down and Cut all our Throats. This apprehension made all the Females of us fly down the River, to be secur'd." Thanks to her absence, Oroonoko is dreadfully whipped, and she is absent because she did not trust his promise. As late as the paragraph before his execution, though, she still expects him to trust her: "We . . . gave him new Assurances." Again she conveniently departs before the barbarity. * * * From the viewpoint of plot, Behn must remove her from the scene to allow spectacular cruelties to take place without totally discrediting her, but this retreat makes her "new Assurances" amount to no more than a trap. * * *

Promises are not the only means by which the narrator domesticates and misleads Oroonoko: * * * "it may not be unpleasant to relate to you the *Diversions* we *entertain'd* him with, or rather he us" (emphasis added). As Oroonko was diverted from suicide by Jamoan's entertainments, from impending enslavement by the entertainments of the English captain, now he will be diverted from thoughts of rebellion and liberty. * * * Here the narrator exercises upon Oroonoko and Imoinda the craft she exercises also upon us. Ranging from history and legend to doctrine and dogma, her discourse defuses a political threat by diverting the oppressed from thoughts of oppression. * * * She will use any discursive tradition ("Lives of the Romans" no less than "Notions of the Trinity") to "divert" him from "Captivity" and "liberty." Though she shares Jamoan's admiration for the prince, she repeats the slaver's aesthetic manipulation: narrative diverts Oroonoko from the politics of slavery, no less than hunting, fishing, and the daring expedition to the Indian village.

This expedition introduces the novel's fourth and final cultural group; presented as another "Digression," it involves many of the terms and issues we have been examining. Immediately following Oroonoko's exploits with "Tygers" and "Numb-Eels," it connects his "Sports" to the theme of viewing other races as exotic fauna. In an ironic inversion of typical exploration narratives, the Indians react to Europeans as Europeans react to aboriginal natives, wondering "if we had Sense, and Wit? If we could talk of affairs of Life, and War, as they could do?" They are thrilled to see the trader who interprets for them: "*we shall now know whether those things can speak.*" Giving them the condescension toward "*those things*" typical of European explorers, Behn sets up a mirror relation: Indians respond to European artifacts and adornments just as the narrator responded to those of Surinam. Indeed, this digression counterpoints the first long digression: both depict introduction to an alien culture; both abound in "wonder," "surprize," "amazement"; and both raise issues of truth, falsehood, and belief.

While the first digression addresses truth telling (in the incident of the "Lyar"), the second complementarily concerns susceptibility to fictions: * * * "by an admiration, that is natural to these People, . . . it were not difficult . . . to impose any Notions or Fictions upon 'em." The Indians, like Oroonoko and the other Surinamese, are characterized by naive susceptibility to appearances.

* * *

But there is throughout *Oroonoko* a kind of truth located on the body, where wit cannot charm nor fiction enthrall. Oroonoko "believ'd it impossible a Man cou'd lose his Force at the touch of a Fish," but where the numb-eel is concerned, touching is believing. Proof on the body becomes increasingly the only kind that counts. Indian self-mutilation displays "a sort of Courage too Brutal to be applauded by our Black Hero" when he first encounters it; but after further disillusionments and betrayals, Oroonoko reproduces it as the only convincing proof of his own courage. As the Indian "Cuts off his Nose, and throws it contemptably on the ground," so Oroonoko "cut a piece of Flesh from his own Throat, and threw it at 'em." For both, contempt of physical pain ironically valorizes the body as the site of visible nobility. Finally, of course, Oroonoko proves his heroic stature by calmly smoking through his dismemberment. Betrayed time and again by "civilized" men of parts, he becomes himself a man of parts in a grotesquely literal manner, adopting the Indian ritual of proving heroism not by verbal assurances but inscription of character on the body.

This ritual evokes less horrible self-embellishments, such as the inscription of class on the body in Coramantien: "those who are Nobly born of that Country, are so delicately Cut and Rac'd all over the forepart of the Trunk of their Bodies, that it looks as if it were Japan'd." * * * To be noble in Coramantien is to be a work of art, literally "figur'd" like the ancestors of the British; to be noble in *Oroonoko* is to merit being "figur'd" in a written "History," as the Picts are in "the Chronicles."

Race and gender, "truths" visible on the body, reflect on one another throughout the novel. The same patriarchy that makes Imoinda a husband's property entitles the King to "rob" him of her; in Surinam, verbal powerlessness shows Oroonoko to be by virtue of race what Imoinda already was by virtue of gender in Africa: property. If the narrative never questions Imoinda's gender status as explicitly as it does racial status, the narrator's posture in patriarchy adumbrates relations of gender and power.

Like Oroonoko, she is brought to Surinam with a promise (of a lieutenant governorship for her father) that never materializes. She too is immobilized, waiting for that colonialist Godot, the Lord Governor. She talks big about "Authority," but never exercises it. Her internally divided sense of womanhood images ambiguous social status. Thus, the pronouns that place her half in and half out of colonial society tell an important truth about her situation, as the oxymoron "Royal Slave" does about Oroonoko's. Her halfway position, like his, is inscribed in her relation to language. She expects her words to be devalued, whereas Oroonoko (reared as a prince) expects no such thing; ironically, though, her language mirrors that of other Europeans (if half out, she is also half in), while his rhetoric (though it asserts European ideals) evinces powerlessness. His race and her gender make their words less valid, allowing an illusion of power but requiring that they continually "prove" themselves.

One prerogative conferred in this novel by perceived superiority is that of presenting discourse as "true" regardless of its actual truth-value. This prerogative, both a function and a source of political power, belongs to the white male; white female and black male expose its structure by half possessing it. This ambiguous half-possession of political "authority" resembles the ambiguous literary "authority" afforded in the Restoration and early eighteenth century to what we now easily accept as prose fiction. In Behn's case, however, critical confusions between rhetorical and moral categories plague the very work that depicts them with such unresolvable complexity. The central sustained irony of the narrative that explodes Oroonoko's assumed congruence between the rhetorical and the moral—his superiority to those who are "superior" to him—does not translate simply into literary terms. Thematic contrast between aesthetic and moral aspects of language and formal contrast between aesthetic and historical aspects of language reflect on one another in various ways, but reflection does not imply, by a glib principle of substitution, an equation between morality and historicity. This spurious equation, which has insinuated itself into the critical discourse of both Behn's detractors and some of her defenders, is inappropriate because the encounter between readers and writers of fiction occurs in an epistemologically misty midregion where a tenuous pleasure principle suspends direct political consequences of belief and disbelief.

Behn creates an image of such suspension early in *Oroonoko*. In Coramantien even Oroonoko, who in the company of Europeans is all Honor, Truth, and Fidelity, deliberately deceives; and the terms in which Behn presents this deception reflect something like a distinction between moral-political falsehood and aesthetic-literary fiction. That the prince contrives to deceive in this society suggests once again that such contrivance is a prerogative of power. * * * The falsehood conveyed to the king is "that the Prince had no more Interest in *Imoinda*, and had resign'd her willingly to the Pleasure of the King"; the fiction conveyed to Onahal is that Aboan has precisely the interest in her that Oroonoko pretends to have relinquished in Imoinda. * * *

* * * The deception of the king is "a Lye," "Falsity," fully "feign[ed]"; it resembles promises, never intended to be kept, made to Oroonoko. Aboan's concurrent "half-feigning" entertainment of Onahal presents an image of a fiction that, though not selfless, resembles Jamoan's tales or the narrator's description of her story in that it sincerely intends to fulfill its audience's desire. And if Aboan gives us the image of a generous fiction, Onahal provides an emblematic posture of half belief toward something one wishes to believe, indeed cannot "forbear" believing. This something, though indeterminate as to truth or falsity, provides satisfaction for those willing to entertain its possibility.

From the novel's opening paragraphs, we see anxiety associated with characteristic literary activities: invention, adornment, management of words and events at the poet's pleasure. The narrator diverts this anxiety with a truth-claim, but proceeds to problematize truth, falsehood, and the grounds of belief throughout her narrative. The anxiety resurfaces in villains who plot, contrive, and enslave with charming language. The narrator who would have our implicit belief tells a tale that depicts the one extraordinary character who gives implicit belief as being utterly at the mercy of those who use language with no fixed relation to truth. In "Digressions" that purport to distinguish groups, she juxtaposes them in ways that make distinctions *less* clear, not only between "civilized" and "primitive" cultures but between the categories of belief, proof, and truth they recognize (including those she invokes to underwrite her own narrative). Placing such categories in volatile relation to one another, she endows key terms—"adorn," "entertain," "divert"—with a range of application that undercuts their presumptive value as indicators of sure distinctions between the aesthetic (toward which she proclaims a profound distrust) and the historical (for which she professes a profound regard).

Oroonoko thus exposes the conceptual underpinnings of European modes of thought as examples not of truth but of ideological and political power, by relentlessly conflating artifice that expresses truth and artifice that dissembles (a conflation the narrator must disregard in order to consolidate her authority as "historian"). Only by ignoring this insistent blurring of conventional distinctions can critics naively question (or naively resolve) the "truth" of this book. And only by ignoring its complex depiction of relations between epistemology and morality can they wrench questions that animate the plot into answers about its author. The scapegoating of fair-tongued villains and the apotheosis of a fair-tongued hero ought to disabuse us of maxims that draw firm correlations between rhetorical and moral categories (this slippage, an intimation of the amorality of narrative, may well be the source of the anxiety associated with "Invention"). The fair-tongued narrator, conversant with European ways, knows that wit ensures neither decency nor its opposite; her more subtle collation marks an equivocal stance between romance extremes of villainy and heroism. *Oroonoko* displays both the political dangers and the aesthetic rewards of such equivocation. Though her truth-claim has diverted critical attention, Behn struggled to stake her true claim on a problematical territory between truth and falsehood, one we must recognize as that of fiction.

LAURA BROWN

The Romance of Empire: *Oroonoko* and the Trade in Slaves†

> *Our victims know us by their scars and by their chains, and it is this that makes their evidence irrefutable. It is enough that they show us what we have made of them for us to realize what we have made of ourselves.*
>
> Jean-Paul Sartre, Preface to Frantz Fanon's
> The Wretched of the Earth

* * *

Although *Oroonoko* is certainly a crucial text in the tradition of women's literature and in the development of the novel; although it supplies us with an interesting early example of the problematic stance of a self-consciously female narrator; and although it demonstrates almost programmatically the tensions that arise when romance and realism are brought together, it demands, at this point in our rereading of eighteenth-century literature, a broader political reevaluation. *Oroonoko* can serve as a theoretical test case for the necessary connection of race and gender, a model for the mutual interaction of the positions of the oppressed in the literary discourse of its own age, and a mirror for modern criticism in which one political reading can reflect another, one revisionist school a variety of revisions. Jean-Paul Sartre's juxtaposition in the epigraph to this chapter of "what we have made of them" and "what we have made of ourselves" suggests the reciprocal movement that must form the basis of such a political revisionism, both within the treatment of specific texts and in the discipline of literary studies at large. In Sartre's reading of Frantz Fanon, that reciprocity is the prerequisite for a relationship of mutual knowledge between the colonizer and the colonized. In this reading of *Oroonoko*, the figure of

† Reprinted (in abridged form) from Laura Brown, *Ends of Empire: Women and Ideology in Early Eighteenth-Century English Literature*, pp. 23–63. Copyright © 1993 by Cornell University. Used by permission of the publisher, Cornell University Press.

the woman in the imperialist narrative—a sign of "what we have made of ourselves"—provides the point of contact through which the violence of colonial history—"what we have made of them"—can be represented.

*   *   *

The aim of this critical project, then, is not simply to reread the problem of race, or the problem of gender, or the problem of race and gender considered as two independent lines of inquiry, but rather to demonstrate the contemporaneity of issues of race and gender in the context of a particular stage in the history of British capitalism associated broadly with commodity exchange and colonialist exploitation. Obviously, other theoratical paradigms, and even other relations of oppression, might usefully be brought to bear here and elsewhere. But the issues of gender and race are crucially connected in this particular text, and, more broadly, their conjunction here is sufficient to demonstrate the value of a pragmatic dialectical criticism, and indeed the political importance of refusing to posit any opposition as absolute.

Oroonoko seems at first to be a rather recalcitrant model for "radical contemporaneity": the novella lends itself with greater readiness to the argument from alterity. Indeed, Behn's opening description of Oroonoko, the "royal slave," is a locus classicus of the trope of sentimental identification by which the native "other" is naturalized as a European aristocrat. In physical appearance, the narrator can barely distinguish her native prince from those of England:

> *   *   *   The most famous Statuary cou'd not form the Figure of a Man more admirably turn'd from head to foot. . . . His Nose was rising and *Roman*, instead of *African* and flat. His Mouth, the finest shap'd that could be seen. *   *   *   The whole Proportion and Air of his Face was so noble, and exactly form'd, that, bating his Colour, there cou'd be nothing in Nature more beautiful, agreeable and handsome.

If this account of Oroonoko's classical European beauty makes it possible to forget his race, the narrator's description of his character and accomplishments further elaborates the act of absolute identity through which he is initially represented:

> Nor did the Perfections of his Mind come short of those of his Person. . . . and who-ever had heard him speak, wou'd have been convinc'd of their Errors, that all fine Wit is confin'd to the *White* Men, especially to those of *Christendom*. . . .
> *   *   *   He had heard of, and admir'd the *Romans*: he had heard of the late Civil Wars in *England*, and the deplorable Death of our great Monarch; and wou'd discourse of it with all the Sense,

and Abhorrence of the Injustice imaginable. He had an extream good and graceful Mien, and all the Civility of a well-bred great Man. He had nothing of Barbarity in his Nature, but in all Points address'd himself, as if his Education had been in some *European* Court.

Oroonoko is not only a natural European and aristocrat, but a natural neoclassicist and Royalist as well, an absurdity generated by the desire for an intimate identification with the "royal slave." * * * The obvious mystification involved in Behn's depiction of Oroonoko as a European aristocrat in blackface does not necessarily damage the novella's emancipationist reputation; precisely this kind of sentimental identification was in fact the staple component of antislavery narratives in England and America for the next century and a half. But the failure of Behn's novella to see beyond the mirror of its own culture in this opening characterization of its hero raises the question of the nature of Behn's relationship with the African slave.

The action of *Oroonoko* forces us to repeat that question at every turn; not only is the novella's protagonist an aristocratic hero, but his story is largely constructed in the tradition of heroic romance. * * * Oroonoko's exploits follow quite closely the pattern outlined by Eugene Waith for the "Herculean hero," the superhuman epic protagonist who plays a major role in heroic form from the classical period through the Renaissance.[1] He is invincible in battle, doing single-handedly "such things as will not be believ'd that Humane Strength cou'd perform." He is also a man of wit and address, governed absolutely by his allegiance to the conventional aristocratic code of love and honor. When he declares his love to Imoinda, for instance, it is voiced entirely in the familiar terms of heroic romance: "Most happily, some new, and, till then unknown Power instructed his Heart and Tongue in the Language of Love. . . . his Flame aim'd at nothing but Honour, if such a distinction may be made in Love."

* * *

Emerging directly from this heroic mystification is the persistent presence of the figure of the woman in the discourse and action of *Oroonoko*. In the ideology of heroic romance, of course, the desirable woman serves invariably as the motive and the ultimate prize for male adventures. As this ideology evolved in the seventeenth-century French prose tradition dominated by women writers such as Madeleine de Scudéry and Madame de LaFayette, women became increasingly central to the romantic action. Behn's novellas, like other English prose works of the Restoration and early eighteenth century, draw extensively upon this

1. Eugene M. Waith, *The Herculean Hero in Marlowe, Chapman, Shakespeare, and Dryden* (New York: Columbia University Press, 1962).

French material, and the foregrounding of female authorship in *Oroon-oko* through the explicit interventions of the female narrator signal the prevalent feminization of the genre.

This narrative must have women, and it generates—or rather ingeminates—female figures at every turn, as observers, beneficiaries, and consumers of Oroonoko's romantic action. Not only is the protagonist represented as especially fond of the company of women, but female figures—either Imoinda or the narrator and her surrogates—appear as incentives or witnesses for almost all of Oroonoko's exploits. In the compact account of his heroic contests, he fights a monstrous, purportedly immortal tiger for the romantic approval of his female admirers: "*What Trophies and Garlands, Ladies, will you make me, if I bring you home the Heart of this Ravenous Beast . . . ?* We all promis'd he should be rewarded at all our hands." * * * On the trip—over which Oroonoko presides as expedition leader—to the Indian tribes, the female figure is again the center of attention. Along with the narrator and her "Woman, a Maid of good Courage," only one man agrees to accompany Oroonoko to the Indian town, and once there, the "*White* people," surrounded by the naked natives, stage a scene of cultural difference in which the fully clothed woman is the central spectacle:

> They were all Naked; and we were Dress'd . . . very Glittering and Rich; so that we appear'd extreamly fine: my own Hair was cut short, and I had a taffaty Cap, with Black Feathers on my Head. . . . from gazing upon us round, they touch'd us, laying their Hands upon all the Features of our Faces, feeling our Breasts and Arms, taking up one Petticoat, then wondering to see another; admiring our Shoes and Stockings, but more our Garters, which we gave 'em; and they ty'd about their Legs.

So ubiquitous and apparently essential is the female eye in the novella that even at the scene of Oroonoko's death, the narrator unobtrusively informs us that, though she was absent, "my Mother and Sister were by him."

The narrator herself, in her account of her position as the female author of Oroonoko's story, makes it even more evident that the romantic hero is the production and expression of a female sensibility, just as his story is a production of "only a Female Pen." The narrator's act of modest self-effacement here, and again on the last page of the novella, is a signal of the special relevance she claims for the female figure as author, character, and ultimate arbiter of Oroonoko's romance, in contrast to the "sublime" masculine wit that would have omitted the crucial naturalness and simplicity of the tale for which the female pen has an innate affinity.

* * *

We must now move, with the help of history, away from the romantic "normalization"[2] that provides the narrative paradigm of *Oroonoko*. Needless to say, the model of heroic romance does not account for all the material in Behn's representation of West Indian slavery. In fact, neither the theme of slavery nor the romantic action explain the extended description of the Caribs, the native Americans of Guiana, with which Behn begins. This opening description deploys another set of discursive conventions and opens another range of ideological expectations than those of romance. The natives are the novella's noble savages, absolutely innocent and without sin, immodesty, or fraud. The notion of natural innocence, which civilization and laws can only destroy, is obviously incompatible with the hierarchical aristocratic ideology of heroic form; Oroonoko, educated by a Frenchman, is admirable for his connection with—not his distance from—European civilization. The account of the Indians belongs in part to the tradition of travel narratives, by Behn's period an established and widely popular mode describing voyages and colonial expeditions to the new world and including detailed reports of marvels, which range from accurate botanical and ethnographic records to pure invention.[3]

Behn's opening account of the Indians establishes her credibility in this context, but in its almost exclusive emphasis on trade with the natives, it also indicates the economic backdrop of the history of the "royal slave":

> trading with them for * * * little Rarities; as Marmosets . . .
> *Cousheries*. . . . Then for little *Parakeetoes*, great *Parrots*, *Muckaws*,
> and a thousand other Birds and Beasts of wonderful and surprizing
> Forms, Shapes, and Colours. For Skins of prodigious Snakes . . .
> also some rare Flies, of amazing Forms and Colours . . . Then
> we trade for Feathers, which they order into all Shapes.
> * * * Besides these, a thousand little Knacks, and Rarities in Nature, and some of Art; as their Baskets, Weapons, Aprons. . . .

The marvels here are all movable objects, readily transportable to a European setting, where they become exotic and desirable acquisitions. Behn's enumeration of these goods belongs to a widespread discourse of imperialist accumulation, typical of both the economic and the literary language of the Restoration and early eighteenth century, in

2. Mary Louise Pratt, "Scratches on the Face of the Country; or, What Mr. Barrow Saw in the Land of the Bushmen," *Critical Inquiry* 12 (1985): 121.
3. In the earlier period, Richard Haklyut's *Principall Navigations* (London, 1589) and Samuel Purchas's *Hakluytus Posthumus; or, Purchas His Pilgrimes* (London, 1616); in the later period, Sir Hans Sloane's *Voyage to the Islands Madera, Barbados, Nieves, S. Christophers and Jamaica* . . . (London, 1707) and A. and J. Churchill's *Collection of Voyages and Travels* (London, 1732).

which the mere act of proliferative listing, the evocation of brilliant colors, and the sense of an incalculable quantity express the period's fascination with imperialist acquisition.[4] But the Indians' goods are at best a small factor in the real economic connection between England and the West Indies; they serve primarily as a synecdoche for imperialist exploitation.

This opening moment of economic and historical contextualization centers around the feathered habit that the narrator acquires, and which, she claims, became upon her return to England the dress of the Indian Queen in Dryden's heroic play of the same name (1664), an artifact of imperialism displayed in the most spectacular manner possible—adorning the female figure of a contemporary actress on the real stage of the Theatre Royal in Bridges Street. This foregrounding of female dress recalls that scene of the expedition to the Indian village, in which the spectacle of the narrator's clothing is similarly privileged. And in general, these items in the opening account of imperialist trade are meant to reflect the acquisitive instincts of a specifically female sensibility—dress, skins, and exotic pets. Pets, indeed, in particular birds, were both sign and product of the expansion and commercialization of English economy and society in the eighteenth century.[5] But this expansion and commercialization found its most frequent cultural emblem in the figure of the woman. Female dress and ornamentation—perfumes, pearls, jewels, silks, combs, petticoats—and the female territory of the tea table with its imported essentials of coffee, tea, and chocolate—came to stand for trade, prosperity, luxury, and commodification in a characteristic synecdoche that pervades the literary culture of this period from Defoe and Rowe to Pope and Swift.[6] And this connection leads to the metonymical association of women, even unadorned, with the ideologically complex phenomenon of mercantile capitalism: goods for female consumption and then women in general come to stand for the massive historical, economic, and social enterprise of English imperialism.

And here, of course, the substantial trade, and the real profit, was not in these exotic objects for female consumption—buffalo skins, *Parakeetoes*, or feathers—but in sugar and slaves. Behn's description of the slave trade, highly accurate in many of its details, is the shaping economic and historical context of *Oroonoko*. A letter written in 1663 to Sir Robert Harley, at whose house at St. John's Hill the narrator claims

---

4. See my *Alexander Pope* (Oxford: Basil Blackwell, 1985), chap. 1.
5. J. H. Plumb, "The Acceptance of Modernity," in Neil McKendrick, John Brewer, and J. H. Plumb, *The Birth of a Consumer Society: The Commercialization of Eighteenth-Century England* (Bloomington: Indiana University Press, 1982), 321–22.
6. See Neil McKendrick, "The Commercialization of Fashion," in McKendrick, Brewer, and Plumb, *The Birth of a Consumer Society*, esp. 51.

to have resided, from one William Yearworth, his steward, may describe the arrival of the slave ship which Behn would have witnessed during her visit to the colony:[7]

> Theare is A genney man [a slave ship from the Guinea Coast] Ariued heare in This riuer of ye 24th of [January] This Instant att Sande poynt. Shee hase 130 nigroes one Borde; ye Comanders name [is] Joseph John Woode; shee has lost 54 negroes in ye viage. The Ladeyes that are heare liue att St Johnes hill.[8]

Behn recounts the participation of the African tribal leaders in collecting and selling slaves to European traders, the prearranged agreements for lots in the colonies, the deliberate dispersal of members of the same tribe around the plantations, the situation of the Negro towns, the imminence of rebellion, and—as we shall subsequently see—the aggressive character of the Koromantyn (in Behn, Coramantien) slaves, the name given to slaves sold at the Gold Coast trading sites from which Oroonoko comes.[9]

Though the uprising Behn recounts—an obvious consequence of the slave trade—has no specific historical counterpart, the situation she presents is typical. Revolts and runaways, or maroons, were commonplace in the West Indies and Guiana throughout this period. In Jamaica rebellions and guerilla warfare, predominantly led by Koromantyn ex-slaves, were virtually continuous from 1665 to 1740.[1] Marronage was common in Guiana as well during the period in which *Oroonoko* is set. In fact, while Behn was in Suriname a group of escaped slaves led by a Koromantyn known as Jermes had an established base in the region of Para, from which they attacked local plantations (Price, *Guiana Maroons*, 23). * * *

The powerful act of "reductive normalizing" performed by the romantic narrative is countered, then, at least in part, by a similarly powerful historical contextualization that we can observe in Behn's account of trade. * * * We cannot read Behn's version of colonialist history uncritically, any more than we can her heroic romance. But we can read them together, because they are oriented around the same gov-

---

7. See Angeline Goreau, *Reconstructing Aphra: A Social Biography of Aphra Behn* (New York: Dial Press, 1981), 56.

8. "Letters to Sir Robert Harley from the Stewards of His Plantations in Surinam (1663–4)," reprinted in *Colonising Expeditions to the West Indies and Guiana, 1623–1667*, ed. V. T. Harlow (London: Hakluyt Society, 1925), 90.

9. *Koromantyn* or *Coromantijn* is a name derived from the Dutch fort at Koromantyn on the Gold Coast; in Suriname it designated slaves from the Fanti, Ashanti, and other interior Gold Coast tribes. For background and statistics on the tribal origins of the Bush Negroes of Guiana, see Richard Price, *The Guiana Maroons: A Historical and Bibliographical Introduction* (Baltimore: Johns Hopkins University Press, 1976), 12–16.

1. Orlando Patterson, "Slavery and Slave Revolts: A Sociohistorical Analysis of the First Maroon War, 1665–1740," in *Maroon Societies: Rebel Slave Communities in the Americas*, ed. Richard Price, 2 ed. (Baltimore: Johns Hopkins University Press, 1979), esp. 256–70.

erning point of reference, the ubiquitous and indispensable figure of the woman. In the paradigm of heroic romance, women are the objects and arbiters of male adventurism, just as, in the ideology of imperialist accumulation, women are the emblems and proxies of the whole male enterprise of colonialism. The female narrator and her proliferative surrogates serve as the enabling point of contact between romance and trade in *Oroonoko*, motivating the hero's exploits, validating his romantic appeal, and witnessing his tragic fate. * * *

We can see these two paradigms intersecting in Oroonoko's anti-slavery speech:

> And why (said he) *my dear Friends and Fellow-sufferers, shou'd we be Slaves to an unknown People? Have they Vanquish'd us Nobly in Fight? Have they Won us in Honourable Battel? And are we, by the Chance of War become their Slaves? This wou'd not anger a Noble Heart; this wou'd not animate a Souldiers Soul: no, but we are Bought and Sold like Apes, or Monkeys, to be the Sport of Women, Fools and Cowards.*

The attack on slavery is voiced in part through the codes of heroic romance: the trade in slaves is unjust only if and when slaves are not honorably conquered in battle. But these lines also allude to the other ideology of *Oroonoko*, the feminization of trade that we have associated primarily with the depiction of the Indians. Oroonoko's resentment at being "Bought and Sold like Apes, or Monkeys . . . the Sport of Women" seems less unprovoked given the prominent opening description of the animals and birds traded by the Indians, in particular the little "Marmosets, a sort of *Monkey* as big as a Rat or Weasel, but of a marvellous and delicate shape, and has Face and Hands like an Humane Creature." In conjunction with the image of the pet monkey, Oroonoko's critique of slavery alludes to one of the most powerful redactions of the critique of colonialist ideology—the representation of female consumption, of monkeys and men.

* * * Because they are marginal and subordinate to men, women have no extrinsic perspective, no objective status, in this narrative, either as the arbiters of romance or as the beneficiaries of colonialism. They have no place to stand.[2] But in their mediatory role, between heroic romance and mercantile imperialism, they generate and enable the mutual interaction of these two otherwise incompatible discourses. They provide the occasion for the superimposition of aristocratic and bourgeois systems—the ideological contradiction that dominates the novella. And in that contradiction we can locate a site beyond alterity, a

2. Myra Jehlen, "Archimedes and the Paradox of Feminist Criticism," in *The "Signs" Reader: Women, Gender and Scholarship*, ed. Elizabeth Abel and Emily K. Abel (Chicago: University of Chicago Press, 1983), 69–75.

point of critique and sympathy effectually produced by the radical contemporaneity of issues of gender with those of romance and race.

On the face of it, the treatment of slavery in *Oroonoko* is neither
coherent nor fully critical. The romance motifs in Oroonoko's story,
based upon the elitist focus on the fate of African "princes," render
ambiguous Behn's attack on the institution of slavery, and open the way
for the development of the sentimental antislavery position of the eighteenth century. But at the same time, the representation of trade and
consumption, readily extended to the trade in slaves and the consumption of Oroonoko himself, and specifically imagined through a female
sensibility, tends to render colonialism unambiguously attractive. This
incoherence in the novella's treatment of slavery can be felt at various
points in the course of the narrative. * * *

* * *

But beyond these multiple ambiguities, at the climactic moment in
the ideological contradiction that dominates the novella, resides a
deeper critique of slavery. This insight originates in the hidden contemporary political referent of the narrative: the party quarrels current in
the colonies of West Indies and Guiana at the time of Behn's visit.
Though the account supplied in the novella is sketchy at best, Behn
names persons whom we can now identify, and animosities that we can
now trace to the political tensions that emigrated to the colonies during
the English revolution and after the time of the Restoration.[3] As a locus
of relative political neutrality, the colonies of the West Indies and Guiana attracted Royalists during the revolution, as the king's cause began
to weaken in England, and Parliamentarians and radicals after the
Restoration—especially those fleeing from prosecution at home. The
narrator's rendering of the colonists' council, and her account of
the contests for jurisdiction over Oroonoko, both before and after his
rebellion, reflect the reigning atmosphere of political tension and confusion in Suriname during the time of Behn's visit in 1663 and 1664,
though without assigning political labels to the disputants. In fact, the
Lord Governor of Suriname to whom the novella refers is Francis, Lord
Willoughby of Parham, an intimate of the royal family and of Lord
Clarendon and a constant conspirator against the Protectorate, who had
received his commission for settlements in Guiana and elsewhere in

---

3. For details on the political issues in Suriname in the 1660s, see the documents reprinted
under "Guiana" in the Hakluyt Society's *Colonising Expeditions to the West Indies and Gui-
ana, 1623–1667*, esp. "The Discription of Guyana," "To yᵉ Right Honourable yᵉ Lords of His
Majesties most Honorable Privy Councel, The Case of yᵉ Proscripts from Surinam wᵗʰ all
Humility is briefely but most truely stated. 1662," and "Letters to Sir Robert Harley from the
Stewards of his Plantations in Suriname. 1663–1664"; V. T. Harlow's detailed introduction
to this reprint collection, esp. xxvii–lv and lxvi–xcv; Goreau, *Reconstructing Aphra*, 66–69;
Cyril Hamshere, *The British in the Caribbean* (Cambridge: Harvard University Press, 1972),
64–65; and James A. Williamson, *English Colonies in Guiana and on the Amazon, 1604–
1668* (Oxford: Clarendon Press, 1923).

the Caribbean from Charles II, at his court in exile. Willoughby is absent during Behn's narrative, but the governor of the colony who orders Oroonoko's execution, William Byam, was a key figure in the Royalist struggle for control of Barbados in the previous decade, and likewise in Suriname battled continuously with the Parliamentarians in the colony. In 1662, immediately before Behn's arrival, Byam had accused a group of Independents, led by Robert Sandford, of conspiracy, and had summarily tried and expelled them from the colony. Sandford had owned the plantation neighboring that of Sir Robert Harley, St. John's Hill, which the narrator mentions as her residence. Harley also was a Royalist, and had been a friend of Willoughby, though a quarrel between the two during Harley's chancellorship of Barbados had resulted in Willoughby's expulsion from that colony in 1664. There were few firm friendships in the British Caribbean in this tumultuous period of colonial adventurism. Indeed in 1665, shortly after Behn left Suriname, Willoughby himself, in a visit to Guiana meant to restore orderly government to the colony, was nearly assassinated by John Allen, who resented his recent prosecution for blasphemy and dueling.

Behn herself may have been engaged with these volatile politics through an alliance with a radical named William Scot, who went to the colony to escape prosecution for high treason in England, and whose father Thomas was a prominent figure on the Parliamentary side in the revolution and during the Commonwealth (Goreau, *Reconstructing Aphra*, 66–69). The radical connection makes some sense in that Byam, the notoriously ardent and high-handed Royalist, is clearly the villain of the piece, and Colonel George Martin, Parliamentarian and brother to "*Harry Martin*, the great *Oliverian*," deplores the inhumanity of Oroonoko's execution. * * *

But there is no simple political allegory available in Behn's novella. Though the Royalist Byam is Oroonoko's enemy, Behn describes Trefry, Oroonoko's friend, who was in fact the overseer of Sir Robert Harley's plantation at St. John's Hill, as an agent of Willoughby's: Trefry must have been a Royalist. His open struggle with Byam over Oroonoko's fate might allude to divisions within the Royalist camp, divisions which were frequent and intense in Barbados, for instance, when Willoughby came to power in that colony. More important than direct political correspondences, however, is the tenor of political experience in the West Indies and Guiana in this period. For Behn and others, the colonies seemed to stage an anachronism, the repetition of the English revolution, and the political endpoint of Behn's narrative is nothing less than the reenactment of the most traumatic event of the revolution, the execution of Charles I.

From almost the instant of his beheading, the king's last days, and the climactic drama of his execution, were recounted by Royalist writers in a language that quickly established the discourse of Charles's suffering as heroic tragedy. *The Life of Charles I*, written just after the Restoration and close to the year in which Oroonoko's story is set, suggests the tenor of this discourse:

> He entred this ignominious and gastly Theatre with the same mind as He used to carry to His Throne, shewing no fear of death . . . [Bloody trophies from the execution were distributed among the King's murderers at the execution and immediately thereafter]; some out of a brutish malice would have them as spoiles and trophees of their hatred to their Lawfull Sovereign. . . . He that had nothing Common in His Life and Fortune is almost profaned by a Vulgar pen. The attempt, I confess, admits no Apology but this, That it was fit that Posterity, when they read His Works . . . should also be told that His Actions were as Heroick as His Writings . . . Which not being undertaken by some Noble hand . . . I was by Importunity prevailed upon to imitate those affectionate Slaves, who would gather up the scattered limbs of some great Person that had been their Lord, yet fell at the pleasure of his Enemies.[4]

Related images appear in a version published in 1681, shortly before the writing of *Oroonoko*:

> * * * he suffered as an Heroick Champion . . . by his patient enduring the many insolent affronts of this subtile, false, cruel, and most implacable Generation, in their Barbarous manner of conventing, and Condemning him to Death; and to see his most blood-thirsty Enemies then Triumph over him. . . . they have made him *Glorious* in his Memory, throughout the World, by a Great, Universal and most durable Fame.[5]

Charles I was evidently a powerful presence for Behn at the writing of *Oroonoko*, even though the story was composed only shortly before its publication in 1688, long after Charles's death, the Restoration, and even the intervening death of Charles II—the monarch with whom Behn's acquaintance and allegiance were much more immediate and personal. Oroonoko's heroism is attached to that of Charles I not just generically—in the affinity of "Great Men" of "mighty Actions" and "large Souls," which has linked all heroes in the epic tradition from Achilles to Anthony—but directly. Behn's slave-name for Oroonoko, Caesar, is the name she repeatedly used for the Stuart monarchs: Charles II is Caesar in her poem "A Farewell to Celladon on His Going Into Ireland" (1684) as is James II in her "Poem to Her Sacred Majesty Queen Mary" (1689). And Oroonoko's character, as we have already

---

4. Richard Perrinchiefe, *The Life of Charles I*, in *The Workes of King Charles The Martyr* (London, 1662), 92–93, 118.
5. William Dugdale, *A Short View of the Late Troubles in England* (Oxford, 1681), 374–75.

seen, is defined by his sympathy for Charles. * * * Sentenced, like
Charles in these Royalist accounts, by the decree of a Council of "notorious Villains" and irreverent swearers, and murdered by Banister, a
"Fellow of absolute Barbarity, and fit to execute any Villainy," "this
great Man" another royal martyr, endures his death patiently, "without
a Groan, or a Reproach." Even the narrator's final apology, though it
refers specifically to female authorship, reproduces the conventional
humble stance of the chroniclers of the king's death. * * * The
"Spectacle . . . of a mangl'd King," then, with which we are finally
presented at the close of the narrative,[6] when Oroonoko is quartered
and his remains are distributed around the colony, evokes with surprising vividness the tragic drama of Charles Stuart's violent death. The
sense of momentous loss that Behn's narrative generates on behalf of
the "royal slave" is the product of the hidden figuration in Oroonoko's
death of the culminating moment of the English revolution.

But the tragedy is double in a larger sense. Abstractly, both Charles
I and Oroonoko are victims of the same historical phenomenon—those
new forces in English society loosely associated with an anti-absolutist
mercantile imperialism. In England the rapid rise of colonization and
mercantile trade coincided with the defeat of absolutism in the seventeenth century. Thus in a mediated sense the death of Charles I makes
that of Oroonoko possible, and Oroonoko's death stands as a reminder
of the massive historical shift that destroyed Charles Stuart and made
England into a modern imperialist power. Ironically, in this context,
both King Charles and the African slave in the new world are victims
of the same historical force.

At this point we might imagine that the account of Oroonoko's death
represents the moment of greatest mystification in the narrative, the
proof of an absolute alterity in the confrontation between the colonialist
and the native "other." What could be more divergent than the fate of
Charles Stuart and that of an African slave? But in fact the violent
yoking of these two figures provides the occasion for the most brutal
and visceral contact that Behn's narrative makes with the historical experience of slavery in the West Indies and Guiana. Merely the information that Oroonoko is a Koromantyn connects his story to

6. I am indebted to Adela Pinch for this reading of these lines. Paul J. Korshin describes Oroonoko's death as an instance of christomimetic martyrology (*Typologies in England 1650–1820*
[Princeton: Princeton University Press, 1982], 213), a typology equally applicable to these
accounts of Charles I's martyrdom; in this sense, these two martyrs could also be connected
as types of Christ. George Guffey sees Oroonoko as a figure for James II ("Aphra Behn's
Oroonoko: Occasion and Accomplishment," in *Two English Novelists: Aphra Behn and Anthony Trollope* [Los Angeles: William Andrews Clark Memorial Library, University of
California, 1975]), an argument that Katharine M. Rogers finds "remarkably far-fetched"
("Fact and Fiction in Aphra Behn's *Oroonoko*," *Studies in the Novel* 20 [1988]: esp. 10 and
n. 46). Rogers's main contention against Guffey is that Behn's treatment of slavery must be
seen as a "serious concern," rather than presuming that the issue for Behn is simply subsumed
by a Royalist allegory. Both sides of this debate, the typological and the serious, support my
argument here.

contemporary historical testimony on slavery and rebellion in the colonies. Bryan Edwards describes the character of slaves from this area:

> The circumstances which distinguish the Koromantyn, or Gold Coast, Negroes, from all others, are firmness both of body and mind; a ferociousness of disposition; but withal, activity, courage, and a stubbornness, or what an ancient Roman would have deemed an elevation, of soul, which prompts them to enterprizes of difficulty and danger; and enables them to meet death, in its most horrible shape, with fortitude or indifference.[7] * * *

Edwards is obviously also drawn to an epic romanticization, but his historical account begins to give us a conviction of the experience behind the romance in Behn's narrative. So common was rebellion among the Koromantyns, that the importation of slaves from the Gold Coast was stopped by the late eighteenth century to reduce the risk of insurrection.

Edwards goes on to recount one such rebellion in Jamaica in 1760, which "arose at the instigation of a Koromantyn Negro of the name of Tacky, who had been a chief in Guiney." He details in particular the execution of the rebel leaders: * * *

> The wretch that was burned was made to sit on the ground, and his body being chained to an iron stake, the fire was applied to his feet. He uttered not a groan, and saw his legs reduced to ashes with the utmost firmness and composure; after which one of his arms by some means getting loose, he snatched a brand from the fire that was consuming him, and flung it in the face of the executioner. (*History* 2:59–61)

* * * And John Stedman, the period's most detailed reporter of the executions of rebel maroons, recounts the request of a man who had been broken on the rack: "I imagined him dead, and felt happy; till the magistrates stirring to depart, he writhed himself from the cross . . . rested his head on part of the timber, and asked the by-standers for a pipe of tobacco."[8]

In the context of these firsthand accounts, Oroonoko's death takes on a significance entirely different from that conferred upon it through the paradigm of heroic romance or the figuration of the death of King Charles: * * * As far as this horrible fictional scene takes us from the image of Dryden's Anthony or that of Charles Stuart, those radically

---

7. Bryan Edwards, *The History, Civil and Commercial, of the British Colonies in the West Indies*, 2 vols. (Dublin, 1793; reprint, New York: Arno Press, 1972), 2:59. * * *

8. John Stedman, *Narrative of a Five Years' Expedition Against the Revolted Negroes of Surinam* (1796; reprint, Amherst: University of Massachusetts Press, 1972), 382. Stedman's book contains the fullest account available in this period of the punishments for maroons in the West Indies and Guiana. Price finds Stedman's descriptions "to have a solid grounding in fact," and he also shows that Suriname was the most brutal of the major plantation colonies of the New World (*Guiana Maroons*, 25. 9).

irrelevant figures are the means by which this narrative finds its way to
the historical experience of the Koromantyn slave—the means by which
this passage offers not merely a fascination with the brutality that is
depicted here and in the other historical materials I have cited, but a
sympathetic memorialization of those human beings whose sufferings
these words recall.

*   *   *

* * * In Charles Stuart and Oroonoko we have seen two beings
who could never meet in this world joined as historical contemporaries
through the contradictory logic of Behn's imperialist romance. We have
used a feminist reading of colonialist ideology, which places women at
the center of the structures of rationalization that justify mercantile
expansion, to ground an account of the formal and ideological contradictions surrounding the representation of race and slavery in this work.
And concurrently we have juxtaposed the figure of the woman, ideological implement of a colonialist culture, with the figure of the slave,
economic implement of the same system. Though Behn never clearly
sees herself in the place of the African slave, the mediation of the figure
of the woman between the two contradictory paradigms upon which
her narrative depends uncovers a mutuality beyond her immediate
awareness or control.

All of these relationships of contemporaneity spring from the failures
of coherence in the discourse of Oroonoko, from the mutual interaction
of the contradictory aristocratic and bourgeois paradigms that conjointly
shape the novella. This interaction—contingent, temporary, and
mediatory—is the dialectical process that my reading of Oroonoko has
aimed to define, the process by which we may imagine Behn's text to
"meet the Other on the same ground, in the same Time."[9] By this
means, we can position the African slave in Behn's novella not as a
projection of colonialist discourse, contained or incorporated by a dominant power, but as an historical force in his own right and his own
body. * * *

9. Johannes Fabian, Time and the Other: How Anthropology Makes Its Objects (New York:
Columbia University Press, 1983), 164.

CHARLOTTE SUSSMAN

The Other Problem with Women: Reproduction and Slave Culture in Aphra Behn's *Oroonoko*†

* * *

* * * Almost any discussion of slavery will eventually call into question the nature of family ties. What finally separates slavery from other kinds of servitude is that while a free person is born into a complex network of social ties and responsibilities, a slave is born into a single legal relationship—that of a servant to his master—over which he has no volition. The ordinary bonds that a slave might enter into, such as marriage or parenthood, have no force in the eyes of his master. The sociologist Orlando Patterson calls this characteristic of slavery "natal alienation."[1] * * * This peculiar horror of slavery is clearly illustrated in *Oroonoko*: The conflict between freedom and slavery is played out along the lines of family ties. Oroonoko reacts against slavery by fighting to reestablish his claim on his own child—to reinvolve that child in a heritage, in a history. It is, then, a measure of the brutality of the relation of slavery that the only way he can make the connection between parent and child evident is through murder.

* * * Precisely because the slave trade was a trade in living human beings, the balance between births and deaths translated directly into economic profit and loss. In the Caribbean colonies, this relationship between people and profit was complicated by the fact that the population of slaves continually decreased despite constant importation of new African captives. This decrease was caused in part by a decision on the part of West Indian plantation owners that importing new slaves was cheaper and more efficient than inducing slaves to raise families. But even when masters tried to cultivate self-reproducing populations, they failed.[2] * * *

Plantation culture depended on the female capacity to reproduce,

---

† Revised and abridged from *Rereading Aphra Behn: History, Theory, and Criticism*, ed. Heidi Hutner (Charlottesville and London: University Press of Virginia, 1993), 212–33. Reprinted with permission of the University Press of Virginia.

I am grateful to Laura Brown for her help with earlier versions of this piece [Author's note].

1. Orlando Patterson, *Slavery and Social Death: A Comparative Study* (Cambridge: Harvard Univ. Press, 1982), p. 7. The phrase "goes directly to the heart of what is critical in the slave's forced alienation, the loss of ties of birth in both ascending and descending generations. It also has the important nuance of a loss of native status, of deracination. It was this alienation of the slave from all formal, legally enforceable ties of 'blood,' and from any attachment to groups or localities other than those chosen for him by the master, that gave the relation of slavery its peculiar value to the master."

2. Orlando Patterson, *The Sociology of Slavery: An Analysis of the Origins, Development, and Structure of Negro Slave Society in Jamaica* (Kingston, Jamaica: MacGibbon and Kee, 1967), p. 109.

but female slaves were themselves workers, brutalized by a cruel economic system. * * * The controversy over whether black women willfully refused to reproduce or whether the slave system itself undermined their actual capacity to reproduce continues among historians today, and I will not resolve it here.[3] I will point out, however, that these problems eventually became a central battleground in the English imperial struggle to maintain a slave culture. Although this crisis did not become acute until the beginning of the nineteenth century, its importance is intimated in Behn's novel by the anxieties provoked by Imoinda's pregnancy. In the struggle over her unborn child, the historical specificity of Caribbean slavery surfaces, if briefly, in a text that otherwise almost completely elides the material facts of that institution. Imoinda's unborn child, made to motivate so much of the later action of *Oroonoko*, also bears with it all the problems of cultural as well as biological reproduction. If the child were to be born in the novel, that birth would signify both the continued captivity of Oroonoko's race and the continued viability of slave culture in Surinam. Its death, in contrast, indicates Oroonoko's continued, princely, control over his race.

Thus, although the problem of reproduction occupies a very small space in *Oroonoko*, it provides a crucial point of intersection between the historical context of the slave trade and an ahistorical heroic romance. Moreover, I choose to focus on this issue because it is a moment when a possible resistance to slavery is glimpsed within a text otherwise quite concerned with maintaining the status quo. The point of coincidence, which is also a window onto the possibilities for resistance, is the body of a woman.[4] * * *

I

Imoinda is a possession even before she is a slave. She, and any children she might have, are inextricably bound by the property definitions of their native culture. Imoinda's exile in Surinam, therefore, is not so much a transition from freedom to slavery as a transition from one code of property relations to another. Of course, the way she is "owned" by Trefry is very different than the way she is "owned" by the king of Coramatien, but in both cases Imoinda remains rigidly confined

3. Cf. Barbara Bush, " 'The Family Tree is not Cut': Women and Cultural Resistance: Studies in the British Caribbean," in *In Resistance: Studies in African, Caribbean, and Afro-American History*, ed. Gary Okihiro (Amherst: Univ. of Massachusetts Press, 1986); Marietta Morrissey, *Slave Women in the New World: Gender Stratification in the Caribbean* (Lawrence: Univ. of Kansas Press, 1989).
4. At this point my argument closely resembles Laura Brown's discussion of the novel, in which she claims that "the figure of the woman in the imperialist narrative . . . provides the point of contact through which the violence of colonial history . . . can be represented," in "The Romance of the Empire: *Oroonoko* and the Trade in Slaves," in *The New Eighteenth Century: Theory *Politics* English Literature*, ed. Felicity Nussbaum and Laura Brown (New York: Methuen Press, 1987), p. 43.

by codes of possession. The novel, however, represents Imoinda as hold-ing a highly unstable position within both of those codes, an unstable position that constantly threatens to disrupt any social system. On the Gold Coast of West Africa, her marriagable body produces an important political crisis as well as a familial crisis. In Surinam, her body as a reproductive vessel again provokes a violent confrontation, this time between Oroonoko's sense of honor and slave culture itself. On both continents the crisis is solved in the same way; not by any change in existing conditions but through the elimination of the offending piece of property—Imoinda's body.

In Africa, the king is troubled by "having been forc'd, by an irresis-tible Passion, to rob his son [grandson] of a Treasure." * * * In this series of events, the conditions for Imoinda's value as property are laid bare; she must be possessed absolutely to be worth being possessed at all. Because of this system of value, Imoinda's chastity becomes an index of the king's authority; his power as a ruler depends on his ability to own the best things and to keep them for his own exclusive use. * * *

When Oroonoko "possesses" her sexually he violates his culture's property laws along with familial sexual prohibitions. The legitimacy of these codes can only be restored by the removal of the property in question. * * *

When Imoinda reappears in Surinam the crisis in property relations also reappears. This time, her progeny rather than her virginity becomes the property in question. Similarly, however, the desirability of this property threatens to upset the existing power structure. When she be-comes pregnant "this new Accident made [Oroonoko] more Impatient of Liberty . . . and [he] offer'd either Gold, or a vast quantity of Slaves, which shou'd be paid before they let him go." * * *

*   *   *

* * * And her pregnancy inspires his first plans for escape because "all the Breed is theirs to whom the Parents belong." In Patterson's terms, Oroonoko rebels against the possibility that his child will be born into a natally alienated state. To Oroonoko's thinking, the child should be the next "of his Great Race," born into the kinship network that makes Oroonoko a powerful prince. For the child to achieve such a status, however, the ties between parent and child as well as between husband and wife must be acknowledged. Only through the recogni-tion of genealogical descent can the child receive its cultural in-heritance. * * *

The resolution to this crisis in property relations is brought about by extraordinary violence. The physical destruction of bodies is, at last, the only way to ascertain their true owners. Oroonoko decides that if he cannot escape he can at least revenge himself on his English captors. A crucial part of this plan to salvage his honor, however, involves Imoinda's death. He resolves to kill her himself rather than leave her to be "a Prey, or at best a Slave" to "nasty Lusts." Thus, he enforces his property claim to Imoinda's body—in both its sexual and its reproductive capacities—by murdering her. He kills this "Treasure of his Soul" by "first, cutting her Throat, and then severing her yet Smiling Face from that Delicate Body, pregnant as it was with the Fruits of tend'rest Love." Although the language here partakes of the nascent conventions of sentimentality, the very cuts between the pieces of her body become the inscription of his proprietorship.

*   *   *

Imoinda's murder, however, in no way changes the conditions of Oroonoko's captivity. The scene, instead, drains Oroonoko of the energy to carry out an actual rebellion. The violence of an uprising is thus absorbed into familial violence. The mayhem of this love scene only works to restore Oroonoko's personal honor, or glory. Furthermore, Oroonoko's liberation from the demeaning conditions of slavery is carried out not against the slave owners but on the body of a woman. Imoinda's dismembered body becomes, strangely enough, the sign of Oroonoko's nobility—of the spiritual liberty that must take the place, for him, of physical liberty.

This effect is most clear in the scene directly following Imoinda's death. When the plantation owners come to recapture Oroonoko, he is far too weak to hurt them; all he can do is hurt himself. The marks Oroonoko makes on his own body, however, mirror the injuries he has recently inflicted on Imoinda. First he cuts a piece of flesh from his own neck, just as he slit Imoinda's throat. Then, in an action that points to the underlying significance of Imoinda's murder, Oroonoko, rather than cutting off his own head, "rip'd up his own Belly; and took his Bowels and pull'd 'em out, with what Strength he cou'd." With this action he recalls that he has just effectively aborted Imoinda's child. Oroonoko is willing to do all this to avoid "the shameful Whip." Thus, the sign of Oroonoko's courage to choose a noble death over the shame of slavery is also a repetition of the sign of his absolute possession of wife and child. The code of nobility that Oroonoko writes on his own body signifies his power over a woman, not his emancipation from slavery.

*   *   *

* * * Imoinda's death paves the way for an ending that allows Oroonoko his glory without seriously challenging the existence of a slave culture. Her mutilation becomes a perfect substitute for violence against the slave owners. Woman's powerlessness seems to be culturally portable. She is a continual threat to the stability of power relations but also, because of her powerlessness, she serves as the ever-reliable instrument of their stabilization.

II

At the same time that the novel imagines Imoinda as a conveniently disposable possession, it also imagines her as an enormously powerful erotic figure. This figuration is achieved by assigning her the conventional features of a romantic heroine. Thus, Imoinda emerges as a character through the established codes of the heroic romance. Larger and more perfect than life, she is characterized not as an African woman of the seventeenth century but rather as the type of the heroine of heroic romance. She is "Female to the noble Male; the beautiful *Black Venus* to our young *Mars*"—an embodiment of a very western ideal. Within the codes of romantic love, however, Imoinda is a very potent figure, in direct contrast to the role she occupies in actual power relations. While still in Africa she carries out "a perfect Conquest over [Oroonoko's] fierce Heart, and made him feel, the Victor cou'd be subdu'd." * * *

* * * In Surinam, "all the Slaves [were] perpetually at her Feet," and the narrator claims to "have seen an hundred *White* Men sighing after her, and making a thousand Vows at her feet, all vain, and unsuccessful." * * *

In terms of this set of conventions, Imoinda directs others' actions instead of being directed by others. She even has the capacity to render Oroonoko powerless by replacing his will with her image. In Africa "his Eyes fix'd on the Object of his Soul; and as she turn'd or mov'd, so did they: and she alone gave his Eyes and Soul their Motions." Imoinda's visual presence has the power to erase any other thought from his mind—his mental capacity does indeed shrink to the space of her body. This power appears inalienable in that the same scene takes place when the lovers meet in Surinam: "In a Minute he saw her Face, her Shape, her Air, her Modesty, and all that call'd forth his Soul with Joy at his Eyes, and left his Body destitute of almost Life: it stood without Motion, and, for a Minute, knew not that it had a Being." Insofar as she exists as an image of beauty, Imoinda's power is extraordinary. The power of love, here a purely erotic affect produced by the visual effect of her presence, is absolute. No other definition of self, no other possibility of action, can exist beside it.

Insofar as the novel describes Imoinda as a romantic heroine, she moves through *Oroonoko* in a kind of alternate universe, a world that runs parallel to the world of slavery and transcends it. Imoinda and Oroonoko "mutually protested, that even Fetters and Slavery were Soft and Easy, and wou'd be supported with Joy and Pleasure, while they cou'd be so happy to possess each other, and to be able to make good their Vows. [Oroonoko] swore he disdain'd the Empire of the World, while he cou'd behold his *Imoinda*." When Oroonoko discovers Imoinda again in Surinam, his physical captivity is elided as its characteristics are recoded in terms of the satisfaction of eros; he is able to replace each term of slavery with what seems to be the complementary term of love. His possession by Trefry is rendered "Soft and Easy" by his possession by Imoinda and his possession of her. The contracts and terms of slavery fade into unimportance beside the lovers' "Vows." The possibility of an "Empire" that could encompass the whole world pales next to the much smaller domain of Imoinda's body. The world of romantic love thus contains all the elements of the world of slavery but reorganizes those elements into "Joy and Pleasure." Imoinda's presence neutralizes, at least momentarily, the pains of slavery. Moreover, her love provides alternate definitions of the crucial terms of "possession" and "empire." As Laura Brown has pointed out, the emphasis on tragic love within *Oroonoko* works to cancel out any connection Oroonoko has to the actual trade in slaves.[5]

Yet, although the conventions of heroic romance allow Imoinda no feature that marks her as distinctly African, the context of slavery makes the erotic power of women seem coercive and constraining. For the alternate world that romantic love creates threatens to block any action in the real world of Surinam: Oroonoko "accus'd himself for having suffer'd Slavery so long: yet he charg'd that weakness on Love alone, who was capable of making him neglect even Glory it self, and, for which, now he reproaches himself every moment of the Day." Despite Oroonoko's protestations of contentment in love, here the category of love becomes the ally of slavery. * * * Imoinda's extraordinary erotic allure is in the service of the coercive violence of slavery. The specific motion she stops with her presence is the action of rebellion.

This configuration—women and love aligned with slavers against men and glory—is acted out in *Oroonoko*. When Oroonoko tries to convince the slaves to rebel, one protests: "Were we only Men, [we] wou'd follow so great a Leader through the World: But oh! consider, we are Husbands and Parents too." Oroonoko assures the other slaves that the women will be able to join the escape, but the fears prove true: "The Women . . . being of fearful Cowardly Dispositions . . . crying out *Yield, yield; and leave Caesar to their Revenge* . . . by degrees the Slaves abandon'd *Caesar*." Imoinda, of course, does not act out the part she takes in Oroonoko's imagination, but remains with him until the end. Still, in this group of images, Oroonoko's romantic love for Imoinda is distinguished from his desire to establish and protect family ties. Although his desire to cement his property ties to her and his child

---

5. ["In Behn's text . . . "reductive normalizing" . . . is carried out through literary convention, and specifically through that very convention most effectively able to fix and codify the experience of radical alterity, the arbitrary codes of love and honor found in heroic romance": Laura Brown, "The Romance of Empire: *Oroonoko* and the Trade in Slaves," in *Ends of Empire: Women and Ideology in Early Eighteenth-Century English Literature* (Ithaca, N.Y., and London: Cornell University Press, 1993), p. 39.]

motivates his original rebellion, in this instance the sentimental attachments between husbands, wives, and children work to keep the slaves in captivity. Romantic love is shown to be dangerous in a slave culture, an enemy to glory and to self-respect. Furthermore, women are the sole agents of this dangerous emotion, inflicting it on men. Imoinda's beauty is a double-edged sword: It makes slavery bearable, but it also prevents any action against slavery.

This second problem posed by women—the disturbing power of their erotic presence—is ultimately managed in the same way as the first problem, the way in which women's bodies threaten property relations. In short, Imoinda dies. She accepts her death quite willingly; "Smiling with Joy," she becomes the "Ador'd Victim." Love effectively channels erotic power into submission. Still, by killing her, Oroonoko acts out his only revenge against slavery. Not only does he prove his power by taking her body out of the grasp of the slave owners, but he also proves his power against her body, insofar as that body has become a surrogate for the coercive power of slavery. The seemingly supererogatory brutality of this love scene is thus explained by the further overdetermination of Imoinda's body. That is, because the text figures Imoinda's sexual allure as complicit with slave culture, it is able to deflect political rebellion against slavery (what Oroonoko sets out to achieve) onto the defeat, or submission, of eros (what Oroonoko ends up achieving).

Cynthia Matlack claims that Imoinda's death scene in Thomas Southerne's dramatic adaptation of *Oroonoko* is only one of a number of similar scenes in heroic dramas of the period. In all the plays in which these scenes of willing sacrifice appear, "the political danger of women's erotic appeal can be seen in the extremely high incidence of metaphors describing the enslavement of the males by love."[6] The context of Behn's novel gives this conventional figure an added force: Imoinda's erotic appeal is figured by the novel to be the only slave-master against which Oroonoko can successfully rebel. Again, women's powerlessness becomes the convenient solution to the problem of slavery. Oroonoko does not have the power to challenge the larger social structures of slavery, but he does have the power to turn an adored "conqueror" into an "Ador'd Victim." Sexual mastery over women is constructed as the perfect double to economic control over slaves.

III

At first glance, the only thing that these images of Imoinda—as a particularly valuable piece of property and as a heart-stopping beauty—have in common is their solution. * * * But the two images are also

6. Cynthia S. Matlack, "Spectatress of the Mischief Which She Made: Tragic Women Perceived and Perceiver," *Studies in Eighteenth-Century Culture* 6 (1977): 319.

involved on another level. Eros is used to mask the possibility of resistance that arises with Imoinda's pregnancy. * * *

Matlack notes the conjunction of politics, eros, and generation in her study of "erotic scenes in which the doomed women embrace their imminent death by willingly presenting their bosoms to the phallic dagger of authority." She claims that "at an elemental level of human semiotic exchange, this act of submission produces a transformation as the breasts which nourish progeny become the sign of domesticated eroticism."[7] We have already seen that erotic authority doubles for political authority in *Oroonoko* and that Oroonoko's power over Imoinda is a substitute for any power he might gain over the plantation owners. But Matlack's observation suggests that a double displacement might occur in the text. Although Imoinda does not present her breasts to be penetrated in the novel as she does in the play, we have already seen the importance of those parts of her body that "nourish progeny" in her mutilation. If Matlack is right, her body is eroticized both to absorb the political tension of the novel and to elide the fact that her body could be a reproductive vessel.

Why would it be important to deflect attention from the generative capabilities of a woman's body? At the beginning of this essay I alluded to the crucial place of reproduction in the slave economy of the Caribbean. Because of the need to reproduce labor through inherited status, a woman's womb played a central role in the economic organization of the slave colonies. And, in at least one instance, that womb became the site of resistance. Orlando Patterson, in the *Sociology of Slavery*, discusses the case of eighteenth-century Jamaica (an English sugar colony like Surinam), where "slave women absolutely refused to reproduce . . . as a form of gynecological revolt against the system."[8] * * *

* * * The possibility that captive women might take their biology into their own hands, either through abortion or the more extreme violence of murder, must have lurked in the imaginations of their white owners. For in this scenario, even the reproductive capacity of the womb—long thought to be the part of woman held in the strictest captivity by patriarchy—falls under suspicion for resistance. Even if the specter of infanticide is an imperialist fantasm, the mechanism through which the colonial mind projected responsibility for the brutality of slavery onto the very bodies it oppressed, the image becomes a sign of the colonist's fear of the consequences of slave culture. * * *

*   *   *

We cannot be sure to what extent such historical material is relevant to *Oroonoko*, of course, but in Behn's text eros does indeed displace

7. Ibid., 322.
8. Patterson, *The Sociology of Slavery*, p. 133. Their refusal to reproduce was accomplished for the most part by self-induced abortion, complimented by widespread veneral disease and malnutrition.

the representation of what I have been calling biology or women's capacity for reproduction—an elision that may be motivated by the desire
to efface the womb as the site of resistance. Despite the length at which
I have discussed them, Imoinda's pregnancy and the crisis in property
relations it provokes take up a very small space in *Oroonoko*. In that
small narrative space, though, the horrors of slavery surface for a short
time. The fate of that unborn child brings the extraordinarily demeaning natal alienation of slavery to the foreground of the text. And through
the highly unstable nature of Imoinda's body, the economic and ideological crisis brought about by the reproductive capacity of slave
women in the Caribbean is brought briefly to bear on the novel.

Yet, when Imoinda is eliminated, all these other problems go with
her. Like the child she bears, the baggage of cultural relevance that her
pregnancy carries is effectively buried with her dead body. The battlefield of reproduction and the issues of cultural inheritance and power
that it involves slide out of sight beneath conventional images of woman
as a sexual icon. Throughout the novel the far more culturally acces-
sible figure of a desirable woman is allowed to overshadow the image
of a black female slave and the contradictions she embodies. In fact, I
have argued here that in *Oroonoko* romantic love generally effaces the
other problem of women as reproductive vessels—the political problem
of biological generation is deflected onto the more conventional problem of managing Imoinda's erotic power.

The narrative of *Oroonoko* mounts a concerted effort on many different levels to refigure what might be the feared consequences of a
brutal slave culture (bloody rebellion, massive escape) as the acknowledged consequences of a doomed love affair (mutual suicide, tragic
self-sacrifice). Imoinda, both as a piece of property and as an erotic
icon, is the instrument the narrative uses to effect this reorganization
or even elision. Because her desirability is the cause of so many of the
problems of the novel, the elimination or submission of her eroticized
body can be constructed as the solution to both Oroonoko's problems
and the narrative's. The political issue of slavery is almost entirely deflected onto the more conventional, more tasteful, and more easily resolved problem of heroic romance.

IV

I would suggest that this deflection is carried out to a large degree
by the other woman in *Oroonoko*, the narrator. * * * In the midst of
the brutal scene of Imoinda's murder—a scene in which I have claimed
that cultural codes are forced to physical extremes—the narrator's voice
observes: " 'tis not to be doubted, but the Parting, the eternal Leave
taking of Two such Lovers, so greatly Born . . . so Beautiful, so Young,
and so Fond, must be very Moving, as the Relation of it was to me

afterwards." * * * The scene is reconstituted as a moving relation, a tragic love story that the narrator hopes will move her reader to sentimental response. In this perspective, Imoinda and Oroonoko are not captive people clinging to some remnant of cultural identity but rather any two noble, beautiful, young lovers doomed to a pitiful end.

* * * The narrator declares, in the last words of the novel, "I hope, the Reputation of my Pen is considerable enough to make his Glorious Name to survive to all Ages, with that of the Brave, the Beautiful, and the Constant Imoinda." She plans for Oroonoko and Imoinda to survive as a couple, possessing only the attributes of a moving relation.

Thus, the narrator herself seems to side with the forces of romance in the conflict between love and rebellion; that is, she sides with the status quo of slave culture. Just as the slave women use love to dissuade their husbands from further bloodshed, the narrator consistently rechannels traces of the pain of a captive culture into romantic conventions. * * * The novel and its narrator consistently place Imoinda so that the African woman can absorb the incipient violence of a slave culture into the tropes of eros.[9]

* * * Imoinda's glorious self-sacrifice and her perfect constancy and love provide the material for the construction of a self-consciously female narrator, a narrator, moreover, enshrined in feminist literary history as among the earliest of feminist individualist heroines. In this way the continual erasure of the African slave by the conventions of a romantic heroine forms the basis of a woman's literary voice, even as early as the end of the seventeenth century. * * * Thus, although we should see Behn's heroine as a crucial female voice in early modern English literature, we must also recognize the burden of racist discourse she must assume to speak as a white English woman.

Yet, the very need to kill Imoinda and the excessive violence of the series of mutilations her death inaugurates paradoxically allow into the text the issues they are designed to keep out. Imoinda's murder conjures up allusions to infanticide as the ultimate horror of slavery that must have been as much present in Behn's day as they are in ours. Furthermore, in the specific physical sites of mutilation—Imoinda's throat, Oroonoko's belly (and later his testicles)—the narrative points out possible sites of resistance. This kind of resistance, which is very different from the armed uprising the novel overtly treats, has nothing to do with conventional tropes of honor or glory. Instead, the circumstances of Imoinda's pregnancy and death demonstrate the lengths to which cap-

9. [The relationship between the white female narrator and the black female slave resembles the relationship Gayatri Spivak describes between Jane Eyre and Rochester's Caribbean first wife, Bertha Mason. . . . The "Reputation" of the narrator's "Female Pen" is surely based on Imoinda as the "self-immolating colonial subject." . . . See Gayatri Chakravorty Spivak, "Three Women's Texts and a Critique of Imperialism," in "Race," Writing, and Difference, ed. Henry Louis Gates, Jr. (Chicago: Univ. of Chicago Press, 1986), p. 270.]

tive persons will resist the appropriation of their reproductive capabilities by their captors. The violence in *Oroonoko* does not spring from a conflict between freedom and slavery but rather from Oroonoko's and Imoinda's need to preserve the property relations of family and culture in a situation that all but destroys them. Theirs is a resistance that tests the limits of a slave's control over his or her own biology and the limits of the connections between body and culture. And, although it can only be expressed negatively in *Oroonoko*, the "gynecological revolt" Patterson records suggests that such control may be much less alienable than one would think and that such resistance can be very powerful. Behind the mask of eros, Behn's novel, perhaps despite itself, allows the threatening image of a rebellious womb to show.

MARY BETH ROSE

Gender and the Heroics of Endurance in *Oroonoko*†

In late seventeenth-century England, traditional forms of male heroics—concerned with movement and adventure, rescue, exploration, and conquest—are undergoing redefinition in a culture in which all power relations involving hierarchy and subjection are being eagerly scrutinized and violently redesigned. Rather than focusing on a phallic heroics of action, many writers instead concentrate on a heroics of endurance which, with its emphasis on resistance, fortitude, and the patient suffering of pain, includes both genders among its protagonists. Indeed it is striking that the terms that constitute the heroics of endurance are precisely those terms used to construct the Renaissance idealization of woman: patient suffering, mildness, humility, chastity, loyalty, and obedience. In *Oroonoko* Aphra Behn deconstructs the phallic heroics of action by presenting a critique of physical strength as the source of male privilege; and she presents compromised agency, or agency inscribed in contradictions, as the defining condition of the heroic. In what follows I argue that this condition is female; and that it is represented first, in the hero's position of being seduced into slavery; and second, in the relation of the hero's slavery to marriage.

Oroonoko presents a problematic critique of late seventeenth-century English colonialism, with a particular emphasis on the slave trade. The story is divided both chronologically and geographically into two parts.

† Adapted from "The Heroics of Endurance in Milton's *Samson Agonistes*, Aphra Behn's *Oroonoko*, and Mary Astell's *Some Reflections Upon Marriage*" by Mary Beth Rose is from *Milton Studies* XXXIII (*The Miltonic Samson*), Albert C. Labriola and Michael Lieb, Guest Editors. © 1997 by University of Pittsburgh Press. Reprinted by permission of the publisher.

The first presents the hero as an honored warrior-prince in his African home, a country called Coramantien, where his happiness with his beloved, Imoinda, is disrupted when the king (his grandfather) desires Imoinda, seizes her, and eventually sells her into slavery, telling Oroonoko she is dead. In the second half, the hero is himself sold into slavery and is transported to the English colony, Surinam, where he meets the English narrator, joyfully discovers and reunites with Imoinda, stages a doomed rebellion, and dies.

Oroonoko was written in 1688, at a time when the project of imperial expansion and the slave trade in England were thriving. As scholars have shown, there was an anti-slavery debate (although not couched in modern terms) in the late seventeenth century; but *Oroonoko* only arguably can be called an abolitionist text.[1] As noted, the African hero and his adored wife are both duplicitously betrayed into slavery, suffer outrages, and die horribly trying to escape their English masters. Aristocratic Coramantiens believe that the degradation of slavery is worse than death. Yet, as an African prince, Oroonoko himself trades in and owns slaves unambivalently, as a matter of right. Laura Rosenthal has demonstrated that slavery more often appears in this text as a class entitlement, rather than human injustice. She argues convincingly that Behn seems to mandate the slavery practiced by the aristocratic Africans, who win their slaves in battle and trade them as part of a gift economy that Behn sentimentally and conservatively idealizes. On the other hand, the author's critique of English slave trading practices takes the form of a Royalist condemnation of the greed and brazenness characterizing the Whiggish merchant forces that propel colonialism.[2]

Moreover, the narrator's own conflicted relation to slavery disturbingly qualifies the consistency of her critique. While struggling to escape the structures of Eurocentrism by sympathizing with Oroonoko and Imoinda and indignantly rejecting the outrages perpetrated upon them by the English, her sympathy and indignation are in fact deeply divided. The narrator's attitudes toward Oroonoko's blackness present a strong example of her ambivalence. Here is one instance of many in which she rhapsodizes about the prince's physical magnificence on one level while undercutting her praise with unacknowledged distaste on the other: "He was adorn'd with a native Beauty so transcending all those of his gloomy Race, that he strook an Awe and Reverence, even

1. See Laura Brown, "The Romance of Empire: *Oroonoko* and the Trade in Slaves," in *The New Eighteenth Century: Theory, Politics, English Literature*, eds. Felicity Nussbaum and Laura Brown (New York, 1987), pp. 41–61 [reprinted in Laura Brown, *Ends of Empire: Women and Ideology in Early Eighteenth-Century English Literature* (Ithaca, N.Y., and London: Cornell University Press, 1993), pp. 23–63 — Editor]; and Moira Ferguson, *Subject to Others: British Women Writers and Colonial Slavery, 1670–1834* (New York, 1992), pp. 3–49.
2. Laura J. Rosenthal, "Owning Oroonoko: Behn, Southerne, and the Contingencies of Property," in *Renaissance Drama*, New Series XXIII (Evanston, 1992), pp. 25–58.

in those that knew not his Quality; as he did in me, who beheld him with Surprize and Wonder, when afterwards he arrived in our World."[3] *Oroonoko*, then, is a very difficult text to sort out in ideological terms. An ambivalent critique of colonialism and slavery, a Eurocentric exposure of Eurocentrism, the text is also complicated by its close relation to Behn's autobiography and the fact that the narrator herself is clearly a surrogate for the author. By contextualizing Behn's novella among contemporary cultural narratives about slavery and women, along with the biography of Behn herself, Margaret W. Ferguson has cogently summed up these complexities as follows: "Behn's professional and economic interests deviated just enough from those we may ascribe to England's dominant male property owners and investors in the colonies to provide a fascinating example of a female author oscillating among multiple subject positions and between complicity with and critique of the emergent institution of New World slavery."[4]

What form does heroism take in a narrative so fractured by ambivalence? The text conjoins the female subject position with slavery and compromised agency and presents the combination as the defining condition of heroism, simultaneously idealizing and scrutinizing the heroics of endurance. The narrator stakes the hero's original claim to audience attention by creating him as a traditional male military champion: "from his natural Inclination to Arms, and the Occasions given him . . . he became, at the Age of Seventeen, one of the most expert Captains, and bravest Soldiers, that ever saw the Field of *Mars*: So that he was ador'd as the Wonder of all that World, and the Darling of the Soldiers." However, the narrative does not sustain the idealization of these phallic qualities, which prove wholly inadequate and are destined never to be realized. In the African half of the story, Oroonoko's military abilities are represented rather obliquely, a point to which I'll return. In the Surinam half of the story, during his career as a slave, his identity as a hero of action is reduced to performing feats like a circus strongman to amuse his captors. Indeed, when Oroonoko stages an abortive, doomed, slave rebellion, it occurs in the text directly following the narrator's account of his strong-man antics. Given the hero's dignity,

---

3. For essays that deal with the complexities of the relation of skin color to conceptions of race in the early modern period, see *Women, 'Race,' and Writing in the Early Modern Period*, eds. Margo Hendricks and Patricia Parker (London, 1994) and two essays in *Renaissance Drama*, XXIII, by Kim F. Hall, "Guess Who's Coming to Dinner? Colonization and Miscegenation in *The Merchant of Venice*," pp. 87–111 and Margo Hendricks, "Managing the Barbarian: *The Tragedy of Dido, Queen of Carthage*," pp. 165–88.

4. Margaret Ferguson, "News from the New World: Miscegenous Romance in Aphra Behn's *Oroonoko* and *The Widow Ranter*, in eds. David Lee Miller, Sharon O'Dair, and Harold Weber, *The Production of English Renaissance Culture* (Ithaca, 1994), pp. 151–89. Cf. her "Juggling the Categories of Race, Class and Gender: Aphra Behn's *Oroonoko*," in eds., Hendricks and Parker, pp. 209–24 and "Transmuting *Othello*: Aphra Behn's *Oroonoko*," in *Cross-Cultural Performances: Differences in Women's Re-Visions of Shakespeare*, ed. Marianne Novy (Urbana, 1993), pp. 15–49. For further valuable discussion of the ideological complexity of the text, see Brown and Moira Ferguson, pp. 27–49.

fierceness, and charisma in generating the rebellion, combined with his ineffectuality in pulling it off, the rebellion tends in its violent inconsequence to resemble those brave and remarkable but politically insignificant feats. Telling his secrets to a woman (the narrator), he is (repeatedly) seduced. Indeed, he occupies a female subject position, particularly when enslaved. Much of his time as a slave is spent in the narrator's household, being diverted and entertained: "He lik'd the Company of us Women much above the Men."[5] As the narrator explains when accounting for Oroonoko's agitation in captivity, "though he suffer'd only the Name of a Slave, and had nothing of the Toil and Labour of one, yet that was sufficient to render him Uneasy; and he had been too long idle, who us'd to be always in Action, and in Arms. He had a Spirit all rough and fierce, that could not be tam'd to lazy Rest." As in Milton's *Samson Agonistes*, the hero's strength proves his bane. Finally, Oroonoko's death bears a close and ambiguous relation to suicide.

In its rejection of the heroics of action as inadequate, *Oroonoko* is an angry and irresolute text, rather than an elegiac one. Behn presents a hero with a lost past composed of high status and military achievement; and *Oroonoko* neither focuses intensely upon, nor mourns the disappearance of, these glories. The structure and story of *Oroonoko* are half-slave, half-free, with the betrayal of the hero taking place almost exactly in the middle. Distinctly divided into two parts, in which the prince loses his country and his birthright and becomes a slave, the text creates a number of links between the subject positions the hero inhabits during his freedom and his slavery.

Oroonoko begins as a handsome, brave, famous soldier, and he remains one for the first half of the story. While the narrator *describes* Oroonoko's valiance at length, however, most of the *dramatized* incidents represent his paralysis. This attenuation of traditional male heroics is in fact applicable to both halves of the story, not simply the second, when the hero is enslaved in Surinam. His African adventures primarily concern his thwarted love for Imoinda. Oroonoko's grandfather is the king in Coramantien; enchanted by Imoinda's beauty, the impotent old man seizes her for his own while Oroonoko is off hunting. Although the African kinship system makes it especially difficult for Oroonoko to defy his grandfather, the narrative nevertheless indicates that defiance is an option that the prince rejects:

> it was objected to him, that . . . *Imoinda* being his lawful Wife, by solemn Contract, 'twas he was the injur'd Man, and might, if

---

5. For a brilliant analysis of Oroonoko's vulnerability to being entertained, see Robert L. Chibka, "'Oh! Do Not Fear a Woman's Invention': Truth, Falsehood, and Fiction in Aphra Behn's *Oroonoko*," in *Texas Studies in Literature and Language*, Vol. 30, No. 4, Winter, 1988, 510–37. (See pp. 220–32 for a revised and abridged version of the Chibka article [Editor's note].)

he so pleas'd, take *Imoinda* back, the Breach of the Law being on his Grandfather's side; and that if he cou'd circumvent him, and redeem her . . . it was both just and lawful for him so to do.

Oroonoko instead responds to Imoinda's loss by proving "pensive, and altogether unpreparing for the Campaign . . . he lay negligently on the Ground, and answer'd very little." Later, he "laid himself on a Carpet, under a rich Pavillion, and remain'd a good while silent," vowing "that henceforth he wou'd never lift a Weapon, or draw a Bow." The point is not that these are the conventional postures of a melancholy lover, but that Behn is interested in exploring heroic agency as paralyzed, grieved, and oppressed. Oroonoko often figures in the narrative as the passive object of the admiring, awe-struck gaze. And his most frequent posture by far is not that of the valiant male conqueror, but of the female object of seduction. In Coramantien he is seduced out of his grief for Imoinda (whom his grandfather tells him is dead) and into slavery; on the slave ship he is seduced into remaining alive with lying reassurances of freedom; in Surinam he is seduced into believing that he and Imoinda will be released; into believing he won't be whipped; and into believing he will be killed, rather than forced to endure further indignities.

Oroonoko's identity as a phallic hero of action is suggestively attenuated in the African half of the novel, then; but the conditions of the heroic as Behn envisions them are starkly and unmistakably revealed during the hero's captivity in Surinam and in the manner of his death. His death occurs in an extended episode of prolonged agony, in which he leads the unsuccessful slave revolt, is deserted by all of the other slaves, kills the pregnant Imoinda in a suicide pact, then fails to kill himself and is captured, tortured, and hideously dismembered by the English colonists.

Why does Oroonoko not kill himself, rather than letting himself be killed?[6] At one point he names revenge as his motive for remaining alive after Imoinda's death; yet he neither avenges his enemies nor takes his own life. Instead he lies paralyzed by his wife's dead body, until his captors discover him. At this point, readers may find themselves wishing that the hero would release himself from further betrayal and torment. Yet, like Job, he refuses to curse God and die. According to John Locke, the ability to commit suicide when captivity becomes intolerable is the "perfect condition of slavery." Thus by resisting suicide, Oroonoko resists self-definition as a slave. This argument is borne out by the fact that a model of the heroics of endurance which valorizes the patient suffering of unspeakable pain is twice singled out for praise by the narrator. The first instance is a description of the proud and horrifying

6. For further discussion of this point, see Moira Ferguson, pp. 40–45.

mutilations that the warriors among the native American Indians who inhabit Surinam are seen to inflict upon themselves:

> being brought before the old Judges, now past Labour, they are ask'd, What they dare do to shew they are worthy to lead an Army? When he, who is first ask'd, making no reply, Cuts off his Nose, and throws it contemptably on the Ground; and the other does something to himself that he thinks surpasses him, and perhaps deprives himself of Lips and an Eye; so they Slash on till one gives out, and many have dy'd in this Debate. And 'tis by a passive Valour they shew and prove their Activity.

Stating that "For my part, I took 'em for Hobgoblins, or Fiends, rather than Men," the narrator with characteristic obliquity (about which more later) assures the reader that the Indians' self-violence presents "a sort of Courage too Brutal to be applauded by our Black Hero; nevertheless, he express'd his Esteem of 'em." However, referring later to Oroonoko's own beatings, woundings, and dismemberments, she states, "I have a Thousand times admired how he liv'd, in so much tormenting Pain." And as the penultimate representation of greatness, the narrator presents Oroonoko's death with admiring awe as a spectacle of the endurance of grotesque and humiliating pain:

> After that, with an ill-favoured Knife, they cut his Ears, and his Nose, and burn'd them; he still Smoak'd on, as if nothing had touch'd him; then they hack'd off one of his Arms, and still he bore up, and held his Pipe; but at the cutting off the other Arm, his Head sunk, and his Pipe drop'd; and he gave up the Ghost, without a Groan, or a Reproach.

Oroonoko's heroic agency, then, is manifested in the non-suicidal (and so non-slavish) endurance of suffering; the one resolution he keeps is that "he wou'd stand fixt, like a Rock, and indure Death so as shou'd encourage them [i.e., his captors] to Dye." Yet Oroonoko *is* a slave and, being human property, cannot escape what Carole Pateman defines as "the contradiction inherent in slavery, that the humanity of the slave must necessarily be simultaneously denied and affirmed."[7] This contradiction is, of course, applicable (with some qualifications) to seventeenth-century women, who were also simultaneously considered both property and persons. Oroonoko's inscription in contradiction becomes apparent when the components of his heroism are broken down in gendered terms. The ambivalent conditions that define the heroic in this text are fully revealed when Oroonoko's destiny is compared with, and elaborated by means of, those of the two women with whom he shares the stage: Imoinda and the narrator.

7. Carole Pateman, *The Sexual Contract* (Stanford, 1988), p. 60.

As has been analyzed extensively elsewhere, the narrator's position in the text is one of discursive incoherence, particularly in her attitudes and behavior toward Oroonoko. Thus while reciting the events of the hero's death with appalled outrage, the narrator also unwittingly clarifies her own complicity in it. Although she claims a special friendship with Oroonoko and Imoinda, among the English colonists, she is the major protagonist in the plot to seduce the royal slaves from thoughts of their freedom. The narrator confides that she assured Oroonoko of his eventual freedom and then speaks with dismay of his being "fed . . . from Day to Day with Promises," as though she were not one of the offenders. Afterwards she confesses, seemingly with no sense of disparity, that she in fact spied on him and schemed against his freedom: "I was oblig'd, by some Persons, who fear'd a Mutiny . . . to discourse with [him] and to give him all the Satisfaction I possibly cou'd"; and that she came to mistrust him: "I neither thought it convenient to trust him much out of our View, nor did the Country, who fear'd him"; and, later, "we were possess'd with extream Fear, which no perswasions cou'd Dissipate, that he wou'd secure himself till Night; and then, that he wou'd come down and Cut all our Throats." Finally, seemingly (and oddly) to exonerate herself, she confesses to abandoning him twice, in instances when he is tortured and at last killed: "For I suppose I had Authority and Interest enough there, had I suspected any such thing, to have prevented it."[8]

Oroonoko and the narrator, then, each possess compromised and strained agency. As noted, Oroonoko is paralyzed by the obvious contradiction that, like a woman, a slave is property while simultaneously remaining a human being. The narrator implicitly recognizes her connections to the hero when she links what she considers to be the inferiority of her female authorship with Oroonoko's destiny as a slave. For example, at exactly the point when the hero is renamed "Caesar" (being renamed and so possessed is the fate of women and slaves) she remarks, "his Misfortune was, to fall in an obscure World, that afforded only a Female Pen to celebrate his Fame." In the final words of the story, she announces cryptically, "Thus Dy'd this Great Man; worthy of a better Fate, and a more sublime Wit than mine to write his Praise." However, identifying with the female position of the slave, the narrator, as discussed above, also identifies with and participates in the European structures that oppress him and, presumably, herself.

Like the narrator, the hero is both slave and slave-master. While his position as an owner is explicit before he himself becomes a slave, Oroonoko enacts his conflicted identity with painful clarity when he kills his wife. As scholars like Orlando Patterson have pointed out, one

8. Cf. Margaret Ferguson, "Juggling," pp. 214–15, where she traces the narrator's inconsistent use of personal pronouns when she (the narrator) uneasily seeks to identify herself both with the slaves and the colonialists.

of the characteristics of slavery is the slave's lack of control over kinship ties.[9] In this sense, as Charlotte Sussman cogently argues, Oroonoko's killing of Imoinda, which also includes aborting their child, proves an act of mastery, a resistance to slavery. The gruesomely ironic fact—that Oroonoko can assert mastery only in this destructive and self-destructive sense—of course points in a circular fashion back to his slavery. Sussman makes the interesting point that Oroonoko acts out this duality when confronting his captors over his wife's dead body: cutting flesh from his own throat, he imitates slitting Imoinda's; disembowelling himself, he "recalls that he has just effectively aborted Imoinda's child. . . . Thus, the sign of Oroonoko's courage to choose a noble death over the shame of slavery is also a repetition of the sign of his absolute possession of wife and child." Yet, "the code of nobility that Oroonoko writes on his own body signifies his power over a woman, not his emancipation from slavery."[1]

If the ambivalent conditions characterizing Oroonoko's identity and agency as owner and slave are displaced onto the white female narrator, Imoinda also enacts displaced parts of her husband's heroic identity: namely, his slavery. Like the narrator's, Imoinda's explicitly female destiny clarifies the multiple meanings of the heroics of endurance. As Ferguson and Sussman have made clear, it is the black slave/wife who unambiguously bears the symbolic brunt of powerlessness in the text. At critical points in the narrative (e.g., during the slave revolt) Imoinda shows herself capable of courageous deeds; she is the only slave who attacks a white male ruler. Indeed, Ferguson has argued convincingly for a causal relation between Imoinda's physical courage and her death.[2] But the major significance of her actions is her willingness to die at her husband's hands, a scene which the narrator describes as follows: "he told her his Design first of Killing her, and then his Enemies, and next himself, and the Impossibility of Escaping, and therefore he told her the Necessity of Dying; he found the Heroick Wife faster pleading for Death than he was to propose it, when she found his fix'd Resolution . . . for Wives have a respect for their Husbands equal to what any other People pay a Deity."

When describing Imoinda's marriage, the narrator romanticizes her subordinate condition as accepted without ambivalence, even joyfully. But Behn also directly connects the violence that defines all slavery

9. Orlando Patterson, *Slavery and Social Death: A Comparative Study* (Cambridge, Mass., 1982), p. 13. See also William D. Phillips, Jr., *Slavery from Roman Times to the Early Transatlantic Slave Trade* (Minneapolis, 1985), pp. 6–14.
1. Charlotte Sussman, "The Other Problem with Women: Reproduction and Slave Culture in Aphra Behn's *Oroonoko*," in ed. Heidi Hutner, *Reading Aphra Behn: History, Theory, and Criticism* (Charlottesville, 1993), p. 220. (See pp. 246–56 for a condensed version of Sussman's article [Editor's note].)
2. See Margaret Ferguson, "Juggling," and "Transmuting," p. 35; and Sussman, pp. 212–33. I am also grateful to Carolyn Swift, who was the first to point out to me the importance of the fact that Imoinda wounds the governor.

with Imoinda's sexuality, including, by implicit extension, female sexuality in general. In Africa, kidnapped by the doting grandfather, Imoinda occupies the status of possession even before she literally becomes a slave. We have already seen how her death at her husband's hand embodies all the tragic ironies of slavery. There is also an earlier, very telling conflation of violence, female sexuality, and slavery. After his capture, Oroonoko befriends his owner, Trefry, and, learning that Trefry is suffering from unrequited love of a slave and not yet knowing that the slave is Imoinda, Oroonoko asks Trefry why he does not simply rape the object of his desires. Trefry replies, "I have been ready to make use of those advantages of Strength and Force Nature has given me. But oh! she disarms me, with that Modesty and Weeping so tender and so moving, that I retire, and thank my Stars she overcame me. The Company laugh'd at his Civility to a Slave." With this conflation of the woman/wife and the slave as vulnerable to sexual violence, Aphra Behn represents male dominance based on physical strength as a figure for all oppression.

Aphra Behn: A Chronology

1640   The baptismal record of Aphra Johnson, near Canterbury, Kent, seems the probable record of her birth. According to a later commonplace-book entry, her mother was wet nurse to a prominent Kent family, the Culpepers. No evidence concerning her upbringing or education.

1649   Trial and execution of Charles I; establishment of the Commonwealth government under Oliver Cromwell.

1660   Charles II is restored to the throne; playhouses reopen under royal patronage with actresses in female parts.

1663   Lord Willoughby of Parham is confirmed coproprietor of Surinam as well as lord governor of Barbados and the Caribbee Islands; he sails for Barbados. No record of an appointed lieutenant general; local colonial officials divide those powers.

1664   A January letter mentions "ladies" in residence at St. John's Hill in Surinam, near Willoughby's Parham Hill estate. In March, Deputy Governor William Byam writes sarcastically that "Celadon," a troublesome Republican named William Scot, has fled the colony in romantic pursuit of "Astrea," in reality escaping his debts.

1666   Signs herself "Behn." Biographies published after her death report her marriage to a London merchant of German or Dutch descent. An otherwise unidentified "Widow Behn" is linked to a seized merchant ship that becomes the subject of a law case in Dutch admiralty court.

           July: sent to Antwerp as a government secret agent. Under code names "Celadon" and "Astrea" (later her literary name) gathers intelligence from William Scot about overseas plots against the Crown. Recalled at the end of the year, appealing for adequate reimbursement.

1668   Threatened with debtor's prison for Antwerp debts; sends urgent petitions on her "more than two years' suffering" as arrest date nears.

1670   Her first play, *The Forced Marriage*, an Arcadian tragicomedy, succeeds with a six-day run, its title marking a frequent theme in her plays and fictions.

1671   A second tragicomedy, *The Amorous Prince*.

1673–75   After the failure of her intrigue comedy *The Dutch Lover*, an interval in which no writings appear. A private chronicler of contemporary events reports it "too publicly known" that in this period she was "kept" by the libertine lawyer and wit John Hoyle, a figure in some of her writings and in satiric squibs against her.

1676   Returns to the stage with *Abdelazer, or The Moor's Revenge*, her one tragedy, about the intrigues of a North African prince at the Spanish court. From 1676 to 1682, brings out ten plays under her name; others are attributed to her.

1677   Her most successful play, *The Rover*, one of the most frequently performed and published Restoration comedies through the mid-eighteenth century.

1678   The "Popish Plot" rouses public feeling against Catholics and the prospect of a Catholic monarch in the king's brother, James. Her comedy *Sir Patient Fancy* appears with a bantering challenge, "pray tell me then, / Why women may not write as well as men."

1680   Her verse paraphrase of Ovid's "Oenone to Paris" is included in Dryden's edition of Ovid's *Epistles*; writes poetic tributes on the death of the earl of Rochester.

1681   The "Exclusion Crisis" intensifies, as Whigs press to exclude James from the throne and Tory resistance stiffens. Shows a sharper vein of anti-Whiggish, anti-Puritan satire in her city comedies *The Roundheads* and *The City Heiress* (1682) and dedicates *The Second Part of the Rover* to James.

1682   The two theater companies consolidate, reducing the demand for new scripts. In August briefly threatened with arrest for "abusive reflections" on the disloyalty of Monmouth, King Charles's bastard son. Thereafter, complaining to her publisher, Jacob Tonson, of "no more credit at the playhouse for money as we used to have," she turns mainly to other forms.

1684   The first part of *Love Letters between a Nobleman and His Sister*, an epistolary roman à clef about a current Whig scandal, and a collected volume of *Poems upon Several Occasions*.

1685   Charles II dies and his brother, James II, is crowned. Behn publishes formal pindarics of mourning and celebration.

1685–88   Prolific period includes two more plays, two sequels to *Love Letters*, complimentary poems and miscellanies, and an increasingly ambitious schedule of translations or adaptations of La Rochefoucauld, Aesop, Fontanelle, and others. Scattered references indicate illness and debt.

1688   *Oroonoko* published, along with two other tales—*The Fair Jilt* and *Agnes de Castro*—and several congratulatory poems to the king and queen on the birth of a royal heir. That event, stirring national anxiety about a Catholic royal succession, and King James's suspension of laws against Catholics and Nonconformists lead to his forced flight and the "Protestant succession" of William of Orange.

1689   Coronation of William and Mary. Behn dies April 16 and is buried in Westminster Abbey (not in Poets' Corner). Posthumous staging of her play *The Widow Ranter*, about heroism and mismanagement in colonial Virginia.

1695   First performance of Thomas Southerne's dramatic adaptation of *Oroonoko*.

1696–98   Sketchy biographies accompanying posthumous works or collections give the earliest references to her family name and husband, repeat with some embellishment the autobiographical claims in *Oroonoko*, and add colorful novella-like material that may be from her unpublished manuscripts.

Selected Bibliography

Works represented in this volume or cited in the headnotes are not included in this bibliography. Biographical and critical studies are listed in chronological rather than alphabetical order to register changing approaches of the last decades.

A concise description of studies of Behn through 1985 is provided by Mary Ann O'Donnell in *Aphra Behn: An Annotated Bibliography of Primary and Secondary Sources* (New York: Garland, 1986). A new edition is in progress.

Montague Summers's incomplete 1915 Behn edition is replaced by Janet Todd's *Works of Aphra Behn* (Columbus: Ohio State, 1992–96).

BIOGRAPHICAL STUDIES

Woodcock, George. *The Incomparable Aphra*. 1948. Reprint, *Aphra Behn: The English Sappho*, Montreal: Black Rose, 1989.

Cameron, W. J. *New Light on Aphra Behn* (University of Auckland Monograph [No. 5]. Auckland: Wakefield Press, 1961.

Duffy, Maureen. *The Passionate Shepherdess: Aphra Behn 1640–89*. London: Jonathan Cape, 1977.

Dhuicq, B. "Further Evidence on Aphra Behn's Stay in Surinam." *Notes and Queries* 26 (Dec. 1979): 524–26.

Goreau, Angeline. *Reconstructing Aphra: A Social Biography of Aphra Behn*. New York: Dial, 1980.

Day, Robert Adams. "Aphra Behn and the Works of the Intellect." In *Fetter'd or Free? British Women Novelists, 1670–1815*, edited by Mary Anne Schofield and Cecilia Macheski, 372–213. Athens: Ohio University Press, 1986.

Mendelson, Sarah Heller. *The Mental World of Stuart Women: Three Studies*. Brighton, UK: Harvester, 1987.

Jones, Jane. "New Light on the Background and Early Life of Aphra Behn." *Notes and Queries* 37 (Sept. 1990): 288–93. Reprint, in *Aphra Behn Studies*, edited by Janet Todd. Cambridge, UK: Cambridge University Press, 1996.

Fitzmaurice, James. "Notes and Documents: Aphra Behn and the *Abraham's Sacrifice* Case." *Huntington Library Quarterly* 56 (1993): 319–26.

Hopkins, P. A. "Aphra Behn and John Hoyle: A Contemporary Mention." *Notes and Queries* 41 (June 1994): 176–80.

Todd, Janet. *The Secret Life of Aphra Behn*. London: Andre Deutsch, 1996.

CRITICAL STUDIES

Link, Frederick M. *Aphra Behn*. New York: Twayne, 1968.

Guffey, George. "Aphra Behn's *Oroonoko*: Occasion and Accomplishment." In *Two English Novelists: Aphra Behn and Anthony Trollope*. Los Angeles: Clark Library, 1975.

Brownley, Martine Watson. "The Narrator in *Oroonoko*." *Essays in Literature* 4 (1977): 174–81.

Hagstrum, Jean H. *Sex and Sensibility: Ideal and Erotic Love from Milton to Mozart*. Chicago: University of Chicago, 1980. 77–80.

Houston, Beverle. "Usurpation and Dismemberment: Oedipal Tyranny in *Oroonoko*." *Literature and Psychology* 32 (1986): 30–36.

Messenger, Ann. "Novel into Play: Aphra Behn and Thomas Southerne." In *His and Hers: Essays in Restoration and Eighteenth-Century Literature*. Lexington: University Press of Kentucky, 1986.

Rogers, Katharine M. "Fact and Fiction in Aphra Behn's *Oroonoko*." *Studies in the Novel* 20 (1988): 1–15.

Stackelberg, Jürgen von. "*Oroonoko* et L'Abolition de L'Esclavage: Le Role du Traducteur." *Revue de Littérature Comparée* 250 (1989): 237–48.

Zimbardo, Rose. "The Late Seventeenth-Century Dilemma in Discourse: Dryden's *Don Sebastian* and Behn's *Oroonoko.*" In *Rhetorics of Order/Ordering in English Neoclassical Literature*, edited by J. Douglas Canfield and J. Paul Hunter, 46–67. Newark: University of Delaware, 1989.

Starr, G. A. "Aphra Behn and the Genealogy of the Man of Feeling." *Modern Philology* 87 (1990): 362–72.

Ferguson, Margaret W. "Juggling the Categories of Race, Class and Gender: Aphra Behn's *Oroonoko.*" *Women's Studies* 19 (1991): 159–81. Rev. ed., in *Women, "Race," and Writing in the Early Modern Period*, edited by Margo Hendricks and Patricia Parker, 209–224. London and New York: Routledge, 1994.

Pearson, Jacqueline. "Gender and Narrative in the Fiction of Aphra Behn." *Review of English Studies* 42 (1991): 40–56, 179–90.

Hutner, Heidi. "Aphra Behn's *Oroonoko*: The Politics of Gender, Race, and Class." In *Living by the Pen: Early British Women Writers*, edited by Dale Spender, 39–51. New York: Teachers College Press, Columbia University, 1992.

Ballaster, Ros. "New Hystericism: Aphra Behn's *Oroonoko*: The Body, the Text, and the Feminist Critic." In *New Feminist Discourses*, edited by Isobel Armstrong, 283–95. London and New York: Routledge, 1992.

Ballaster, Ros. *Seductive Forms: Women's Amatory Fiction, 1684–1740.* Oxford, UK: Clarendon, 1992.

Ferguson, Moira. "*Oroonoko*: Birth of a Paradigm." *New Literary History* 23 (1992): 339–59. Reprint, in *Subject to Others: British Women Writers and Colonial Slavery, 1670–1834.* New York: Routledge, 1992.

Rosenthal, Laura J. "Owning Oroonoko: Behn, Southerne, and the Contingencies of Property." *Renaissance Drama*, n.s., 23 (1992): 25–58.

Athey, Stephanie, and Daniel Cooper Alarcón. "*Oroonoko's* Gendered Economies of Honor/ Horror: Reframing Colonial Discourse Studies in the Americas." *American Literature* 66 (1993): 415–43.

Ferguson, Margaret. "Transmuting Othello: Aphra Behn's *Oroonoko.*" In *Cross-Cultural Performances: Differences in Women's Re-Visions of Shakespeare*; edited by Marianne Novy, 15–49. Urbana: University of Illinois, 1993.

Todd, Janet. "Spectacular Deaths: History and Story in Aphra Behn's *Love Letters, Oroonoko*, and *The Widow Ranter.*" In *Gender, Art and Death.* New York: Continuum, 1993.

Ferguson, Margaret. "News from the New World: Miscegenous Romance in Aphra Behn's *Oroonoko* and *The Widow Ranter.*" In *The Production of English Renaissance Culture*, edited by David Lee Miller, Sharon O'Dair, and Harold Weber, 151–89. Ithaca, N.Y.: Cornell University Press, 1994.

Fogarty, Anne. "Looks that Kill: Violence and Representation in Aphra Behn's *Oroonoko.*" In *The Discourse of Slavery: Aphra Behn to Toni Morrison*, edited by Carl Plasa and Betty J. Ring, 1–17. London and New York: Routledge, 1994.

Kaul, Suvir. "Reading Literary Symptoms: Colonial Pathologies and the *Oroonoko* Fictions of Behn, Southerne, and Hawkesworth." *Eighteenth-Century Life* 18, n.s., no. 3 (Nov. 1994): 80–96.

Gallagher, Catherine. "The Author-Monarch and the Royal Slave: *Oroonoko* and the Blackness of Representation." In *Nobody's Story: The Vanishing Acts of Women Writers in the Marketplace 1670–1829.* Berkeley and Los Angeles: University of California, 1994. Excerpted in "Oroonoko's Blackness." In *Aphra Behn Studies*, edited by Janet Todd. Cambridge, UK: Cambridge University Press, 1996.

Pacheco, Anita. "Royalism and Honor in Aphra Behn's *Oroonoko.*" *Studies in English Literature* 34 (1994): 492–506.

Paxman, David. "Oral and Literate Discouse in Aphra Behn's *Oroonoko,*" *Restoration* 18 (1994): 88–103.

Hoegberg, David E.. "Caesar's Toils: Allusion and Rebellion in *Oroonoko.*" *Eighteenth-Century Fiction* 7 (1995): 239–58.

Ferguson, Margaret. "Feathers and Flies: Aphra Behn and the Seventeenth-Century Trade in Exotica." In *Subject and Object in Renaissance Culture*, edited by Margreta De Grazia, Maureen Quilligan, and Peter Stallybrass, 235–259. Cambridge, UK: Cambridge University Press, 1996.

Lipking, Joanna. "Confusing Matters: Searching the Backgrounds of *Oroonoko.*" In *Aphra Behn Studies*, edited by Janet Todd, 259–81. Cambridge, UK: Cambridge University Press, 1996.

Pearson, Jacqueline. "Slave Princes and Lady Monsters: Gender and Ethnic Difference in the Work of Aphra Behn." In *Aphra Behn Studies*, edited by Janet Todd, 219–34. Cambridge, UK: Cambridge University Press, 1996.

ADDITIONAL READING

An essential guide to the interrelated West African sources is provided by Adam Jones, "Semper Aliquid Veteris: Printed Sources for the History of the Ivory and Gold Coasts, 1500–1750," *Journal of African History*, 27 (1986), 215–235, supplemented by articles in the special edition of *Paideuma*, "European Sources for Sub-Saharan Africa before 1900: Use and Abuse," edited by Beatrix Heintze and Adam Jones, 1987.

Elizabeth Donnan, ed., *Documents Illustrative of the History of the Slave Trade to America*, vols. 1–2 (Washington: Carnegie Institution, 1930–31) is an extraordinary trove of primary materials. A recent brief bibliographical guide to books on slavery appears in James Walvin's *Slaves and Slavery: The British Colonial Experience* (Manchester, UK, and New York: Manchester University Press, 1992); relevant new studies appear regularly in such periodicals as *History in Africa* and *Journal of African History*. An introduction to some issues in the interpretation of early colonial societies is provided in a review article by Jack P. Greene, "Society and Economy in the British Caribbean during the Seventeenth and Eighteenth Centuries," *American Historical Review* 79 (1974): 1499–1517.

Barker, Anthony J. *The African Link: British Attitudes to the Negro in the Era of the Atlantic Slave Trade*. London: Frank Cass, 1978.

Bridenbaugh, Carl, and Roberta Bridenbaugh. *No Peace Beyond the Line: The English in the Caribbean 1624–90*. New York: Oxford University Press, 1972.

Chinard, Gilbert. *L'Amérique et le Rêve Exotique dans La Littérature Française au XVII et au XIII Siècles*. Paris: Hachette, 1913.

Craton, Michael. *Testing the Chains: Resistance to Slavery in the British West Indies*. Ithaca, N.Y.: Cornell University Press, 1982.

Curtin, Philip D. *The Atlantic Slave Trade: A Census*. Madison: University of Wisconsin, 1969.

Daaku, K. Y. *Trade and Politics on the Gold Coast*. London: Clarendon, 1970.

Dabydeen, David. "Eighteenth-century English Literature on Commerce and Slavery." In *The Black Presence in English Literature*. Manchester, UK: Manchester University Press, 1985.

Dabydeen, David. *Hogarth's Blacks: Images of Blacks in Eighteenth-Century English Art*. Mundlestrup, Denmark: Dangaroo Press, 1985.

Davies, K. G. *The Royal African Company*. 1957. New York: Athenaeum, 1970.

Davis, David Brion. *The Problem of Slavery in Western Culture*. Ithaca, N.Y.: Cornell University Press, 1966.

Fryer, Peter. *Staying Power: Black People in Britain Since 1540*. Atlantic Highlands, N.J.: Humanities Press, 1984.

Gaspar, David Barry, and Darlene Clark Hine, eds. *More Than Chattel: Black Women and Slavery in the Americas*. Bloomington and Indianapolis: Indiana University Press, 1996.

Gay, Peter. "Abolitionism: A Preliminary Probing." In *The Enlightenment: An Interpretation*, vol. 2. New York: Knopf, 1969.

Grafton, Anthony, *New Worlds, Ancient Texts: The Power of Tradition and the Shock of Discovery*. Cambridge, Mass., and London: Belknap-Harvard University Press, 1992.

Grant, Douglas. *The Fortunate Slave: An Illustration of African Slavery in the Early Eighteenth Century*. London: Oxford University Press, 1968.

Hall, Kim F. *Things of Darkness: Economies of Race and Gender in Early Modern England*. Ithaca, N.Y.: Cornell University Press, 1995.

Heuman, Gad, ed. *Out of the House of Bondage: Runaways, Resistance, and Marronage in Africa and the New World*. London and Totowa, N.J.: Frank Cass, 1986.

Hobby, Elaine. *Virtue of Necessity: English Women's Writing, 1649–88*. Ann Arbor: University of Michigan Press, 1988.

Hoffmann, Léon-François. "En Marge d'Un Article du *Pour et Contre*: Prévost et l'Esclavage Colonial." In *Essays on the Age of Enlightenment in Honor of Ira O. Wade*, edited by Jean Macary, 155–68. Geneva: Droz, 1977.

Honour, Hugh. *The New Golden Land: European Images of America from the Discoveries to the Present Time*. New York: Pantheon, 1975.

Hulme, Peter. *Colonial Encounters: Europe and the Native Caribbean, 1492–1797*. London: Methuen, 1986.

Hulton, Paul. *America, 1585: The Complete Drawings of John White*. Chapel Hill: University of North Carolina; London: British Museum, 1984.

Law, Robin. *The Slave Coast of West Africa 1550–1750*. Oxford, UK: Oxford University Press, 1991.

McKeon, Michael. *The Origins of the English Novel 1600–1740*. Baltimore and London: Johns Hopkins University Press, 1987.

Morgan, Philip D. "British Encounters with Africans and African-Americans." In *Strangers within the Realm: Cultural Margins of the First British Empire*, edited by Bernard Bailyn and Philip D. Morgan, 157–221. Chapel Hill: University of North Carolina, 1991.

Mintz, Sidney W. *Sweetness and Power: The Place of Sugar in Modern History*. New York: Viking, 1985.

Pagden, Anthony. *European Encounters with the New World*. New Haven, Conn.: Yale University Press, 1993.

Patterson, Orlando. *Freedom*, vol. 1. New York: Basic Books, 1991.

Porter, Robert. *English Activity on the Gold Coast, 1620–1667*, 2 vols. Ann Arbor, Mich.: University Microfilms, 1989.

Puckrein, Gary A. *Little England: Plantation Society and Anglo-Barbadian Politics 1627–1700*. New York: New York University Press, 1984.

Sandiford, Keith A. *Measuring the Moment: Strategies of Protest in Eighteenth-Century Afro-English Writing*. Cranbury, N.J.: Associated University Presses, 1988.

Seeber, Edward D. *Anti-Slavery Opinion in France During the Second Half of the Eighteenth Century*. 1937. Reprint, New York: Greenwood, 1967.

Zook, George Frederick. *The Company of Royal Adventurers Trading into Africa*. Lancaster, Pa.: New Era, 1919.

NOTES ON PLANTER PERSONNEL

Basic documents appear in *Calendar of State Papers, Colonial*; James A. Williamson, *English Colonies in Guiana and on the Amazon 1604–1668* (Oxford, UK: Clarendon, 1923); and V. T. Harlow, ed., *Colonising Expeditions to the West Indies and Guiana 1623–1667* (London: Hakluyt Society, 1925). The biographies of Behn by Maureen Duffy and Angeline Goreau summarize much of what is known.

Lord Willoughby: His complex career is carefully traced in the *Dictionary of National Biography*. Although he himself strongly backed free trade, he was often caught between home government policies and concerned or resentful colonists. Lady Willoughby died in 1661.

John Trefry: His August 1662 letter on the public spirit of Surinam, which credits "our noble Governor" (Byam) with "having won every one not only to himself but also to industry," appears in *Historical Manuscripts Commission, 10th Report*, 6: Bouverie Manuscripts. His later career is examined in Maureen Duffy's *The Passionate Shepherdess* (1977), 37–40.

George Marten (or Martin): His life and early correspondence are traced in "Documents and Letters in the Brotherton Collection," *Journal of the Barbados Museum and Historical Society* 24 (1957), 175–87, with further information in P. F. Campbell, "Two Generations of Walronds," *Journal of the B. M. H. S.* 38 (1989), append. C. In Barbados he was a member of the assembly and, in 1655, its speaker; but there is evidence of significant later debt. He cannot with entire certainty be identified as same Martin whose property is marked on the Surinam map.

William Byam: His early career is traced by P. F. Campbell, "Two Generations of Walronds," *Journal of the B. M. H. S.* 38 (1989). Although Behn describes him as an upstart, he held two plantations in Surinam and land in Antigua. His wife, Dorothy Knollys, was described by Father Biet as "one of the most beautiful women I have ever seen." He wrote two works on attacks by aggrieved planters against himself and Lord Willoughby and a manuscript journal of the colony's last years, and he successfully vindicated himself in a court-martial instigated by the Willoughby heirs. He died in 1670 or 1671 in Antigua. The family became prominent; "A Genealogy of the Byam Family" appears in an appendix to *Antigua and the Antiguans* by Mrs. Flannigan (or Lanaghan) (London, 1844). A later slave ship was named the *Byam*.

James Banister: His origins remain untraced. He was appointed acting governor of Surinam in 1668 as "the only remaining eminent person" (C.S.P.). After detention by the Dutch, in 1671 he led more than a hundred Surinam families to Jamaica, where he joined the governor's council, was commissioned major general, and reorganized the militia. He was among the biggest planters, owning at least two thousand acres. In 1674 he was murdered by the island's surveyor general, who was hanged. Sources: Stephen Saunders Webb, *The Governors-General: The English Army and the Definition of the Empire, 1569–1681* (Chapel Hill: University of North Carolina, 1979), 255, 259; Richard S. Dunn, *Sugar and Slaves* (New York: Norton, 1972), 176; and "A Journal Kept by Colonel William Beeston," *Interesting Tracts Relating to the Island of Jamaica* (St. Iago, Jamaica, 1800), 288–90.